GOOD GOVERNANCE
GONE BAD

A Volume in the Series
Cornell Studies in Political Economy
Edited by Peter J. Katzenstein

A list of titles in this series is available at cornellpress.cornell.edu.

GOOD GOVERNANCE GONE BAD

How Nordic Adaptability
Leads to Excess

Darius Ornston

CORNELL UNIVERSITY PRESS   ITHACA AND LONDON

Copyright © 2018 by Cornell University

All rights reserved. Except for brief quotations in a review, this book, or parts thereof, must not be reproduced in any form without permission in writing from the publisher. For information, address Cornell University Press, Sage House, 512 East State Street, Ithaca, New York 14850. Visit our website at cornellpress.cornell.edu.

First published 2018 by Cornell University Press

Printed in the United States of America

Library of Congress Cataloging-in-Publication Data

Names: Ornston, Darius, 1978– author.
Title: Good governance gone bad : how Nordic adaptability leads to excess / Darius Ornston.
Description: Ithaca : Cornell University Press, 2018. | Series: Cornell studies in political economy | Includes bibliographical references and index.
Identifiers: LCCN 2018015846 (print) | LCCN 2018016562 (ebook) | ISBN 9781501726118 (pdf) | ISBN 9781501726125 (epub/mobi) | ISBN 9781501726101 | ISBN 9781501726101 (cloth : alk. paper) | ISBN 9781501730177 (pbk. : alk. paper)
Subjects: LCSH: Scandinavia—Economic policy. | Europe—Economic policy. | Scandinavia—Economic conditions—21st century. | Europe—Economic conditions—21st century. | States, Small—Economic policy.
Classification: LCC HC345 (ebook) | LCC HC345 .O76 2018 (print) | DDC 338.0948—dc23
LC record available at https://lccn.loc.gov/2018015846

To Eric

Contents

Acknowledgments	ix
Introduction: The Nordic Paradox	1
1. Good Governance Gone Bad: Overshooting in Nordic Europe	11
2. Manufacturing a Crisis: Planning in Sweden	25
3. Connecting People: Innovation in Finland	58
4. From Banking on Fish to Fishy Banks: Liberalization in Iceland	101
5. Overshooting in Comparative Perspective: Contrasting Cases	141
6. Overshooting beyond Nordic Europe: Ireland and Estonia	160
Conclusion: Lessons for Large States	180
Appendix 1: Measuring Cohesive, Encompassing Networks	203
Appendix 2: Characterizing Economic Adjustment	211
Notes	215
References	227
Index	253

Acknowledgments

This book was inspired by fieldwork in Denmark, Finland, Sweden, and Ireland in the early 2000s. In seeking to understand how these countries engineered "big leaps" into new industries, I was struck by the informal ties that united my interviewees. Across the business system and ideological spectrum, the people I spoke with responded to open-ended questions about economic competitiveness by identifying common challenges, proposing similar solutions, and even employing identical metaphors. Although I did not anticipate it at the time, these observations would prove useful when I sought to make sense of the Danish housing crisis, the Irish banking crisis, the decline of the Finnish ICT industry, and the Icelandic hedge fund debacle. I am thus indebted to those who funded and guided that earlier work, including the German Marshall Fund of the United States, the American-Scandinavian Foundation, the Berkeley Department of Scandinavian Studies, the Swedish Embassy in Washington, DC, the University of California at Berkeley, the Research Institute of the Finnish Economy, Copenhagen Business School, Mandag Morgen, University College Dublin, and the Swedish Institute for Working Life.

I transformed this puzzle into a book at the University of Georgia and the University of Toronto. The University of Georgia, UGA's Department of International Affairs, the University of Toronto, the Munk School of Global Affairs, and the Connaught Fund financed additional fieldwork in Finland, Greece, Iceland, Ireland, Portugal, and Sweden between 2012 and 2016. I also benefited from an exceptionally collegial working environment at the Department of International Affairs and the Munk School of Global Affairs, both of which encouraged me to investigate the Nordic paradox identified at the beginning of this book.

Indeed, this project depended more on people than places, and it was ultimately my colleagues, students, and hundreds of interviewees who made this work possible. For a project six years in the making, and whose origins stretch back even earlier, the number of individuals who volunteered their time and contributed to the book are too numerous to name. Some, principally interviewees, requested anonymity. But a list would certainly include Chris Allen, Vicki Birchfield, Danny Breznitz, Shiri Breznitz, Markus Crepaz, Keith Gehring, Gernot Grabher, Eskil Ekstedt, Peter Katzenstein, Paulette Kurzer, Niamh Hardiman, Roger Haydon, Wade Jacoby, Florian Justwan, Bill Kissane, Peer Hull Kristensen, Jonah Levy, Cas Mudde, Dann Naseemullah, Sean O'Riain, Christopher Palmberg,

Øve Kaj Pedersen, Erik Rasmussen, Olli Rehn, Martin Rhodes, Petri Rouvinen, Sebastian Royo, Herman Schwartz, Zak Taylor, Mark Vail, Vesa Vihriälä, Toby Schulze-Cleven, David Wolfe, Joseph Wong, Pekka Ylä-Anttila, Nick Ziegler, and John Zysman, as well as the referees who commented on this and related work.

From this long list, I should single out Peter Katzenstein, whose work on small states inspired my interest in European politics (as well as Bruce Morrison, who recommended it). Peter's detailed remarks on this manuscript strengthened the book considerably. Danny Breznitz also deserves special mention, acting as a sounding board and helping develop the argument from the earliest stages of the project until the final draft.

Finally, I thank my family, who endured my idiosyncratic interests with patience and grace. I am particularly grateful to my mother, who has delivered detailed feedback since I started writing and provided line-by-line commentary on a far less readable draft of this book. I am also grateful for Eric, to whom this book is dedicated. His wide-ranging and enthusiastic intellectual adventures are an enduring source of joy and inspiration in work and play. To Eric, my mother, and the rest of my family, thank you, and I promise to speak about something other than policy overshooting in small states, at least for a few years.

GOOD GOVERNANCE GONE BAD

Introduction
THE NORDIC PARADOX

The Nordic states have attracted attention for their capacity to adopt best practice in a wide variety of policy domains. The *Economist* recently labeled the region a "supermodel" (*Economist* 2013), as organizations such as the World Bank, the International Monetary Fund, and the OECD have singled out Nordic achievements in labor-market policy, education, and innovation policy, among others (Dahlman, Routti, and Ylä-Anttila 2006a; OECD 2010; Zhou 2007). Partly as a result of these reforms, Nordic countries have seized leadership in a diverse array of dynamic knowledge-intensive industries including biotechnology, financial services, software, and telecommunications equipment. Rapid innovation has, in turn, contributed to robust economic growth and low unemployment, with the result that these economies are routinely ranked among the most "competitive" in the world by organizations such as Institute for Management Development and the World Economic Forum.

Although illuminating, these laudatory accounts often overlook the region's inconsistent and troubled economic history. Contemporary high-technology leaders such as Finland and Sweden were heavily dependent on low- and medium-technology industries such as metal-processing and papermaking in the early postwar period. Policy makers and business leaders were slow to adapt to new challenges in the 1970s, and the decision to double down on established strategies led to unsustainable fiscal and trade deficits by the 1980s. By the end of the century, the diminutive Nordic region had generated three of the "big five" postwar banking crises (Rogoff and Reinhart 2009, 160). The Nordic countries responded effectively to those shocks, but they continue to exhibit similar vulnerabilities. Sweden fueled one of the largest ICT bubbles in Western Europe in the late 1990s, Denmark created an American-style housing bubble in the mid-2000s, and Finland proved exceptionally susceptible to a single technological innovation, the iPhone, in 2007. Not to be outdone, Iceland managed to establish a new standard for economic mismanagement by inflating bank assets from 100 percent to 800 percent of GDP between 2000 and 2007.

These crises are even more perplexing because they cannot be attributed to "crony capitalism," rent-seeking, or the other ills that commonly plague crisis-prone countries. On the contrary, the Nordic countries routinely rank among the most trusting and least corrupt societies in the world (Rothstein and Stolle 2003, 11; Transparency International 2010), with a capacity to deliver high-quality collective goods from education to infrastructure. Naturally, international openness increases their exposure to disruptive economic shocks, and the downturns described above can, to some extent, be attributed to "bad luck" (Schwartz and Becker 2005b, 17). But this book demonstrates that these crises were also shaped by poor policy choices, sharply at odds with the conventional image of the Nordic region. How do we explain this Nordic paradox? Why are the Nordic states so successful economically?[1] And why do these paragons of good governance make such terrible policy choices and poor investment decisions? In short, how can we reconcile these two, contradictory images of Nordic capitalism?

Nordic economic success is a puzzle in its own right. Often treated collectively, the Nordic countries have thrived in very different ways. Some countries, such as Iceland, have prospered under state intervention. Others, such as Denmark, have favored more market-oriented arrangements. Sweden successfully incorporated organized labor within a generous welfare state, whereas Finland flourished for decades by repressing it. Partly as a result of this, the Nordic countries have excelled in very different industries. Iceland and Norway continue to rely heavily on low-technology, resource-based industries such as fishing and oil, while Finland and Sweden have assumed leadership in radically innovative high-technology markets and knowledge-intensive services. In fact, the same countries have prospered with fundamentally different institutions and industries, as evidenced by Finland's evolution from a heavily regulated, labor-repressive, resource-extractive economy into a more equitable, but highly competitive, high-technology leader (see chapter 3).

The most common explanations for Nordic success, focusing on the state, labor, or industry, fail to capture the region's diversity. The most popular narrative among economists focuses on the benefits of robust market competition, attributing Nordic success to high levels of foreign trade and investment (*Economist* 2013). Without denying that the Nordic countries have benefited from economic openness, it is important to recognize that they also boast some of the largest public sectors in the world. Even more importantly, some Nordic countries, such as Finland and Iceland, thrived for decades under relatively closed economic regimes, with heavily regulated product and financial markets.[2]

An alternative approach views the public sector as an asset and emphasizes the benefits of universal social policies. Broad-based investments in collective goods such as childcare and continuing education represent a valuable resource for entrepreneurial individuals and the firms that employ them (Kristensen 2011, 221).[3] This statist explanation, however, also falters when situated in comparative and historical perspective. As this book relates, iconic welfare states such as Sweden ranked among the most laissez-faire societies in Western Europe before World War II.

Theories that privilege social democratic ideology or working-class "power resources" are problematic for similar reasons.[4] Finnish political and industrial elites marginalized organized labor until the 1960s and they continued to prioritize industry-friendly instruments such as subsidies for research and development (R&D) over more social democratic measures such as continuing education into the twenty-first century (Ornston 2012a, 694–98). Social democracy played an even more peripheral role in Iceland, where the conservative Independence Party played a near-hegemonic role in Icelandic politics.

More recent scholarship has shifted attention away from the size and power of working-class organizations such as trade unions to the organizational capacity of employers (Hall and Soskice 2001, 15). Coordination, where production is influenced by long-term nonmarket relationships among firms and other actors, enables countries to invest in sophisticated collective goods from specialized equipment to vocational training and high-quality standards (Hall and Soskice 2001, 39). The Nordic experience, however, challenges the "Varieties of Capitalism" literature in two ways. First, the literature is insensitive to the diverse ways Nordic firms coordinate economic activity.[5] Second, the Varieties of Capitalism framework argues that coordinated market economies compete by gradually upgrading established, century-old industries such as automobiles or machine tools. This works well for Central European states such as Austria and Switzerland (see chapter 5), but it offers little insight into the sharp institutional and economic shifts that characterize Nordic economic history (Ornston 2013, 705).

The literature on small states offers an alternative way to understand Nordic success (Katzenstein 1985). Instead of emphasizing the state, organized labor, or employers, this work focuses on the relationship among them. More specifically, geographic proximity and geopolitical vulnerability lead to a high level of interconnectedness and support national cooperation (Campbell and Hall 2017, 6). As I relate in chapter 5, this is not true of all small states. In the Nordic region, however, late industrialization, external threats, and a common ethnic, linguistic, and religious heritage have led these societies to develop particularly cohesive and encompassing networks.[6] Relationships are cohesive in the sense that they are characterized by a high level of trust; they are encompassing in the sense that they transcend regional, political, socioeconomic, and sectoral cleavages (see appendix 1).[7]

The literature on small states (Bodley 2013), and on political economy more broadly (Ostrom 1990; Putnam 1993), suggests that these cooperative relationships improve economic performance by enabling governments and private-sector actors to invest in collective goods. Widely distributed networks permit policy makers to access high-quality expertise from across society as well as local information from ordinary citizens. The threat of exclusion from dense networks raises the cost of free riding, shirking, and other opportunistic behaviors, which are easier to identify with a relatively small number of actors (Jalan 1982). Finally, the ability to coordinate across multiple policy domains and actors enables these societies to produce complex, sophisticated collective goods ranging from ambitious innovation policies to comprehensive, green infrastructure. These social structures are particularly effective when subject to market competition. In the Nordic countries, international openness acts as a safeguard against economic mismanagement (Andersen et al. 2007, 17).

In this book, I argue that this work on small states provides a more compelling explanation for Nordic economic success than theories that focus exclusively on markets, the state, trade unions, or employers. Even as the settings, instruments, and even objectives of public policy and corporate strategy have varied, cohesive and encompassing social networks have remained a defining feature of Nordic economic governance for over a century. These dense relationships have enabled public and private actors to invest in a variety of high-quality public goods, supporting fundamentally different growth regimes. After relying on natural resources to industrialize, the Nordic countries thrived during the era of Fordist-style, large-scale manufacturing, using statist instruments to compete in a variety of heavy industries. In the late twentieth century they again adapted public policy and corporate strategy, liberalizing their economies and redefining themselves as leaders in high-technology manufacturing. When those markets were transformed by disruptive technological innovations and low-cost competitors, they reinvented themselves anew, entering knowledge-intensive services.[8]

At the same time, this book exposes two shortcomings in the literature on small states. First, even as scholars consistently emphasize flexible adaptation, the transformative capacity of these tight-knit relationships is often understated. Perhaps because cooperation is generally conceptualized as an incremental force in political economy (Hall and Soskice 2001, 39), scholars of small states commonly emphasize incremental upmarket movement within established, stable niches (Katzenstein 1985, 79; Kristensen and Levinsen 1983). This work accurately reflects Central European economies such as Austria and Switzerland, but it does not capture the pace and scope of change articulated above.[9] The Nordic countries have adapted to disruptive economic shocks by fundamentally restructuring their economies, shifting from natural resources to heavy industry, and then from Fordist-style manufacturing to rapid technological innovation and sophisticated services.

I argue that the Nordic countries can do so, because the information-gathering, consensus-building, and coordinating capacities described above are more dynamic than we recognize. Scholars have historically focused on "welfare capitalism," in part because of their interest in cross-class relations (Katzenstein 1985, 48–53; Thorhallsson 2010, 380). But tight-knit networks can also support investments in innovation or, even more counterintuitively, radical market-oriented reform. Meanwhile, cross-regional and cross-sectoral ties facilitate the diffusion of new business models within the private sector. Far from delaying the pace of restructuring, these cohesive social structures can accelerate it.

This more dynamic vision of cooperation illuminates a second limitation. Because cooperation is widely perceived to delay the pace of reform and restructuring, scholars focus on the risk of political paralysis and economic stagnation (Grabher 1993, 260–64). In Nordic Europe, and elsewhere, this danger is addressed by subjecting communities to market competition (Andersen et al. 2007, 17). I argue, however, that cohesive, encompassing relationships can lead to *too much* change. Widely distributed networks expose policy makers to bad ideas as well as good ones. Even more importantly, the ability to coordinate public and private sector activity can lead societies to scale the best ideas to dangerous and unsustainable heights. In short, the Nordic countries, and tight-knit communities more generally, are vulnerable to policy overshooting and overinvestment. Unfortunately, international markets, the most popular solution to political paralysis, are less effective in diagnosing these problems, particularly during good times.

As a result, I argue that cohesive, encompassing social networks lead to a distinctive pattern of adjustment in Nordic Europe. While international markets eventually identify flawed institutions or misallocated resources, this often occurs after the Nordic countries have scaled new ideas to dangerous extremes. Consensus building and coordination enable these societies to respond quickly and effectively to the resulting economic crisis. These societies use dense, widely distributed networks to thoroughly overhaul their policies and fundamentally transform their economies, all within the span of a decade. But with few checks against the misallocation of resources as the economy booms, the Nordic countries are vulnerable to a new round of overshooting and overinvestment. The result is an admirable but volatile pattern of economic adjustment. The same forces that facilitate rapid reform and restructuring generate new excesses in a recurring pattern of overcorrection.

These findings have important consequences for how we understand and conduct economic policy in small and large states alike. First, the book contributes to the growing recognition that size is an important variable (Campbell and Hall 2009; Katzenstein 1985) and, perhaps more importantly, that state size is socially constructed (Brown and Purcell 2005, 607; Kuokstis 2015, 114). The literature on international relations often defines small states by objective criteria such as population, gross domestic product, or economic openness, and there are advantages to doing so. The case studies in this book, however, suggest that comparably sized countries have responded to similar structural conditions in very different ways. The Nordic countries developed collective responses to capital scarcity and geopolitical vulnerability, whereas similar challenges divided their Southern European counterparts (see chapter 5). The effects of constrained geopolitical space are not uniform.

Second, closer attention to cohesive and encompassing social networks demystifies the much-discussed "Nordic model." By examining different Nordic countries across several different time periods, I suggest that economic growth cannot be attributed to a specific ideology or policy. Instead, I argue that the Nordic region is defined by widely distributed, high-trust social networks, which have enabled these countries to invest in a variety of high-quality collective goods. By isolating the politics of interconnectedness, I suggest how other countries can learn from and copy Nordic strategies. The lessons are most obvious for small countries such as Estonia and Ireland with dense, informal networks (chapter 6), but even large countries can replicate Nordic success by leveraging tight-knit interpersonal networks at the local level (conclusion).

Third, I challenge the widespread perception in business, economic sociology, geography, political science, and innovation studies that dense, high-trust networks delay reform and restructuring (Grabher 1993, 260–64; Hall and Soskice 2001, 65; Hommen and Edquist 2008, 477; Katzenstein 1985, 47). I argue that cohesive, encompassing networks can also lead to paradigmatic institutional shifts, from competition to coordination, investment to innovation, and statism to liberalism. These comprehensive reforms have enabled the Nordic countries to develop fundamentally new products, services, and industries within a remarkably short period of time. In other words, nonliberal economies are considerably more dynamic than we recognize, and policy makers seeking to accelerate restructuring may benefit from considering the politics of cooperation as well as the politics of (market) competition.

At the same time, I seek to counterbalance the celebratory literature on small states and the Nordic countries in particular. To date, this work has been overwhelmingly positive, highlighting their flexibility, pragmatism, and superior policy-making capacity (Bodley 2013; Campbell and Hall 2009; Pekkarinen, Pohjola, and Rowthorn 1992). To the extent that the literature identifies problems, it often focuses on their vulnerability to larger, more powerful actors or external forces (Thorhallsson 2010, 384). By contrast, I argue that many of the crises these societies experience are also self-generated. The same cohesive, encompassing networks that underpin good governance also lead to policy errors and terrible investment decisions. It is important for policy makers to acknowledge this risk, as international markets provide few checks against policy overshooting and overinvestment during good times.

Finally, this focus on cohesive, encompassing social networks has important implications for how we understand good governance in *all* societies. The Nordic countries illuminate a novel problem with the cooperative relationships celebrated in literatures on economic coordination (Hall and Soskice 2001), network-building (Ansell 2000), social capital (Putnam 1993), and associative democracy (Rogers and Cohen 1995). Commonly believed to delay change, dense social networks can accelerate the diffusion of bad ideas and lead communities to scale good ideas to dangerous, unsustainable heights. The Nordic countries represent an important counterpoint to the common argument that more cooperation would help larger countries navigate contemporary problems, from financial regulation (Rosenthal, Poole, and McCarty 2013) to "grand challenges" (Deak and Peredy 2015). The Nordic countries also highlight the very real risk of policy overshooting and overinvestment in tight-knit local communities within large societies. In short, overshooting is not just a Nordic problem.

I develop this argument in six steps. In chapter 1 I resolve the "Nordic paradox" by turning to the literature on small states. I begin with the unusually cohesive and encompassing social networks that characterize the Nordic states and explain how this social structure supports effective policy making and successful economic adjustment. More specifically, I discuss how dense, high-trust relationships facilitate reform and restructuring through three mechanisms: the politics of persuasion, the politics of compensation, and the politics of coordination. At the same time, these dynamic forces increase the region's vulnerability to policy overshooting, overinvestment, and economic crises. For additional information on the measurement of cohesive, encompassing networks and economic volatility, I refer the reader to two appendices at the end of the volume.

In chapter 2 I begin the empirical section of the book with the Swedish case. This case study performs two roles. As the largest and most pluralist of the three Nordic countries in this book, Sweden functions as a contrasting case. Readers looking for a more extreme example of reform, restructuring, and overshooting should skip ahead to Finland or, better yet, Iceland. Relative to most other countries, however, Sweden is a cohesive, tight-knit society and the industrial policies of the early postwar period reflect this. Beginning in the 1930s, policy makers across the world turned to credit rationing, state aid, and planning. This volte-face away from free markets was particularly pronounced in Sweden, which could rely on tight-knit networks to implement and scale new ideas through the politics of persuasion, compensation, and coordination. In many respects, Sweden eclipsed even France, the paradigmatic statist economy, both in its capacity to reform public policy as well as its ability to foster the growth of large, capital-intensive manufacturing enterprises. At the same time, state intervention proved increasingly dysfunctional over time, generating unsustainable trade and fiscal deficits and a deep economic crisis.

In chapter 3 I turn to Finland, a smaller and more tight-knit society that relied even more heavily on state intervention and low-technology industry in the early postwar period and experienced an even deeper crisis by the early 1990s. To advance the argument, this chapter focuses instead on the emergence of innovation policy and new digital technologies in the late twentieth century. Finland was among the most aggressive and successful countries in the world in converting traditional industrial policies into new innovation policies. I identify the specific ways in which policy makers used tight-knit networks to fundamentally restructure Finnish economic institutions. Together with entrepreneurial private-sector actors, namely Nokia, they transformed Finland from one of the lowest technology economies in the OECD into one of the most research-intensive societies in the world. At the same time, I reveal that Finland relied so heavily on technological innovation that it increased its vulnerability to adverse economic shocks, most notably the invention of the iPhone.

In chapter 4 I examine Iceland. Characterized by exceptionally tight-knit informal networks, it developed the most extreme form of statism of these three cases. Although slower than Finland or Sweden to embrace new innovation policies, this is mainly because its policy makers reacted to the failure of statism in a very different way. Iceland instead prioritized liberalization and deregulation, suggesting that policy overshooting and overinvestment is not simply a story about state intervention. On the contrary, Icelandic policy makers used formal and informal networks to liberalize their economy even more rapidly and radically than neoliberal icons such as Ronald Reagan or Margaret Thatcher. Institutional reform spurred movement into new industries, such as financial services, partly because of the policy innovations described above and partly because of the speed with which new ideas diffused within dense interpersonal networks in the private sector. At the same time, public- and private-sector actors were slow to recognize the ensuing financial bubble, and Iceland suffered the largest banking economic crisis in human history, eclipsing not only financial powerhouses such as the United Kingdom and the United States but also the Swedish and Finnish banking crises of the early 1990s.

The book gains analytic leverage by comparing relatively fragmented Nordic societies (Sweden) to tight-knit ones (Iceland), but in chapter 5 I increase the range of the independent variable by examining several small, open societies without cohesive, encompassing networks. Austria and Switzerland have developed a consensual approach to economic adjustment that enables them to resolve basic collective action problems, but these federal, sectorally coordinated societies are also marked by more salient regional, linguistic, and industrial cleavages. These divisions have created a pronounced status quo bias, favoring the gradual modernization of established niches rather than Nordic-style reform and restructuring. In addition to eliminating alternative explanations for Nordic volatility such as economic openness, the Austrian and Swiss cases suggest that countries can prosper without Nordic levels of social cohesion. The Greek and Portuguese cases, however, reveal that excessive fragmentation can also pose a problem. Although small and ethnically homogeneous, these societies are far more polarized than their Nordic or Central European counterparts and have struggled to resolve even the most basic collective action problems such as industrial peace and macroeconomic stability. As a result, these countries experienced recurring economic crises, albeit for very different reasons from those of their Nordic counterparts. Here, the issue has not been too much reform and restructuring but too little.

The formidable barriers to cooperation in Southern Europe raise the question whether any country can learn from Nordic Europe. To this end, chapter 6 identifies two non-Nordic societies with cohesive and encompassing networks. I begin with Ireland, a liberal market economy characterized by exceptionally strong informal relationships between public- and private-sector actors. Ireland clearly varies from Nordic Europe in its heavy reliance on foreign direct investment, but I identify a strikingly similar series of abrupt policy reversals and dramatic boom-bust cycles. I then turn to Estonia, where tight-knit relationships among Estonian speakers supported comprehensive reform and restructuring. In addition to outpacing its Central and East European peers in liberalization and deregulation, dense, widely distributed ties also facilitated the exceptionally rapid digitalization of Estonian society. In doing so, they also increased the country's vulnerability to external shocks, including the 2007–2009 credit crunch and the emerging threat of cyberwarfare.

I conclude by examining the lessons for large countries. At first glance, large states such as France, Germany, and the United States appear very different from their Nordic counterparts. Although these societies have evolved over time, I demonstrate that reform and restructuring has proceeded at a slower pace, overshooting has been less pronounced, and economic volatility has been lower. At the same time, I suggest that even fragmented, polarized countries may resemble the Nordic region at a local level, where individuals are more likely to know and trust one another. Examining the politics of economic adjustment in San Diego, California, and Waterloo, Ontario, I illustrate how local communities can use the politics of interconnectedness to accelerate restructuring, as well as the risks associated with this.

1
GOOD GOVERNANCE GONE BAD
Overshooting in Nordic Europe

Why are the Nordic countries so economically successful? And why do these seemingly well-governed societies suffer such severe economic crises? In this chapter I argue that the cause of these two apparently contradictory phenomena is one and the same: the tight-knit relationships that connect elites (and masses) across different regions, sectors, and socioeconomic classes. I begin by explaining how cohesive, encompassing networks facilitate investment in a wide range of collective goods, from peaceful industrial relations to human capital. If anything, the literature on small states (and cooperation more generally) understates the benefits of these social structures. Dense ties can accelerate policy reform and industrial restructuring by enabling entrepreneurial actors to persuade skeptics, compensate losers, and coordinate activity. These same processes, however, can lead to policy overshooting, overinvestment, and economic volatility. Although international openness guards against economic mismanagement in hard times, it does little to check excess in good times. The result is a distinctive pattern of economic volatility in which the Nordic countries respond effectively to economic crises but are prone to policy errors and bad investments when things are going well.

Small States, Interconnectedness, and Good Governance

As I relate in the introduction and subsequent chapters, Nordic success is intrinsically perplexing, because the Nordic countries have succeeded in contrasting ways using different economic models. Denmark, Finland, Iceland, Norway, and Sweden have prospered under highly interventionist regimes and laissez-faire ones, opening themselves to international trade and developing behind protective tariffs. They have relied on lightly processed natural resources and excelled in cutting-edge high-technology markets. Partly because of this diversity, scholars have cycled among competing explanations, alternately emphasizing the strength of the state (Rothstein and Stolle 2003, 19), labor power resources (Korpi 2006, 202), or employer organization (Hall and Soskice 2001, 15). In fact, these characteristics have varied considerably, both cross-nationally and over time.

The literature on small states suggests that the unifying thread in the Nordic region is not a particular industry, economic model, or even a single actor but rather the relationship among them. More specifically, elites (and masses) are connected within cohesive, encompassing networks (Campbell and Hall 2017, 34). These relationships are *cohesive* in the sense that actors trust one another and have an easy time cooperating. They are *encompassing* in the sense that they transcend political, regional, and sectoral divisions. In other words, Nordic societies' dense, high-trust relationships take the form of "bridging" rather than "bonding" capital, cutting across salient social cleavages rather than reinforcing them (Rothstein and Stolle 2003, 9).

In appendix 1 I discuss the conceptualization and measurement of these cohesive, encompassing relationships, making the case that the Nordic countries are unusually interconnected. It is worth emphasizing, however, several key differences between this book and other research on small states. First, small size may be a necessary condition for the creation of cohesive, encompassing networks (Campbell and Hall 2009, 548), but it is most certainly not a sufficient one. This is most obvious in the highly polarized small states of Southern Europe such as Greece and Portugal, but it also applies to Austria and Switzerland, where industry is generally organized along regional or sectoral lines rather than national ones (see chapter 5). In Nordic Europe, however, constrained geopolitical space has interacted with external security threats and cultural homogeneity to foster the development of unusually broad, dense, and high-quality social ties.

Scholars historically have used the language of "neocorporatism," a formal system of interest intermediation in which policy makers cooperate with large, encompassing producer associations, specifically trade unions and employers, to characterize these relationships (Fioretos 2013, 312; Katzenstein 1985, 91; Thorhallsson and Kattel 2013, 84). The Nordic countries rank high on measures of neocorporatism and this captures an important form of interconnectedness.[1] This emphasis on industrial relations and cross-class cooperation, however, does not directly address the corporate linkages that might accelerate (or inhibit) the diffusion of new business models within the private sector. As a result, we need to consider interfirm relations and the degree to which these do (or do not) transcend political, regional, or sectoral cleavages.

This interest on interfirm relations is reminiscent of the Varieties of Capitalism literature, which seeks to measure the degree of strategic coordination among firms. In appendix 1, however, I outline several problems with coordination, not least of which is the insensitivity to the dense informal ties that structure life in small states.[2] Scholarship and interviews alike suggest that individuals are more likely to be connected through professional associations, military service, common courses, soccer clubs, informal roundtables, and even family ties (Gingrich and Hannerz 2017, 13). Even when not directly connected, concentrated media markets bind actors by generating shared experiences and values (Gingrich and Hannerz 2017, 24). Widely acknowledged in the literature on small states (Katzenstein 1985, 89; Rehn 1996, 234), these informal ties lie at the center of my analysis, which uses 335 interviews to characterize social relations instead of relying exclusively on quantitative measures of neocorporatism or coordination (see appendix 1).

Whether employing the language of neocorporatism, coordination, or informal networks, research on small and large states alike has argued that cohesive, encompassing ties can improve the quality of governance by facilitating investment in collective goods. Neocorporatism has been linked to peaceful industrial relations, price stability, lower unemployment, higher growth, and a host of other positive economic outcomes as very large producer associations internalize the cost of their demands (Soskice 1990, 37). When this pattern of organization extends to the corporate sector, the Varieties of Capitalism literature suggests that dense interfirm relationships permit investment in more specialized inputs such as human capital, technological development, and product standards (Ornston and Schulze-Cleven 2015, 562–63).

Research suggests that dense informal relationships deliver similar benefits. Economists point out that tight-knit networks facilitate investment in collective goods by making it easier to detect opportunistic behavior and raising the reputational cost of free riding or shirking. For example, opportunistic firms jeopardize access to training, legal representation, standard setting, as well as other collective benefits (Soskice 1990, 45). Sociologists suggest that membership within a cohesive community encourages actors to sacrifice short-term individual interests in order to achieve long-term collective goals (Campbell and Hall 2009, 559). In the Nordic region, these instrumental and other-regarding motivations reinforce one another. A Finnish research director, describing his decision to participate in a large collaborative research project, began with an appeal to economic patriotism, citing his commitment to his country. He concluded on a more individualistic note, acknowledging not only the ease of cooperation in a small society but also the high reputational cost of free riding in a tight-knit community:

> One aspect, which I forgot to mention, is that everybody knows everybody. We are five million people. It's not Luxembourg, but it's still easy to establish cooperative networks between suppliers and customers. It's never possible in bigger countries and it doesn't have anything to do with bribes. We have been studying in the same university . . . so natural forms of cooperation are easier to establish in that sense since [we] know each other relatively well. And it is such that people have to perform. Your reputation is on the line. (interview with research director, 19 October 2005, Finland)

In addition to delivering benefits, these informal relationships also mitigate the worst features of neocorporatism, a highly centralized system of interest intermediation which may be unrepresentative and insensitive to local conditions (Pontusson and Swenson 1996, 237). Dense interpersonal connections, of the sort that characterize Nordic Europe, reduce the distance between top-level leaders and rank-and-file members. Widely distributed networks that cut across political, regional, and sectoral cleavages are particularly beneficial. In addition to increasing access to local information (Scott 1999, 38), they expose decision makers to a wider variety of economic (and noneconomic) perspectives (Breznitz 2007, 16). At the same time, ordinary citizens are more likely to trust experts in a high-trust environment, contributing to pragmatic and flexible policy making (Campbell and Hall 2017, 14).

As a result, the literature on small states provides a compelling way to understand good governance in Nordic Europe. Although the specific nature of these ties has varied over time and space, actors are connected through formal institutions and, more importantly, dense interpersonal ties. Transcending political, regional, and sectoral cleavages, these connections exemplify best practice as identified by business scholars (Kristensen and Lilja 2011), economists (Rodrik 2007), sociologists (Safford 2009), and political scientists (Burt 2005; Ostrom 1990), enabling decision makers to access high-quality local information and motivating individuals to contribute to collective goods. These ties not only enable the Nordic countries to invest in goods such as industrial peace and wage moderation but also support the development of more sophisticated and complex inputs such as infrastructure, machinery, education, research, and risk capital.

The literature on small states provides a nice explanation for Nordic prosperity, highlighting the constant cohesive, encompassing networks that connect different countries, time periods, and economic models. But it offers little insight into one of the region's most distinctive features. In Nordic Europe, prosperity is not merely a story about the gradual accumulation of productive inputs. Rather, the last century has witnessed sudden shifts in both policy making and comparative advantage. Sweden, for example, transformed itself from one of the most laissez-faire societies in Western Europe to one of the most statist during the interwar years. In the late twentieth century, Finland redefined itself from a paper producer and supplier to the Soviet Union into a high-technology leader. These two examples suggest that the Nordic countries exhibit not only a capacity for investing in collective goods but an aptitude for radical reform and restructuring. How do we explain this dynamism?

The Politics of Interconnectedness and Systemic Change

The connection between cohesive, encompassing networks, comprehensive institutional reform, and radical restructuring is not immediately obvious. Tight-knit relationships are more often perceived to delay change. Historically, heightened connectedness in small states was associated with generous social policies that cushioned the pace of economic adjustment to a socially acceptable level (Katzenstein 1985, 47). This is most obvious in the social democracies of Scandinavia, but even welfare laggards such as Switzerland developed alternative private-sector instruments, such as long-term bank loans, to slow the rate of adjustment (Katzenstein 1984, 96). These compensatory social policies are embedded within consensual political systems that discourage comprehensive reform. Reliance on proportional representation, multi-party governments, and the institutionalized participation of large producer associations all represent "veto points" that can be used to block reform (Immergut 1992, 391). As a result, institutional change is generally perceived to occur gradually, unfolding at the margins of society through incremental processes of layering, conversion, drift, or erosion (Streeck and Thelen 2005).

In small states, the impact of generous social policies and consensual political institutions is compounded by informal relationships, which increase the number of veto points. An Icelandic policy maker described how interconnectedness could inhibit reform:

> In a sense, you would think that a small state would make it easier. Everyone knows everyone and the lines of communication are very short.... But a problem with smaller states is that everything is personal. In a large state you can decide to make some reforms and it is easier because you don't have to deal with the individuals. Here even if you are talking about joining programs or merging universities, you have to deal with all of the individuals that are affected. And they can be very well connected, even to political leaders. (interview with policy maker, 5 March 2012, Iceland)

Collectively, these institutions are perceived to delay the redistribution of resources to new firms and activities. Scholars of business, economics, and innovation repeatedly conclude that consensus-based societies, small and large, are struggling to adapt to an increasingly fast-paced and dynamic global economy (Alesina and Giavazzi 2006; Eichengreen 2006). This is not limited to literature on formal institutions. Research on informal relationships consistently draws similar conclusions, arguing that dense high-trust networks restrict individual freedom (Portes 1998), increase resistance to new ideas (Gargiulo and Benassi 1999), stifle innovation (Kern 1998), and contribute to regional "lock-in" (Grabher 1993, 260–64). With their consensual political systems, cooperative economic institutions, and high levels of social capital, the Nordic countries appear uniquely vulnerable to this kind of political and economic sclerosis.

Proponents of relational capitalism, influenced chiefly by the German case (and other Central European countries), have accepted many of these claims and responded by reconceptualizing incrementalism as an economic asset. More specifically, the cooperative relationships described above, formal and informal, are perceived to protect asset-specific investments. Firms (and workers) are more willing to invest in specialized equipment, skills, and knowledge, knowing that other enterprises, large banks, or the state are willing to protect them against opportunistic behavior, international economic shocks, and other negative events (Zahariadis 2002, 607). These commitments are more credible to the extent that consensual political institutions, large producer associations, and a general spirit of social solidarity discourage policy makers from introducing any sudden large-scale institutional reforms (Cusack, Iversen, and Soskice 2007, 379).

Countries (and regions) with consensual political systems, cooperative economic institutions, and dense informal networks can rely on these asset-specific investments to insulate themselves from economic competition, entering stable low- and medium-technology industries with high barriers to entry such as machine tools or automobiles. They react to economic shocks not by dismantling industries, but rather by upgrading preexisting investments in specialized skills and equipment (Streeck 1991, 26). Scholars have argued that this tendency is particularly pronounced in small states, which have successfully defended century-old niches such as Austrian steel (Katzenstein 1984, 210), Dutch electronics (Dalum 1988, 117), and Swiss watchmaking (Porter 1990, 324).

This incremental view of cooperation does an excellent job of explaining how Central European countries such as Austria and Switzerland compete in the international economy (see chapter 5), but it yields little insight into Nordic Europe, where comprehensive reform and restructuring is commonplace. Late industrializers, the Nordic countries relied on the rapid diffusion of new organizational innovations such as the universal bank to enter capital-intensive low- and medium-technology industries with high barriers to entry in the late nineteenth and early twentieth centuries (Fellman et al. 2008). Then, in the late twentieth century, the Nordic countries systematically dismantled many of these institutions, including their heavily regulated financial systems, in a bid to promote innovation and market competition. These days, they are more commonly associated with fundamentally new and often radically innovative industries, such as biotechnology, software, and telecommunications equipment (Ornston 2012b, 13). How do we make sense of this fundamentally discontinuous pattern of institutional reform and economic adjustment?

I argue that cohesive, encompassing networks, the constant that governs the adoption of new policy instruments and business models, can facilitate reform and restructuring in three ways: through the politics of persuasion, the politics of compensation, and the politics of coordination. First, reform-oriented actors can rely on persuasive appeals to mobilize support. The politics of persuasion is particularly effective in tight-knit societies, because reform-oriented actors can more easily identify the actors who oppose reform and their motives (Culpepper 2002, 778). Having done so, they can then use high levels of trust to convince skeptics, draw on the shared values that may have special resonance in a cohesive community, or appeal to a spirit of social solidarity (Campbell and Hall 2009, 552). This applies not only to policy reform but also to the private sector, where new business models diffuse quickly within dense social circles. To cite one example that is not covered in the book, Finnish banking representatives argue that the country's pioneering role in electronic banking could only have happened in a small state. High-trust relationships among a very small number of financial institutions made it easier to convince skeptics about the benefits of electronic banking, agree on a single, common standard, and collaborate on technological development (interview with bank representative, 2 November 2005, Finland).[3]

Second, when the politics of persuasion fails, dense social structures make it easier to generate consensus by delivering side payments to adversely affected actors. Scholars have long recognized that small states can use generous social policies to neutralize opposition to free trade (Katzenstein 1984). But the politics of compensation can facilitate other reforms as well. For example, Swedish industry supported the construction of a massive welfare state in exchange for industry's right to "direct and allocate work" (Magnusson 2000, 187), while Finnish trade unions supported massive public investments in corporate R&D with the understanding that corporate profits would be invested in a way that increased wages and employment (Ornston and Rehn 2006, 94).[4] These bargains are easier to strike in tight-knit societies where actors know and trust one another, as evidenced by the role that personal relationships played in the Icelandic Social Contract of the early 1990s (see chapter 4). Trust makes actors more willing to exchange large short-term costs for uncertain future benefits (Saari 2001, 198–99) and facilitates policy linkage, in which policy makers adjust several policies simultaneously (Wilensky 2002, 104).[5] Meanwhile, harmonious labor relations and the short distance between leaders and ordinary citizens ensure that the benefits of reform and restructuring are widely distributed. Just like the politics of persuasion, these compensatory strategies are not limited to the public sector. In chapter 4 I describe how Icelandic banks were able to compensate adversely affected actors without the state, distributing low-interest loans to traditional industries, generously patronizing the arts, investing in education, and delivering other public goods.

Finally, by using the politics of persuasion and the politics of compensation to build a broad consensus, reform-oriented actors can use the politics of coordination to accelerate reform and restructuring. Although obviously constrained by the compensatory deals described above, consensus and the ease of communication enables reform-oriented actors to adapt multiple policies at the same time.[6] In chapter 2 I illustrate how virtually every aspect of Swedish public policy was modified to support the growth of large capital-intensive firms. The result was not simply a story about "regulatory capture," in which a single industry controls a public agency or two (Stigler 1971, 5), but rather the conversion of the entire state apparatus. In the Finnish and Icelandic cases, it makes more sense to speak of "societal capture" to describe the way in which Nokia independently reoriented much of the Finnish business system around its vision and the degree to which Iceland's banks influenced seemingly unrelated fields from the media to university research.

The politics of persuasion, compensation, and coordination have very different implications for politics and economic adjustment. Instead of delaying institutional change, reform-oriented actors can use tight-knit networks to accelerate it. This is clearest in the case of the welfare state, where the Nordic countries developed unusually robust systems of social protection within a relatively short period of time. But it also applies to other areas, from the adoption of systemic innovation policies to financial deregulation. By fundamentally altering the environment in which firms compete, these systemic changes have enabled the Nordic countries to engineer big leaps into new industries. They industrialized with remarkable speed, exploiting unprocessed natural resources and quickly moving into capital-intensive manufacturing. In the late twentieth century, they exited traditional industry just as abruptly, entering knowledge-intensive services. Of course, all countries experience institutional and economic change (Streeck and Thelen 2005), but the Nordic countries have experienced reform and restructuring on a pace and scale with few parallels in the developed world (see appendix 2). These moves have earned them high praise (*Economist* 2013b), but also expose them to unique risks that are widely overlooked by political economists.

When Good Governance Goes Bad: From Adaptation to Overshooting

Although the adaptive capacities described above have enabled the Nordic countries to respond effectively to a wide variety economic challenges, they can also have dysfunctional effects. Scholars have long criticized cohesive and encompassing networks for inhibiting change, but the preceding account suggests that these social structures can also cause *too much* change. The same connections that accelerate the diffusion of good ideas can also facilitate the spread of bad ones (Berman 1997, 419), as evidenced by the ability of several American-trained economists to popularize risky financial strategies in 1980s Finland (Tainio, Lilja, and Santalainen 2002). In fact, the Finnish credit bubble and banking crisis is an excellent example of how a willingness to trust experts, conceptualized as an asset in the literature on small states (Campbell and Hall 2017, 14), can also represent a liability. Moreover, even the best ideas, such as the decision to favor capital-intensive manufacturing firms in early postwar Sweden or the emphasis on technological innovation in late twentieth-century Finland, can be carried to dangerous extremes. These weaknesses are even more striking when we revisit the politics of persuasion, compensation, and coordination.

Although the Nordic countries have a history of implementing some excellent ideas, they have also fallen prey to the persuasive appeals of less scrupulous entrepreneurs, from the Swedish "Match King," Ivar Kreuger, to Iceland's "Corporate Vikings." These charismatic reformers used the politics of persuasion, manipulating national symbols to mobilize public support. The American-trained economist Pentti Kouri, for example, used informal roundtables to successfully sell his attractive image of a "Fortress Finland" to bankers, industrialists, and politicians (interview with roundtable participant, 20 October 2005, Finland). Once an idea enters the mainstream, critics are quickly dismissed. At the height of the bubble, Icelandic authorities, journalists, and ordinary citizens famously attributed critical financial reports from Danish banks to "jealousy" and systematically ignored warnings by foreign financial regulators, economists, and investment banks (Bergmann 2014, 91–92). Domestic critics do not necessarily fare any better. Asked about a successful Finnish businessman who criticized industrial and innovation policies, a journalist remarked, "He is a very creative man and I think very clever. He is doing very good business so he should be listened to more than he is now. [But] he has a reputation as a freak. It is a pity, because he was the only [Finn] who was invited by [a foreign government] as a consultant" (interview with journalist, 9 November 2005, Finland). A bank executive who challenged Finnish monetary policy in the early 1990s remarked:

> It was sort of like what I would expect in the politburo of the Chinese Communist Party. There is room for debate in certain areas but in other areas debate is not acceptable or if you debate you run the risk of becoming excluded. . . . It's a question of whether you belong or don't belong and for most people it becomes important to belong, because they do not have the self-confidence or assets to run the risks of not belonging. (interview, bank executive, 12 June 2012, Finland)

The politics of compensation increases the cost of social exclusion in a tight-knit community by jeopardizing access to a much broader array of collective goods. For example, corporate executives that failed to "play by the rules" risked exclusion from public industrial policies and private research consortia (interviews with R&D director, technology firm, 19 October 2005, and executive, software firm, 23 November 2005, Finland). Critically minded individuals faced even bigger obstacles ranging from a curtailment of their professional responsibilities to the loss of their job (interviews with bank director, Iceland, 7 March 2012; professor, Iceland, 8 March 2012; and bank executive, Finland, 12 June 2012). This represents an existential threat in a tight-knit society, because one faces the prospect of being blacklisted, not from an individual firm or even an entire industry but rather the entire economy (Árnason 2015, 53).

Finally, the elimination of dissent and the ability to coordinate across a wide range of organizations can lead to policy overshooting and overinvestment. Sweden's decision to favor large capital-intensive manufacturing firms in the early postwar period was entirely reasonable, but the ability to coordinate virtually every aspect of economic policy stifled the kinds of new growth-oriented firms that might have protected the country from rising oil prices, technological change, and shifting patterns of competition in the 1970s (Henrekson and Jakobsson 2001, 355). This form of coordination is arguably even more problematic when it extends to the private sector. Iceland's financial crisis was exacerbated by the fact that the banks not only accumulated Swiss-sized liabilities in less than a decade but, in contrast to other countries, firms pursued the exact same business model. Iceland's three main commercial banks not only targeted the same asset classes but, in several cases, chased the exact same assets. In short, the same adaptive capacities that enable the Nordic countries to reform public policies and restructure their economies contribute to some of the most extreme cases of policy overshooting and overinvestment in the developed world.

If this is true, why aren't the Nordic countries complete basket cases? The Nordic countries, and small states more generally, combine cohesive, encompassing internal networks with relatively open economies (Andersen et al. 2007, 17). International openness (and market competition in general) performs two valuable functions. First, it guards against cognitive lock-in, exposing policy makers to new ideas (Breznitz and Ornston 2014, 252). Robust market competition is a particularly effective monitoring device because it exposes inefficient strategies, discrediting established routines and creating windows for new actors and ideas. For example, developmental agencies such as the Finnish Agency for Technology and Innovation (Tekes) target export-oriented firms in part because it is easier to measure success (interview with Tekes representative, 28 November 2006, Finland). In fact, Tekes owes its existence to international competition. It was created after a foreign investor withdrew from a joint venture with the Finnish state, sending a clear and visible signal about the (in)efficiency of traditional state-led industrial policies (Rehn 1996, 283).

Second, when trade approaches or exceeds a country's gross domestic product, policy makers literally cannot afford to defend bad policies or vulnerable firms (Schrank and Kurtz 2005, 684). For example, defensive economic strategies based on state aid and passive social benefits proved too costly in Denmark and Sweden during the late 1970s and early 1980s. Mounting fiscal and current-account deficits not only alerted policy makers to a problem but compelled them to reform industrial, social, and labor-market policies (Schwartz 1994, 528). Denmark and Sweden responded admirably to this challenge, liberalizing more rapidly than larger Western European countries with less cohesive, encompassing networks (Campbell and Pedersen 2007, 317–18; Glimstedt and Zander 2003, 110). In the conventional literature, the small, open Nordic countries appear to represent the optimal combination of social solidarity and market competition (Andersen et al. 2007, 17). No wonder they are presented as a "supermodel" worthy of emulation (*Economist* 2013b).

The problem with this happy formula is that market competition is an imperfect disciplinary device. Even though markets quickly expose flawed policies and troubled firms in hard times, they are notoriously inept at exposing inefficiencies during good times. During periods of "irrational exuberance," markets systematically discount political risks, overinvest in specific industries, and generate massive asset bubbles. All economies are vulnerable to these shifts in market sentiment, but these dynamics are even more exaggerated in highly interconnected societies. In these communities, there are few mechanisms to guard against overshooting or overinvestment. As a result, I argue that the Nordic countries and other cohesive, open economies are characterized by a distinctive pattern of economic adjustment. They respond effectively to crises but are vulnerable to exaggerated policy shifts, the misallocation of resources, and asset bubbles during good times.

This theory has clear, observable implications. First, I predict that the Nordic countries are characterized by unusually rapid restructuring. Although they will not chase every trend (Iceland was too preoccupied with financial liberalization to systematically pursue new opportunities in the digital economy during the 1990s), these societies are more likely to surpass incumbents and establish themselves as clear leaders in their field. Second, they are characterized by overshooting, scaling new policies and business models to unsustainable levels, prompting sharp crises. Far deeper than the garden-variety downturns that affect all economies, these are record-setting downturns that stand out in comparative perspective.

Finally, these dynamics persist over time. When confronted with a crisis, countries will respond with radical reform and restructuring. Crises empower hitherto marginalized actors, experimenting with new ideas at the periphery of the public and private sectors.[7] These reform-oriented agents can use the politics of persuasion, compensation, and coordination to transform public policy and private business once again, leapfrogging leaders and fundamentally redefining comparative advantage. "Successful" adjustment, however, brings little stability. Instead, these societies are likely to overcorrect, triggering a new round of policy overshooting and overinvestment. In appendix 2 I present cross-national evidence to support these claims, documenting rapid restructuring, deep crises, and greater economic volatility in the Nordic region between 1979 and 2009.

To more closely examine the relationship between interconnectedness and economic volatility, however, I analyze three boom-bust cycles in three countries. Chapter 2 examines the rise and fall of traditional industrial policies and heavy industry in Sweden. I then move forward in time to discuss the shift to high-technology competition (Finland) in chapter 3 and financialization (Iceland) in chapter 4. I open each case study by documenting the presence of cohesive and encompassing networks and then connecting these dense relationships to reform and restructuring through the politics of persuasion, compensation, and coordination. The chapters conclude by illustrating how the same mechanisms that accelerated change led to overshooting.

Examining multiple boom-bust cycles in several tight-knit societies enables me to eliminate many alternative explanations. First, I demonstrate that overshooting was never simply a story about comparative advantage.[8] Although the Nordic countries specialized in low-technology, resource-extractive industries in the past, overshooting also occurred within high-technology and nontradable industries.[9] Second, I argue that volatility does not follow automatically from economic openness. Overshooting also occurred under relatively closed, heavily regulated regimes such as early postwar Iceland.[10] Finally, I argue that overshooting is not synonymous with state intervention. Heavy-handed industrial policies may have contributed to overinvestment in the early postwar period, but recent banking crises illustrate how private-sector entrepreneurs can also use the politics of persuasion, compensation, and coordination to independently transform tight-knit societies.

Instead, the Swedish, Finnish, and Icelandic cases highlight the importance of interconnectedness. This is also true when we compare Finland, Sweden, and Iceland to each other. Although all three countries are tight-knit by the standards of large, diverse societies such as Germany, the United Kingdom, or the United States, Sweden is significantly more fragmented and polarized than Finland. Iceland, at the other extreme, is the most interconnected, particularly when we take informal relationships into account. As I relate in chapters 2 through 4, this has predictable implications for economic adjustment. Iceland exhibited the greatest capacity for reform and restructuring, but also the greatest vulnerability to overshooting and overinvestment. By contrast, developments were more muted in Sweden at each stage in history, whether we are discussing the statist turn of the early postwar period or its retreat and the financialization of the economy at the end of the century.

Of course, three cases alone are not enough to satisfy more skeptical readers. Given the ubiquity of crises in contemporary capitalism, some might question whether the Nordic countries are truly unique in their vulnerability to overshooting. To be sure, small, open economies are more volatile than their larger counterparts.[11] Could overshooting reflect a hitherto overlooked variable such as population size or the timing of industrialization? To address these questions, I compare the Nordic countries to four small, open economies without cohesive, encompassing networks (Austria, Greece, Portugal, and Switzerland) in chapter 5.[12] In the concluding chapter I illustrate how the Nordic region differs from three large countries, France, Germany, and the United States.

Other readers might wonder whether overshooting reflects some idiosyncratic pan-Nordic variable and, as a result, question its relevance for other societies. To this end, I present two non-Nordic cases, Ireland and Estonia, in chapter 6. Institutionally, these liberal market economies look very different from Nordic Europe and have also adopted divergent economic strategies. But they are also exceptionally small and cohesive societies, characterized by strong informal ties that unite different political parties, regions, sectors, and industries. These social structures facilitated Nordic-style reform and restructuring, but they have also contributed to deep crises. The conclusion generalizes the argument to an even wider set of cases, identifying parallels between the politics of interconnectedness in Nordic Europe and small and medium-sized cities within large states. Before expanding the geographic scope of the argument, however, we begin in Nordic Europe with the politics of planning and Sweden's emergence as a manufacturing powerhouse in the mid-twentieth century. As noted above, this is the least tight-knit of my three Nordic cases. Readers looking for a more extreme example of overshooting should skip ahead to chapter 3 (Finland) or 4 (Iceland).

2

MANUFACTURING A CRISIS
Planning in Sweden

The defining feature of twentieth-century economic policy was the rise of the state. In discrediting nineteenth-century liberalism and market competition, the economic turmoil of the interwar years triggered unprecedented state intervention. The statist turn was most revolutionary in the developing world, where capitalism was associated with imperialism and exploitation. But even market-oriented, advanced industrialized countries in Western Europe and North America reconsidered the benefits of unfettered market competition. Postwar France exemplified this new model with its selective industrial policies, but the shift to the state reshaped Western capitalism more generally. Germany institutionalized its commitment to a "social state" in its postwar constitution, the United States complemented the "New Deal" and "Great Society" with countercyclical monetary policies, and the United Kingdom nationalized a wide variety of strategic industries such as coal and steel.

Statist ideas proved particularly transformative in Nordic Europe, however, which turned to the public sector with even greater gusto than its larger, more fragmented peers. From the 1930s to the 1980s, these historically laissez-faire societies used the state to comprehensively restructure systems of social protection and production. This shift was most conspicuous in social democratic societies such as Denmark, Norway, and Sweden, which constructed the most generous and encompassing welfare states in the world. But even welfare laggards with weak labor movements such as Finland and Iceland turned to the public sector, adopting selective industrial policies that eclipsed paragons of statism such as France and Japan. Moreover, unlike France and Japan, which witnessed regime change after World War II, Nordic Europe was characterized by a relatively high degree of political continuity. How did they manage to introduce such sweeping reforms?

In this chapter I argue that cohesive, encompassing networks enabled the small states of Northern Europe to engineer a dramatic volte-face in the middle of the twentieth century. Like all countries, these societies were influenced by new ideas about market failure and the power of the state. Those ideas, however, diffused more quickly within tight-knit social circles as ideational entrepreneurs used persuasive appeals to convince policy makers, industrialists, and labor representatives about the benefits of state intervention. Although not everyone was converted, repeated interaction enabled pro-reform advocates to neutralize the most influential opponents with side payments. Once they did so, dense relationships made it easier to isolate and marginalize any remaining dissenters. As a result, these countries were able to adopt a highly coordinated approach to the politics of planning, synchronizing developments across a staggering array of policy domains. This pattern of comprehensive institutional reform facilitated exceptionally rapid economic restructuring and postwar growth, with the result that the Nordic countries were widely celebrated by postwar political economists.

These pragmatic reformers, however, struggled to grapple with new challenges beginning in the 1970s, resulting in sluggish growth and severe imbalances. What happened to the reform capacity that these countries exhibited in earlier decades? The same dense, high-trust relationships that enabled them to expand the state and capital-intensive industries contributed to structural imbalances and fiscal deficits. Tight-knit ties blinded decision makers to these weaknesses, obscured policy alternatives, and hindered reform. As a result, initial responses reinforced flawed, existing economic policies, with predictable results. In short, postwar planning in Nordic Europe exemplifies how good governance goes bad. The same mechanisms that enabled these tight-knit societies to adopt innovative policies in the mid-twentieth century contributed to policy overshooting and delayed reform.

I develop this argument by examining developments in Sweden from 1932 to 1982. At first glance, the country appears to be a poor example of "planning," as well-organized employers successfully resisted French-style selective industrial policies (Pontusson 1992). Sweden, however, constructed one of the most generous, encompassing, and extensively studied welfare states in the world. Focusing on the politics of persuasion, compensation, and coordination within cohesive, encompassing networks complements accounts that have hitherto emphasized the role of medieval legacies (Iversen and Soskice 2009), labor power resources (Korpi 2006), or employer organizations (Swenson 1991).

This explanation also highlights how the welfare state was part of a broader, deliberate, and highly coordinated strategy to restructure Swedish industry by strengthening large firms in established capital-intensive, export-oriented industries. In this sense, Swedish "planning" was even more comprehensive and effective than archetypical statist societies such as France (as I discuss in the conclusion). At the same time, these "successful" industrial policies heightened Swedish vulnerability to shifting economic conditions during the 1970s. Tight-knit networks made it more difficult to identify and respond to new challenges, with the result that Sweden was transformed from a paragon of pragmatism in the early postwar period into the worst performer in the OECD and a symbol of economic sclerosis by the early 1980s.

Antecedents: Forging Sweden, Inc.

Sweden is significantly larger and less tight-knit than other Nordic countries such as Finland or Iceland, but it exhibits a high level of interconnectedness relative to other advanced industrialized economies. Although commonly equated with postwar neocorporatism (Gourevitch 1986; Katzenstein 1985), heightened interconnectedness can be traced back to the pre-industrial era, long before the rise of organized labor. The country's small population and unusually capacious, absolutist monarchy supported the development of a coherent national administrative structure. Weak feudal traditions further narrowed the divisions between different estates (Magnusson 2000, 21), while the early and permanent adoption of Lutheranism tempered religious conflict. The Lutheran emphasis on literacy further eroded divisions between elites and masses, fostering a relatively strong sense of national identity and facilitating the diffusion of new ideas (Sjögren 2008, 26).

In the late nineteenth century, these tight-knit networks facilitated the rapid adoption of German-style universal banking. Hitherto dominated by merchant houses that provided only working capital, universal banks issued large long-term loans to their clients. Pioneered by André Oscar Wallenberg's Stockholm's Enskilda Banken (SEB) in 1856, other entrepreneurs quickly pounced on this model. By the 1870s, Sweden boasted over forty modern commercial banks (Magnusson 2000, 170). This reflected a coordinated effort by a broad cross-section of Swedish society, including rivals keen to copy Wallenberg's success as well as politicians concerned with Sweden's overwhelmingly agrarian economy (Sjögren 2008, 34). For example, Skandinavisk Kredit connected Wallenberg, a bishop's son, with other commercial bankers, traditional Gothenberg-based merchant houses, conservative aristocrats, and liberal politicians (Magnusson 2000, 83). Bolstered by patriotic coverage in *Aftonbladet* and *Post-Tidningen*, these new entities had no trouble mobilizing deposits in a homogenous, literate society with a high degree of social capital (Magnusson 2000, 171). By the end of the century, Sweden had eclipsed its original role model. With 75 percent of credit to large enterprises flowing through Swedish banks (Sjögren 2008, 40), Sweden possessed one of the most concentrated financial markets in the world (Magnusson 2000, 175).

These new banks used their privileged economic position to organize Sweden's largest and most important enterprises into a relatively small number of cohesive industrial blocs (Ottosson 1997, 61–62). The Wallenberg family, whose holdings have included not only SEB but also ASEA (ABB), Atlas Copco, Electrolux, Ericsson, and Saab, played an especially prominent role in Swedish politics and economics.[1] But competitors pursued similar strategies, organizing networks around holding companies such as Industrivärden (Handelsbanken, Sandvik, SCA, Skanska) and Melker Schörling AB (Securitas, Assa Abloy, Hexagon). These industrial groups represent an important foundation for both intra- and intersectoral cooperation, consolidating small and medium-sized enterprises into larger conglomerates during the early twentieth century and coordinating activity among larger firms in later years (Ottosson 1997, 54). After the Wallenberg family assumed control of Ericsson, for example, the firm reached an agreement to focus exclusively on lower-voltage devices, while its rival, ASEA, concentrated on higher-voltage equipment (Tell 2008, 114–15).

A relatively small number of powerful financial actors also facilitated cooperation across industrial families. This was particularly evident following the centralization of industrial relations in the middle of the twentieth century. Sweden ranks high on measures of employer organization (Martin and Swank 2012, 19); a single industry confederation, Svenskt Näringsliv, represents 60,000 firms, employing over half of Sweden's private sector workers. Collaboration is, if anything, even more intensive at the sectoral level, where organizations such as the Association of Swedish Engineering Industries and the Swedish Forest Industries Association have a tradition of exchanging ideas and cooperating on a wide range of issues from wage setting to research, despite belonging to rival industrial families (Rehn 1996, 170). These official neocorporatist bodies were flanked by less formal fora, such as the Big Five (Tell 2008, 114) and the Executive's Club (Rehn 1996, 170), which leading multinationals used to coordinate political strategy during the interwar and postwar years.

This pattern of cooperation extends to the public sector as well. Policy makers have proven responsive to industry demands, from the introduction of universal banking in the 1850s (Magnusson 2000, 100–101) to the present day. The government and business have forged particularly close relations in the realm of procurement, using public utilities such as Televerket and Vattenfall to support the development of new communications and electrical technologies (Berggren and Laestadius 2003, 91; Sjögren 2008, 30). Combined with extensive patterns of interfirm collaboration, it is no surprise that Swedish economists popularized the concept of a "development block" (Dahmén 1950).

Finally, these dense relationships were extended to cover organized labor in a series of bargains during the 1930s (see below). Trade union density in Sweden, which exceeded 80 percent for most of the postwar period, remains among the highest in the developed world (see table A.1). Sweden was most famous for a highly centralized system of wage bargaining, but cooperation extended beyond production to a wide array of policy-making bodies. For example, the social partners collaborated within the tripartite Labor Market Board (AMS) to shape Sweden's ambitious active labor-market policies (Lindvall and Sebring 2005, 1061). For this reason, Sweden is often classified as a prototypical case of neocorporatism, exemplifying institutionalized cooperation between centralized, encompassing producer associations (Katzenstein 1985; Pekkarinen, Pohjola, and Rowthorn 1992).

These formal neocorporatist institutions have weakened in recent years. The Swedish Trade Union Congress (LO)'s proposal to introduce "wage earner funds" was perceived as a ploy to socialize control of Sweden's largest firms and polarized Swedish industrial relations during the 1980s (Vartiainen 1998b). Swedish employers responded by decentralizing collective wage bargaining and withdrawing from virtually all tripartite boards (Lindvall and Sebring 2005). At the same time, Sweden remains a highly interconnected society, even within a postcorporatist environment. Employers, for example, remarked that decentralization and their retreat from tripartite policy making was predicated on strong collaborative relationships with organized labor that enabled them to negotiate change at a sectoral level and within individual enterprises (interview with representative, Swedish industry association, 8 May 2012, Sweden).

Enduring patterns of industry-labor cooperation reflect the fact that Swedish interconnectedness was always rooted in informal relationships as well as formal institutions. One employer remarked, "The positive thing [about Sweden] is that you always know everyone. . . . I can call anyone" (interview with executive, financial firm, 8 May 2012, Sweden). Even high-technology industry, which does not conform to the traditional model of Swedish corporate governance, is well connected. An observer commented:

> Well, it's a small country of course and it's easy to know everybody that has to be known in the field. . . . If you look at the top [tech] companies on the Stockholm exchange it's more or less the same people sitting

on every board. . . . A lot of the kids that started the companies, their fathers were executives at IBM in Stockholm, [they] became icons at the same time and had to know each other because they were attending the same seminars, fairs, and events. (interview with reporter, 16 May 2012, Sweden)

Although similar phenomena occur in larger countries, many interviewees maintained that Swedish networks were distinctive. A banker, for example, argued that Swedish financial firms enjoyed cozier relationships with their regulators than their American counterparts (interview with representative, financial firm, 10 May 2012, Sweden). Policy makers concurred, noting that it was easier to access information and coordinate activity with a smaller number of players (interviews with representative, financial regulator, 10 May 2012, and former employee, Ministry of Finance, 15 May 2012, Sweden). Meanwhile, politicians highlighted the ease of collaboration across different political camps (interview with former employee, Ministry of Finance, 15 May 2012). In the words of one policy maker:

> Talking about the last financial crisis we had the 1990s, one of the big reasons we were so successful in handling that was that there was an agreement between the political parties. It was a couple of guys writing press releases and the closeness and that kind of social cohesion really helped to take radical measures when it was doomsday feeling. It worked. There, the small country situation was helpful. (interview with former employee, financial regulator, 11 May 2012, Sweden)

Although most visible within elite circles, these networks extend to ordinary citizens. Swedes use the expression "bicycle monarchy" to capture these serendipitous interactions within constrained geopolitical space (Hannerz 2017, 322). Sweden thus exhibits cohesive and encompassing social networks in ways that both predate and survive neocorporatism. These networks are encompassing in the sense that they connect firms across multiple different sectors and link industry to policy makers and organized labor. They are cohesive in the sense that actors trust one another in ways that encourage emulation and facilitate cooperation.

Of course, it is important not to exaggerate the coziness of Swedish society. Interviewees were quick to note that Sweden is less interconnected than other Nordic countries, and in subsequent chapters I take advantage of this variation to contrast Sweden with more tightly knit communities such as Finland and Iceland. Swedish politics, for example, is more polarized, with fewer coalition governments (Anthonsen and Lindvall 2009). Even though rival ideological camps know and trust one another, they rarely fraternize in the same way as their Finnish counterparts (interview with former minister, 11 May 2012, Sweden). Swedish industry is also less monolithic. Historically divided between accommodationist and confrontationalist wings, executive officers such as Curt Nicolin of ASEA criticized Swedish industrial policy during the 1960s and 1970s more prominently and vociferously than his Finnish counterparts (Tell 2008, 122). To some extent, this reflects Sweden's greater size and diversity. Ten times closer to Copenhagen than Stockholm, regions such as Skåne are economically and culturally distinct from the rest of the country (interview with executive, financial firm, 8 May 2012, Sweden). A Mälmo-based director quipped that Sweden was small enough to seek consensus, but too large to do it effectively:

> If you have a meeting in Sweden and invite people, there will always be someone who complains. That is contrary to what I have heard in Åland or Finland, where you know approximately what groups there are, you invite one from each group and you are fine. In Sweden we try to discuss, but unfortunately you don't know who to discuss with. You can see that in the regulatory process. The number of appeals in Sweden is significantly higher. (interview with research director, ICT firm, 7 May 2012, Sweden)

At the same time, Sweden is clearly more interconnected than larger societies. For example, whereas French policy makers are famously cohesive as a result of their common experiences at *grandes écoles* such as the École Nationale d'Administration (ÉNA) (Hall 1986), Swedish networks extend to well-organized industrial actors. The United States is also characterized by cozy ties, for instance between Wall Street and the Treasury Department (Lewis 2011), but in Sweden these relationships span multiple industries. Finally, unlike France and the United States, Swedish policy makers and industrialists enjoy high-trust relations with encompassing labor unions, effectively integrating the masses into elite negotiations. Several interviewees, seeking to distinguish Sweden from these larger countries as well as the other Nordics, suggested that the country was big enough to sustain different views, but the high level of interconnectedness enabled the country to entertain "only one conversation at a time" (Hannerz 2017, 320).[2]

Remodeling Sweden, Inc.: The Politics of Planning

These tight-knit relationships shaped economic adjustment long before the incorporation of organized labor into centralized collective wage bargaining and policy formulation in the 1930s. For example, Sweden industrialized with remarkable speed during the late nineteenth century. The number of manufacturing firms more than quadrupled from 900 in 1872 to 3,800 by 1897 as universal banks financed a wave of start-ups (Magnusson 2000, 154). Sweden was also unique in the proliferation of so-called genius companies, which used mechanical or electrical inventions to penetrate international markets. Scholars have attributed this distinctive pattern of competition to cohesive industrial networks (Erixon 1997, 10), as entrepreneurs were goaded by the banks (Gustavson 1986, 286), influenced by rivals (Erixon 1997, 10), and actively supported by the state and other firms (Sjögren 2008, 30).[3]

These dense cross-sectoral ties were not unambiguously positive. The lightly regulated financial markets that channeled resources to genius companies during the late nineteenth century funneled capital into less profitable projects during the 1920s. In particular, the "Match King" Ivar Kreuger, with the support of Sweden's commercial banks (Sjögren 2008, 40–42), constructed a sprawling and unsustainable empire that included four of Sweden's largest industrial firms. Sweden was only modestly affected by the decline of international demand in the early 1930s, but Kreuger's collapse was devastating. His fall endangered Sweden's banks, dozens of industrial firms, and hundreds of thousands of individual investors, all of whom were implicated in his ambitious ventures (Magnusson 2000, 168).

Although suggestive, a detailed account of the rapid rise and subsequent crisis of Swedish capitalism is beyond the scope of this book. In this chapter I focus specifically on the remarkable rise of the state in the twentieth century. Few would have anticipated this development in 1932. Policy makers worked closely with industry, deregulating financial markets in the late nineteenth century and investing heavily in infrastructure such as railroads, communication networks, and electricity (Magnusson 2000, 175). Beyond this, however, Sweden was a decidedly laissez-faire society. At 18.9 percent of gross national income in 1933, total taxation was significantly lower than practically any other advanced industrialized economy, including Italy (30.6 percent), the United Kingdom (25.2), the United States (23.4), Germany (23.0), and France (21.1) (Magnusson 2000, 196).

By 1975, toward the end of our period of study, Sweden could not have looked more different. In taxing 46.6 percent of GDP, Sweden had eclipsed all of the economies listed above, generating almost a full ten percentage points of revenue more than that paragon of statism, France (Magnusson 2000, 189). Moreover, taxation obscures the myriad other ways in which Sweden directed the allocation of resources, using credit rationing, investment funds, labor-market policy, collective bargaining, and other instruments to systematically favor large, established capital-intensive enterprises. Swedes were so enamored with the state that a liberal-conservative coalition responded to the OPEC oil crisis of the 1970s with a program of nationalization and subsidies totaling 6 percent of GDP (Rehn 1996, 196). This spectacular volte-face is all the more surprising because Sweden, unlike France, Germany, Italy, and many other European countries, did not experience regime change during or after World War II. In contrast to France, where de Gaulle exploited postwar turmoil to craft a powerful, autonomous civil service, or Germany, where a new constitution committed policy makers to a "social state," Swedish policy makers confronted powerful, well-organized interest groups. These dense social structures should have militated against reform. How, then, do we explain this dramatic transformation?

The proximate causes of this shift are clear. The Great Depression of the early 1930s, and the "Kreuger crash" in particular, discredited the liberal economic order, which had already failed to accommodate an increasingly restive working class. In this environment, the Social Democrats won a decisive victory over their liberal and conservative rivals in 1932. The incoming government abandoned its commitment to balanced budgets, instead attempting to stabilize economic activity by running deficits during economic downturns (and surpluses during good times). Countercyclical fiscal policies were flanked by increased taxation and greater public-sector involvement in unemployment insurance, health care, and housing (Magnusson 2000, 196). In the early postwar period, Sweden deepened its commitment to macroeconomic stabilization by regulating financial markets and unveiling an ambitious system of state-managed investment funds (Erixon 1997, 29–31). By the 1960s, Sweden had developed what was arguably the most generous and universal welfare state in the world.

Because of this, many political scientists and sociologists attribute the rise of the state to "labor power resources" or the Swedish trade union movement. The largest and second most centralized labor movement in Western Europe used their bargaining power to secure concessions from Swedish industry during the 1930s. Those concessions, from generous social benefits to the growth of public sector employment, in turn enhanced the position of the working class in Swedish politics and economics (Korpi 1983). It is worth emphasizing, however, that working-class organization reflected the solidaristic ties described above, including low levels of regional, religious, and ethnic polarization as well as a strong sense of national identity. Moreover, an emphasis on labor power resources does not explain why Social Democrats enthusiastically championed austerity before 1932.[4] Finally, labor-based theories obscure the degree to which Social Democrats relied on cross-class cooperation in their efforts to expand the public sector.

As a result, others have highlighted the limits of Social Democratic control, prioritizing the interests of Swedish business and large export-oriented firms in particular. According to this interpretation, employers deliberately promoted the centralization of the labor movement and collective bargaining in an effort to control restive workers in nontradable industries (Swenson 1991). The massive expansion of the public sector was also structured in a way that benefited large export-oriented firms (Henrekson, Jonung, and Stymne 1996). When Swedish institutions no longer conformed to employer preferences, they collapsed (Pontusson and Swenson 1996). These are compelling insights, to such a degree that even labor-centric theorists acknowledge the importance of cross-class alliances, albeit with agriculture and then the middle class rather than industry per se (Esping-Andersen 1990). At the same time, this required a high level of coordination among large export-oriented enterprises. These theories do not explain why employers were able to coordinate across a wide variety of different sectors.

More recent scholarship has emphasized the role of ideas in transforming Sweden from a laissez-faire society into a strikingly statist one. Ideas predisposed the Swedish Social Democrats to cross-class cooperation (Berman 1998) and enabled them to recruit nonsocialist allies (Blyth 2002). Yet this compelling account raises several questions. Why were Swedish Social Democrats so inclined to collaborate with other parties and how did they successfully diffuse those ideas within the broader labor movement? What enabled the Swedish Social Democrats to engage nonsocialist actors more effectively than moderate left-of-center parties in other countries such as the United States? And why were their capital-owning counterparts able to speak with a relatively unified voice?

I resolve these questions by shifting attention to the dense, widely distributed networks that not only unified workers and employers but also narrowed the distance between these two camps. Informal relationships predisposed industrialists and social democratic leaders to cross-class collaboration, while making it easier to sell new ideas to their members. In a high-trust environment, powerful agrarian, business, and labor interests that did not readily embrace new ideas could be accommodated with generous side payments. Once a critical mass of actors embraced the Swedish model, dissenters were easily marginalized. In this environment, Sweden was able to adopt an unusually comprehensive approach to institutional reform, coordinating across a staggering array of policy domains and enlisting private sector support. The result was one of the most comprehensive and effective industrial policies in the developed world, even as Sweden eschewed French-style planning.

Interpersonal Networks and the Politics of Persuasion

Sweden looked like one of the most inhospitable environments to challenge liberal orthodoxy in the 1920s. Although the heterodox economist Knut Wicksell had conducted pioneering work in macroeconomics and influenced a number of promising young disciples, these voices were marginalized within contemporary policy-making circles. Instead, classical economists such as Gösta Bagge, Eli Heckscher, and Gustav Cassel dominated popular discourse. These scholars argued against countercyclical fiscal and monetary measures as well as any social policies that might reduce labor-market flexibility. Interestingly, these beliefs were largely unchallenged by the Social Democratic Party. Influenced in part by orthodox Marxist views that capitalism should be allowed to collapse under the weight of its own contradictions, Social Democrats supported fiscal austerity and the adoption of the gold standard as late as the 1920s (Blyth 2002, 102–4). Why then did the ideological landscape change so rapidly and comprehensively in interwar Sweden?

When increasing unemployment and social unrest delegitimized orthodox liberal and Marxist views in the late 1920s, Social Democrats challenged classical economics by elevating young academics at the Stockholm School of Economics such as Gunnar Myrdal, Erik Lindahl, and Bertil Ohlin. A 1927 government-sponsored "Committee of Inquiry into Unemployment" gave these scholars a public forum to explore how fiscal policy could combat business cycles (Blyth 2002, 105–7). Inspired in part by this work, the Social Democratic Party resolved to overhaul the Swedish Unemployment Commission in 1930 (Magnusson 2000, 197). Pledging that "the state should be given a totally different role than it had before in order to stabilize employment on a higher level" in the run-up to the 1932 election (Blyth 2002, 108), the Per Albin Hansson administration subsequently introduced an ambitious program of public works to combat unemployment in 1933 and rolled out an array of complementary social programs over the course of the decade (Magnusson 2000, 197).

This new, unorthodox approach to economic management diffused quickly within a large and cohesive Swedish labor movement. Comparative studies suggest that the Swedish Social Democratic Party (SAP) was more unified than its continental counterparts and tightly linked to LO in particular (Berman 1998, 64–65). Although officially separated in 1898, their personnel remained closely intertwined even following their formal division (Berman 1998, 54). This relationship made it easier for Social Democratic politicians such as prime minister Hansson and finance minister Ernst Wigforss to enlist LO support. During the 1930s, the latter not only provided an electoral boost but also delivered wage moderation and industrial peace. Both would prove integral to the success of the Swedish model (see below). In subsequent decades, LO would prove even more valuable, generating original ideas such as the Rehn-Meidner model of solidaristic wage bargaining (see below) and using the Workers' Educational Association to educate vast swaths of the population about the goals and achievements of the Swedish labor movement (Blyth 2002, 122).

Close ties to LO enabled elites to develop and diffuse popular ideas among workers, but the Swedish Social Democrats could not have succeeded by relying on organized labor alone. On the contrary, Social Democrats were unusually committed to cross-class cooperation, working closely with liberals to expand the suffrage as early as 1918 and striking deals with agriculture and industry to increase public expenditure during the 1930s. The next section elaborates on these deals, but it is worth highlighting these cross-class connections here. The influential SAP leader Hjalmar Branting was a committed Marxist, but he had forged friendships with future leaders of the Swedish Liberal Party at university and maintained those relationships in later years (Berman 1998, 45). Meanwhile, former Liberals such as Erik Palmstierna and Carl Lindhagen pushed Social Democrats to build bridges with Swedish agricultural interests (Berman 1998, 61–62), establishing a foundation for the famous "cow trade" of the early 1930s (see below).

As a result, even though the Swedish Social Democrats are often credited with their bold and visionary response to interwar economic challenges (Berman 1998; Blyth 2002), many of their innovative policy proposals were originally developed by liberal economists rather than Marxists. Myrdal was closely linked to SAP, but his nonsocialist colleague Lindahl played an instrumental role in introducing the role of aggregate demand to young Swedish economists. Swedish Social Democrats, such as finance minister Wigforss, drew on these insights in developing policies to stabilize the Swedish economy during the 1930s (Blyth 2002, 106–7).

This liberal influence on Social Democratic thinking proved important, because bourgeois ideas proved more palatable to nonsocialist politicians and economists. For example, the fact that Wigforss, Myrdal, and other Social Democrats prioritized price stability in their theorizing and policy proposals made it easier to woo their bourgeois counterparts. In fact, Social Democrats leaned heavily on bourgeois economists to educate their nonsocialist colleagues about the feasibility of state intervention. For example, Lindahl and Ohlin used the 1927 Committee of Inquiry into Unemployment to successfully persuade future Conservative Party chairman and classical economist Bagge that "even if unemployment had been caused by a wage rise . . . a wage reduction was probably not the best antidote." Wigforss called on these liberal economists to educate the Swedish legislature about multiplier theory, while Lindahl lobbied his academic colleagues by presenting to the Swedish Economic Society. By 1933 their testimony had "crystallized public opinion and support for a positive recovery program" to such a degree that even orthodox stalwarts such as Cassel acknowledged deflationary risks during "crisis times" (Blyth 2002, 107–9).

By this point, virtually all political parties had embraced countercyclical economic policies (Sjögren 2008, 45). In 1936 the Social Democrats, with the support of nonsocialist economists, expanded their initial program of public works and social policies to introduce a budget-balancing fund that would permit deficit spending during economic downturns (Blyth 2002, 110). High corporate taxation dampened economic activity during booms, while the government relied on housing investment and active labor-market policy to stimulate demand during downturns. Tax incentives encouraged firms to allocate profits to special investment reserve funds that could be released by the Bank of Sweden during economic downturns (Pontusson 1992, 12). These countercyclical fiscal measures, which were expanded during the 1940s and 1950s, were complemented by heavy financial regulation. While interest rates were fixed below market clearing levels, the Bank of Sweden used quotas to limit private-sector lending (Magnusson 2000, 252).

Consequently, the statist turn in Swedish policy cannot be attributed solely to Social Democratic electoral dominance. As described below, SAP did not always command a parliamentary majority. For example, they relied on the Farmer's League to introduce countercyclical fiscal policies and public works programs in the early 1930s and bourgeois parties to adopt a "bridge policy" in response to the OPEC-induced oil crises of the 1970s. In fact, these bourgeois parties adopted an even *more* statist stance when they assumed power in 1976. A center-right coalition broadened public intervention from macroeconomic, social, labor, and housing policy to industrial policy. State aid increased to 10 percent of public expenditure by 1980 as policy makers distributed adaptation grants and nationalized troubled firms (Pontusson 1992, 139). Public debt soared from a modest 20 percent of GDP in the mid-1970s to over 60 percent by the mid-1980s (Henrekson, Jonung, and Stymne 1996, 255). Although conservative willingness to experiment with Keynesian policies during the 1970s was hardly unique, the Swedish center-right proved unusually committed to defending the Swedish model. Blyth argues that this cannot be attributed merely to the clout of the Swedish labor movement. Rather, it reflects the remarkable inability of the bourgeois parties to develop any compelling alternative strategy. SAP and LO had proven so effective in diffusing new ideas within Swedish society that even the most recalcitrant, anti-socialist parties were "imprisoned" within a social democratic paradigm (Blyth 2002, 208).

In sum, the highly interconnected nature of Swedish society accelerated institutional reform. When the Great Depression discredited traditional policies, new ideas about the stabilizing influence of the state spread quickly within dense interpersonal networks. These ideas not only were embraced by a cohesive labor movement but enabled socialist leaders to persuade orthodox economists, bourgeois politicians, agricultural organizations, and business leaders. Of course, broad-based support reflected much more than persuasive rhetoric. Even ideational scholars are quick to describe how SAP used side payments to satisfy the material interests of nonsocialist actors (Berman 1998; Blyth 2002). The following section develops this point, explaining how the same tight-knit networks that enhanced persuasive appeals simultaneously made it easier for reform-oriented actors to neutralize opposition by striking deals.

Coopting the Opposition: The Politics of Compensation

Although the politics of persuasion encouraged liberals and employers to look at the state in a new way, hard-nosed bargaining was just as important. The highly interconnected nature of Swedish society facilitated negotiation in several ways. First, the relatively small number of actors made it easier for reform-oriented agents to identify and negotiate with opponents. Second, repeated interaction made it easier to determine what, exactly, would satisfy skeptics. Repeated interaction with bourgeois partners, plus dense cross-sectoral linkages within the private sector, enabled SAP leaders to develop solutions that would placate liberal, agricultural, and industrial interests. Finally and perhaps most importantly, partners could make credible commitments. Long-term commitments to respect private property, maintain industrial peace, or secure full employment were based on a high level of trust, and these agreements were easier to monitor and enforce in a tight-knit society with relatively few moving parts. In this environment, reform-oriented actors could use side payments to cultivate exceptionally robust support for state intervention. Although not universal, the breadth and strength of this postwar consensus made it much easier to marginalize any dissenting actors.

The first and most iconic deal was struck in 1933, when SAP negotiated the "cow trade" with the Farmer's League. SAP had performed strongly in the 1932 election, but it lacked the legislative majority it required to increase expenditures on public works and other social programs. Finance minister Ernst Wigforss persuasively argued that increasing working-class purchasing power would benefit agricultural producers, but agrarian support was ultimately predicated on import restrictions and other nontariff barriers designed to stabilize agricultural prices (Berman 1998, 171–81). SAP receptivity to agricultural interests and its capacity to deliver on its promises enabled the Social Democrats to command a legislative majority throughout the 1930s. At the same time, agricultural support, although still significant in 1930s Sweden, was hardly sufficient to introduce the kinds of sweeping institutional changes that would characterize the postwar era. Even though the Farmer's League accepted increased expenditure on public works, it was hardly in a position to endorse the expensive, active labor-market policies that would redistribute labor from agrarian regions to industrial districts in the early postwar period. The expansion of the public sector required reform-oriented Social Democrats to construct an even broader alliance, engaging industry and, eventually, the middle class.

Industry was an unlikely ally. Employers initially opposed not only increased expenditure on public works but social democracy more generally, which they viewed as a threat to capitalism. A key turning point occurred when the Social Democratic Hansson administration, worrying that European-leading levels of industrial conflict could endanger Sweden's economic recovery, prepared legislation to reduce strike activity. The threat of state intervention prompted the Swedish Employers' Association (SAF) to reach an independent agreement with LO, negotiating a deal at the resort town of Saltsjöbaden in 1938.[5] The initial agreement was a watershed in Swedish industrial relations for the way it incorporated organized labor, exchanged industry's right to "direct and allocate work" for labor's right to an "equitable" share of production, and provided an institutional framework to peacefully resolve future disputes (Magnusson 2000, 187). At a time when industrial relations in larger Western European countries remained highly polarized, Saltsjöbaden represented a remarkable example of cooperation. SAF agreed to abandon its push to legislate against unionization (Rehn 1996, 171). At the same time, they expected LO to moderate wage demands, limit strike activity, and respect managerial prerogatives. LO, in turn, trusted Swedish employers to reinvest their profits in ways that would support employment and wage growth (Magnusson 2000, 235). In safeguarding bourgeois control over private property, the Saltsjöbaden Agreement not only diffused industrial conflict but also reduced resistance to the expansion of the Swedish public sector (Pontusson 1992, 38).

In fact, this relatively narrow agreement exchanging the right to manage for the right to organize was broadened in subsequent years in ways that would transform Swedish economic institutions. Once incorporated into Swedish industrial relations, LO struck deals with SAF regarding employee protection, works councils, and apprentice training (Magnusson 2000, 234). More importantly, the social partners settled on a division of the labor with the Swedish state, effectively neutralizing opposition to public spending (Pontusson 1992, 39). Industry accepted the government's commitment to full employment and the unprecedented expansion of the Swedish welfare state. In exchange, the governing SAP abandoned its plans to introduce discretionary industrial policies, tempering its commitment to nationalization and selective credit allocation. By the end of the 1940s, virtually all actors accepted more robust social policies and these constraints on planning (Rehn 1996, 171).

Why was Swedish industry so quick to support socialist policies? Certainly, SAF's newfound sympathies could be attributed to the political success of SAP and the specter of more radical anti-capitalist legislation. This explanation, however, does not explain why the bourgeois parties protected the Swedish welfare state and expanded state aid during the 1970s (Rehn 1996, 196). In fact, industry supported the expansion of the Swedish public sector because policies were designed in a way that benefited the largest and most influential Swedish firms.

The Great Tax Reform of 1938, a key turning point in Sweden's transition from a low-tax to a high-tax country, is an instructive example. The new legislation increased income tax progressivity and subjected corporate profits to taxation (Magnusson 2000, 188–90), but also included generous depreciation allowances, the ability to deduct inventory, and the option to direct profits toward tax-free pension and investment funds (Pontusson 1992, 46). These measures, exceptionally generous by international standards, neutralized opposition by large capital-intensive firms (Erixon 1997, 29). When Swedish policy makers pushed tax rates even higher to fund public investment and stabilize economic activity during the 1950s, this system of "investment reserve funds" was enhanced, increasing from 640 firms in 1956 to 2,566 by 1965 (Pontusson 1992, 71). Released during economic downturns, the funds enabled firms to reinvest their profits with minimal tax liability (Henrekson, Jonung, and Stymne 1996, 260). Even the revenue that the state did collect benefited large capital-intensive firms as public procurement stimulated demand, while housing investment and active labor-market policies facilitated the movement of workers to emerging industrial centers in southern Sweden (Magnusson 2000, 223–24).

Policy makers and the social partners struck similar deals to deepen their commitment to full employment and social protection in the postwar period. Initially, rapid economic growth threatened to undermine competitiveness as sheltered sector workers took advantage of their insulated position in the Swedish economy to push for higher wages. While the government dampened demand by increasing taxes, SAF and LO worked collectively to centralize collective wage bargaining in ways that would restrain wages in nontradable sectors (Pontusson and Swenson 1996, 225). As noted above, wage moderation was predicated on the understanding that companies would reinvest profits in ways that would permit wage and employment growth (Magnusson 2000, 235). To compensate low-productivity workers in nontradable sectors, SAF and LO endorsed the principle of equal pay for equal work or solidaristic wage bargaining. Although less profitable firms that could not afford to pay higher wages were directly threatened by this arrangement, unemployed workers were rewarded with some of the most ambitious, active labor-market policies in the developed world, which increased from 0.2 percent of GNP in 1950 to 1.5 percent by 1970 (Magnusson

2000, 239). Sweden's leadership in this area reflected an exceptionally strong consensus among policy makers, industrialists, and labor representatives, who jointly administered programs through the Labor Market Board.

Centralized collective wage bargaining was not particularly appealing to high-productivity workers, who initially opposed a solidarity wage (Rehn 1996, 175). Gösta Rehn and Rudolf Meidner's persuasive appeals, adopted by LO in 1951, converted some skeptics (Pontusson 1992, 63), but white-collar trade unions also secured their own targeted side payments. A supplemental pension scheme, adopted in 1959, rewarded middle-class workers with generous earnings-related benefits. This earnings-related pension program was fiercely contested in 1959, but it proved highly durable. The scheme effectively bound the Swedish middle classes to the welfare state by crowding out private-sector alternatives. And even Swedish employers eventually embraced the ATP program, as the funds were reinvested in private industry and public housing (Pontusson 1992, 124). The capacity of reform-oriented Social Democrats to strike deals, first with farmers, then industry, and finally the Swedish middle classes enabled them to expand the public sector at an unparalleled rate in the early postwar period.

Their capacity to do so was based in large measure on the small and cohesive nature of the Swedish elite. SAF and LO's dominant position in the Swedish labor market made it easier to negotiate and enforce centralized labor-market agreements. SAF's ability to speak with a common voice in turn reflected the organized state of Swedish industry. The Wallenberg family controlled leading firms in a wide variety of sectors through SEB and its industrial family. At the height of their influence in 1979, they employed nearly a quarter of the Swedish industrial workforce (Larsson, Lindgren, and Nyberg 2008, 78). They maintained a cordial relationship with Social Democratic leaders, to such a degree that the latter jested about their physical proximity in press photographs (Sejersted 2011, 220). Competitors such as Handelsbanken were also organized along cross-sectoral lines, organizing firms in a wide variety of industries. This encompassing structure not only made it easier for employers to speak with one voice but also reduced opposition to public policies that shifted resources from declining sectors to expanding ones.

At the same time, the expansion of the public sector represented much more than interelite bargaining. Swedish society was also characterized by a relatively short distance between elites and ordinary citizens, as evidenced by the influential role of mass membership–based organizations such as LO. As a result, the positive effects of increased state intervention were not confined to a small number of industrialists. On the contrary, benefits were widely distributed, reaching the influential middle class as well as blue-collar workers. This wide-ranging bargain not only enabled the Swedish Social Democrats to increase public expenditure at an unprecedented rate but also made it difficult to restructure the state until confronted with a clear crisis. As noted above, even the bourgeois parties found themselves defending the Swedish welfare state and increasing state aid during the 1970s.

This is not to imply that all benefited from or embraced this postwar model. As the following section relates at length, labor-market cooperation and public-sector expansion were negotiated in a way that systematically disadvantaged new, small, and low-productivity enterprises. These actors were not particularly fond of Social Democratic ideas, were not well-represented within industrial circles, and were excluded from the comprehensive bargains described above. In contrast to Finland and Iceland, some of these actors publicly challenged the Swedish model. For example, the Bonnier family maintained a competitive and critical relationship with the Social Democratic–controlled media (Larsson, Lindgren, and Nyberg 2008, 99), while ASEA CEO Curt Nicolin used his company's annual reports to criticize Swedish industrial policy during the 1970s (Tell 2008, 122). But these actors were never significant enough to challenge the broad coalition that supported the postwar model and were easily marginalized within postwar Swedish society.

In fact, contemporaries describe a stifling, even "dangerous" environment in which criticism could generate negative media publicity, jeopardize employment prospects, or threaten access to capital. One veteran industrialist remarked:

> When we had a very socialist parliament, it was a very small country, and the socialists controlled everything, so as a businessman you had very little room for maneuver and all of the institutions were controlled from the top. It was a very dangerous situation in the 1960s and 1970s and that's the problem with a small place like this. If you get the wrong people in, it becomes very, I get the feeling that the US, with all of its problems, is always a democracy in some way. But a small place like this can strangle you. (interview, industry representative, 8 May 2012, Sweden)

Another industry representative underscored the risks associated with challenging the postwar consensus: "If you were a business person at the time, which my father was, he was really scared of doing something that he wasn't supposed to do" (interview, industry representative, 8 May 2012, Sweden). Although their recollections may be colored by antisocialist sentiment, other examples are documented in the public record. The Bonnier family never employed Finnish-style self-censorship, but it deliberately limited its share of the Swedish media market to avoid provoking a reaction by the Social Democratic Party (Larsson, Lindgren, and Nyberg 2008, 97–98). This restrictive environment hardly afforded entrepreneurial agents or other critically minded actors the space to challenge the economic institutions and policies described above.

Scaling the Swedish Model: The Politics of Coordination

By persuading and compensating skeptical actors, the cohesive social structures described above enabled Social Democrats and other ideational entrepreneurs to restructure Swedish institutions more effectively, synchronizing multiple policy domains and coordinating with private-sector actors. In other words, increased state intervention extended beyond a few high-profile successes, such as active labor-market policy, to touch virtually all aspects of Swedish economic and social life. The Swedish welfare state is considered SAP's crowning achievement, not only by virtue of its generosity but also because of its extensive scope (Esping-Andersen 1990). SAP introduced more generous unemployment benefits, early education, retraining, pensions, disability insurance, affordable housing, health care, and child care (Magnusson 2000, 241–45). This commitment to equality transcended the public sector, however, as private-sector allies such as LO and SAF independently reduced pay differentials through solidaristic wage bargaining (Sejersted 2011, 224).

By looking beyond the politics of social protection to the politics of production, this section demonstrates that Swedish policies were even *more* highly coordinated than we recognize. To date, analysts have focused heavily on the welfare state (Berman 1998; Blyth 2002), going so far as to assert that Sweden rejected planning (Pontusson 1992, 11) and lacked an industrial policy (Rehn 1996, 171). This is true in the sense that Swedish policy makers never achieved French levels of discretion in their ability to target specific firms or overrule private-sector preferences in the allocation of resources. The generous social policies described above, however, represented part of a broader, highly coordinated strategy to restructure the Swedish economy, systematically redistributing resources to large established firms in capital-intensive export-oriented manufacturing industries. Social Democrats, bourgeois politicians, labor representatives, industrial leaders, and virtually all Swedish elites prioritized economic growth, believed that large, modern enterprises were best positioned to do so, and sought to restructure Swedish society accordingly (Magnusson 2000, 241). Although the preceding sections have provided individual examples of how Social Democrats secured the support of large capital-intensive firms, it is worth retracing the contours of postwar Swedish economic policy to highlight the country's exceptional capacity for coordination.

The Swedish welfare state favored large export-oriented manufacturing firms to such a degree that some have characterized postwar Swedish economic policy as a strategy to "reallocate labor, not capital" (Rehn 1996, 175). The active labor-market policies that represent the hallmark of the Swedish welfare state facilitated the movement of workers from low-productivity enterprises in nontradable and import-competing industries into highly profitable export-oriented firms (Rehn 1996, 175). The strategic reallocation of labor to large capital-intensive firms was by no means limited to labor-market policy. The supplementary pension fund scheme introduced in 1959 was used to invest in affordable housing on a massive scale (Henrekson and Jakobsson 2001, 341), facilitating the movement of workers from sparsely populated, agrarian northern provinces to urban districts in southern Sweden populated by large manufacturing firms (Magnusson 2000, 223–24). Private labor-market institutions also favored large firms. Solidaristic wage bargaining, proposed by LO and embraced by SAF, was explicitly designed to drive low-productivity firms out of business and facilitate the expansion of highly profitable enterprises (Pontusson 1992, 32). In practice, these policies disadvantaged smaller firms in nontradable, import-competing, or service-based industries and rewarded larger capital-intensive export-oriented manufacturing firms.

In fact, Swedish economic policy was never simply a story about the reallocation of labor, as evidenced by other domains such as capital taxation. As noted above, high corporate taxes were offset by accelerated depreciation allowances, the generous treatment of inventory, and the right to deposit profits in tax-sheltered investment reserve funds (Pontusson 1992, 46). These provisions systematically favored large export-oriented manufacturing firms that were more likely to accumulate inventory, invest in capital equipment, and dispose of funds within the narrow window during which the investment reserve funds were opened. High marginal tax rates and tax-deductible interest payments also advantaged established firms because they made debt-based financing more attractive. Large manufacturing enterprises were most likely to capitalize on this, because these enterprises possessed physical collateral, enjoyed lower borrowing costs, and invested more heavily in capital equipment (Henrekson and Jakobsson 2001, 338–39).[6]

Public policies rewarded debt-based financing in more ways than one. In addition to allowing firms to deduct interest payments, the Bank of Sweden maintained real interest rates at low or even negative levels (Henrekson and Jakobsson 2003, 83). These arrangements favored large manufacturing firms with easy access to Swedish credit markets and encouraged them to increase their reliance on capital-intensive corporate strategies. At the same time, the Swedish tax code discouraged alternative forms of external financing such as equity. By the 1970s, the tax treatment of new share issues was so punitive that household investors faced a negative after-tax return on their equity investments (Henrekson and

Jakobsson 2001, 339). The fact that corporate governance favored creditors and did little to protect minority shareholders hardly favored equity financing. Together with the heavy taxation of retained earnings, Swedish legislation thus made it considerably more difficult for entrepreneurs, particularly those relying on labor-intensive strategies or intangible assets, to develop new businesses (Henrekson and Jakobsson 2003, 339).

The punitive treatment of new share issues was not universal. Sweden taxed households heavily, but other actors enjoyed a more privileged position in tax and regulatory policy. Institutional investors, including pension funds, insurance companies, and banks, were taxed at significantly lower rates (Henrekson and Jakobsson 2001, 340).[7] Banks occupied a particularly advantageous position, as tax, regulatory, and monetary policy systematically favored deficit financing. In addition to allowing enterprises to deduct interest payments and protecting creditors, policy makers channeled massive public-sector surpluses back to banks, fixing interest rates below market-clearing levels in ways that caused the demand for credit to outstrip supply. This form of "credit rationing" not only subsidized loans in a way that favored capital-intensive enterprises but allowed decision makers to selectively allocate resources to strategic industries. Unlike France, where autonomous policy makers used state-owned banks to reshape French industry (Zysman 1983), private-sector banks such as SEB and Handelsbanken were allowed to allocate credit as they saw fit (Rehn 1996, 193). Because the major commercial banks were also interested in protecting established capital-intensive firms, however, any policies that enhanced their position as financial gatekeepers effectively advanced Social Democratic interests as well.

In fact, this is an excellent example of how public- and private-sector actors could work in tandem to restructure the Swedish economy. Because banks issued large long-term loans to their commercial clients, they preferred to target mature industries with relatively clear and predictable technological trajectories. Once committed, these banks faced strong incentives to protect their investments, extending credit to upgrade operations during difficulties times. In bolstering the position of the major commercial banks and other institutions investors, Swedish policy makers ensured that large capital-intensive firms would enjoy an even more privileged position in the Swedish financial system at the expense of their younger, smaller service-based counterparts. Although it was theoretically possible for firms to circumvent these constraints by growing through the reinvestment of retained earnings, Swedish tax and regulatory policy ensured that this was only feasible for Sweden's largest enterprises (Henrekson and Jakobsson 2001, 341–42).

Formal industrial policy remained underdeveloped in Sweden, as the state refrained from widespread nationalization or the selective allocation of credit.

But the industrial policy measures that Sweden did pursue further advantaged large, established firms in heavy industry. Public research funding, for example, prioritized basic research, which is more easily commercialized by large enterprises with superior absorptive capacity (Gergils 2006, 313). Swedish public policy was so strongly oriented toward incumbent firms that strategies to promote industrial renewal focused largely on modernizing established industries. The Swedish Board for Technical Development (STU), established in 1968, publicly lobbied against targeting new high-technology enterprises (Eklund 2007, 75–76). This defensive orientation is less shocking than it appears when one considers that the government was converting the historically marginal State Enterprise Corporation into a vehicle for rescuing troubled low- and medium-technology industries. Textiles, shipbuilding, steel, iron ore, and forest products alone absorbed over 95 percent of public spending on sectoral aid during the 1970s (Pontusson 1992, 138).

The State Enterprise Corporation, STU, and the panoply of other agencies that were created or expanded to facilitate industrial renewal at this time may have paled in comparison to the selective industrial policies employed by other countries such as France.[8] This section, however, suggests that Swedish labor-market, social, fiscal, monetary, and regulatory policies were so highly coordinated that the country hardly required a selective industrial policy. Virtually every aspect of Swedish public policy was structured to systematically favor the large capital-intensive export-oriented manufacturing firms that were perceived to bolster Swedish prosperity and security. Moreover, and in contrast to countries such as France, powerful, encompassing private-sector actors such as LO, SAF, and the major commercial banks worked alongside the public sector to favor incumbent capital-intensive firms. In doing so, they nearly eliminated the space entrepreneurs required to develop alternative business models. In short, the compromises that were perceived to inhibit planning ironically enabled Sweden to develop one of the most comprehensive and effective industrial policies in the developed world.

Good Governance Gone Bad: From Success to "Swedosclerosis"

This coordinated approach to economic restructuring proved highly successful during the interwar and early postwar period, when Swedish policies were hailed as a pragmatic response to contemporary challenges (Childs 1936; Montgomery 1962). In this era, the Great Depression had just highlighted the risks of unfettered market competition. Policy makers were charged with stabilizing the economy to prevent any shortfall in aggregate demand and minimize social disruption. Large, diversified conglomerates were ideal in this respect, as they possessed the resources to weather economic shocks and could distribute risk across more product lines (Lewellen 1971). Large firms were also perceived as an important source of growth, particularly in a small export-oriented economy, because of their capacity to achieve economies of scale and outmuscle smaller rivals (Bain 1950).[9] This emphasis on large firms is not surprising, as other countries also viewed manufacturing as a leading industry, delivering the technological innovations and capital inputs that spurred economic expansion (Hall 1999, 216).

But Sweden adapted its public policies to meet those objectives more effectively than almost any other developed country. As a result, Sweden enjoyed rapid economic growth from the 1930s until the 1970s. Although Sweden had grown before 1930 (see above), average per capita income growth accelerated sharply from 2.1 to 3.2 percent (Sjögren 2008, 47). Wartime neutrality helped, but incomes grew even more rapidly between 1960 and 1970, eclipsing many Western European states. This is surprising, because one would expect Swedish growth to taper off as it converged with other advanced industrialized economies. Instead, Sweden continued to equal or outpace its European peers, even after surpassing them in per capita GDP (Henrekson, Jonung, and Stymne 1996, 243). This remarkable performance fueled Sweden's reputation as an economic model and industrial powerhouse.

Swedish growth, however, was built on a skewed industrial base. The share of the labor force employed in manufacturing increased from 26.2 percent in the early 1930s to 35 percent by the early 1950s. When manufacturing employment shrank as a share of the population in subsequent decades, it was eclipsed by public services, the fastest-growing employer of labor in the postwar period. Private nonmanufacturing employment, including services, stagnated. Agriculture illustrates the pace of restructuring, experiencing a rapid decline from 34 percent of the labor force in the early 1930s to less than 7 percent by the 1970s (Sjögren 2008, 48).

Swedish industry was more diverse than that of Finland or Iceland, in the sense that firms populated a wide range of industries such as aerospace, automobiles, power generation, forestry, metals, mining equipment, shipbuilding, and telecommunications. Comparative advantage, however, was narrower than most large states and even smaller economies such as Switzerland (Rehn 1996, 190–92). Postwar Sweden was highly specialized in basic manufacturing, with a much weaker presence in services or consumer goods (Sölvell, Zander, and Porter 1991, 341–42). Even if manufacturing firms could be research-intensive, they generally focused on improving cost-efficiency in mature industries rather than entering new areas or developing new product lines.[10] Forestry and steel are particularly famous for relying on capital inputs to improve productivity, but even Swedish engineering industries were surprisingly low tech by conventional classifications (Erixon 1997, 38–39).

Sweden's industrial structure appears even more distorted when we examine enterprise size. As recently as 1991, corporations with more than 500 workers employed 58 percent of private sector workers, as opposed to 37 percent in Germany, 34 percent in France, and 34 percent in the United Kingdom (Sjögren 2008, 61). The vast majority of these enterprises were established before World War II (Erixon 1997, 42).[11] Sweden had always relied on large firms, partly as a result of its dependence on capital-intensive, resource-extractive industries. Postwar policies, however, caused entrepreneurship to plummet. The formation rate of new manufacturing firms fell from 4 percent during the 1920s to 1.5 percent by the 1970s. The perception that "big is beautiful" was not confined to corporate boardrooms. Only 30 percent of the population believed it was "important to encourage entrepreneurship and firm creation" by 1978. Partly as a result, nonagricultural self-employment was the lowest in the entire OECD (Henrekson and Jakobsson 2001, 344–51).

The policies that enabled Sweden to flexibly adapt to interwar and early postwar challenges thus heightened its exposure to new threats. Sweden was uniquely vulnerable to three economic developments during the 1960s and 1970s. First, the OPEC-induced oil crises of the 1970s significantly increased energy costs. This supply shock was felt across most of the developed world, but rising energy prices proved particularly problematic for Sweden because the country had specialized in capital-intensive heavy manufacturing industries that consumed a lot of energy. Forestry, mining, steel, and shipbuilding were all heavily affected by increasing energy costs (Pontusson 1992, 101).

Second, Sweden's struggles to adapt to a post-OPEC world were compounded by the fact that the country confronted new competitors in traditional niches. Low-cost rivals, most notably in East Asia, entered manufacturing, targeting heavy industries such as steel and shipbuilding where Sweden had specialized. These countries adopted similar capital-intensive strategies, enabling them to achieve economies of scale while simultaneously benefiting from lower wage costs (Pontusson 1992, 106–7). Swedish manufacturing was affected by East Asian industrialization as early as the 1960s. Increased competition, coupled with rising energy costs, proved even more problematic in the 1970s. Swedish steel output plummeted by 30 percent between 1975 and 1977 alone (Sjögren 2008, 53).

Third, shifting patterns of international economic competition were shaped in part by new technologies that facilitated communication and trade. In many advanced industrialized economies, this represented an important source of employment and productivity growth (OECD 2005). Sweden, however, was poorly positioned to capitalize on these developments. As described above, Swedish conglomerates were slow to move into new industries, preferring to rationalize existing activities (Sölvell, Zander, and Porter 1991, 135). Although Swedish firms were quick to embrace new technologies such as computers and robots in production processes, they generally lagged in the production of high-technology goods (Erixon 1997, 38–39).

Of course, Sweden did compete in several high-technology industries such as electro-technical equipment. But its presence was based on large, incumbent firms such as ASEA and Ericsson, which were founded in 1883 and 1876 respectively. Even though these firms would eventually adapt to new digital technologies, they were slow to introduce radical innovations during the 1970s, with the result that Swedish specialization in high-technology production actually decreased during this time (Bitard, Hommen, and Novikova 2008). The fact that public policies caused firm creation to plummet exacerbated this structural crisis by suppressing the entrepreneurial forces that might have facilitated industrial renewal.

These headwinds challenged virtually all advanced industrialized economies in the 1970s, but the reversal of fortune was particularly sharp in Sweden. Lauded as a miracle in the 1960s, the country was presented a cautionary tale by the 1980s. Per capita income growth slowed to an average of 1.7 percent per annum between 1970 and 1992, almost half the OECD average. Productivity growth was even less impressive. Although practically every country struggled, no large, advanced industrialized economy fared as badly as Sweden during this time period (Henrekson, Jonung, and Stymne 1996, 244–45).

One could attribute Sweden's deteriorating economic performance to the country's long-standing comparative advantage in resource-extractive, low- and medium-technology industries, most notably metal-processing activities such as steel and shipbuilding (Erixon 1982). Focusing exclusively on Sweden's industrial structure, however, obscures the degree to which comparative advantage was politically constructed. As I demonstrate in this chapter, Sweden relied on universal banking to enter capital-intensive industries during the late nineteenth and early twentieth centuries, while interwar and postwar policies systematically favored large, incumbent heavy manufacturing firms. Cohesive and encompassing political and social networks enabled Swedish elites to implement these policies more quickly and comprehensively than virtually any other advanced industrialized economy. These same bargains narrowed Sweden's comparative advantage and heightened its vulnerability to disruptive economic shocks.

In addition to increasing vulnerability, cohesive, encompassing networks blinded Swedes to the structural nature of the slowdown. This is not to deny divisions and debate. High-productivity workers within LO, encouraged by SAF, struck to protest solidaristic wage bargaining. Efforts to dampen labor militancy with legislation, most notably the controversial "wage earner funds," provoked the wrath of SAF, which declared the Saltsjöbaden agreements dead (Blyth 2002, 211).[12] All the major actors, however, including SAF and the bourgeois parties, continued to believe that large capital-intensive manufacturing firms were central to Swedish prosperity and that the state could play a constructive role in protecting those enterprises. Actors who challenged this dominant paradigm were marginalized by a "dangerous" political and social climate (interviews with industry representatives, 8 May 2012, Sweden).

As a result, policy makers attempted to resolve Sweden's deteriorating economic performance, and the social tensions it generated, by doubling down on their postwar bets. Swedish policy makers not only defended preexisting commitments to the welfare state and credit rationing but actually deepened their commitment to Keynesianism by launching an ambitious bridging strategy to carry Sweden, and large capital-intensive enterprises in particular, through the OPEC-induced oil crisis. Government spending increased sharply in the 1960s and 1970s (Magnusson 2000, 258–60). Demand stimulus was coordinated across multiple domains, with the government simultaneously releasing investment funds to stimulate the Swedish economy (Pontusson 1992, 114).

In addition to increasing spending, the Social Democrats broadened the scope of the public sector, introducing an array of selective industrial-policy instruments, including a state-owned investment bank in 1967, the Swedish Board for Technical Developmental (STU) in 1968, and a holding company to manage the steadily increasing number of state-owned enterprises in 1970. Ostensibly committed to promoting innovation in technologically intensive sectors, the instruments were also responsible for targeting "areas with employment problems" (Pontusson 1992, 132–33). As a result, STU interpreted its mandate as promoting the diffusion of new technologies to modernize established industries (Eklund 2007, 75–76). Modest state-owned ventures in emerging sectors such as pharmaceuticals and nuclear power were dwarfed by even larger commitments to iron ore, steel, and forestry (Pontusson 1992, 136).

The nonsocialist coalition that assumed power in 1976 disagreed with the Social Democrats in important ways, most notably over the latter's efforts to restructure workplace relations through the 1973 Worker's Protection Act, the 1974 Work Environment Act, the 1976 Codetermination Act, and the proposed wage earner funds. But the postwar model was broadly accepted. The bourgeois parties did little to alter the Keynesian macroeconomic policies of the previous administration and increased expenditure on state aid. Industrial policy expenditure grew from 8.8 billion Swedish crowns in 1974–75 to 16.9 billion

Swedish crowns by 1979–80 (Pontusson 1992, 139), as the center-right government nationalized more industry during their short administration than the Social Democrats had in forty-four years (Pontusson 1992, 140–41). By 1980 Sweden, which was supposed to be uniquely opposed to nationalization (Pontusson 1992), employed nearly as many workers in state-owned enterprises as France and the United Kingdom (Clifton, Comín, and Fuentes 2003, 107). Instead of fixing the structural problems described above, these policies were overwhelmingly defensive in nature, using investments and mergers to modernize large, incumbent firms in mature low- and medium-technology industries such as forestry, shipbuilding, steel, and textiles (Pontusson 1992, 138). In short, both Social Democrats and their bourgeois rivals failed to diagnose or remedy the country's difficulties in a timely fashion. Both governments not only maintained flawed policies but effectively doubled down on them.

This counterproductive response transformed a slow-moving structural crisis into an acute fiscal one. Competitive devaluations and increased government expenditure caused inflation to more than double (Henrekson, Jonung, and Stymne 1996, 249). At the same time, Sweden's fiscal situation became progressively less tenable. The "bridging strategy" of the early 1970s and increased state aid caused public sector outlays to reach 66 percent of GDP by 1983 (Henrekson, Jonung, and Stymne 1996, 269). A significant portion of this expenditure had to be financed through borrowing, as taxation already approached 50 percent of GDP (Magnusson 2000, 189). With debt as a share of GDP breaching 60 percent and annual deficits approaching double digits by the early 1980s (Henrekson, Jonung, and Stymne 1996, 255), Sweden faced a clear and existential crisis (interview with former employee, Ministry of Finance, 11 May 2012, Sweden). Stated bluntly, the country could no longer rely on the state and large, established enterprises to drive growth.

Epilogue: Economic Adjustment after 1980

Although the highly coordinated campaign to strengthen established capital-intensive manufacturing enterprises greatly increased Sweden's vulnerability to changing economic circumstances during the 1970s, this is not to suggest that Sweden was a total basket case. Consistent with the argument in chapter 1 and contrary to depictions of "Swedosclerosis," policy makers and societal actors did an effective (if belated) job of tackling structural problems once confronted with a clear fiscal crisis. Beginning in 1982, policy makers pivoted away from the large, established export-oriented manufacturing firms that defined postwar growth and experimented with several fundamentally different growth models. This reflected a sudden and decisive shift in public opinion as the share of the population believing that it is "important to increase entrepreneurship and firm formation" increased from 30 percent in 1978 to 74 percent by 1985 (Henrekson and Jakobsson 2001, 351). Policy makers promoted entrepreneurship in two ways, by liberalizing financial markets and reorienting traditional industrial policies. In chapters 3 and 4 I cover the politics of innovation and financialization in greater detail, presenting Finland and Iceland as even more extreme cases of overshooting. Dynamics were more moderate in Sweden, but we can preview these findings here. In doing so, we can also establish that overshooting was not an anomaly, nor was it specific to the rise of organized labor, neocorporatism, Social Democratic hegemony, the presence of large export-oriented firms, or other factors specific to the early postwar period.

Like their predecessors in the 1930s, a newly elected Social Democratic government responded to the economic crisis of the early 1980s (in this case, a fiscal one) with radical reforms. First and foremost, the government reversed the policies of the 1970s, seeking to tame inflation by stabilizing government expenditures and committing itself to a hard currency regime. Second, the government went even further in dismantling regulatory apparatus that underpinned the postwar Swedish model. In contrast to other continental European economies that moved more gradually, such as Austria, France, or Germany, Sweden liberalized its financial system in just a decade (Englund and Vihriälä 2009, 77).[13] The 1985 "November revolution" was particularly decisive, as the government eliminated the comprehensive system of credit rationing that empowered Sweden's leading banks and their large corporate clients (Jonung, Kiander, and Vartia 2009, 34).

Although this reform fundamentally transformed the Swedish financial system, it attracted little criticism. One might have expected actors that benefited from the old system to block reform or at least protest these changes. By the 1980s, however, all actors recognized that the status quo was unsustainable (in no small part due to policy overshooting in earlier years). A policy maker summarized:

> The whole regulatory system in 1985 was completely deficient. It didn't produce what we wanted, it didn't produce lending restraint. . . . So it was counterproductive. Everyone who worked with this was totally disillusioned. I think that is something that politicians haven't explained, the total disaster of the state of regulation in 1985. It was a complete mess, it didn't work, and they didn't know what to do. And then they said, let's get rid of the whole thing. (interview with former policy maker, Ministry of Finance, 11 May 2012, Sweden)

Like other small, cohesive societies with a high level of social capital, actors placed a great deal of trust in the relevant experts (Campbell and Hall 2017, 14). Scholarly accounts, commenting on the lack of debate, note that politicians, organized labor, and industry were all willing to defer to the discretion of the Bank of Sweden, the Ministry of Finance, and their assurances that the reforms would not be disruptive (Jonung, Kiander, and Vartia 2009, 37).

Any concerns were further mollified by the fact that the benefits of financial liberalization were widely distributed. Generous social policies, which were preserved by the Palme administration (and its successors), reduced resistance to fiscal austerity and market-oriented reform. Like Finland and Iceland in chapters 3 and 4, this is an excellent example of how continuity in some policy domains, such as social policy, can permit comprehensive reform in other areas. Financial markets were a particularly easy target for reformers, because the abolition of credit rationing democratized access to capital (interview with economist, 11 May 2012, Sweden). Consumers could secure loans that were once unattainable and rising asset prices benefited almost all actors. Banks were unlikely to object to the opportunity to service growing financial markets, while the government used the boom to achieve a modest fiscal surplus by the late 1980s (Jonung, Kiander, and Vartia 2009, 35).

In contrast to Finland and Iceland, there was relatively little in the way of policy coordination during the 1980s. But there is some evidence that new attitudes toward credit spread quickly within tight-knit private-sector networks. Pioneered by mortgage lenders in the early 1980s, weaker commercial banks quickly increased lending, and by the late 1980s even SEB was expanding its balance sheet (Englund and Vihriälä 2009, 81–85).[14] Meanwhile, traditional industry was caught in the bubble as foreign exchange loans among firms proliferated (Englund and Vihriälä 2009, 87). The shift in corporate strategy was not as pronounced as in Finland or Iceland, but it nonetheless marked a sharp break with the early postwar period. The exporters that drove the Swedish economy until 1982 suffered under this inflationary hard currency regime, as policy makers pivoted to nontradable services to stimulate growth (Jonung, Kiander, and Vartia 2009, 35). By way of illustration, the share of value-added attributed to financial intermediation (4.6 percent) rivaled manufacturing juggernauts such as France (4.4) and Germany (4.5) in 1980. In just ten years, it stood at 6.9 percent, surpassing not only France (5.4 percent) and Germany (4.4) but also leapfrogging financial centers such as the United States (6.0) and the United Kingdom (6.6) (OECD 2016).

Unfortunately, this new supply of credit was not invested prudently. Because capital had been so heavily regulated before the 1980s, defaults were rare. Banks thus had no experience assessing lender risk in a deregulated environment (interview with former employee, Ministry of Finance, 11 May 2012, Sweden). Although Swedish policy makers did not actively fuel the bubble like their Finnish or Icelandic counterparts, these deficiencies were nonetheless exacerbated by a failure to adequately tighten fiscal policy, monetary policy, or financial regulations (Jonung, Kiander, and Vartia 2009, 36; interview with former employee, Ministry of Finance, 11 May 2012, Sweden). On the contrary, repeated assurances about the health of the economy did little to encourage proper risk management (Jonung, Kiander, and Vartia 2009, 57). As a result, Sweden suffered a massive banking crisis in the early 1990s. The boom and bust may not have been as severe as in Finland or Iceland, but table A.4 demonstrates that Sweden was still an outlier among larger advanced industrialized economies (as well as many smaller ones), securing a place in the "big five" until 2007 (Rogoff and Reinhart 2009, 160). Sweden's financial-services industry shrank as quickly as it grew. By 1995 financial intermediation represented just 4.5 percent of value-added, comparable to Germany rather than the United Kingdom or the United States.

If Sweden differed from other crisis-affected countries such as the United States in the scale of its banking crisis, it also differed in its response. Although interviewees argued that groupthink delayed recognition of the crisis and contributed to a costly and ineffective defense of the Swedish crown, they also claimed that these tight-knit ties were also an asset once the scale of the problem was clear (interviews with economist, 11 May 2012, and three former employees, Ministry of Finance, 11 and 15 May 2012, Sweden). Sweden was hailed for its pragmatic and innovative approach to bank recapitalization. The government also addressed the macroeconomic errors that contributed to the crisis, most notably with the addition of expenditure ceilings and a budgetary surplus target of 2 percent of GDP (Jonung, Kiander, and Vartia 2009, 51).[15] But it went even further in championing a completely different growth model in the early 1990s, based not on large, established exporters or nontradable services, but rather entrepreneurial high-technology enterprises.

To be clear, there was always more space for high-technology enterprises (Astra, Ericsson, Saab) in Sweden than neighboring Finland, and the latter represents an even more extreme case of reform and restructuring. By conventional standards, however, Sweden's performance is still impressive. As noted above, the country was heavily dependent on century-old conglomerates, and its position in high-technology markets steadily weakened over the course of the postwar period, trailing the United States, the United Kingdom, and even Germany in 1980 (see table A.3). By 2000, however, the share of high-technology exports had increased by 269 percent and Sweden had rebranded itself a "wireless wonder" (Glimstedt and Zander 2003). Ericsson spearheaded growth, but restructuring also reflected the unlikely proliferation of high-technology start-ups (Augustsson 2005) competing in radically innovative markets such as middleware software

(Casper 2007a). This was not merely a departure from the growth regime of the early postwar period, it was almost diametrically opposed to it.

Like the financialization of the Swedish economy in the 1980s, Sweden's improbable entry into new high-technology markets was shaped by cohesive, tight-knit networks (Skog et al. 2016, 11). At first glance, this sounds implausible. Political economists often depict the 1980s and 1990s as a period of intense conflict, focusing on bitter debate over the wage-earner funds and the subsequent breakdown of formal neocorporatist institutions (Pontusson and Swenson 1996). Although accurately capturing the breakdown of the traditional postwar model, this narrative obscures the country's unusually broad and strong commitment to innovation, particularly after 1991. The government's official slogan, "IT for everyone, before anyone else," embraced by all major parties, captures both the country's ambitions as well as the perception that the benefits of ICT-based growth would be widely distributed (Augustsson 2005, 66).

Restructuring can be traced back to the Palme administration's draconian cuts to traditional industrial policy and the subsequent reorientation of funding toward small and medium-sized enterprises (Pontusson 1992, 142–45), but high-technology competition achieved even greater salience under the center-right Carl Bildt administration of the early 1990s. Innovation policy was never as ambitious or comprehensive as Finland, but the government signaled its commitment to technological innovation by sending the first email to another head of state, convening national and local ICT committees, promoting successful high-technology entrepreneurs, and engaging in other symbolic gestures (Augustsson 2005, 88). Unlike other high-technology enthusiasts such as the United States, this lofty rhetoric was matched by significant public investments. For example, the government invested in high-speed broadband, doubled expenditure on higher education, established public venture capital funds, and created three new research foundations.[16] To placate opponents, the benefits of this ICT-intensive strategy were widely distributed. The government subsidized computer purchases and introduced a massive ICT-focused retraining initiative to assist workers adversely affected by economic and technological change (Augustsson 2005, 69; Gergils 2006, 334–39; Steinmo 2010, 71).

These initiatives provide a sense of the scale and scope of Swedish innovation policies, but it is important to recognize that digital initiatives represented much more than a modern-day upgrading of traditional investments in human capital and infrastructure. In a sharp break with earlier practices, policy makers specifically targeted new high-technology firms by promoting the development of early-stage venture capital markets. The government established two public funds, Atle and Bure, in 1992, followed by Industrifonden in 1995 (Gergils 2006, 338–39). Like the industrial policies of the early postwar period, these measures worked because they enjoyed the support of the private sector. For example, industry and labor agreed to convert one pension fund, the Sixth AP Fund, into a dedicated venture capital investor and other funds soon followed its lead into early-stage risk capital markets (Cetindamar and Jacobsson 2003, 127).

They did so, in part, because private entrepreneurs used nationalist imagery to capture the popular imagination and attract investor interest, much like Finnish banks had done in the nineteenth century and Icelandic banks would do in the twenty-first. The ICT entrepreneur Jonas Birgersson, for example, challenged Microsoft by throwing a brick through a glass window while wearing a national ice hockey jersey (Augustsson 2005, 82). Birgersson's commitment to creating a digital *folkhemmet* (people's home) was an extreme case, but Staël von Holstein used mercantilist rhetoric in insisting that Sweden could and should become a net exporter of ICT, and organizations such as the "Silicon Vikings" harkened back to a golden age of international conquest (Augustsson 2005, 106). Like in Finland, interest in ICT was a broad-based social phenomenon, although one firm, Ericsson, towered above the rest. Perceived as a source of national pride and repeatedly compared to the "genius companies" of the nineteenth century in Swedish media, Ericsson dominated public discourse (Linden 2012, 121). Fredrik Augustsson writes:

> IT was one of the dullest topics people could think of. But within a few years, IT went from infrastructural negotiations between Ericsson, Televerket, and government officials to intense dinner conversations between more or less initiated Swedes. . . . Not a day went by without the news showing the current value of [Ericsson's] stock and it seemed as if more or less everyone knew that value. The IT sector became a matter of national pride. (Augustsson 2005, 106)

Collectively, these ambitious public policies and a dramatic shift in public opinion not only paved the way for Ericsson's growth but also created unprecedented opportunities for small start-ups. Early-stage risk capital increased from 0.021 percent of GDP in 1989, less than any Western European country except Austria and Finland,[17] to 0.857 percent by 2000. By this point, Sweden exceeded every Western European country except Finland and Iceland (Eurostat 2016). Abundant risk capital enabled Sweden to move beyond telecommunications hardware into fundamentally new industries such as digital media (Augustsson 2005) and middleware (Casper 2007a).

If the resulting dot-com boom was one of the largest in the Western world, it was also one of the most fragile. The share of high-technology manufactured exports fell from 28.8 percent in 2000 to 21.7 percent by 2003, when demand for Ericsson's handsets collapsed and its network equipment business stumbled

(OECD 2016). Meanwhile, venture capital investment plummeted, from 0.857 percent of GDP in 2000 to 0.364 percent in 2003, less than half of British levels (Eurostat 2016). The sudden reversal of fortune hit Sweden's dot-com start-ups, many of whom did not have viable business models, particularly hard. For example, half of the firms in the digital media industry disappeared after 1999 (Augustsson 2005, 113).

In the long run, the crisis would strengthen high-technology industry. Sweden now boasts a higher (population-adjusted) rate of start-ups with billion-dollar valuations than any other region in the world. Contemporary success is based less on massive injections of public risk capital than a complex combination of specialized inputs delivered through dense private-sector networks (Skog et al. 2016). But the path to high-technology leadership has not been a smooth one. In chapter 3 I present an even more extreme example of the rise, collapse, and renewal of high-technology industry, focusing on the politics of innovation in late twentieth-century Finland.

3

CONNECTING PEOPLE
Innovation in Finland

If the first half of the twentieth century illuminated the dangers of unfettered market competition, the second half highlighted the limits of the state. Sweden's slowdown was not unique, as efforts to steer the economy were perceived to suppress growth across the world. Advanced industrialized economies faced two broad problems. First, capital-intensive strategies failed to protect these countries from new cost-competitive rivals. As a result, the manufacturing industries that fueled postwar prosperity hemorrhaged jobs after 1970. Second, heavy-handed regulation was perceived to inhibit the development of the new high-technology industries that might sustain growth in the future. These challenges were particularly acute in Nordic Europe, which had relied most heavily on the public sector and heavy industry. Sweden, once a model, was reclassified a "small state in big trouble" in the 1990s (Schwartz 1994) while Finland was rebranded a "failure" (Tainio, Pohjola, and Lilja 1997).

As I foreshadow in chapter 2, Sweden and the other Nordic countries responded to the economic slowdown of the 1970s in two ways. First, policy makers looked to the market to boost growth. This neoliberal strategy sought to bolster competitiveness by shrinking the state and opening the economy. Although pioneered by Anglo-Saxon countries such as the United Kingdom and the United States, neoliberals found a receptive audience in Nordic Europe. In the 1980s and 1990s, Nordic policy makers virtually eliminated traditional forms of state aid, opened the economy to international competition, and perhaps most significantly, deregulated financial markets. Open, competitive financial markets promised to accelerate the redistribution of resources to new growth-oriented enterprises and restructure old ones. In fact, in a deregulated environment, finance would become a growth industry in its own right. Rapid liberalization was not limited to Sweden. Finland also experienced a massive credit boom and banking crisis, and in chapter 4 I describe how Iceland constructed a (short-lived) Swiss-sized financial empire in the span of a decade.

Late twentieth-century economic policy, however, was never simply a question of rolling back the state. Drawing on the insights of Joseph Schumpeter, economists also focused on innovation as a second alternative to capital-intensive manufacturing. By the 1970s, growth in advanced industrialized economies was based on the creative recombination of existing resources rather than the mobilization of additional labor and capital. These developments led academics and policy makers to identify a new role for the state, investing in relevant public goods and fostering collaboration within a "national innovation system." Like the market-oriented reforms described above, these new ideas were initially developed by Anglo-Saxon scholars such as Christopher Freeman and Richard Nelson but were quickly embraced by Nordic scholars and policy makers (Edquist 1997; Lundvall 1992). Over the course of the 1980s and 1990s, several Nordic countries dramatically increased investment in research, risk capital, and higher education.[1] Together with new network-oriented industrial policies, these inputs enabled policy makers and private-sector entrepreneurs to transform historically low-technology countries, heavily dependent on resource-extractive industries and capital-intensive manufacturing, into unlikely high-technology leaders, leapfrogging larger economies such as France, Germany, the United Kingdom, and, by some measures, even the United States (Ornston 2012b).

In this chapter I examine this second shift, the rise of innovation policy and high-technology industry, focusing specifically on late twentieth-century Finland. Several decades ago, this would have seemed like an odd choice. In 1980 Finland was even more heavily regulated than Sweden and its economic structure reflected this. Large, incumbent firms dominated the economy, using economies of scale to compete in low- and medium-technology industries such as forestry, mining, and metal processing. At 3.6 percent, the share of high-technology exports exceeded only Greece (1.0 percent) and Iceland (0.4 percent) within Western Europe, and the country spent just 1.16 percent of GDP on R&D, less than the average OECD member (OECD 2016). Moreover, Finland lacked the characteristics commonly associated with high-technology production such as a large domestic market, incumbent producers, heavy defense spending, or close ties to high-technology leaders such as the United States. By the end of the millennium, however, Finland ranked among most the innovative countries in the world, not only in terms of exports but also research expenditure, patenting, and services. Nor was it unique within the Nordic region, as Sweden and Denmark experienced similar (albeit more modest) shifts (Ornston 2012b).

Rapid reform and restructuring makes more sense when we focus on the cohesive and encompassing relationships that characterize Finnish society. Although these tight-knit ties rendered Finland even more dependent on state intervention and heavy industry than Sweden, reform-oriented actors could use these same networks to engineer an even sharper about-face during the 1980s and 1990s. Confronted with a clear geopolitical and economic crisis, policy makers liberalized their financial system more rapidly than their Swedish counterparts and adopted more ambitious innovation policies. More importantly, reform-oriented actors used formal and informal networks to scale these new innovation policies, investing heavily in technological innovation. The politics of persuasion, compensation, and coordination enabled Finland to transform itself from one of the least research-intensive countries in the developed world into a high-technology leader.

Unfortunately, this same pattern of coordination rendered Finland exceptionally vulnerable to policy overshooting and overinvestment. Most obviously, the country mobilized resources around a single firm (Nokia). This was not necessarily a bad thing, as the benefits of Nokia's growth were widely distributed and lifted the country from a devastating recession. But the dependence on a single firm increased the fallout from Nokia's decline. More problematically, coordination led public- and-private sector actors to focus on technological development at the expense of social, organizational, and other nontechnological forms of innovation. This narrow technological orientation not only undermined any efforts to diversify away from Nokia but heightened Nokia's own vulnerability to disruptive shocks such as the Internet-enabled smartphone.

In addition to providing another example of overshooting, the Finnish case is theoretically significant for several reasons. First, the Finnish experience suggests that overshooting cannot be attributed to natural resources or inherited comparative advantage. Unlike the rich ore deposits that supported Swedish movement into mining and metal processing, Finnish specialization in mobile communications was not geographically predetermined. Second, overshooting cannot be attributed to traditional industrial policies, as these were largely abandoned by the 1990s. In fact, the rise and fall of the Finnish ICT industry was driven just as much by the private sector as the state. Nokia demonstrated an independent capacity to leverage tight-knit networks, reorienting firms, knowledge-bearing institutions, and even public policies around its strategic vision. Finally, Finland represents an important counterpoint to the celebration of "systemic" action in innovation studies (Edquist and Hommen 2008; Lundvall 2002).[2] While the benefits of coordination are formidable, so are the risks.

Antecedents: Interconnectedness in Finland

To understand Finland's remarkable transformation from a low-technology, resource-based economy into a high-technology powerhouse, we need to situate the country in comparative perspective. Although not as cozy as Iceland (chapter 4), Finnish society is significantly more tight-knit than Sweden. Historically, Finland was even more dependent on bank-based finance than Sweden; private banking blocs cooperated even more closely with the state, and public disagreements were even rarer, as evidenced by Finnish reliance on super-majority coalitions, centralized, collective wage bargaining, and a distinctive tradition of self-censorship in the media. This consensual approach to politics and production enabled Finland to introduce new policies and restructure its economy even more rapidly than Sweden, but it also led to even greater overshooting, first in its dependence on capital-intensive manufacturing during the 1970s and then in a massive banking crisis during the early 1980s. After documenting the presence of cohesive, encompassing networks, this section reviews each boom-bust cycle in turn.

"Finland Is Not a Country, It's a Club"

To an even greater degree than Sweden, Finland epitomizes the tight-knit ties that are the subject of this book manuscript (see appendix 1). Finland was never dominated by a single family such as the Wallenbergs, but the Finnish financial system was more concentrated in other ways. For example, Finnish firms were even more dependent on bank-based financing than Swedish counterparts (Hyytinen et al. 2003, 398). As a result, there was even less space in Finland for entrepreneurial actors such as Ingvar Kamprad or Erling Persson. Whereas postwar commentators spoke of Sweden's "fifteen" families (Sejersted 2011, 219), two commercial banks, the National Share Bank (Kansallis Osake Pankki) and the Union Bank of Finland (Suomen Yhdyspankki), dominated Finnish financial markets (Rehn 1996, 230).[3] These banks used their clout to construct encompassing industrial families that enveloped nearly all of Finland's large private-sector enterprises (Rehn 1996, 231) and cooperated closely with one another within peak-level neocorporatist federations and sectoral associations such as the Central Association of Finnish Forest Industries (Rehn 1996, 229).[4]

The National Share Bank and Union Bank of Finland did not completely monopolize postwar credit allocation. Three other blocs jockeyed for influence in postwar Finland, including a savings bank group, Säästöpankki (SKOP); a cooperative banking group, Osuuspankki; and a state-owned banking group, Postipankki.[5] Closer attention to these rivals, however, illustrates just how interconnected Finnish financial markets were. The SKOP group was the most distinctive, but it was largely relegated to retail markets until the 1980s. The cooperative movement played a more important role in financing industry. In sharp contrast to other countries such as Denmark, however, the Finnish cooperative movement did not attempt to decentralize political and economic power (Ornston 2012b, 32). While funding farmers and small businesses, it also channeled capital to Metsä Serla, one of Finland's largest forestry firms. This distinctive history stems in part from the fact that the Confederation of Finnish Cooperatives was established in the capital by political and economic elites. Its initial membership list reads like a Who's Who of fin de siècle Finnish society. The 1899 roster included not only farmers but also senators, civil servants, university professors, and prominent industrialists (Kuisma 1999, 32). The cooperative movement was thus tightly integrated into Finnish politics, enjoying close links to the Agrarian Union party and Finland's longest-serving president, Urho Kekkonen.

Organized labor was late to join these cohesive networks. A civil war between German-backed Whites and Russian-supported Reds in 1918 soured Finnish industrial relations, to the point that the Finnish Employers' Confederation prohibited its members from negotiating with Finnish trade unions. The labor movement was internally divided among several competing factions (Rehn 1996, 227), fueling the highest levels of industrial unrest in Nordic Europe (Stokke and Thornqvist 2001). Conditions changed, however, after the Social Democratic Party won a resounding electoral victory in 1966. Viewing the Confederation of Finnish Trade Unions as a valuable ally in the battle against Communism, the Social Democrats and their coalition partners introduced reforms to encourage trade union growth and consolidation (Bergholm 2003, 53). The 1968 Liinanmaa Agreement further reduced industrial unrest by trading wage restraint for social policy concessions.

Tripartite bargaining among the state, industry, and labor became an important vehicle for integrating the working class. By the 1980s Finland closely resembled Sweden in trade union density, employment protection, and social benefits (Fellman 2008, 182). To be clear, Finland was less social democratic in its commitment to de-commodification (Esping-Andersen 1990), Keynesian demand management (Rehn 1996, 244), and active labor-market policy (Ornston 2012b, 76–77). But organized labor was actively involved in and supported a wide range of policies, including wage setting, training, pensions, social policy, fiscal policy, and even innovation policy. In sharp contrast to Sweden, where employers withdrew from neocorporatist boards in the 1990s, Finnish neocorporatism persisted into the twenty-first century (Ornston and Rehn 2006).

This pattern of collaboration extends to Finnish political life as well. In contrast to Sweden, where minority governments are common, postwar Finnish politicians relied heavily on supermajority coalitions. The reliance on oversized governments was partly a function of pre-1992 constitutional requirements, but it also reflected a genuine convergence of views. Finland's precarious geopolitical position next to the Soviet Union forged a remarkably strong consensus among the major political parties on a nonaligned foreign policy (Rehn 1996, 235). This consensus was actively cultivated by the Finnish government, which used two- to three-week courses to educate leading industrialists, trade union representatives, politicians, and journalists on foreign policy. These programs, originally designed to integrate Communist politicians and trade union representatives into Finnish society, became an important vehicle for narrowing policy options among mainstream elites (Rehn 1996, 234). For example, although Finland ranked high in measures of press freedom, self-censorship was pervasive throughout the postwar period (Salovaara-Moring 2009, 215–16).

Self-censorship was most pronounced in foreign policy, but extended to other aspects of Finnish politics and society as well (interview with journalist, 19 June 2012, Finland). As a result, this consensual approach to politics outlived the Cold War and constitutional reform. The increasing frequency of "rainbow coalition" governments, uniting the National Coalition Party on the right and the Social Democratic Party on the left, reflects broad consensus on an array of contemporary issues from European integration to income policy (Rehn 1996, 235). The tendency of mainstream parties to adopt a pro-European stance was by no means limited to Finland, but the Finnish media provided less room for dissenting views. Whereas Sweden engaged in a more robust debate over EU membership and opted out of the Euro during the 1990s, Finland exhibited a familiar pattern of self-censorship (Salovaara-Moring 2009, 217).[6]

This consensual approach could be attributed to formal neocorporatist institutions of the sort that characterized postwar Finland. But it also reflects the dense, high-quality informal ties that connect Finnish elites as well as ordinary citizens. These connections are harder to quantify, but feature prominently in interviews, often in contrast to Sweden. Individuals that did not grow up attending the selective Helsinki primary school that trained many of Finland's most powerful decision makers are often connected to each other through mandatory military service, student unions, or informal associations such as the Hyvä Veli and Hyvä Sisko associations of the early postwar period (Rehn 1996, 234). A journalist summarized:

> Everybody knows each other, so to speak. When it comes to the educational system, we go to the same universities. We don't have elite universities, but we go to the same schools. Another very important aspect is, or used to be, the army.... As a [journalist], it's easy for me to get access

to all of those people in the various branches of the administration or the business life or trade unions or NGOs. In that sense, the doors are more or less open. (interview with journalist, 19 June 2012, Finland)

Several interviewees opened conversations by noting that Finland should be seen as a "club" rather than a country (interviews with journalist, 9 November 2005; professor, 12 June 2012; and economist, 20 June 2012, Finland). A civil servant, sensing my familiarity with the concept, remarked, "So you have heard that Finland is not a country, it is a club. That is true. Everybody knows everybody. That is because we are a small state and class differences are very low in Finland compared to, for instance, Sweden" (interview with civil servant, 11 June 2012, Finland).

It might seem odd that a less social democratic country would be characterized by weaker class cleavages, but the remark makes sense when one examines informal relationships. Although Sweden is also characterized by encompassing organizations representing capital and labor, cross-class fraternization is less common (interview with former minister, 11 May 2012, Sweden). During my time at Swedish and Finnish research institutes, I was stuck by the degree to which Finnish economists not only knew their counterparts at "rival" research institutions but also attended the same social functions. Even organizations associated with a particular "camp" were more encompassing than they initially appeared. When asked about one such group, the journalist cited above remarked:

> The group that you mentioned was the G10 and it consisted of economists from various parts of society, from trade unions, employer organizations, economic research institutes, and certain ministries. They have an informal discussion group to ventilate all kinds of issues. The participants were academic economists, except for three or four journalists who participated in those discussions and [represented] the man in the street. For me, it was very rewarding because I could see economists from the trade unions and the economists from the employer organizations trying to find a common understanding on certain aspects of the economy. (interview with G10 participant, 19 June 2012, Finland)

These tight-knit networks are a clear asset, but it is important to recognize that they can also marginalize dissenting views and the individuals who express them. A business journalist with experience in Sweden and Finland remarked: "It's quite a big difference in Finland and Sweden with journalism. In Sweden journalists are much harder. They don't look up to the company leaders and authority as much as Finns do" (interview with journalist, 14 May 2012, Sweden). Another journalist was even more blunt, describing how a businessman, whose right-of-center views might fit comfortably within the American Chamber of Commerce or even the Swedish Center for Business and Policy Studies, was treated as a "freak" within Finland (interview with journalist, 9 November 2005, Finland).

Traditional Industrial Policy and the Crisis of Low-tech Production

Like Sweden, cohesive and encompassing social networks can be traced back to the pre-industrial period, which was marked by a high level of literacy, low levels of religious conflict, and a relatively coherent administrative apparatus (Larsen 2001, 12).[7] Finland leveraged these assets to reform and restructure its society with remarkable speed. After World War II, Finland used an exaggerated form of statism to modernize established resource-extractive industries such as forestry and mining and target capital-intensive heavy industries such as steel and transportation equipment. These policies paid dividends in the early postwar period. A country that used the primary sector to employ nearly half its population and was almost half as prosperous as Sweden in 1950 had nearly closed the gap between the two countries by the 1980s (Fellman 2008, 182; Vartiainen 1999, 277). Finnish prosperity, however, came at a heavy price. The country was even more dependent on low- and medium-technology industries than Sweden, as tight-knit networks discouraged policy experimentation and economic diversification. By the early 1990s, the country was mired in the worst banking crisis in the history of the OECD.

This turn to statism and heavy industry was scarcely conceivable in the nineteenth century. Poorer and more agrarian than Sweden, in the 1860s Finland was the last Western European country to experience a peacetime famine (Fellman 2008, 140). Although Swedish-speaking entrepreneurs copied their counterparts across the Gulf of Bothnia by establishing the Union Bank of Finland in 1862, financing was modest and the bank exercised relatively little influence over its clients. As a result, Finland relied principally on foreign capital to industrialize and specialized in unfinished or lightly processed raw materials (Schybergson 2001, 147). The banking industry changed rapidly in the late nineteenth century, however, when the Fennoman, or Finnish nationalist movement, swept the country. Seeking to elevate Finnish speakers to positions of political and economic power, the Fennoman leaders established the National Share Bank in 1889. The National Share Bank used the *Fennoman* movement to mobilize deposits from across the country, establishing larger firms in more capital-intensive activities such as papermaking. The Swedish business community quickly responded by using the Union Bank of Finland to merge three paper mills into Nordic Europe's largest forestry firm, Kymmene, in 1904 (Fellman 2008, 150).

State intervention remained limited until World War I. Like their Swedish counterparts, nineteenth-century Finnish elites did an excellent job of applying contemporary economic theories, and analysts characterized the late 1800s as an "ultra-liberal" era (Fellman 2008, 151). While policy makers invested in education, transportation, and communication infrastructure, they simultaneously dismantled traditional and mercantilist regulations. For example, the government removed restrictions on the establishment of sawmills in 1857, eliminated obligatory employment in 1865, abolished the guild system in 1868, joined the gold standard in 1878, and allowed the free movement of labor by 1879 (Fellman 2008, 146–49). In two decades Finland, like Sweden, transformed itself from one of Europe's most heavily regulated and mercantilist societies into one of its most liberal ones.

As in Sweden, this laissez-faire stance changed abruptly during the interwar period. The abrupt collapse of Russian markets, which absorbed 45 percent of Finnish exports before World War I, posed an existential threat to Finnish industry and the nation more generally. In addition to a civil war and the threat of foreign invasion, Finland suffered a famine in 1918 (Fellman 2008, 154–55). Finnish business responded to the economic shock by working together. Finland had exhibited some cartelistic tendencies before, but after 1918 rival banking blocs consolidated control over their holdings and collaborated with one another within a dense network of sectoral associations, export boards, marketing organizations, and price-fixing cartels (Schybergson 2001, 144). Collectively, these organizations controlled 80 percent of Finnish exports (Fellman 2008, 161). The industrialists, such as Gösta Serlachius, who organized these joint ventures worked closely with policy makers. The state, for example, not only tolerated cartelization but passed legislation that favored the large commercial banks and devalued the currency to protect resource-based industries (Fellman 2008, 155–59).

Policy makers also intervened more directly, nationalizing privately held enterprises. To some extent, this was an extension of the nineteenth-century Fennoman movement, designed to elevate Finnish speakers to positions of power (Fellman 2008, 160). But it also reflected concerns about Finnish dependence on foreign investment, Finland's inability to manufacture more sophisticated products, and the conviction that industrialization was essential to protect Finland from an increasingly menacing Soviet Union. The nationalization of the Norwegian-owned forestry giant Gutzeit in 1918 not only asserted sovereignty over Finland's natural resources but also spearheaded movement from lightly processed timber exports to pulp and paper production (Schybergson 2001, 121–22). Within a decade, policy makers had founded another forestry firm, modernized a loss-making copper firm, and established state-owned corporations in power, chemicals, and armaments.

State intervention increased even more dramatically after 1939. While war and heavy reparations payments led policy makers to sharply increase taxes, politicians deliberately elected not to lower rates in the 1950s and relied on the statutory pension system to raise additional capital. Public savings were channeled back to industry through the main commercial banks and a new state-owned investment bank, Postipankki (Vartiainen 1999, 277–78). The latter enabled policy makers to establish a new generation of state-owned enterprises in power generation, copper, steel, paper machinery, and petrochemicals. By the early 1990s, state-owned enterprises represented 23 percent of manufacturing value-added, 27 percent of manufacturing investment, and 30 percent of manufactured exports (Rehn 1996, 282).

The establishment of state-owned enterprises represents just one way in which the Finnish state overshadowed its Swedish counterpart. As in Sweden, policy makers rationed credit and used tax policy to favor large capital-intensive enterprises (Fellman 2008, 176–77). But they went further in restricting foreign investment and using credit quotas and access to foreign exchange to favor strategic sectors. Furthermore, credit was hardly the only resource that was rationed. Postwar planning committees regulated the use of foreign exchange, imported goods, and even domestic resources such as energy (Fellman 2008, 168; Skippari and Ojala 2008, 244). Originally designed to facilitate postwar reconstruction and complete reparation payments, regulation persisted even after these immediate challenges were met in the 1950s. The government instead adopted French-style numerical targets in strategic industries in 1951 (Rehn 1996, 280). While price regulations and trade restrictions were relaxed later in the decade, the economy remained heavily managed. Bilateral trade with the Soviet Union, which increased steadily throughout the postwar period, played a particularly important role. These agreements, which were negotiated at the highest level, enabled the Ministry of Trade and Industry to directly manage up to a quarter of Finnish exports (Fellman 2008, 170–75). In this strategically important sector, postwar Finland more closely resembled a Soviet-style command economy (Steinbock 2000, 28).

In contrast to other planned economies, such as France, Finnish policy makers collaborated closely with private-sector actors. To some degree, this reflected a spirit of shared sacrifice within a small, vulnerable community (Campbell and Hall 2009). Finnish industry, sensitive to the threat of foreign invasion, recognized the need to contribute to the "national interest" (Fellman 2008, 187). Differences between Finnish and Swedish speaking blocs evaporated as the Swedish speakers who opposed the initial nationalization of Enso-Gutzeit supported statist policies (Fellman 2008, 178). Leading Swedish-speaking industrialists such as Rudolf Waldén and Gösta Serlachius managed the Finnish economy during the war, and private-sector actors were heavily involved in postwar planning efforts (Vartiainen 1999, 227).

Private-sector backing was also based on the capacity of policy makers to satisfy business interests. As in Sweden (and unlike France), state intervention strengthened the traditional banking blocs and their clients rather than threatening them. The rationing of credit, and foreign exchange, enhanced the position of the main commercial banks as gatekeepers in Finnish society. Meanwhile, exchange-rate policy was so heavily influenced by the powerful Central Association of Finnish Forest Industries that commentators dubbed it the "pulp cycle" (Fellman 2008, 173–76). Even the decision to establish state-owned enterprises was not incompatible with private-sector interests, as policy makers focused on complementary industries such as steel, paper machinery, chemicals, petrochemicals, and power generation. Meanwhile, private-sector firms such as Nokia, Wärtsilä, and Tampella were deeply implicated in bilateral trade with the Soviet Union, which linked the private and public sectors in ways that surpassed other capitalist societies (Steinbock 2000, 28).

While postwar policies clearly benefited Finnish industry, support was not confined to big business. All the major political parties endorsed this developmental strategy. Former prime minister and four-time president Urho Kekkonen enthusiastically championed heavy manufacturing even though his Agrarian Party represented agrarian interests and smallholders. Like industry, agrarian support was based partly on a willingness to sacrifice to secure Finnish sovereignty. Echoing late nineteenth-century Fennoman appeals, Kekkonen reframed industrialization as a collective project in an influential pamphlet entitled "Do We Have the Patience to Prosper?" (Rehn 1996, 279). Agrarian interests were also satisfied with generous side payments, including broadly distributed ownership rights to forest resources, agricultural protectionism, and the decision to situate state-owned enterprises in rural districts (Fellman 2008).

Even organized labor, which received few benefits in the early postwar period, embraced this statist strategy. Although obviously disagreeing over issues such as pay and social policy, the Social Democratic Party did not challenge fundamental aspects of the model, including high taxes, credit rationing, and nationalization. On the contrary, the Social Democrats became one of statism's biggest supporters, particularly once they began to receive side payments through centralized collective wage bargaining in the 1960s and 1970s (Fellman 2008, 182–84). For example, Social Democratic–led governments in the 1970s followed the same model that had succeeded in copper, steel, and oil by establishing national champions in televisions and telecommunications equipment (Rehn 1996, 282–83).

By then, statist policies had transformed the country. Even if Finland never surpassed its more prosperous neighbor, its performance was even more impressive. Finland enjoyed the highest growth rate of any European country in the twentieth century, more closely resembling the tiger economies of East Asia (Fellman 2008, 139). In 1900 Finland was 43 percent poorer than an average of thirty Western European countries. By the late twentieth century, Finland had not only eclipsed that benchmark but surpassed northern Italy, Spain, the United Kingdom, and Germany (Bolt and Zanden 2013).[8] Rapid economic growth was based on radical restructuring, as Finland transformed itself from an overwhelmingly agrarian economy in the first half of the twentieth century into a manufacturing powerhouse. As in Sweden, cheap credit fueled the growth of industry. Exceeding 25 percent of GDP in the early postwar years, Finland boasted the second highest investment rate in Europe after Norway (Boltho 1982, 33).

At the same time, this state-led strategy introduced even greater imbalances into the economy. Although slightly less dependent on large firms than Sweden, the coordinated redistribution of resources to strategic sectors rendered Finland even more reliant on low- and medium-technology industries. Pulp and paper alone represented a third of Finnish exports in the 1970s, while another quarter was based on wood products and basic metals (Koski and Ylä-Anttila 2006, 19). Although Finland exported processed goods, many of these industries (particularly metal processing) relied on heavily regulated bilateral trade with the Soviet Union. Nokia, one of Finland's most diversified firms, sent half of its exports to the USSR in the 1970s (Steinbock 2000, 28). Finland's share of high-technology exports, 3.6 percent, was among the lowest in the developed world in 1980 (OECD 2016).

The mobilization of public- and-private sector resources around large capital-intensive firms left little room for entrepreneurial actors to rectify this situation. Nokia, for example, was only able to experiment with televisions and telecommunications because joint ownership by the Union Bank of Finland and the National Share Bank gave it unusual latitude (Fellman 2008, 178). In the words of one historian, "The big boys were in the forest industry . . . Electronics was young and small. It was left over. There was no interest by the major banks. It was a little playground" (interview, historian, 10 November 2005, Finland). A diversified, century-old conglomerate such as Nokia could rely on internal revenue to fund experimentation in this space, but new enterprises were not so fortunate. One ICT entrepreneur noted that it was virtually impossible to secure an uncollateralized loan until the 1980s (interview with former owner, ICT firm, 20 November 2006, Finland).

The lack of alternative funding instruments reflects the degree to which Finnish society prioritized heavy industry. These views were encapsulated by the famous claim of one veteran industrialist and employer association leader that

Finland should "export nothing smaller than a horse." Individuals who questioned that view faced fierce resistance. One ICT representative described his experience with a different association leader when he attempted to mobilize support for new innovation policies, "The president listened to us carefully, he was a lawyer by training. And suddenly he said, 'If you come back and tell me about networks, I will get my gun and pull the trigger'" (interview, 10 November 2005, Finland). Not surprisingly, the most innovative efforts to develop alternative industries occurred at the margins of Finnish society, in small, peripheral agencies such as Sitra (Breznitz and Ornston 2013). Mainstream efforts to diversify the Finnish economy, to the extent that they existed, replicated traditional industrial policies, using state-owned corporations to achieve economies of scale in high-technology industries such as televisions and telecommunications equipment (Rehn 1996, 282–83).

As a result, Finland entered the 1970s in an even more precarious situation than Sweden. Although bilateral trade with the Soviet Union insulated Finland from the worst of the OPEC-induced oil crises, dependence on this historic enemy reached troubling levels. When the share of exports to the Communist bloc reached 25 percent, policy makers and industrialists alike recognized that Finland's developmental model was not only economically unsustainable but also geopolitically unacceptable. Executives at firms such as Nokia realized that they could no longer send half of their exports to Communist markets (Steinbock 2000, 45), while policy makers fretted about the country's independence (Rehn 1996, 246). The mounting sense of crisis was compounded by the failure of state-led high-technology ventures in televisions and telecommunications equipment in 1979 and 1981 (Sabel and Saxenian 2008, 61). As a result, when "high-technology" enterprises such as Nokia spearheaded calls for reform (Moen and Lilja 2005), policy makers and even traditional industries were receptive to these new ideas (interview with bank executive, 12 June 2012, Finland). A former forestry executive remarked:

> This is very typical in Finland in that it's a consensus society. We've seen that in so many phases of our history. . . . Once you agree silently or explicitly that we have a crisis, then people pull together, labor unions, industry, politicians, and everybody else. . . . In the 1980s, the labor unions and government understood that we can no longer remain an exporter of more or less commodities. And so in a way the shift from an investment-based economy into an innovation-based economy started pretty early and there was broad consensus for the need for this shift. All sectors, even the construction industry, liked this. (interview with former forestry executive, 31 October 2005, Finland)

Financial Liberalization and the Banking Crisis of the Early 1990s

Like their Swedish counterparts, the Finns responded to the "crisis" of the early 1980s in two ways, deregulating financial markets and introducing new innovation policies. In the 1970s, financial liberalization seemed even more implausible in Finland than Sweden, because the economy was so heavily regulated. A veteran economist at the Bank of Finland remarked that proposals to reform the Finnish financial system were quickly shut down by "an elite consensus" until the 1980s (interview with economist, 20 June 2012, Finland). By the 1980s, however, declining competitiveness, macroeconomic imbalances, and increasing dependence on the Soviet Union gave reform-oriented actors the space they needed to attack traditional industrial policies. These actors persuasively argued that repeated devaluations and credit rationing were preventing restructuring by favoring large, established firms in mature capital-intensive industries (interview with economist, 20 June 2012, Finland). They responded by adopting a hard currency regime, opening up the financial system to international competition, and deregulating interest rates, effectively dismantling the most distinctive characteristics of Finland's postwar model (Moen and Lilja 2005, 367).

Like Sweden, this was not a simple case of convergence with the rest of the developed world. First, Finland liberalized financial markets with remarkable speed. In some respects, it leapfrogged Sweden, despite a later start. For example, the Bank of Finland started to deregulate lending rates in 1983. Within three years the Bank of Finland abolished credit rationing, and by 1987 permitted all firms to borrow freely from international markets (Englund and Vihriälä 2003, 9). Like the heavy-handed regulation of financial markets in the early postwar period, there was surprisingly little debate. Although the shift to a hard currency regime was highly contentious, few questioned the benefits of liberalizing Finnish financial markets or the need to do so as quickly as possible (interview with economist, 20 June 2012, Finland).

Second, this rapid policy reversal was all the more remarkable because the Bank of Finland and other organizations introduced few countervailing measures to regulate risk-taking until the crisis hit in 1991. For example, policy makers were even slower to raise capital requirements than their Swedish counterparts (Englund and Vihriälä 2003, 11), while financial supervision was largely unaltered (Englund and Vihriälä 2003, 12). Like Sweden, no effort was made to reform debt-friendly tax policies (Rehn 1996, 254). But policy makers went even further in fueling the bubble by adopting actively *pro*-cyclical policies (Kuusi 2015).[9]

Much like Sweden and Iceland (chapter 4), high-trust networks and deference to expertise inhibited effective regulation. Officials at the Ministry of Finance, for example, trusted that the Bank of Finland was regulating credit in a responsible fashion (interview with policy maker, 11 June 2012, Finland). Economists at the Bank of Finland relied on the discretion of the Financial Supervisory Authority, a separate department responsible for monitoring the banks (interview with economist, 20 June 2012, Finland). The supervisory authority in turn trusted the banks to monitor their own lending (interview with former financial supervisor, 20 June 2012, Finland), to such a degree that even Finland's lenient regulations were not always enforced (Englund and Vihriälä 2003, 12).

The transformation from one of the most heavily regulated financial systems in Western Europe to one that failed to meet even the minimal standards articulated by the Bank of International Settlements created space for entrepreneurial private-sector actors to introduce revolutionary new business models. In a classic example of the politics of persuasion, MIT-trained economist Pentti Kouri used the same roundtables that popularized new technology policies to present a highly leveraged vision of "Fortress Finland" to corporate leaders and politicians (interview with roundtable participant, 20 October 2005, Finland). This high-risk financial strategy quickly spread across Finnish society, leading to a lending frenzy during the second half of the 1980s.

SKOP Bank, a savings bank confederation servicing households that had historically been overshadowed by Finland's two large commercial banks, moved first and most aggressively. In an interesting example of isomorphism, they used newly available credit to mimic Finland's two more prestigious commercial banks by acquiring their own flagship paper machinery firm, Tampella, in 1987 (interview with former banking executive, 15 June 2012, Finland).[10] The commercial banks in turn copied SKOP Bank, bidding up the price of commercial assets and extending credit to consumers.[11] This is an important point of contrast with Sweden and other, larger countries. Whereas Finnish bank managers closely monitored and mirrored their domestic counterparts (interview with former banking executive, 15 June 2012, Finland), Handelsbanken executives focused on their traditional business model and were uninterested in their rivals (interview with former employee, Handelsbanken, 8 May 2012, Sweden). As a result, Handelsbanken was largely unaffected by the Swedish banking crisis. By contrast, all major Finnish banking blocs bought into the "new paradigm," expanding credit by at least 80 percent between 1985 and 1990 (Vihriälä 1997, 59) and accumulating losses exceeding 15 percent of assets by 1993 (Vihriälä 1997, 57).

While it is understandable why the banks would copy each other, why did not nonfinancial actors intervene to curb lending? In addition to the discursive mechanisms elaborated above, Finnish banks also employed a familiar strategy of compensation. Contemporaries quipped that the largest political party in Finland during the 1980s was the "Savings Bank Party," which (contrary to Sweden) delayed the implementation of new capital requirements recommended by the

Bank of International Settlements (interviews with economists, 15 June 2012, 17 June 2012, and 18 June 2012, Finland).[12] Indeed, all parties benefited from an environment in which lending and stock prices were increasing by 20 percent a year (Englund and Vihriälä 2003, 14; Rehn 1996, 251). In fact, cross-class alliances ensured that gains from the bubble were widely distributed, as the government compensated organized labor with new transfer programs and the expansion of old ones in the late 1980s (Englund and Vihriälä 2003, 20).

Although Finland's historically underdeveloped financial services industry never eclipsed its Swedish counterpart, the country surpassed its traditional rival on virtually all other metrics. Bank lending as a share of GDP in Finland increased from less than 50 percent of GDP in 1982 to over 90 percent by 1992, whereas Swedish credit as a share of GDP increased from 70 percent to just over 80 percent of GDP (Hyytinen and Pajarinen 2003, 24). By extension, the bust was also more extreme. All of Finland's major banking blocs, and many nonfinancial firms, facing severe losses, required government support (Englund and Vihriälä 2003, 19; Vihriälä 1997, 57). The 11 percent decline in output between 1990 and 1993 set a record for the worst banking crisis in the history of the OECD. Even today, after the 2007–2009 financial crisis, Finland retains its unenviable top five ranking (Laeven and Valencia 2012, 20).

Of course, it is important to recognize that bilateral trade with the Soviet Union, which was not fully addressed by the reforms of the 1980s, compounded the crisis (Honkapohja et al. 1999, 405).[13] Bilateral trade, which plunged by 70 percent in 1991, is often used to distinguish between the two countries (Gorodnichenko, Mendoza, and Tesar 2012; Honkapohja et al. 1999). Partly because of this, I examine the politics of financialization in Iceland in chapter 4, which was not heavily dependent on the Soviet Union or any other single export market in 2007. For now, it is important to note that credit expanded more rapidly in Finland during the 1980s, *before* the collapse of the Soviet Union. Also, the preceding section described how bilateral trade was not predetermined, but politically and socially constructed by the economic policies and business decisions of the early postwar period. When it collapsed, Finland would radically restructure its economic policies and corporate strategies, competing in a new but equally coordinated way.

From Industrial Policy to Innovation Policy: Explaining Radical Reform and Rapid Restructuring

After Finland's economy was presented as a clear "failure" with deep-rooted structural flaws in the mid-1990s (Pohjola 1996; Tainio, Pohjola, and Lilja 1997), few would have anticipated it would be hailed a "model" less than a decade later

(Castells and Himanen 2002). This new narrative reflected a fundamentally different Finnish economy. By 2000 electronics had surpassed forestry as Finland's largest industry and the share of high-technology exports had more than quintupled to 27.3 percent (see table A.3). The country trailed manufacturing hubs such as Ireland or Hungary, but Finland ranked first in Europe in more knowledge-intensive measures of high-technology production, including high-technology patenting and value-added.

It is difficult to overstate the magnitude of these changes. Although experts correctly identify pockets of innovative activity in early twentieth-century Finland (Rehn 1996, 286–87), the country lagged on most measures of technological development. As recently as the 1970s, public R&D appropriations stagnated as politicians used fiscal pressure to justify cutbacks (Lemola 2004, 275). Between 1981 and 2006, however, publicly funded R&D as a share of GDP nearly doubled, from 0.56 percent to 0.97 percent. As a result, Finland not only caught up to the EU and OECD average but jumped to the top of the table. Equally implausible developments occurred in other areas, such as early-stage risk capital funding and tertiary education, where Finland emerged as an unlikely leader (Eurostat 2016).

Perhaps the most remarkable aspect of Finland's shift from technological laggard to model innovator, however, was the way it transformed Finnish society. Private-sector R&D as a share of GDP increased from 0.63 percent of GDP in 1981 to 2.48 percent by 2006. Collectively, gross expenditure on R&D increased more rapidly than in any other EU member state, from an EU-lagging 1.16 percent in 1981 to 3.48 percent by 2006, second only to Sweden (Eurostat 2016). Increasing R&D expenditure represented a fundamental transformation, as traditional capital-intensive low-technology ventures yielded to emerging high-technology industries such as biotechnology, software, and, most importantly, telecommunications equipment. By the turn of the century, this low-technology late developer was the most ICT-intensive country in the world and a model in the emerging field of innovation policy (Dahlman, Routti, and Ylä-Anttila 2006b, 3). Moreover, it did so without the characteristics commonly associated with high-technology production, such as a large domestic market (Kristensen and Levinsen 1983), incumbent producers (Dalum 1992), heavy defense spending (Weiss 2014), or close ties to high-technology leaders such as the United States (Taylor 2004).

Finland's sudden emergence as a high-technology powerhouse also undermines several of the alternative explanations I identify in chapter 1. Clearly, we cannot place too much emphasis on natural resource endowments. Although Finland's forests may have supported the pulp and paper industry in the past, it is hard to link the country's more recent successes to natural resources. A more plausible explanation prioritizes international openness and market competition. This theory is more compelling in that it highlights the primacy of private-sector actors such as Nokia, as well as their access to international markets and capital (Häikiö 2002).[14] This "liberal" narrative, however, does not explain why Finland was so successful in adopting market-oriented reforms (see above). It also overlooks the fact that Finland remains less open than other European states, such as Sweden. In fact, "market-oriented reform" was accompanied by a healthy dose of state intervention, including one of the most ambitious innovation policies in Western Europe (Ornston 2006).

As an alternative to natural resources and economic openness, one could emphasize luck (Schwartz and Becker 2005a). Finland certainly benefited from bad luck, in the sense that the economic crisis of the early 1990s triggered comprehensive reform and economic restructuring. The depression redistributed capital and labor from unproductive traditional industries to rapidly growing high-technology sectors. At the same time, it is important not to overlook the policy decisions that got Finland into trouble in the first place, most notably a highly coordinated statist developmental model (Tainio, Pohjola, and Lilja 1997). A purely crisis-based explanation also fails to explain why deteriorating economic performance triggered sweeping policy reform rather than the pattern of political paralysis and incremental reform observed in Greece (chapter 5). As a result, even scholars using this luck-based prism highlight Finland's unusual capacity for collective action (Kiander 2005).

Others have focused on more fortuitous conditions, such as the pan-Nordic mobile telephone standard, on which the world-leading GSM digital standard was based (Beise 2004). Without denying that Nokia benefited from the GSM standard and Finland profited from Nokia's success, these accounts ignore increasing research intensity in traditionally low-technology industries such as food processing as well as the recent proliferation of new high-technology start-ups. Moreover, even if we accept that Finland is principally a story about a single firm, this conclusion raises more questions than it answers. For example, why did Nokia succeed where other firms with access to the GSM standard, such as Motorola, failed?[15] How did Nokia manage to grow so rapidly within the confines of an economy of five million people? And what enabled Nokia to create a supporting cluster of four thousand ICT-based firms and complementary public policies? To answer these questions, we must examine how cohesive, encompassing networks influenced reform and restructuring.

Prioritizing Innovation: The Politics of Persuasion

Innovation was not entirely neglected during the early postwar period. Sitra, the Finnish National Fund for Research and Development, had experimented with technology policies on a modest scale since the late 1960s. But this tiny agency was marginalized from mainstream policy-making circles until growing dependence on the Soviet Union and high-profile industrial policy failures prompted a national search for alternative economic strategies (Breznitz and Ornston 2013, 1227).[16] Technology policy entered mainstream discourse in 1979, when a parliamentary committee, seizing on Sitra's work and international reports, identified a "technology gap" between Finland and its competitors (Rehn 1996, 288). Originally assembled to address the concerns of left-of-center parties that technological innovation would destroy jobs, the 1979 Technology Committee and its successors concluded that technology would in fact create jobs, converting Social Democrats and their trade union allies from skeptics to supporters (interview, former member, STPC, 18 October 2005, Finland). In 1984 the same Parliament that sought to promote restructuring by abandoning credit rationing and other forms of public support established Tekes, the Finnish Funding Agency for Technology and Innovation, to subsidize corporate R&D. At forty million Euro its budget was four times larger than that of Sitra, and it would increase rapidly in subsequent years (Murto, Niemelä, and Laamanen 2006).

Tekes's impact might have remained limited if not for the fact that reform-oriented actors could use neocorporatist institutions to diffuse new ideas about technological innovation throughout Finnish society. During the 1980s, the 1979 Technology Committee and the ad hoc deliberative bodies that followed it were superseded by the Science and Technology Policy Council (STPC). Originally established in 1963 as the Science Policy Council, the STPC (now the Research and Innovation Council) acquired a broader mandate and a tripartite structure between 1986 and 1987. By incorporating the prime minister, cabinet officials, and social partners, the STPC emerged as a powerful vehicle for generating consensus and transforming Finnish innovation policy (Murto, Niemelä, and Laamanen 2006).

The STPC's ability to bridge divisions among a handful of powerful top-level actors was enhanced by Sitra's seminar program. These seminars, which invited elites from across Finnish society to participate in a series of short, weeklong classes, were introduced in the 1960s to forge consensus in defense policy. In 1977 they were adapted to educate Communist politicians and trade union leaders about the benefits of capitalism and, by extension, the dangers of planning (Rehn 1996, 234). Initially directed at leftists, the seminars also engaged corporate executives, politicians, and journalists across the political spectrum. As a result, they became an important mechanism for diffusing new ideas about technological innovation in the 1980s and 1990s (Moen and Lilja 2005, 373).

These public consensus-building bodies were complemented by private-sector initiatives. For example, during the early 1980s, Nokia's energetic new CEO Kari Kairamo used his position as head of the Confederation of Finnish

Employers to successfully lobby for new technology policies (Moen and Lilja 2005, 372). This encompassing organization provided Kairamo with a powerful vehicle to transform Finnish public opinion. At the same time, he used informal channels to persuade skeptical colleagues. For example, Kairamo took advantage of a private roundtable with other executives, politicians, economists, journalists, and agricultural representatives to educate them on the benefits of technological innovation (interview with economist and roundtable participant, 20 October 2005, Finland).

Collectively, these top-level bargains, elite courses, and informal discussions thoroughly transformed Finnish politics and society. In sharp contrast to the overtly hostile attitudes that prevailed in the 1970s, a Finnish politician remarked:

> I became [an MP] when these efforts started to be implemented with Tekes. All were enthusiastic that now we have new tool to develop our economy, to develop our resources.... I have the impression that all parties on the right or conservatives, liberals, Center Party, and social—at least Social Democrats and maybe even Communists of that time were able to support that policy orientation. There was even a competition, who was most favorable political movement to support that! (interview with former member of Parliament, 10 October 2005, Finland)

Although it is possible to identify a convergence of views as early as the 1980s, the banking crisis of the 1990s sharpened and deepened this shift. The depression increased interest in high-technology industries as an alternative to the capital-intensive manufacturing that was most heavily affected by the collapse in bilateral trade. In fact, support for innovation was so strong that the STPC was able to persuade the Finnish government to increase R&D expenditure at the height of an economic crisis (Ylä-Anttila and Palmberg 2005, 5). A former member summarized their power thusly:

> [During the recession] we were able to make decisions that normal Western societies can only dream of. [Some] public expenditures were cut by 25 percent. You can imagine what that means if you think of any normal Western democracy. [Cutting] 25 percent of public expenditure, it's quite a hard thing. But at the same time the government decided to increase R&D expenditure.... [This was] supported by the analysis that we were very involved in at the time. Finland was ready to do anything to create jobs.... We were able to convince the government that the best way to create new jobs was to invest in high tech. (interview with former member, STPC, 18 October 2005, Finland)

This decision to increase public R&D expenditure during a crisis, at odds with the rest of the OECD (Koski et al. 2006, 46), was only conceivable with broad private-sector support. In interviews, chief technology officers consistently described a marked shift in the attitudes of top-level management, in which R&D was no longer viewed as a cost but an investment (interviews with former director, forestry firm, 10 October 2005; executive officer, engineering firm, 25 October 2005; former executive officer, forestry firm, 31 October 2005; director, forestry firm, 2 November 2005; executive officer, software firm, 3 November 2005; and director, engineering firm, 4 November 2005, Finland). Naturally, these attitudes were most pronounced in high-technology enterprises such as Nokia, which accounted for the lion's share of private R&D investment in Finland. But R&D investment as a share of GDP would have exceeded the EU average even without Nokia as traditional industries attached growing importance to technological innovation (Ali-Yrkkö 2010, 30). The food processing industry, a heavily regulated low-technology backwater during the early postwar period, was investing a remarkable 3.5 percent of turnover in R&D by the late 1990s (Saarinen 2005, 29). A wide variety of historically low- and medium-technology process-based industries linked corporate competitiveness to new-to-market product innovations (interviews with former research director, forestry firm, 13 October 2005; former executive, forestry firm, 31 October 2005; executive, engineering firm, 4 November 2005; and executive, food processing firm, 29 November 2006, Finland). A former research director in forestry characterized the shift from capital investment to knowledge-based growth in the following terms:

> It used to be so that if you take "software" investments which means education, research, and marketing, they were less than 10 percent of the total investment of the company. Now they are increasing the share, not to the level of Nokia or the medical companies where only 10 percent is [physical capital] investment. But it is going to 20 percent and maybe 30 percent. This change started in the 1990s. (interview with former research director, forestry firm, 13 October 2005, Finland)

By the time I started conducting interviews in 2005 and 2006, one could observe remarkably broad support for technological innovation across the entire scope of Finnish society. For example, technological innovation was repeatedly credited with rescuing Finland from its low-technology trajectory and the crisis of the early 1990s in particular (interviews with former STPC planning officer, 18 October 2005; former director, Confederation of Finnish Employers, 19 October 2005; and economist, metalworkers union, 28 October 2005, Finland). It was also seen as central to Finnish growth in the future and an important source of competitive advantage relative to other firms and other countries (interviews with research director, electronics firm, 19 October 2005; representative, Finnish Forest Industries Federation, 9 November 2005; and research director, forestry firm, 24 November 2006, Finland). Although Finland already led the EU in public R&D expenditure, interviewees responded to open-ended questions about competitiveness by recommending that the public sector should do even more to promote corporate research (interviews with former executive officer, electronics firm, 17 October 2005; former member, STPC, 18 October 2005; and two industry association representatives, 19 October 2005, Finland).

Of course, one should not overstate this apparent convergence of public opinion. For some firms, the decision to prioritize R&D was motivated not by a newfound interest in technological innovation but rather an opportunistic strategy to tap new forms of state aid. One chief technology officer, who framed his personal decision to participate in a Tekes-sponsored research consortium in patriotic terms,[17] secured the support of his multinational parent company by emphasizing the pecuniary benefits of the project (interview with research director, 20 October 2005, Finland). In fact, an exclusive focus on the "politics of persuasion" obscures the degree to which powerful actors, who might have suffered under new innovation policies, were generously compensated. Cohesive, encompassing networks, such as the STPC, made it much easier to strike these kinds of deals.

Placating Labor and Low-tech Industry: The Politics of Compensation

Market-oriented reform and large-scale investments in R&D enabled Finland to diversify its economy, but the benefits of reform were not evenly distributed. The 1979 Technology Committee and related bodies may have persuaded traditional industries that Finland could no longer compete by exporting low- and medium-technology products to the Soviet Union and convinced trade unions that technological innovation could increase job growth, but these actors also received significant side payments. For example, although early innovation policies devoted unprecedented attention to emerging industries such as telecommunications equipment, they also made a point of including traditional industries. A former Tekes director remarked:

> We were so heavily into process industries and wood-based production and shipbuilding and so on. When one major industrialist said that you should not sell articles smaller than the horse when you export from Finland, I said, "Why don't we make horses with some electronics or high tech inside?" (interview with former Tekes director, 1 November 2005, Finland)

The figures confirm his story. Although electronics received over a quarter of the funding that Tekes allocated to new product development during the 1980s, forestry, chemicals, mining, and metal-processing received approximately twice as much. In the first two years, Tekes launched new programs on the use of wood as a raw material, steel casting, manufacturing automation, mechanical wood-processing, functional paper, and metal working (Murto, Niemelä, and Laamanen 2006, 96–102).

These initiatives helped convert low- and medium-technology opponents into supporters. For example, veteran forestry executives credited Tekes with modernizing the industry by diffusing new technologies such as nonchlorinated bleaching (interview with former R&D director, forestry firm, 13 October 2005, Finland). A former Tekes director suggested that similar dynamics occurred in the metal processing industry, which benefited from the incorporation of university mathematics into the casting process (interview with former Tekes director, 1 November 2005, Finland).

These deals were easier to strike in a tight-knit community where key actors knew and trusted one another. For example, interpersonal ties made it easier for civil servants to identify side payments that would satisfy low- and medium-technology enterprises. The former director above continued:

> That's normally a problem in such projects. A project goes but the industrialists are not interested and there is no flow of information.... [But firms] were positive, especially in early days, because of the committee. It was more or less a steering committee, consisting of half academic and half industry representatives. In the early days, they were really active industrialists so that they had something to say. They made de facto decisions even if the decisions were officially made in Tekes's board. (interview with former Tekes director, 1 November 2005, Finland)

If tight-knit interpersonal networks enabled civil servants to identify side payments that low- and medium-technology industries actually wanted, they also reassured corporate executives that this bargain would be protected over time. Finland would focus more heavily on new high-technology industries such as biotechnology, software, and telecommunications equipment after the recession of the early 1990s, but large low- and medium-technology industries continued to receive significant support from Tekes for product- and process-based innovation (Murto, Niemelä, and Laamanen 2006).

Labor also benefited from the modernization of traditional low- and medium-technology industries and supported reform with the understanding that corporate profits would be reinvested in ways that would support future wage and job growth (interview with economists, 22 August 2005 and 26 September 2005, Finland). This commitment was more credible because by this point unions were regularly cooperating with industry within neocorporatist fora and on the corporate boards of large firms. Moreover, just like the postwar Swedish model, this bipartite agreement was reinforced by public policies that redistributed the benefits of innovation-driven growth. The same coalition governments that adopted a hard currency regime, liberalized financial markets, reduced state aid, and invested in R&D simultaneously expanded social safety nets. Authorities increased unemployment benefits and employment protections over the course of the 1980s, narrowing the gap between Finland and the Scandinavian social democracies (Kiander and Pehkonen 1999; 100 Vartiainen 1998a, 44).

Of course, authorities were hardly in a position to purchase labor's consent with expensive social policies during the recession of the early 1990s. On the contrary, it was widely accepted that Finland needed to retrench public expenditure, including popular social programs.[18] The politics of compensation changed to reflect this more austere environment. More specifically, trade unions viewed new innovation policies as an alternative to more controversial market-oriented reforms (interviews with trade union directors, 21 October 2005 and 28 October 2005, Finland). Any move to reduce unemployment benefits or increase labor-market flexibility was effectively tabled (Rehn 1996, 269).[19] In exchange, organized labor enthusiastically endorsed Finnish innovation policies through the STPC and other tripartite bodies.

Just as it is possible to overstate the power of persuasion, it is also possible to exaggerate the degree of compensation. Large, influential actors were accommodated, but small, peripheral ones were marginalized. For example, Finnish authorities did an excellent job of compensating low- and medium-technology industries as well as the employees who worked there. Other sectors, however, were not so fortunate. The Finnish software product industry, for example, was largely excluded from national innovation policies until the turn of the century. Although Tekes invested aggressively in software that was embedded in concrete, exportable, physical products, such as the GSM protocol in a Nokia phone (Ornston 2012b, 80–83), software was not viewed as a product in its own right and received limited support (interview with professor, Helsinki University of Technology, 22 November 2006, Finland).

That negative attitude would change, quite profoundly, in the twenty-first century, particularly following the success of Angry Birds (Ben-Aaron 2010), but many representatives from the software product industry did not view Finnish innovation policies as particularly relevant or useful in the mid-2000s (interviews with software executives, 31 October 2005 and 24 November 2006, Finland). In fact, they were among the only industry representatives to openly criticize Tekes at this time. One executive stated:

> I have a pretty gloomy opinion about Tekes. My feeling is that they are totally incapable people who do not understand anything about the high-tech industry itself. It's a politically driven organization, which does not give anything to the Finnish economy or society.... If you are Vaisala or Nokia or Martis, you get more interest. I think that somehow it's easier for people to understand when you can see a concrete thing. (interview with software executive, 23 November 2006, Finland)[20]

The marginalization of the software product industry during the 1980s and 1990s suggests that not everyone was included in the deals that supported Finnish innovation policies, although the largest and most important actors received generous side payments. This explains why, although specific individuals and industries may have expressed skepticism, all the major parties enthusiastically supported greater investment in technological innovation and complementary public policies. This consensus, which spanned both public and private sectors, enabled Finland to coordinate technological innovation to an unparalleled degree.

The Politics of Coordination and Systemic Innovation Policy

For scholars and practitioners, Finland exemplifies the "systemic" approach to innovation policy (Dahlman, Routti, and Ylä-Anttila 2006a; Gergils 2006). This is no accident. In a sense, Finnish innovation policy had assumed a systemic dimension as early as the 1980s. Although initial technology policies revolved around just a couple of organizations, mainly Sitra and Tekes, these bodies used dense interfirm networks to mobilize support among private-sector actors. The same connections that enabled the Finns to construct marketing associations and price-fixing cartels in the early twentieth century made it easy to construct research consortia in the late twentieth century. Personal ties and repeated cooperation among firms raised the reputational cost of intellectual theft, shirking, and other opportunistic behaviors (Ornston 2012b, 70). In 1990 Finland went one step further, becoming the first country to embrace the concept of a "national innovation system." Instead of delegating responsibility to a single organization, such as the Ministry of Trade and Industry or Tekes, policy makers reconceptualized innovation as a society-wide process, involving multiple ministries as well as educational institutes, financial intermediaries, consumers, and a wide array of other actors (Science and Technology Policy Council 1990, 64–65). To illustrate this shift, in this section I describe how Finnish universities and financial firms were integrated into the policy-making process.

Industry and academia might look like logical partners in innovation, but academics are fiercely protective of their autonomy and corporations often view researchers as naive or irrelevant. Finland was no exception in this respect. In the words of one policy maker:

> If you go twenty or twenty-five years back, it was almost a sin or not politically correct if the university would cooperate openly with business, fraternizing with the enemy. When did this change happen? Was it after the banking crisis? (interview with representative, Academy of Finland, 29 November 2006, Finland)

His colleague immediately confirmed:

> This turn to industrial R&D really boomed after that. When I was at the university, computer science students would only study for one or two years before being recruited by Nokia, because they wanted to train their own employees and didn't want them spoiled by old-fashioned university teaching. (interview with representative, Academy of Finland, 29 November 2006, Finland)

The tense arm's-length relationship between Finnish industry and universities changed rapidly in the 1990s as the Science and Technology Policy Council narrowed the distance between the Ministry of Trade and Industry and the Ministry of Education. Although the majority of public R&D is administered through Tekes under the supervision of the Ministry of Trade and Industry, Tekes requires its clients to cooperate with Finnish research institutes and universities in order to receive funding (interview with former Tekes director, 1 November 2005, Finland).

Partly a result of increasing cooperation between the Ministry of Trade and Industry and the Ministry of Education, Finland boasted OECD-leading levels of industry/university cooperation (Koski et al. 2006, 50). Firm-level representatives were quick to emphasize not only public-sector coordination but also informal interpersonal connections, which effectively reduced the gap between academia and the corporate world. After describing how their firm utilized university research, a technology officer concluded, "If you look at this Finnish system, this technology system, all the key players, companies, and universities know each other. So this kind of networking is key. It's quite easy to make these kinds of deals" (interview with director, engineering firm, 4 November 2005, Finland). These tight-knit ties distinguish Finland not only from other advanced industrialized economies but also from Sweden, where academics successfully resisted any efforts to increase funding for applied R&D (Carlsson, Elg, and Jacobsson 2010, 23).

Finland's impressive capacity to synchronize corporate and university research was reinforced by complementary investments in human capital. Finland responded to the crisis of the early 1990s by doubling university enrollment and tripling polytechnic intake (Dahlman 2006, 102). This massive commitment to education, achieved via the consensus-building mechanisms described above, is impressive in its own right. But Finland went even further in tailoring capital investments to industry needs. Because universities cap the number of seats in a specific major, they were able to manipulate enrollment to fit the strategic vision of the STPC and the needs of local industry. For example, as the banking crisis and the subsequent rise of Nokia led Finnish decision makers to stake their future on high-technology industry, authorities quickly adjusted the educational curriculum. Between 1993 and 1998, admittance to ICT-based programs increased by 126 percent (Koski et al. 2006, 62), and this figure does not include the extensive use of conversion courses and other instruments to retrain older adults (Lehtonen et al. 2001, 111).

Parallel developments occurred in financial markets, which were also subsumed under the concept of a "national innovation system" in the early 1990s.[21] The recession not only increased interest in small and medium-sized enterprises (SMEs) as a source of growth and renewal but also generated concerns about their access to capital in the middle of a financial crisis (Science and Technology Policy Council 1993, 54). Tekes was already in the process of redirecting support toward SMEs to comply with EU regulations, but the crisis encouraged policymakers to think more broadly. Sitra's venture capital activities, which the organization had quietly adopted when Tekes took over its program of R&D subsidies, represented an attractive template. Early-stage risk capital markets, woefully underdeveloped within Finland's bank-based financial regime (Hyytinen and Pajarinen 2003, 37), became a priority in the 1990s.

Inspired by Sitra, policy makers established several new public venture capital funds, including the Start Fund of Kera in 1990 and Finnish Industry Investment in 1995 (Luukkonen 2006, 6). Like the decision to promote corporate R&D, public initiatives succeeded because they could draw on robust private-sector support. Sitra not only continued to finance private-sector venture capital firms but also organized them into an industry association in 1990. Collectively, they lobbied the Ministry of Trade and Industry to reduce restrictions on institutional investors and urged Finnish pension funds to invest in this new asset class (interview with director, venture capital fund, 22 November 2006, Finland). Motivated partly by these persuasive appeals and partly by the growth of Nokia, which received widespread, universally positive coverage in the Finnish media, pension funds entered Finnish venture capital markets en masse. In the words of an industry veteran:

These pension funds monitor each other very jealously and there's a lot of group behavior.... With the success of Nokia as the catalyst or symbol, it became very easy to jump on the high-tech wagon and start investing into venture capital, to start investing into private equity, which actually occurred more or less at the same time. This is very typical of a small group. (interview with executive officer, financial firm, 12 June 2012, Finland)

Collectively, these public- and private-sector investments caused early-stage venture capital investment to surge from 0.003 percent of GDP in 1989 to 0.103 percent of GDP by 2000, leapfrogging every EU member-state for which data is available (Eurostat 2016).[22] These massive outlays were tightly linked to the R&D policies described above. Consistent with the coordinated approach to innovation policy described above, Sitra focused exclusively on technology-intensive firms. Every one of its clients received a Tekes grant to fund R&D (Hyytinen and Väänänen 2003, 342). This type of coordination was less explicit in the private sector, but favorable media coverage of Nokia ensured that venture capital investment was overwhelmingly focused on high-technology firms, and ICT-based enterprises in particular, during the late 1990s (interviews with executive officer, financial firm, 12 June 2012, and venture capitalist, 8 June 2016, Finland).

As a result, Finland did much more than increase public (and private) expenditure on R&D. Dense social networks enabled reform-oriented actors to adapt educational policy and financial markets in ways that systematically rewarded technological innovation and, with the rise of Nokia, new technology-intensive firms. This significant shift in public policy had profound consequences for Finnish society, fueling unprecedented and unparalleled movement into new ICT-based industries. As the following section relates, however, these deals increased Finland's vulnerability to disruptive economic shocks by mobilizing resources around a single firm, Nokia, and privileging technological innovation over other forms of value creation.

Too Much Innovation? The Limits of High-tech Competition in Finland

The innovation policies described above, together with the market-oriented reforms I cover in chapter 4, enabled entrepreneurial actors to thoroughly restructure Finnish society during the 1980s and 1990s. This section focuses on Nokia, which exemplifies the country's transformation from a predominantly low- and medium-technology manufacturing juggernaut into a high-technology leader. Focusing on Nokia also illustrates how the politics of overshooting is not limited to the public sector. Nokia used tight-knit networks to fuel growth, securing supportive public policies and mobilizing a massive network of Finnish subcontractors around its strategic vision. There is no question that Nokia's growth lifted Finland, paving a clear path from the banking crisis of the early 1990s. At the same time, it rendered the country dangerously dependent on a single industry and a single enterprise. Even more importantly, any efforts to diversify the economy were undermined by a narrow, near-universal obsession with technological innovation. This constricted focus would hurt Finland and Nokia alike in the 2000s.

Like Finland more generally, Nokia was an unlikely high-technology leader. Although its unique position between the two major banking blocs gave the diversified conglomerate enough leeway to experiment with new technologies such as microcomputers as early as the 1960s, Nokia lacked the capital to make a serious run in capital-intensive high-technology industries. Instead, the firm was best known for producing cable, rubber boots, and toilet paper. By the late 1970s, the company was so dependent on bilateral trade that it sent half of its exports to uncompetitive Communist markets (Steinbock 2000, 28). Although the acquisition of the state-owned telecommunications firm Televa gave the firm a foothold in telecommunications equipment in the early 1980s, the decade was defined mainly by a catastrophic foray into television manufacturing. More specifically, CEO Kari Kairamo used newly liberalized financial markets to embark on a risky M&A spree that culminated in his suicide in 1988 (Häikiö 2002). How, then, did the firm redefine itself as a global leader in mobile communications?

Financial liberalization was vital as the firm used external capital to restructure its operations and penetrate newly opened telecommunication markets during the 1990s. Nokia also relied on Finnish technology policies, the ones it had helped construct in the early 1980s. For example, Tekes cofunded the research between Nokia and the Public Technical Research Center (VTT) that led to the development of a software protocol for the GSM mobile telephone standard (interview with former executive officer, electronics firm, 17 October 2005, Finland). Finnish technology policies proved even more important in sustaining long-term research during the early 1990s, when Nokia reeled following the collapse of its television business, the Soviet Union, and the Finnish market (Ali-Yrkkö and Hermans 2004, 107).

Once the firm recovered, it could use foreign capital and internal revenue to expand its operations. Nokia, however, remained heavily dependent on Finland until the end of the millennium. In 1999, for example, Nokia retained 55 percent of production in Finland. By contrast, competitors such as Ericsson only manufactured 3 percent of their products in Sweden (Steinbock 2004, xxxiii). Nokia's commitment to retain not just its headquarters but also a significant portion of its R&D and manufacturing capacity within the confines of a nation of five million reflects the firm's unique ability to restructure Finnish public policies, and Finnish society more generally, around its strategic vision.

Nokia used its close ties to Finnish policy makers to secure a supportive environment that would have been difficult to replicate elsewhere (interview with former member, STPC, 18 October 2005, and Nokia executive, 24 November 2006, Finland). Human capital proved particularly important as firms struggled to keep pace with the expanding telecommunications industry during the 1990s (Häikiö 2002, 119). Firm representatives consistently cited the country's responsive educational system, described above, as one of the main advantages of operating in Finland (interviews with former executive officer, 17 October 2005; manager, 25 October 2005; and executive officer, 24 November 2006, Finland).

Although education was Nokia's top priority, the firm's influence extended to other fields as well. Examples of regulatory capture abound (Stigler 1971), but few firms rival Nokia in the breadth of their influence. For example, Nokia successfully lobbied for an ICT center of excellence (interview with Nokia executive, 24 November 2006, Finland), more liberal immigration policies (Bärlund and Brewis 2013, 21), and reductions in capital taxation (Pelkonen 2008, 407). Nokia even influenced seemingly unrelated domains such as data privacy, where lawmakers made it easier for firms to monitor their employees' electronic communications (Lee 2009).[23] The "Lex Nokia" proved controversial, but few publicly questioned the firm's leadership in "modernizing" the Finnish economy until the late 2000s.[24] Instead, the firm was depicted as central to the Finnish nation, likened to classic icons such as the hoe, the marsh, and a spirit of *sisu* or determination (Linden 2012, 243). The *Helsingin Sanomat* went so far as to amend its editorial policy, "negotiating" content with Nokia in a way that resembled the self-censorship of the Cold War (Linden 2012, 271). In this environment, it was hard for Nokia *not* to influence Finland. A former employee remarked:

> What bothered me the most when I was working at Nokia was that the industry associations, the federation of technology industries, and even the Finnish government would approach us and ask "What is the next thing that we need to do?" And I thought, "Why are you asking me? Shouldn't you have a plan of your own?" (interview with former employee, Nokia, 14 June 2016, Finland)

Nokia's remarkable role in Finnish society, eclipsed only by the Icelandic banks in chapter 4, enabled it to independently restructure the private sector in its image. Beginning with manufacturing and then extending into software development, Nokia assembled a sprawling network of three hundred first-tier

Finnish subcontractors and a broader ICT cluster of four thousand firms (Ali-Yrkkö and Hermans 2004, 113). In the 1990s, this networked structure distinguished Nokia from its competitors and underpinned its success in the industry (Steinbock 2000). This dense supplier network was distinctively Finnish for several reasons. Finnish innovation policies made it easier for Nokia to identify reliable subcontractors, talented employees, and promising technologies. In the words of one employee:

> [Technology policies] have been very valuable with the networking. The national programs have helped us create a network. That's the reason why I started to work with Nokia. . . . I had a lot of subcontracting projects for Nokia, I was participating in the GSM standards competition and I was [hired] by Nokia. (interview with Nokia employee, 24 November 2006, Finland)

Others emphasized informal networks. An economist argued that Finnish-speaking networks reduced transaction costs, particularly during the 1990s (interview with economist, 17 June 2016, Finland). A subcontractor confirmed: "One thing that is always an issue is [intellectual property]. In Finland, you can trust very much. We have trusted relationships. But this is not the case in France or Germany. It's even more difficult in Italy" (interview with director, high-technology firm, 10 November 2005, Finland). These high-trust relations were so important that they shaped foreign direct investment. A policy maker charged with promoting the Finnish ICT industry confessed that buyers were not interested in cutting-edge Finnish technology or know-how; instead, they sought access to Nokia's network:

> One thing you have to remember is that everybody knows everybody in this business. These guys graduated from the same faculties at the same time. A fellow student is working for Nokia and buying services from you. So it's very networked, which is great if you have the access and not so great if you don't have the access. This is what the Indian companies have in mind. By buying the personnel you get immediate access, because word of mouth is still very important here. (interview with policy maker, 23 November 2005, Finland)

In a tight-knit community, Nokia also emerged as an important role model and a resource for other firms. The sewing machine manufacturer, Elcoteq, for example, followed Nokia into mobile communications and transformed itself into Europe's largest electronics manufacturing services provider (Ali-Yrkkö 2003). By 1998 Nokia's first-tier subcontractors employed almost as many Finns (14,000) as Nokia itself (21,000) (Paija 2000, 4). When Nokia moved to internationalize its supplier network at the turn of the millennium, its subcontractors followed suit (Seppälä 2010).

Although Nokia and its subcontracting network dominated the Finnish economy at the turn of the millennium, the firm's mythic status inspired other high-technology entrepreneurs and even traditional low- and medium-technology enterprises. The late 1990s witnessed a wave of ICT start-ups, fueled by supportive innovation policies, an enthusiastic public, and an infusion of venture capital (interviews with venture capital managers, 20 November 2006 and 22 November 2006, Finland). Spinouts from Nokia included Benefon, Bothnia High Tech, Elektrobit, Jabra, Martis, and Net Hawk (interview with executive, Nokia, 24 November 2006, Finland). Even traditional manufacturing firms followed Nokia's lead as a "modernizing agent" (Linden 2012) by elevating novel product innovation to the center of their business models (interviews with executive, manufacturing firm, 25 October 2005; executive, manufacturing firm, 4 November 2005; and director, food processing firm, 29 November 2006, Finland).

Collectively, these developments transformed Finland within the span of a decade. The share of high-technology exports more than tripled from 8.8 percent in 1990 to 27.3 percent by 2000 as electronics replaced forestry as Finland's dominant export (Bitard, Hommen, and Novikova 2008, 490–92). At the height of the dot-com bubble, Finland was more specialized in ICT than any other country in the OECD (Paija 2000, 6). Nokia single-handedly accounted for much of this growth, representing half of business R&D expenditure, 20 percent of Finnish exports, and 4 percent of GDP at the peak of the dot-com bubble (Ali-Yrkkö 2010, 10). As described above, however, Nokia was embedded within a broader network of more than four thousand ICT firms and represented only half of the cluster's turnover (Paija 2000). Parallel developments in low- and medium-technology industries lifted Finnish R&D expenditure above the EU average, even without Nokia (Ali-Yrkkö 2010, 30).

By the turn of the millennium, Finland was hailed as a miracle (Kiander 2005) and a model (Castells and Himanen 2002). Per capita GDP growth was the second fastest in Western Europe in the late 1990s, trailing only Ireland (Eurostat 2016). Unlike other success stories, growth was based on knowledge generation rather than natural resources, nontradable industries, or cheap credit. In this sense, the country benefited from its tight-knit networks. At the same time, all was not well in Finland and it is important to recognize the risks associated with this highly coordinated strategy. More specifically, the same deals that transformed the country into an innovation leader increased its vulnerability to disruptive shocks in two ways.

First and most obviously, the mobilization of resources around Nokia hindered the development of other enterprises, industries, and technologies. Smaller enterprises in nonestablished industries were quick to comment on this. As noted above, many software start-ups viewed Tekes as either irrelevant or incompetent (interviews with software executives, 24 and 31 October 2005, 11 and 27 November 2006, Finland).[25] In 2005 a frustrated executive at one of Finland's most successful non-ICT start-ups concluded:

> There are a lot of government programs. There's so much support for R&D, for internationalization and other activities, but it is always about telecoms. I mean, what the hell? Why is that? It's as if telecoms companies are the only growth-oriented, high-tech firms in Finland. I was at a meeting in India and about 60 percent of the meeting was only about telecoms. But there are other companies that could probably benefit even more from connections in India. (interview with executive, engineering firm, 24 October 2005, Finland)

Although entrepreneurial start-ups in nonestablished industries argued that the public sector's focus on mobile communications (and other large industries) left them at a disadvantage, it is not clear that small and medium-sized enterprises in the telecommunications industry fared any better. Tekes-brokered networks diffused knowledge from Nokia to small and medium-sized enterprises, but they also enabled Nokia to access technologies developed by smaller firms. One venture capitalist glumly remarked:

> We won't invest in any company that supplies to Nokia [because] the company has grown into a monster.... Look at how much money we've poured into Nokia's research, how much venture money has been put into the R&D effort. They then used that without any gains for [our] companies. (interview with director, venture capital firm, 22 November 2006, Finland)

Nokia's status as a large, prestigious firm in a small society proved particularly problematic in the case of human capital, which Nokia often identified through Tekes-sponsored research partnerships (interviews with Nokia employees, 8 and 24 November 2006, Finland). Venture capitalists and executives at smaller enterprises argued that Nokia's ability to recruit the best talent made it extremely difficult to develop new high-technology enterprises (interviews with venture capitalists, 4 November 2005 and 22 November 2006, and software executives, 24 and 27 November 2006, Finland). One interviewee characterized the firm as a "black hole," while another quipped that the firm's motto (the title of this chapter) should have been changed to "Nokia: Collecting People" (interviews with venture capitalist, 8 June 2016, and software industry representative, 10 June 2016, Finland). A venture capitalist described the grim environment for start-ups thusly:

> Nokia has been all the time a big tree in the electronic industry that has been shadowing and killing almost everything. It has been a very high risk, especially in the 1990s, it was really a huge risk for the start-ups, and the main reason was that Nokia was hiring so many engineers. For example, we were investing in one design house. . . . In one year, Nokia hired more than one third of the company! I called Jorma Ollila and said you must prevent your people from hiring them, because you will kill all of the small companies. I know him very well and I could say that directly. But of course he said, "We cannot do anything about that." (interview with director, venture capital firm, 20 November 2006, Finland)

Policy makers were aware of the country's unusual reliance on a single firm, but no politician was willing to directly confront it so long as it continued to receive universally positive coverage in the Finnish media. The media periodically fretted about the country's exceptional dependence on a single firm, but any concrete criticisms of the company's management or proposals to reduce the firm's influence were effectively suppressed. In a pattern that echoes postwar practices, critics found their most pointed remarks were systematically excised by the time articles appeared in print. In one extreme case, a student magazine was sanctioned by the university chancellor when it made a passing reference to Jorma Ollila's "slender" shoulders (Linden 2012, 172–73). To identify parallel examples, we must turn to Iceland in chapter 4. The Swedish media was never as supportive of Ericsson (Linden 2012, 13). Even after Nokia struggled to adapt to the increasing popularity of clamshell phones in 2004, press coverage was muted relative to Sweden (Linden 2012, 234). Finnish papers were as likely to defend Nokia against foreign criticism as they were to report on the company's missteps (Linden 2012, 193). If this avalanche of positive press coverage was not formidable enough, private threats to relocate its headquarters discouraged any serious efforts to reduce its influence (Sajari 2009).

Second, any efforts to diversify the Finnish economy were undermined by a narrow focus on technological innovation. In theory, the early adoption of a national innovation system led policy makers to acknowledge that innovation can take many forms (Science and Technology Policy Council 1990). In practice, Finnish policy makers and firms focused almost exclusively on technological change, to the exclusion of design, marketing, user-driven innovation, organizational reform, and other forms of value creation. Echoing a sentiment expressed by many colleagues, a Tekes veteran remarked: "Tekes was established in 1983 and was very focused on technology, technology was the name.... Today, a huge amount of trouble comes from 1983 where we just looked at new technology" (interview with director, Tekes, 9 June 2016, Finland). This exceptionally narrow view of innovation made it more difficult to develop new firms and new industries and also helps explain Nokia's struggles.

Labor-market reform represents just one example of how narrowly the Finns conceptualized innovation. As noted above, Finnish trade unions supported new innovation policies with the implicit understanding that policy makers would not pursue significant labor-market reform. But the belief in technological innovation was so strong that stakeholders never considered alternative strategies such as Danish-style unemployment benefit reform or continuing education (Ornston 2012a). When asked about Danish "flexicurity," an economist remarked: "I recently [researched] what we know about the economic effects of company-provided training. I could not refer to even one Finnish study, because there are none" (interview with economist, Research Institute of the Finnish Economy, 26 October 2005, Finland). The dearth of research on this topic reflected a lack of private-sector interest. In sharp contrast to his Danish colleagues, who repeatedly emphasized the quality of their workers, an industry representative bluntly concluded:

> One thing you have to recognize to be honest is the amount of money used for active labor-market policy. In Denmark, they are using quite a lot of money for that.... And one might wonder how that could be afforded, if there is not enough growth going on. [Active labor-market policies] are mainly concerning, it is the low-productivity side (of the economy). And if you think of R&D, in Finnish economy, it represents the high-end of the economy.... From one Euro you get more through R&D. (interview with economist, Technology Industries of Finland, 19 October 2005, Finland)

The failure to implement Danish-style labor-market reforms proved problematic in several ways. First, the failure to restructure collective bargaining or social benefits contributed to macroeconomic imbalances. For example, Finland's labor costs increased more rapidly than its competitors during the 2000s (Milne 2015). Second and arguably even more importantly, the failure to conceptualize workers as an asset deprived Finnish firms of an important resource. In Denmark workers represent an important source of innovation because of their proximity to end users (Lundvall 2002). The lack of interest by Finnish firms was symptomatic of a broader neglect of marketing, managerial experience, and other assets that are integral to commercialization. One industry representative concluded, with a touch of exasperation: "Marketing [is] our biggest problem.

We are not capable of selling anything. We should hire people from Denmark, that is what I learned when I was studying.... I studied international marketing and I never marketed anything anywhere!" (interview with forestry association representative, 11 October 2005, Finland).

This narrow emphasis on technological innovation constrained Finnish firms in several ways. The commitment to aesthetically pleasing, consumer-friendly designs that underpinned Nokia's early success faded in a strongly engineer-driven driven environment (Bilton 2011). Nokia's industry-leading R&D budget enabled it to assemble a massive patent portfolio, but it proved unable to adapt to shifting consumer preferences after 2000 (Orlowski 2011). The firm's weak user interface and dearth of software applications can be directly linked to its notoriously poor relations with mobile phone users in the United States, as well as the failure to cultivate a cadre of committed application developers that helped strengthen Apple and Google's mobile platforms (Boutin 2010). These weaknesses would prove fatal to Nokia's handset business after 2007.

Finnish emphasis on technological innovation was even more problematic for new firms in emerging industries, where soft skills were more important and less developed. Just as 1970s-era policy makers blindly applied the same state-led, capital-intensive model that worked in low-technology industries such as copper and steel to telecommunications equipment and television, 1990s-era policy makers naively believed that technological innovation would generate "new Nokias" in emerging industries such as biotechnology. This turned out to be a mistake, not least because Nokia's success was never simply about technological innovation. Although it may have focused too heavily on R&D, the diversified conglomerate also had competent management, an experienced sales department, and strong international connections (Steinbock 2000).

Biotechnology start-ups possessed none of these assets. Despite this, Finland privileged R&D to a greater degree than any European country except Belgium (European Commission 2007, 63). Comparative studies describe a "surprising" lack of attention to business development (Breznitz and Tahvanainen 2010, 26). One-sided investments in R&D propelled Finland to third in the EU in per capita biotechnology patent applications to the United States Patent and Trademark Office (USPTO) by 2001, surpassing biotechnology "success stories" such as Germany and the United Kingdom (Eurostat 2016). But the Finnish biotechnology industry trailed its peers in employment and turnover, precisely because it lacked the business experience and supporting infrastructure that other countries enjoyed (Breznitz and Tahvanainen 2010). A former Tekes employer concluded:

> When biotech became very hot ... it was simply a collective illusion that what was done in the ICT sector could be repeated in other sectors

> without anyone objecting to it. So it was, how to put it, a common belief that you could simply do it and no one really looked at whether we have all the necessary competencies needed in order to make it a global success story as well. That was forgotten. It was a time when we generally believed in the power of technology and science. . . . There was ignorance and stupidity in that no one thought how different it would be in this business. (interview with former Tekes employee, 22 June 2016, Finland)

Finland's struggles in biotechnology were exacerbated by the decision to focus on pharmaceuticals, the most research-intensive form of biotechnology, at the expense of more viable but less glamorous fields such as food processing and forestry, where Finnish firms had greater experience working with enzymes (interview with policy maker, 20 November 2005, Finland). This puzzling decision makes more sense when viewed in the context of Nokia's phenomenal growth, the narrative it generated, and the country's consistent collective emphasis on technological innovation.

The first warning signs were visible during the dot-com crash of 2000, which exposed the extreme fragility of the Finnish start-up scene. Policy makers and private investors had ploughed venture capital into technological innovations with little attention to managerial expertise, commercial viability, or other characteristics.[26] As a result, the Finnish venture capital industry suffered one of the steepest declines in the OECD. Early-stage risk capital investment plummeted from 135.4 million Euro in 2000 to 40.2 million by 2004, an even steeper decline than other crisis-hit countries such as the United States and United Kingdom (Eurostat 2016). The failure to develop a cluster of independent start-ups in either biotechnology or ICT should have alarmed Finnish stakeholders, but the actual impact of the dot-com crash was muted as Nokia escaped largely unscathed. Increasing cost pressures led the company to offshore most of its manufacturing activity, devastating its subcontractors. But Finland remained an important center for R&D, design, and other executive functions. As a result, employment in high-technology industry actually grew between 2001 and 2006, albeit only slightly from 6.59 percent to 6.67 percent (Eurostat 2016). The firm's apparent health reinforced Finnish faith in Nokia and technological innovation more generally (Linden 2012). As recently as 2005, interviewees responded to open-ended questions about competitiveness with statements such as this:

> For future competitiveness, countries like Finland should increase our R&D inputs every year. [Physical] investment should also be attractive, but this is difficult because there are better investments outside of

Finland. (interview with representative, Technology Industries of Finland, 18 October 2005)

Circumstances changed, however, when Nokia's market share shrank from a seemingly unassailable 41 percent in 2006 to less than 20 percent by 2012. By 2016 the firm's handset unit, sold to Microsoft, was effectively dead. Although Finnish manufacturing subcontractors had shuttered their operations earlier in the decade, Nokia remained a giant and mass layoffs devastated the Finnish ICT industry (Moen 2011a). Nokia alone accounted for a third of the 8 percent decline in Finland's GDP in 2009 (Pajarinen and Rouvinen 2013, 3) as the share of high-technology exports plummeted from 17.3 percent in 2008 to 10.0 per cent by 2010 (Eurostat 2016). Finland retained a reputation as a well-managed country, in that it had avoided the real estate bubbles, banking crises, and fiscal problems that plagued other countries along the European periphery (partly as a result, it was among the most vocal in criticizing fiscal mismanagement in Southern Europe). The mobilization of private- and public-sector resources around Nokia, however, proved no less problematic. As Nokia's struggles continued, Finland lagged crisis-hit economies such as Ireland, Portugal, and Spain. Macroeconomic performance was the sixth-worst in the European Union as real per capita GDP fell by 8.25 percent between 2007 and 2014. Only Croatia, Cyprus, Greece, Italy, and Slovenia fared worse. Ironically, Finland found itself in danger of violating the Stability and Growth Pact by 2014 as the budget deficit exceeded the 3 percent threshold and government debt reached 59 percent of GDP (Eurostat 2016). Commenting on the quality of Finnish economic governance, an economist glumly concluded:

> With this general adrenaline rush created by Nokia and the ICT cluster, the economy seemed so strong and invincible that nobody thought of politically uneasy reforms. Now we sit in a situation where we have insufficient labor supply and a cost level that is too high. We should have done all these reforms ten to fifteen years earlier, but we have not. (interview with economist, 22 June 2016, Helsinki, Finland)

Epilogue: Adjustment after Nokia

Like its dependence on the Soviet Union in the early 1980s and the financial crisis of the early 1990s, Finland's dismal economic performance has triggered a sharp shift in public opinion. By 2010 the laudatory coverage of Nokia was replaced with a tidal wave of negative press. Nokia's statements were greeted with skepticism as former employees raced to publish scathing critiques of the company (Linden 2012, 289). Subcontractors that were once willing to violate the law to protect Nokia (Linden 2012, 282) feuded openly in the media (interview with journalist, 14 June 2012, Helsinki, Finland). Jorma Ollila's "slender" shoulders were no longer off-limits as *Iltalehti*, a mainstream outlet, published articles referring to the former CEO as a "short-tempered control freak" (Linden 2012, 173–74).

This unprecedented criticism of Nokia reflected a broader shift in Finnish economic policy, as academics, politicians, and industry representatives have begun to publicly question the primacy of technological innovation. Peter Vesterbacka, the marketing director of Rovio, one of Finland's most successful gaming firms, used his heightened profile to question the utility of Tekes funding at the beginning of the crisis (Hölttä 2011). By 2014 he was joined by three prominent economists, who argued that Finland could more effectively promote restructuring by reducing public R&D support and exposing firms to greater market competition. Finland's OECD-leading commitment to R&D, consistently articulated as an asset and a strategic priority by interviewees in 2005 and 2006, has now been reconceptualized as a weakness.

As a result, the center-right government that assumed power in 2015 launched reforms that would have been unthinkable a decade ago. For example, the government weakened the Research and Innovation Council by abolishing its secretariat, kicking out private-sector representatives, and refusing to convene the body. The government has also proposed unprecedented cuts to Tekes, more than halving its budget (Liimatainen and Teivainen 2015). Although some attribute this anti-intellectual attitude to the populist Finns Party, neither the National Coalition Party nor its private-sector allies objected to these reforms. Technology Industries of Finland, which argued forcefully for greater R&D investment in 2005, was virtually silent ten years later (interviews with director, employers' organization, 22 June 2016; researcher, Confederation of Finnish Trade Unions, 22 June 2016; and senior policy maker, 21 June 2016, Finland). Employer representatives claimed that they were working to reverse those budget cuts, but this claim was not supported by other interviewees. The following comment was more typical:

> Even [the Confederation of Finnish Employers and Technology Industries of Finland] were not very active in lobbying for Tekes. Whenever I say something critical about enterprise support that involves energy, I cannot get to my desk before some lobbyist calls me. On three separate occasions I had to go in and explain what I said. There was nothing even remotely like this with Tekes. It was an easy cut. (interview with economist, 7 June 2016)

If the crisis has clearly repudiated the narrow, technologically driven approach to growth that defined early twenty-first-century Finnish economic policy, it remains unclear what strategy Finnish stakeholders will adopt going forward. It is already possible to identify several radical changes. Industry and government have both identified labor costs as a key determinant of Finnish competitiveness. Although industry always kept an eye on worker compensation, few interviewees expressed concern about wage levels in the mid-2000s and employers signed off on very generous increases in collective bargaining. Today, Finnish stakeholders are adapting neocorporatist institutions to undercut their competitors, most notably Germany and Sweden. The 2016–17 "Competitiveness Pact," for example, freezes wages for two years (after several years of wage freezes), extends working time by twenty-four hours, and reduces employer social contributions. This tripartite agreement is flanked by steep cuts to public expenditure and follows a series of corporate tax cuts and increased allowances. As one interviewee related:

> There was this tax reduction scheme that was introduced in 2013 and that was something the industry was very heavily pushing. . . . And since then I would say that the discussion has been mainly on what is the cost level of our labor force and that has been on the top of the agenda of industry. They are not concerned, publicly, in R&D or innovation. So clearly that's number or two or three on their agenda. (interview with director, Tekes, 9 June 2016, Finland)

This new lobbying strategy reflects a more fundamental change in corporate priorities away from investment- and innovation-driven growth toward cost competiveness:

> There was a big shift that happened in 2008 . . . when the shit hit the fan in the Finnish economy. The Finnish companies suddenly shifted their focus and realized "Oh no, we need to be really cost competitive to survive." And now the companies are stuck on that point. So there are a lot of these CEOs that are proud of how their companies survived the crash and it was excellent crisis management, but they have been saving their way out of trouble. (interview with representative, Technical Research Center of Finland, 21 June 2016, Helsinki, Finland)

This strategy could transform Finland into a cost-competitive country, but it is also fraught with peril. Most obviously, fiscal austerity and corporate cutbacks could jeopardize investments in collective goods from research to education. Others worried that Finland's obsession with cost competitiveness would prevent it from addressing more pressing problems, specifically demographic change and labor-market reform (interviews with economists, 7 and 22 June 2016, Finland).

Finally, excessive cost cutting could prevent Finnish corporations from capitalizing on new business opportunities. When I conducted research on digitalization in 2016, interviewees argued:

> When all those investments for the ICT have been made, they have been made from the perspective that we need to save money. We have seen that we are implementing those tools to be able to save. . . . [Firms] have this cost-cutting perspective for productivity, and they do not see digitalization as market expansion or creating new market perspectives. That's one of the biggest problems that we are facing in Finland as an industry, we don't see digitalization as an opportunity to grow. (interview with economist, 17 June 2016, Finland)

Another interviewee confirmed, "[I see] many cool business opportunities are out there that require R&D and business innovation, but those may take five to ten years. I don't see Finnish companies taking those kinds of bets and leaps" (interview with representative, Technical Research Center of Finland, 21 June 2016, Helsinki, Finland).[27]

If large Finnish enterprises may be slow to experiment with new business models, this is not necessarily true of Finland as a whole. Small entrepreneurial firms at the margins of Finnish society have developed a very different, collective vision of the future and, in so doing, have fundamentally changed economic discourse. The remarkable rise of the Finnish gaming industry exemplifies this transformation. Rovio's breakthrough hit, *Angry Birds*, presented entrepreneurs with an attractive alternative business model as Nokia fell apart in 2009. More than two hundred firms (84 percent of the Finnish gaming industry) followed in its wake, most notably Supercell, the maker of *Hay Day*, *Clash of the Clans*, and *Boom Beach*.[28] Between 2009 and 2014, employment in the largest 110 gaming companies increased from 1,120 to 2,500.[29] Turnover increased from 87 million Euro to 1.8 billion Euro, representing 20 percent of the turnover in the Finnish ICT industry (Neogames 2014). Nokia's collapse likely contributed to the growth of the Finnish gaming industry, as the firm released talented engineers and managers, with valuable international experience, into the Finnish economy (Pajarinen and Rouvinen 2013). But the Finnish gaming industry could also use tight-knit networks to generate its own collective goods, much as Nokia and its partners did two decades earlier. Commenting on the advantages of operating in a small state, an interviewee described how Finnish gaming firms assist each other by making referrals, organizing conferences, and branding themselves. He concluded:

> In a small country, it's very easy to speak with one voice and when you are doing branding it's all about the story. It's not about inventing a story but wording the story. Wording the story is the key issue, and in

> Finland we can do that in tight networks.... I think it's one of the keys when it comes to the Finnish game industry brand as such. (interview with software industry representative, 10 June 2016, Finland)[30]

This branding campaign has proved highly effective, attracting the attention of international investors and national policy makers. Tekes has identified the gaming industry as a strategic priority, effectively immunizing it from budget cuts. More fundamentally, policy makers have prioritized entrepreneurship in unprecedented ways. Since the decline of Nokia and the rise of Rovio, Tekes has devoted an entire division to start-ups, launching an accelerator program (Vigo) and a venture capital vehicle. Between 2005 and 2012, funding for entrepreneurship more than tripled, from 40 million Euro to 130 million Euro (interview with director, Tekes, 9 June 2016, Finland). These activities are less vulnerable to budget cutting as the head of government publicly champions entrepreneurship by attending Slush, the largest start-up conference in Europe (Gehring 2015, 72).

To be clear, however, increasing interest in entrepreneurship reflects the rapid diffusion of new ideas within tight-knit social circles rather than a master strategy developed by the government or Rovio. When asked to explain the start-up boom, interviewees pointed to Finland's student body, shaken by Nokia's decline and inspired by successes such as Rovio and Supercell (interviews with venture capitalist, 8 June 2016, and adviser, Tekes, 9 June 2016, Finland). Rovio's own marketing director is alleged to have commented on this:

> The marketing guy at Rovio has been saying that during the last ten years, when he started on the marketing side, he's always asked in the university who wants to be an entrepreneur. When he started, one or two hands went up and everyone else wanted to go to Nokia or some bank. Now more than half the hands go up. So clearly a lot has happened in the thinking of people. (interview with CEO, start-up, 21 June 2016, Finland)

Finnish university students have demonstrated an independent capacity for collective action by establishing organizations such as the Aalto Entrepreneurship Society. The driving force behind the wildly successful Slush conference, the organization has also been credited with providing a stronger support network for aspiring entrepreneurs (Toivonen 2014).

Although the recent start-up scene may bear a superficial resemblance to the dot-com boom of the late 1990s, there are important differences. Whereas policy makers, venture capitalists, and entrepreneurs prioritized technological innovation in the late 1990s, industry leaders now recognize that successful entrepreneurship requires experienced investors, skilled management, effective marketing, and other inputs, and may not require much technological innovation at all. The Slush conference, the Vigo accelerator program, and the Aalto Entrepreneurship Society are all more focused on connecting aspiring entrepreneurs to a wide range of resources and human capital rather than prioritizing technological innovation per se. A venture capitalist remarked:

> If I compare to start-ups [a decade] ago, the mindset is much more commercial. People realize R&D is not the only thing that matters and it doesn't have to be perfect when you hit the market. Ten years ago they developed, developed, and developed without ever having met a customer. And then, oops, there's no demand for this. (interview with venture capitalist, 8 June 2016, Finland)

These new attitudes have penetrated the highest levels of government. An official at Tekes, increasingly involved in funding young enterprises, noted:

> I have been here [for roughly a decade] and the application process at Tekes has changed a lot. Before, we were primarily interested in the technology, how new and promising the technology was. Today, we hardly focus on the technology at all. There needs to be a solid business model and market potential. There is a lot more attention to commercialization. (interview with director, Tekes, 16 June 2016, Finland)

This more balanced approach to entrepreneurship has, by all accounts, fueled the largest and most sustainable start-up boom in postwar history (Bosworth 2012). In the words of one venture capitalist, "[A decade ago,] I saw every single start-up in Finland, either me or my team. Now I'm happy if we see one in five or one in ten. [Perhaps] we've become a little lazy, but so much is happening. The start-up scene is sizzling" (interview with venture capitalist, 8 June 2016, Finland). Quantitative analysis of Nokia's labor outflows supports his claims. The share of employees leaving for small and medium-sized enterprises has increased from 37 percent at the height of the dot-com boom to an unprecedented 61 percent (Pajarinen and Rouvinen 2013, 18).

Of course, much like episodes of radical policy reform and restructuring in the past, the "sizzling" start-up scene is not without risks. Finland has adopted a more balanced approach to entrepreneurship, but the start-up industry is still relatively small and extremely young. It is unclear whether the ambitious investments that are being made today will prove profitable a decade from now or whether the fledgling industry can survive any change in credit conditions. By themselves, start-ups are also unlikely to solve the kinds of challenges described above, including demographic change, labor-market reform, and continuing education. But the Finnish gaming industry, and the start-up scene more generally, certainly represents a radical break from the country's historic reliance on large, established firms[31] and could redefine the economy going forward.

4

FROM BANKING ON FISH TO FISHY BANKS

Liberalization in Iceland

Although the growth slowdown of the 1970s generated interest in technological innovation, the late twentieth century was also characterized by a more fundamental shift from state intervention to market competition. This neoliberal revolution was most conspicuous in English-speaking liberal market economies that had struggled to adopt and execute *dirigiste* policies in the early postwar period (Levy, Kagan, and Zysman 1997). Charismatic leaders such as Ronald Reagan and Margaret Thatcher privatized state-owned enterprises, lowered taxes, promoted free trade, deregulated financial markets, reduced social spending, and confronted organized labor. Market-oriented reform facilitated restructuring, challenging traditional manufacturing firms and creating space for new growth industries such as information technology (see chapter 3) and financial services. The Reaganite and Thatcherite revolutions inspired similar experiments across the developed world, but market-oriented reform was particularly rapid and comprehensive in Nordic Europe.

This is surprising, as there are reasons to believe that Nordic Europe should be less susceptible to market-oriented reform. As described earlier, well-organized business communities in Finland and Sweden could rely on strategic coordination rather than market competition to penetrate international markets. Meanwhile, a competent, well-trained civil service enabled policy makers to execute the statist policies of the early postwar more effectively than their Anglo-Saxon counterparts. Finally, public policies such as the welfare state were wildly popular with the electorate and defended by large, powerful labor unions. The failure of the Carl Bildt and Esko Aho administrations to dismantle social safety nets in the early 1990s suggests that Sweden and Finland should have been largely unaffected by the neoliberal revolution. As a result, many scholars writing on Nordic Europe juxtapose the region's enduring commitment to social solidarity with market-oriented reform in Anglo-Saxon and central European societies (Martin and Thelen 2007; Pontusson 2011).

By other measures, however, the Nordic countries rank among the most committed and successful neoliberals. In chapters 2 and 3 I describe how Finnish and Swedish policy makers, while defending generous social policies and repurposing traditional industrial policies to facilitate innovation, simultaneously deregulated financial markets with remarkable speed. In a matter of years, they transformed some of the most closed and heavily managed financial markets in the developed world into some of the most competitive and lightly regulated. Market-oriented reform was even more radical in Iceland, where an extreme form of neoliberalism enabled a small and isolated island, heavily dependent on natural resources, to construct a Swiss-sized financial empire in less than a decade. Unfortunately, this impressive achievement also led to one of the biggest financial crises in modern history.

Iceland's remarkable and unlikely transformation from fish exporter to financial services center is theoretically important for several reasons. First, it suggests that the pattern of adjustment in chapters 2 and 3 is not simply a function of excessive state intervention. In Iceland, cohesive and encompassing social networks not only facilitated the growth of the public sector in the early postwar period but also accelerated the rollback of the state during the 1990s. Privatization and liberalization was clearly a state-directed process, but the *absence* of state intervention was arguably more important in fueling the rapid expansion of the Icelandic financial services industry than its presence in the early 2000s.

Second, the Icelandic case highlights how private-sector actors can use cohesive, encompassing relationships to accelerate restructuring, independently from the state. In chapter 3 I demonstrate how Nokia used dense social ties to construct a sprawling supplier network. This phenomenon was not unique to Finland and its reliance on a single flagship firm. In Iceland three commercial banks exercised even greater influence, shaping everything from media coverage to human capital accumulation and the corporate strategy of nonfinancial firms. Partly because of their capacity to transform Icelandic society on their own, they lobbied against government intervention as often as they lobbied for it.

Finally, Iceland provides another opportunity to test the relationship between cohesive, encompassing networks, adaptability, and excess by examining an even more tight-knit society. Formal neocorporatist institutions may be underdeveloped in Iceland, but elites and ordinary citizens are nonetheless connected within exceptionally dense, widely distributed social networks (see appendix 1). As I relate in the beginning of this chapter, these cozy interpersonal ties facilitated the expansion of the state and contributed to an even greater dependence on resource-extractive exports than Finland (or Sweden) during the early postwar period. By extension, Iceland's economic performance was also significantly more volatile. During the 1990s, the heavily regulated, old-fashioned economy was abruptly transformed into a neoliberal pioneer and a financial services center. This coordinated shift into financial services stimulated growth, but ultimately led to the largest banking bubble in the history of the OECD.

Antecedents: The Politics of Interconnectedness and Icelandic Industrialization

Iceland's ability to construct a Swiss-sized financial empire in less than a decade may have been unprecedented, but it was not the country's first experience with radical reform and restructuring. During the early postwar period, elites and ordinary citizens across the political spectrum embraced state intervention. Although many were driven by the conviction that this was the best policy for a small, vulnerable state, this consensus also reflected the government's ability to mobilize support with generous side payments. By the late postwar period, the Icelandic economy was even more heavily planned than its Finnish (or Swedish) counterpart. The postwar regime did an excellent job of increasing seafood exports, but this left the country vulnerable to disruptive economic shocks, including dwindling fish stocks and sudden shifts in international demand.

The Power of Informal Networks

The claim that Iceland leveraged cohesive, encompassing social networks merits explanation, as Icelandic scholars often emphasize conflict and discord (Bergmann 2014; Thorhallsson 2010). This contentious image of Icelandic society is often based on the weakness of the formal neocorporatist institutions that characterize other small states (Katzenstein 1985). For example, employers and trade unions struggled to achieve a negotiated solution to the country's persistent inflation until relatively recently, prompting the government to intervene unilaterally in the labor market (Thorhallsson and Kattel 2013). The resulting distrust between the government and organized labor contributed to high levels of industrial unrest, eclipsing even those of Finland (Mjøset 1987, 417).[1] Meanwhile, Iceland never developed the system of bank-based finance that underpinned interfirm coordination in twentieth century Finland and Sweden (Bergmann 2014, 39).

By other measures, however, Iceland was an exceptionally cohesive economy. Whereas corporate Sweden was divided among fifteen families and its Finnish counterpart was governed by two commercial banks, virtually all large individually owned firms belonged to a single bloc, "the Octopus," until the 1990s. This informal but cohesive network of enterprises controlled Iceland's most important industries, including fishing and shipping (see table A.1 for data on interlocking directorates). Through the Confederation of Icelandic Employers and numerous informal ties, the Octopus was further connected to the Icelandic Independence Party, a center-right party that consistently received the highest share of the vote and frequently participated in postwar coalitions (Bergmann 2014, 31). The Independence Party, in turn, dominated a concentrated media market through its control over *Morgunblaðið*, Iceland's most prestigious daily publication.

Although sometimes characterized as a hegemonic force in postwar politics, the Independence Party never ruled alone. Like Finland (and unlike Sweden), Iceland generally relied on majority coalitions rather than minority governments. The Progressive Party, based in rural Iceland, represented a natural coalition partner for the Independence Party. The Progressive Party was in turn linked to a powerful cooperative movement, "the Squid," based in agriculture and fishing (Boyes 2010, 35). As most remaining enterprises were owned by the state, these two economic blocs effectively controlled postwar Icelandic politics through the so-called "rule of halves" (Bergmann 2014, 35).

With a divided left that received a much lower share of the vote than its Nordic counterparts (Karlsson 2000, 306) and a trade union movement that openly embraced the individual pursuit of wealth (Bergmann 2014, 31), Iceland was hardly a paragon of social solidarity. But the left spent more years inside governing coalitions than outside them. To an even greater degree than in Finland, Icelandic governments bridged class divisions, as the Progressive Party frequently cooperated with the communist Socialist Party People's Alliance and the Independence Party often partnered with the social democratic Labour Party (Karlsson 2000).[2] In fact, Iceland's most conservative party was not wedded to big business, but routinely attempted to woo working-class voters with its commitment to full employment and the encompassing slogan "class with class" (Bergmann 2014, 39).

This unusual pattern of cross-class cooperation makes more sense when one shifts attention from formal neocorporatist institutions such as collective bargaining, codetermination, and corporate governance to the informal ties that connect individuals in a community of just 330,000. Like Finland, civic associations played an important role in binding Iceland's corporate and political elite. In Iceland the Freemasons served as a bridging organization, connecting different economic sectors as well as many bureaucrats within the civil service (Baldvinsdóttir 1998, 62–63). Family ties were arguably even more significant (Grímsson 1976, 18). For example, in the 1990s virtually all managers in the financial services industry were connected either by overlapping board memberships or family ties (Baldvinsdóttir 1998, 68).

These personal friendships and kinship rendered formal, Swedish-style coordination less necessary. To cite just one example of how interconnected Icelandic society is, most of Iceland's political and business class can be traced to one of two grammar schools. Sigillum Scholae Reykjaviciensis's alumni network, which includes almost all of Iceland's former prime ministers, extends from Iceland's largest high-technology firms to its major banks (Boyes 2010, 30). A former newspaper editor remarked:

> I just went into school. . . . I was on the right. One of my closest friends became the chairman of the Communist Party in Iceland, which became the People's Alliance and the other became the chairman of the Social Democratic Party. . . . We all had very different views, but all were close friends. They all became ministers and members of parliament for many decades. One was a financial minister, one was a transport minister, and so on. We have been fighting each other, publicly and privately, but there is this very strong friendship. This in a nutshell gives you a sense of what society we are in. It depends on common ties, on friendship from school, and also on ties which have come along because of common financial and economic interests. So this is a very tightly knit society and there are such contacts all over the place. (interview with former editor, 15 March 2012, Iceland)

Of course, not everyone is so fortunate, prompting some to argue that Iceland is governed by a narrow (albeit cross-sectoral) elite (Grímsson 1976, 9; Wade 2009, 25). But Iceland is fundamentally different from larger societies such as France that are governed by a remote, ÉNA-educated caste. In a society of just several hundred thousand individuals, ordinary citizens interact with decision makers on a daily basis and have no trouble accessing elites. The Icelandic media market is exceptionally concentrated, but it is also famously open to individual citizens and virtually anyone can publish an opinion piece (Árnason 2015, 58). This extends to the policy-making process as well, explaining why the powerful Independence Party might have been so keen to advance working-class objectives such as full employment (see above). In the words of one civil servant:

> In a large, multimillion [person] state you decide to make some reforms and it's easier because you don't have to deal with the individuals. Here

even if you are talking about joining programs, it's all these individuals that are being [affected]. Here, I think it is interesting that the general public can interview the minister. I would think in a large state you would never have such a direct access to the minister. Of course [the minister] sees all sorts of people. But sometimes it strikes people, not even heads of organizations or whatever, but the general public, that you can write an email. And [the minister] will answer you. (interview with civil servant, 5 March 2012, Iceland)

These informal ties bound rather divided actors, in part because they were connected by a strong sense of national identity. Like Sweden, Iceland was characterized by a coherent administrative structure and weak feudal cleavages, while the early adoption of Lutheranism insulated the country from religious conflict and contributed to mass literacy (Karlsson 2000). Like Finland, this cohesive foundation was reinforced by a clear external threat. Governed by Norway and then Denmark from 1262 until 1944, Icelandic sovereignty is recent and precarious. This perception has been reinforced by an educational curriculum which connects Iceland's medieval golden age to independence and attributes its subsequent decline to foreign domination. The so-called "cod wars" with the United Kingdom between 1958 and 1976 (see below) sharpened this sense of vulnerability (Bergmann 2014, 23). Collectively, this resulted in an exceptionally strong sense of national solidarity, as exemplified by the fact that 99.8 percent of the country tuned in to watch Iceland's quarterfinal match with England in the Euro 2016 soccer competition.

It is important not to overstate the degree of consensus in Iceland. The fact that politics is personal generates fierce feuds and fuels an image of Iceland as a bitterly divided society (Boyes 2010). For example, Central Bank governor and former prime minister Davíð Oddsson's policy decisions during the 2000s appear to have been motivated by a personal grudge against one bank owner, Jón Ásgeir Jóhannesson (Bergmann 2014, 102–4). Oddsson's relations with the minister of commerce were so poor than the two famously refused to appear in the same room together (Bergmann 2014, 114). These intense rivalries, freely acknowledged in interviews and widely publicized in the Icelandic media, clearly compromised Iceland's response to the crisis (Bergmann 2014; Boyes 2010). They also represent a sharp contrast from Finland, where politicians and industrialists went to great lengths to portray an image of consensus, downplaying individual differences and policy disagreements (interviews with former prime minister, 6 October 2005; former executive, 31 October 2005; and trade union representative, 21 October 2005, Finland).

That said, one could argue that Iceland's brand of personalized politics reflects a fundamental agreement on most major economic issues, as exemplified by cooperation among all the large political parties. In other words, Finland had to develop robust consensus-building institutions and an ideology of social partnership to bridge fundamental cleavages in the wake of a violent civil war and respond to a pressing geopolitical threat. In Iceland, the relative absence of deep-rooted social cleavages enabled individuals to engage in personal attacks and score settling.[3]

Moreover, because personal rivalries cut across major social cleavages, so did friendships (Grímsson 1976). This supported cross-sectoral deals that mirror Sweden and Finland rather than the cases I survey in chapter 5. Naturally, these bargains are most visible within traditional economic blocs. For example, the Icelandic Independence Party was able to connect its political activities to Iceland's largest business association (the Confederation of Icelandic Employers) and most prestigious newspaper (*Morgunblaðið*). Because kinship and friendships transcended these blocs, however, personal relationships also permitted broader patterns of cooperation. For example, the heads of Iceland's main employer association and trade confederation traditionally dine together at home in an example of cross-class socialization that eclipses that of not only Sweden but even Finland (Baldvinsdóttir 1998, 4). In politics, Davíð Oddsson repeatedly cooperated with the Social Democratic Alliance during his tenure as prime minister and struck a deal with trade unions, trading market-oriented reform for social benefits (see below). This long-term agreement, between a champion of neoliberalism and organized labor, reflected a high degree of trust between the two parties that is difficult to envision in less cohesive societies.[4]

Furthermore, the fact that even the fiercest rivals operated within the same small social circles and shared fundamentally similar national values rendered them susceptible to the politics of persuasion. Again, this was most pronounced within Iceland's traditional blocs. For example, Davíð Oddsson and his allies used external speakers such as Milton Friedman; a journal, *Locomotive*; and informal dialogue to diffuse neoliberal ideas throughout the Independence Party (Bergmann 2014, 41). Oddsson was able to reach Icelandic industry through the Confederation of Icelandic Employers and, with *Morgunblaðið*, Icelandic society more generally. Even rivals proved surprisingly susceptible to these kinds of persuasive appeals. When confronted with an entrepreneurial new rival—Jón Ásgeir Jóhannesson and his Octopus-eating "Orca" group—the Octopus did not use its formidable political and economic power to defend established business models. Instead, they abandoned old routines and copied his highly financialized strategy (Boyes 2010, 50–57).

In short, tight-knit personal networks enabled reform-oriented actors to transform Icelandic society even more rapidly and comprehensively than their counterparts in Finland and Sweden. Icelandic history is full of examples of radical change, many of which have nothing to do with economics.[5] Until recently, Iceland was the most homophobic country in the Nordic region and one of the least tolerant in Western Europe (Rydström 2011, 46). Attitudes toward homosexuality changed very late in Iceland,[6] but changed quickly when they did. Activists attribute the sudden reversal to extended family ties. Many Icelanders were personally connected to the AIDS epidemic, because social circles are so tight (Rydström 2011, 49). Meanwhile, the lesbian and gay movement had an easy time cultivating contacts in the Icelandic parliament (Rydström 2011, 51–52). By the time the Althing voted to legalize gay marriage in 1996, only one parliamentarian opposed the bill (Rydström 2011, 56). Today, Iceland is arguably the most tolerant society in Nordic Europe. A quarter of the population participates in annual pride celebrations, and tolerance has become an important part of the country's national identity (Rydström 2011, 21, 163).

A similarly abrupt shift in social attitudes appears to underpin the country's recent emergence as a soccer contender. A single successful role model, Eiður Guðjohnsen, fundamentally transformed the country's sporting culture, inspiring Icelandic youth to enter soccer. He also sparked a coordinated campaign to invest in soccer infrastructure, from indoor playing facilities to a marked expansion in the number of licensed coaches (Blickenstaff 2014). Ranked 131 as recently as 2012, Iceland not only became the smallest country to qualify for a major soccer tournament but advanced to the quarterfinals of Euro 2016.

Changing attitudes toward homosexuality and soccer highlight the transformative power of cohesive and encompassing social relationships, transcending regional, class, and sectoral divisions. In this chapter I demonstrate how entrepreneurial actors could use these interpersonal ties to transform economic policy and restructure the Icelandic economy. Unfortunately, adaptability came at a price. Even the most sensible economic ideas, such as financial liberalization, could be carried to unsustainable extremes when embraced by Icelandic society writ large. Meanwhile, interpersonal ties facilitated the diffusion of very bad ideas, such as the highly leveraged business models that transformed Icelandic banking. Friendship blinded some actors to fraudulent activity, whereas others who recognized these problems faced the risk of marginalization if they spoke out. These threats, in some cases quite explicit, carried extra weight in a small society, where troublemakers could find themselves blacklisted not just from a specific sector, but society more generally.

Postwar Economic Adjustment: Banking on Fish

This exaggerated pattern of adaptability and excess was already visible in the early postwar period. As I describe in chapter 2, all Western economies responded to the Great Depression and its immediate aftermath by turning to the state, increasing social spending, nationalizing enterprises, and regulating finance. Few countries, however, not even Finland, leaned as heavily on the state as Iceland. To be clear, Icelandic policy makers were not pursuing a socialist agenda. Although Iceland developed a comprehensive modern welfare state, social expenditure, and public spending as a share of GDP more generally, remained lower than in the other Nordic countries (Karlsson 2000, 334). By virtually any other measure, however, state intervention in Iceland was unparalleled.

There was little reason to anticipate the growth of the state in the early twentieth century. Like Finland, Iceland relied on foreign capital and a consistently laissez-faire policy framework to develop its natural resources. English entrepreneurs, Norwegian businessmen, and Danish capital mechanized the Icelandic fishing fleet between 1899 and 1929 (Karlsson 2000, 289). Like Finland and Sweden, however, this liberal model changed following the Great Depression. Iceland was heavily affected by decreasing international demand for fish, particularly after the outbreak of the Spanish Civil War (Karlsson 2000, 308). Simultaneously, Icelandic nationalists were struggling to achieve independence from Denmark, a convenient scapegoat for the country's economic woes (Bergmann 2014, 33).

The initial response, including the cartelization of the fishing and agricultural industries, protectionist trade measures, and the establishment of a modern welfare state in the mid-1930s (Karlsson 2000, 311, 331), was typical of the times. But Iceland went further, moving beyond investment in lighthouses and supporting infrastructure to nationalize most of the fish-processing industry, the country's leading manufacturing activity (Jóhannesson 2013, 113). The fishing industry itself was privately owned but did not escape the long arm of the state. Viewing foreign capital as a threat to the country's prosperity and independence, policy makers imposed capital controls and regulated domestic financial markets. Unlike Sweden and Finland, policy makers went even further in nationalizing most of the Icelandic financial system. In doing so, Iceland's major political parties were able to directly control the allocation of credit to virtually every business and individual in the country. Whereas Finnish entrepreneurs may have complained about the difficulty of obtaining start-up capital before the 1990s, a study of Iceland concluded, "Apart from the black market, there was no way to get a loan to build a fence or buy a car, or to obtain foreign exchange to go abroad except by going through the party functionaries in charge of rationing" (Gylfason et al. 2010, 141).

Public control of finance, the lifeblood of a modern economy, immediately sets Iceland apart from its Nordic counterparts, but it is hardly the only example of state intervention. Credit rationing was flanked by additional regulations that shaped virtually all aspects of Icelandic life. For example, the postwar government introduced a comprehensive system of import quotas, tariffs, rationing, and export subsidies to manage economic adjustment (Jónsson 2004, 65). Customs and import duties represented a staggering 33.5 percent of tax revenue in 1965, higher than the heavily regulated Finnish economy (6.5 percent), Sweden (3.5 percent), or any other OECD country for which data is available.[7] These onerous restrictions extended beyond trade in ways that made postwar Sweden and Finland resemble a libertarian paradise. For instance, privately run radio and television channels were not legalized until 1986. Until that time, the state monopolized television, broadcasting only several hours a day and never on Thursday evenings (Jóhannesson 2013, 125). Beer was not legalized until 1989 (Boyes 2010, 32).

Iceland's evolution into a hyper-regulated society presents a puzzle in its own right. Unlike papermaking, fishing is not a particularly capital-intensive industry, and the country's founding myth celebrates independent, rugged individuals fleeing political persecution and high taxes in Norway (Loftsdóttir 2015, 7–8). Like Finland and Sweden, however, the Great Depression, which was particularly deep and long-lasting in Iceland, shattered faith in free market capitalism (Karlsson 2000, 311). In Iceland the persuasive appeal of these illiberal critiques was strengthened by the ability to scapegoat foreign capital.[8] Icelandic political activists, journalists, literary figures, academics, and, eventually, even history textbooks consistently linked the country's poverty to its domination by foreign powers (Bergmann 2014, 23). This widely accepted mythology made it easy to justify the nationalization of foreign-dominated industries such as banking and fish processing, as well as the regulation of external trade and even mass media.

The ideological consensus described above was reinforced by the politics of compensation. This was clearest in the case of the Octopus, which dominated the shipping industry, controlled the lucrative trade with the American military base at Keflavik, and thus benefited heavily from an illiberal trade regime (Bergmann 2014, 31). But the "rule of halves" also reflected the interests of the Progressive Party, sheltering their agricultural interests from foreign competition and channeling cheap credit to favored firms through their own financial institutions (Bergmann 2014, 35). These policies were part of a broader effort to discourage depopulation of the Icelandic hinterland, a side payment to rural regions that might be adversely affected by industrialization (Gylfason et al. 2010, 140).

As noted above, organized labor was weaker in Iceland than Finland or Sweden, but the working class was hardly excluded from these arrangements.

For example, left-wing political parties supported measures to prevent rural depopulation with the understanding that limiting migration would improve the living standards of urban workers. More importantly, workers enjoyed a progressively more generous system of social benefits, including the introduction of modern social security, educational, and health care policies in the late 1940s and a generous system of occupational pensions, introduced to restrain wage demands in 1969 (Ólafsson 2011, 8, 13). Although Iceland may have lagged behind the other Nordic countries in social expenditure as a share of GDP, its underperformance partly reflects the broad political commitment to full employment (Bergmann 2014, 39). With an unemployment rate of less than 3 percent until the 1990s, inequality was comparable to other Nordic societies (Gylfason et al. 2010, 139).

This strong consensus, achieved through persuasive appeals and generous side payments, enabled Iceland to adopt a highly coordinated economic strategy. In 1944 the Innovation Regime, an Independence-Labor Party coalition responsible for the modernization of the welfare state, launched a massive investment campaign focused on the fishing and fish-processing industries. Subsidies to the fishing industry alone consumed over 40 percent of public expenditure until the 1960s (Gylfason et al. 2010, 142). Although export subsidies were eventually reduced when Iceland gradually dismantled trade barriers, the fishing industry continued to benefit from a wide range of supporting policies, from subsidized credit to deep devaluations.[9] Even foreign policy was subordinated to economic policy as Iceland confronted Britain in a bid to unilaterally extend its fishing grounds to four miles in 1950, twelve in 1958, fifty in 1972, and two hundred in 1975 (Karlsson 2000, 342–47).

As a result, Iceland was even more dependent on a single natural resource than Finland. In 1980 fish represented over 70 percent of Icelandic exports and approximately 15 percent of GDP (Agnarsson and Arnason 2007, 240). To put this in perspective, forest related industries (including chemicals, machinery, and automation) represented only 42.4 percent of exports and 6.6 percent of GDP in Finland (Paija and Palmberg 2006, 64). A veteran policy maker shared his impression of the Icelandic economy in the 1970s:

> I [sat on a committee] and we were questioning how we can use fisheries as a market basis to develop industries that relate to fisheries, manufacturing industries. They didn't exist, except for a few people in the steel industry who could make services to the fishing industry. And that was based entirely on imported machinery, a lot of it from Germany. (interview with former official, Ministry of the Economy, 24 May 2016, Iceland)

This was partly a consequence of geography, but it also reflected a coordinated, near-universal campaign by public- and private-sector actors to boost fishing exports. An Icelandic historian summarizes the postwar Icelandic political economy thusly:

> With a few notable exceptions, governments followed similar economic policies from [1947] on and until the 1990s. Knowing the track record but not the composition of the coalitions, an outside observer would find it next to impossible to guess which party was in power at any given moment. At the obvious risk of oversimplifying, it could be said that the Icelandic economy relied, for better or worse, on fishing and the sale of fish. (Jóhannesson 2013, 113)

Massive investment in the fishing industry was successful in the sense that it increased growth. At the beginning of the twentieth century, Iceland was even poorer than Finland. In 1904, the year it acquired home rule and electricity, Iceland was half as prosperous as Denmark. By 1980 Iceland had converged with its colonial master (Gylfason 2015, 311). The problem, of course, was that growth was heavily based on a single activity, the exploitation of its fishing stocks. As a result, Iceland was highly sensitive to volatile fish prices. Unlike other advanced, industrialized countries, 5 percent contractions were not unusual in postwar Iceland. Per capita GDP plummeted by 14.7 percent in the late 1940s and 9.5 percent in the late 1960s (Ólafsson 2011, 9).

With a few exceptions, such as the construction of a single aluminum smelter in 1969, Iceland generally responded to these disruptive economic shocks by doubling down on the fishing industry. The specific instruments varied, but the objective remained the same. When a massive public investment campaign (centered on the fishing industry) created a balance of payments crisis in the early postwar period, policy makers responded by using subsidies to increase fish exports (Gylfason et al. 2010, 142). When Iceland liberalized its trade regime in the 1960s, massive devaluations became the preferred instrument for restoring competitiveness in the fishing industry (Ólafsson 2011, 10–11). Iceland was even more dependent on the devaluation cycle than Finland. Since 1939 the Icelandic crown has lost 95.95 percent of its value against the Danish crown (Gylfason 2015, 318). Meanwhile, subsidized credit enabled firms to modernize their fishing fleet with stern trawlers in the 1970s (Jóhannesson 2013, 117), and Icelandic diplomats successfully expanded the country's territorial waters as noted above.

By the early 1980s, however, it was clear that this widely accepted developmental strategy was no longer sustainable (interview with former policy maker, Ministry of the Economy, 24 May 2016, Iceland). Unlike the large but temporary decline in commodity prices that had triggered previous recessions, Iceland now confronted a potentially catastrophic, broad-based collapse of its fishing stocks. Meanwhile, the devaluation cycle contributed to rampant inflation, peaking at 85 percent in 1983. Policy makers responded with several major reforms, beginning with the adoption of an individual fishing quota system in 1983. Confronted with a clear crisis, this politically difficult approach to resource management enjoyed the support of all the major stakeholders within the Icelandic fishing industry and passed the legislature with little debate. Although the system of individual transferrable quotas (ITQ) that followed in the 1990s proved more controversial, few questioned the initial adoption of individual quotas, and the system's ability to improve the efficiency and sustainability of the Icelandic fishing industry is widely accepted (Eythórsson 2000).

Economic Adjustment after the Quotas: A Short History of Innovation in Iceland

The adoption of a progressively more stringent quota system in response to repeated recessions during the 1980s marks a more fundamental shift in Icelandic economic policy, as growth could no longer be based on the more extensive exploitation of the country's fishing stocks. It was evident that Iceland would have to rely on other industries to fuel growth, and this would require a fundamentally new set of economic policies. Like Finland and Sweden, Icelandic policy makers and firms turned to technological innovation at this time. Until the early 1980s, Icelandic enterprises viewed R&D as a waste of money and opposed any systematic efforts to develop Icelandic innovation policy. A veteran policy maker recalled:

> I remember talking to people in the fisheries in the 1970s, that industries might be developed to serve their interests, and they said, "We don't have the time to play with industry which cannot do anything. It's an incompetent field." And it was. They didn't know what product development was. We had to set up committees to educate them on product development. "What's innovation? How do you approach it?" I had to run [project management] courses (interview with former official, Ministry of Economy, 24 May 2016, Iceland)

Once confronted with a clear crisis, however, the tight-knit networks that stifled adjustment could be adapted to increase research expenditure. Commenting on Iceland's transformation into a more knowledge-intensive economy, the policy maker cited above continued:

> Well, it was really the short lines of communication, convincing key individuals to start investing [in innovation]. We got this [public] money in 1985 to finance projects and we decided to use it in three

major sectors, IT, in biotechnology, and in health. Information technology was primarily concerned with IT in the fisheries . . . so I personally went to these three conglomerates in the fishing industry that were set up for marketing. . . . They recognized that this was a new opportunity for them. (interview with former official, Ministry of Economy, 24 May 2016, Iceland)

By the 1990s, the Icelandic economy looked very different. The public sector was channeling nearly one percent of GDP to R&D, one of the most ambitious commitments in the OECD. Total expenditure on R&D more than quadrupled, from 0.67 percent in 1983 to 2.88 percent by 2001 (OECD 2016), as enterprises not only established a presence in food processing equipment (Marel) but also diversified into unrelated industries such as prosthetics (Ossur) and generic pharmaceuticals (Actavis). Perhaps the most visible symbol of this transformation, however, was DeCode Genetics, whose influence within Iceland eclipsed even Nokia in Finland.

Established in 1996 following a decade of ambitious public-sector investment in medical research, the firm planned to mobilize Iceland's homogeneous population to investigate genetic diseases. CEO Karí Stefánsson, a former classmate and close friend of prime minister Davíð Oddsson, leveraged interpersonal connections, collective myths about Iceland's unique genetic heritage, and a national obsession with genealogy to secure a variety of policy concessions. For example, the legislature voted to establish a national database in 1998 to support the company's business model. Although the database itself proved controversial and was ruled unconstitutional in 2003, over half of Iceland's adult population participated in this project. The firm was even more successful in attracting institutional and individual investors, lured by its appealing narrative and soaring stock price (Bergmann 2014, 67; Boyes 2010, 40). Inspired by its example, private and public venture capital investors catapulted Iceland from virtual irrelevance to the top of the OECD, exceeding Sweden, Finland, and even the United States at the height of the dot-com boom (OECD 2006, 85–88).[10]

Unfortunately, DeCode, and Iceland's status as a high-technology leader, rested on shaky foundations. Although it was no longer the low-technology economy of decades past, Iceland never eclipsed Finland (or Sweden) in research intensity and trailed on other measures of innovation, including R&D personnel, patenting, high-technology employment, and exports (Eurostat 2016). There are several reasons for this. First, DeCode's share value plummeted by 97 percent in the bursting of the dot-com bubble as the firm suffered a series of setbacks. Knowledge-intensive enterprises such as Marel and Ossur were unaffected by its collapse, but venture capital investment evaporated. By 2003 the industry was in such poor shape that the private equity association disbanded and the European Venture Capital Association stopped compiling statistics on the sector (OECD 2006, 85–88). In this climate, few if any policy makers, investors, or entrepreneurs championed the cause of high-technology industry.

Second, even at the height of the dot-com boom, Icelandic policy makers and business leaders sought to modernize the Icelandic economy in a different way. Whereas their Finnish and Swedish counterparts placed greater emphasis on OECD-commissioned reports about technology policy and national innovation systems, Icelandic policy makers attached greater weight to American economists, such as James Buchanan and Milton Friedman. This is not so surprising, as Iceland is geographically, politically, culturally, and economically closer to the United States than Finland or Sweden. For example, the Keflavik air base generated up to a fifth of the country's foreign exchange during the early postwar period and had a profound impact on the country's culture (Bergmann 2014; Boyes 2010). As a result, investments in research and education were overshadowed by more comprehensive, far-reaching market-oriented reforms, including privatization, liberalization, and deregulation.

These market-oriented reforms also facilitated restructuring, but did more to bolster the growth of financial services rather than high-technology industry. To a certain extent, this was even true of DeCode, Iceland's flagship high-technology firm. Even as he credited DeCode for putting Iceland's medical research community on the map, an innovation policy expert remarked: "You mention DeCode as an example of an innovative company. But DeCode never produced any product. It sold some services, maybe, but it didn't do what it was set up to do" (interview with former official, Ministry of Economy, 24 May 2016, Iceland). In fact, the firm is just as often depicted as an early example of the financialization of the Icelandic economy (Boyes 2010, 40).

These dynamics were even more pronounced after 2003 as financial services replaced medical technology as Iceland's next great industry. Lured by the promise of short-term profits in financial markets, few firms expressed interest in risky long-term research and development. In a comment that sounded strikingly similar to the 1970s, a policy maker remarked: "In 2003 or 2004, I was trying to convince the manager at one of the banks to invest in innovation and he said 'We don't have time for innovation, we're too busy developing new financial products'" (interview with former official, Ministry of Economy, 24 May 2016, Iceland). In the following section I focus specifically on the rapid liberalization and financialization of the Icelandic economy. Why were policy makers able to reform such a heavily regulated economy? And how does a small country of 330,000 with virtually no experience in international banking transform itself into a financial services center?

Iceland's Neoliberal Revolution: Explaining Radical Reform and Rapid Restructuring

In 1980 Iceland was the most statist of the three countries examined in this book and one of the most heavily regulated in Western Europe more generally. By 2000 Iceland had become a paragon of neoliberalism. Reform began with the stabilization of the Icelandic economy, where inflation had reached 85 percent by 1983. A more restrictive monetary policy reduced inflation and reliance on the devaluation cycle. This shift in macroeconomic policy was reinforced by a classic tripartite social pact among labor, business, and the state to contain real wage growth, negotiated in the shadow of dwindling cod stocks in 1990 (Ólafsson 2011, 16–17).[11] Coupled with fiscal consolidation during the 1990s, these developments brought Icelandic inflation below the OECD average for the first time since independence (OECD 2016).

Macroeconomic stabilization was accompanied by even deeper market-oriented reforms. Although liberalization can be traced back to the introduction of an ITQ-based fishing regime in 1983 or even earlier to the liberalization of trade in 1960, market-oriented reform accelerated sharply under the stewardship of prime minister Davíð Oddsson between 1991 and 2004. Accession to the European Economic Area enabled Iceland to catch up with its European peers in fields such as trade policy and product market regulation. In other areas, Iceland raced ahead of its continental counterparts. Until the 1990s, the government controlled virtually the entire banking industry, in addition to interests as varied as fish processing, fertilizer, travel, radio, and television (Boyes 2010, 37). By 2003 Iceland (2.01) still trailed the United Kingdom and the United States, but it closely resembled liberal market economies such as New Zealand (1.97) and Canada (2.03) in measures of public ownership (OECD 2014, 30).[12]

Privatized enterprises flourished under a capital-friendly tax and regulatory regime. The corporate tax rate was gradually lowered from 51 percent to 15 percent, eclipsing the United Kingdom (Sigurjónsson 2011, 28). By the turn of the century, revenue from corporate taxation was the lowest in the entire OECD at 1.3 percent of GDP. Cuts to income taxation followed between 2004 and 2007 and the property tax was abolished in 2006 (Bergmann 2014, 77). Consistent with neoliberal theory, Iceland instead generated more tax revenue from consumption taxes (16.7 percent of GDP) than any other country in the OECD (OECD 2001, 54). To develop the financial services industry, capital taxation was reduced to a flat 10 percent, again undercutting the UK (Sigurjónsson 2011, 28).

Furthermore, whereas Thatcher grappled with proliferating regulations (Vogel 1996), the retreat of the Icelandic state was complemented by a light regulatory framework. In finance, for example, Iceland assumed a more relaxed approach to prudential regulation than the United Kingdom (de Serres et al. 2006, 86), particularly as it related to capital requirements, supervision, liquidity, and diversification (Rüdiger, Arnold, and Murtin 2009, 36–37). Moreover, Iceland systematically failed to enforce these modest regulations (Gylfason 2015, 323–25). Between 1980 and 2005, Iceland increased its position on the Fraser Economic Freedom of the World Index from fifty-seventh to eleventh. Although fueled in part by Iceland's commitment to "hard money," the country stood out in its commitment to property rights and deregulation, ranking fourth in the world in both categories (Gwartney, Lawson, and Hall 2015).

Restructuring was no less dramatic as market-oriented reform created space for entrepreneurial actors to fundamentally restructure the Icelandic economy. Throughout the postwar period, Icelandic banks had played a peripheral role in the economy, channeling cheap credit to the fishing industry but restricted by state ownership, capital controls, and extensive regulation. In the mid-1990s, bank assets represented just 30 percent of GDP, trailing most of Western Europe. Financial intermediation represented just 3.6 percent of value-added, exceeding only Poland, the Czech Republic, and Hungary within the OECD. By 2007 the share of value-added had climbed to 8.8 percent, surpassing frothy banking centers such as the United Kingdom (8.3 percent) and the United States (7.9 percent). Within the OECD, only Ireland, Switzerland, and Luxembourg ranked higher. The growth in bank assets was even more impressive, rivaling Switzerland and exceeding the United Kingdom by a factor of two at over 800 percent of GDP (Wade 2009, 15).

The growth of the Icelandic banking industry was unprecedented. Unlike the United States, the United Kingdom, Luxembourg, and Switzerland, which accumulated financial and human capital over a period of decades, if not centuries, Iceland had transformed itself from a financial backwater to a global player in thirteen years.[13] Of course, the unprecedented pace of economic restructuring in Iceland also rendered it exceptionally vulnerable to disruptive economic shocks. By 2008 Iceland's three leading banks had collapsed and the country faced the deepest financial crisis in the developed world. Although relative measures of the country's rise and fall are skewed by its diminutive GDP, absolute metrics are no less remarkable. Individually, the bankruptcies of Glitnir, Landsbanki, and Kaupthing were the eleventh largest in the world and collectively they were exceeded only Lehman Brothers and Washington Mutual in the United States (Bergmann 2014, 125). Landsbanki's owner Björgólfur Guðmundsson had the dubious distinction of setting the record for the largest personal bankruptcy in world history (Gylfason 2015, 321). This was an impressive achievement for a country with just 330,000 citizens and a GDP comparable to Papua New Guinea.

Before describing Iceland's remarkable fall from grace, however, we need to explain the country's unlikely emergence as a financial services center. Like

Swedish industrialization and Finland's transformation into an ICT leader, the financialization of the Iceland economy was based in part on radical reform. In this section I describe how policy makers used the politics of persuasion, compensation, and coordination to pursue an ambitious and comprehensive program of liberalization. In contrast to Sweden and Finland, however, this new vision was based not on interventionist industrial or innovation policies but rather on public-sector retrenchment. This extreme, neoliberal vision restructured Icelandic society by creating space for private-sector actors to convince their colleagues, transform traditional business practices, neutralize opponents, and work collaboratively to assemble a massive financial empire.

Recreating Iceland's Golden Age: The Politics of Persuasion

Iceland's transformation into a financial services center began in the 1970s, when young reform-oriented actors at the margins of Icelandic society experimented with new neoliberal ideas. In 1972 future prime minister Davíð Oddsson worked with other young Independence Party members Geir Haarde, Thorsteinn Pálsson, Hannes Hólmsteinn Gissurarson, Brynjólfur Bjarnason, and Kjartan Gunnarsson to establish *Locomotive*, a magazine devoted to libertarianism (Bergmann 2014, 41). Like the heterodox Swedish economists of the 1920s and innovative policy makers at Sitra in the 1970s, their influence proved limited and their magazine was discontinued after three years. Commenting on Hannes Hólmsteinn Gissurarson, a colleague remarked, "For a long time he was considered a strange outcast, because these ideas that he was talking about sounded like they do in the other Nordic countries, pretty far-fetched, pretty extremist" (interview with professor, 14 March 2012, Iceland). Collapsing fishing stocks and the clear failure of traditional economic policies in the 1980s, however, created an opportunity for hitherto marginal actors such as Gissurarson and Oddsson to influence mainstream Icelandic politics and society.

When Davíð Oddsson was elected mayor of Reykjavik in 1982 and Thorsteinn Pálsson assumed control of the Independence Party in 1983, they used their positions to advance market-oriented reforms such as the adoption of a hard currency regime, an individual quota system, and the elimination of Iceland's most onerous regulations. These initial reforms were modest, as the Independence Party was still divided between libertarians and more conservative actors who benefited from postwar regulations (interview with journalist, 6 March 2012, Iceland). As a result, young libertarians launched a coordinated campaign to influence Icelandic public opinion, bypassing party elites. The recently established Libertarian Association published a new magazine, translated the works of neoliberal economists James Buchanan, Milton Friedman, and Friedrich Hayek, and invited them to visit Iceland during the 1980s (interview with professor, 14 March 2012, Iceland).

Marketed as Nobel Prize winners to increase their credibility, these visitors had a profound effect on Icelandic society. Ironically, state regulation of the media ensured that a large number of Icelanders tuned in to watch skilled orators such as Milton Friedman, debating in his native tongue, outmaneuver the left-leaning Icelandic academics pitted against him (interview with professor, 14 March 2012, Iceland). Asked to comment on the period, a journalist associated with the Independence Party remarked, "The left wingers brought their experts, but there were always fewer of them and they were less convincing" (interview with journalist, 6 March 2012, Iceland). Meanwhile, Oddsson's and Pálsson's rising influence within the Independence Party enabled them to secure control over Iceland's most prestigious publication. In the words of one observer:

> They had the big media power behind them, *Morgunblaðið*, which has traditionally been the political press of the Independence Party.... So yeah, they managed to take over the national debate. In a way, what you are left with is that it's fairly easy to take over a society like this. That's what it is. (interview with professor, 14 March 2012, Iceland)

By the time Oddsson assumed the helm of the Independence Party in 1991, there was surprisingly little opposition to more ambitious, market-oriented reforms such as trade liberalization, financial deregulation, and even privatization. Organized labor, for example, supported the government by signing a neo-corporatist pact in the early 1990s and offered little resistance when market-oriented reform accelerated at the turn of the century. Whereas Finnish and Swedish trade unions opposed right-of-center governments with threats of a general strike in the early 1990s, their Icelandic counterparts behaved very differently:

> The unions just sat on the side and weren't active in anything policy-wise. I can give one example of that, like in taxation policy. There was a taxation policy which was systematically run by governments from 1995 up until 2006 which involved reducing the personal tax allowance, either letting it stay put or even cutting it nominally and also cutting child benefits and interest rebates on mortgage loans. The unions didn't do anything about this. (interview with professor, 14 March 2012, Ireland)

Oddsson was adept at using the "politics of compensation" to neutralize opposition (see below), but in many cases consensus reflected genuine convergence between left and right. A journalist described a consensus among like-minded economists within the trade union movement, employers' confederation, and government that resembled the informal fraternization that I observed in Finland (interview with journalist, 6 March 2012, Iceland). Meanwhile, Oddsson governed in coalition with the Social Democrats in the early 1990s, who supported liberalization as a strategy to internationalize and modernize Icelandic society (Bergmann 2014, 66). A trade union representative remarked:

> When we joined the EEA . . . we opened up our economy in a more extensive manner than we did before and that was totally backed up by the social partners. We needed to open our borders and encourage more competition and that actually laid a basis for a growth period in business here, having better market access for our products. So we enjoyed very good growth. We had a difficult period because of our fisheries. We knew that in 1990. We couldn't use our natural resources to bail ourselves out of bad policy choices. (interview with trade union representative, 8 March 2012, Iceland)

There were exceptions, such as the controversial ITQ system. But there was little in the way of principled opposition to the government's agenda. A left-leaning professor concluded:

> The policy currents are all neoliberal ideas, even still after the collapse. The left doesn't really have any ideology here anymore except, perhaps, a general, vague notion of protecting the welfare state, which is protecting their old achievements. The neoliberal ideology has pretty much drowned out all other policy options. (interview with professor, 14 March 2012, Iceland)

Market-oriented reform also created space for entrepreneurial private-sector actors to influence Icelandic public opinion, most notably newly privatized banks with aspirations to become "the Merrill Lynch of Iceland" (Mixa 2015, 38). Fueled by cheap credit, their aggressive international expansion represented an attractive alternative to an increasingly unstable, old-fashioned developmental model based on Iceland's fickle fishing stocks. Just as Davíð Oddsson used *Morgunblaðið* to champion the cause of neoliberalism, the banks increased their appeal by acquiring Icelandic television stations and newspapers, which dutifully reported on their corporate dealings, emphasizing their business acumen and financial health (Mixa 2015, 39). Just as Hannes Hólmsteinn Gissurarson had legitimized neoliberalism by inviting prestigious foreign economists to Iceland, the Icelandic Chamber of Commerce commissioned favorable reports by prestigious American economists such as Richard Portes and Frederic Mishkin (Árnason 2015, 56).

This media campaign succeeded because the banks were able to tap into powerful national myths that united a tight-knit society. The international expansion of Iceland's three largest banks was routinely characterized as an *útrás* or "outvasion," the term used to describe the exploits of the Vikings a millennium before. This was an explicit reference to what is widely depicted in Icelandic history textbooks as a golden age, before Norwegian and Danish colonizers impoverished the country (Loftsdóttir 2015, 7–8). Iceland's "conquest" of Nordic Europe, and Denmark in particular, resonated with the postcolonial narrative that Icelanders learned as schoolchildren (Bergmann 2014). Bank executives were perfectly aware of this and exploited these symbols to reshape public opinion. Jón Ásgeir Jóhannesson renamed his bank Glitnir and placed a statue of Leif Ericsson in his London headquarters, Björgólfur Thor Björgólfsson used Thor's hammer as his corporate logo, and Hannes Smárason attributed his success to the "Viking spirit" (Bergmann 2014, 26).

It is difficult to overstate the degree to which the Icelandic banks were able to capture the popular imagination. In addition to the consistently favorable media coverage, politicians raced to associate themselves with Iceland's financial services industry. A report commissioned by the prime minister referred to Iceland's founding myth in 2007, while Iceland's minister of trade was even more blunt, attributing the country's success to the "power, guts, and good knowledge of the Icelandic business Vikings" (Loftsdóttir 2015, 10). Government support is not surprising given that two of Iceland's banks enjoyed tight links to the Independence Party and Progressive Party (see below). But even Social Democratic politicians such as Ingibjörg Gísladóttir promoted Iceland's banks on the international stage (Bergmann 2014, 102). The banking industry's influence was so pervasive that President Ólafur Ragnar Grímsson, a left-leaning academic who had debated against Milton Friedman in 1984 and lobbied against the "whitewashing" of Iceland's history, was converted. He lionized the banks as an example of Icelandic greatness in a series of speeches. To cite just one example, in 2005 he argued:

> Unique qualities [give our] businesses a competitive edge, enabling us to win where others either failed or did not dare to enter. Our entrepreneurs have thus been able to move faster and more effectively, to be more original and more flexible, more reliable but also more daring than many others. (qtd. in Bergmann 2014, 85)

As a result of these developments, Iceland's banks not only enjoyed the widespread support of Iceland's political class and the broader public but also inspired others to emulate their success. The banks vacuumed up human capital, as workers left traditional industries for the financial services sector and students trained to work in finance (Lewis 2011). One professor remarked: "We [looked] at the banks as great places, wonderful places. I worked in one for a year and gave up and no one understood why. It was like, what's wrong with you?" (interview with professor, 7 March 2012, Iceland). Even traditional actors admired and emulated Iceland's banks. Instead of resisting the financialization of the Icelandic economy, trade unions bet heavily on the new banks through their occupational pension funds (Bergmann 2014, 71). Meanwhile, traditional industries mimicked their more successful modern counterparts:

> Some big companies started to play with the money not in their sector but within the banking sector. We saw some [fishing] companies, because they generate a lot of cash flow, they played the difference between the *króna* and the foreign currency. They were playing the currency market and ended up with huge debts because of that. (interview with journalist, 9 March 2012, Iceland)

Just like Oddsson and his neoliberal colleagues in the 1980s and 1990s, Iceland's newly privatized banks were able to use the media to transform public opinion within a remarkably short period of time. Within the span of a decade, it seemed like everyone wanted to work for an investment bank, invest in one, or start one.

"The Money Just Silenced It": The Politics of Compensation

Of course, not everyone in Iceland was a committed libertarian or investment banker. Organized labor and other left-leaning actors were not necessarily convinced that Iceland required lower corporate tax rates, higher consumption taxes, or looser financial regulations. Reform and restructuring was also based on the politics of compensation, in which entrepreneurial public- and private-sector actors used tight-knit networks to compensate organized labor, traditional businesses, and rival political parties such as the Progressives and Social Democrats. By the same token, reform-oriented agents could threaten to withhold resources, marginalizing opponents and stifling dissent. In the words of one journalist: "When the banks started to show this enormous growth, they were almost like creating money, pumping huge amounts of money. Then the criticism got dwarfed, just got run over. The money just silenced it" (interview with journalist, 9 March 2012, Iceland).

The politics of compensation helps explain one of the most puzzling aspects of Davíð Oddsson's reign: the virtual absence of union opposition to market-oriented reform. With the highest trade union density in Nordic Europe, and the OECD more generally, organized labor was a force to be reckoned with and had used its clout to secure generous wage increases and compensatory social policies in earlier decades. Commenting on the Swedish government's efforts to link social contributions to the risk of unemployment, a trade union representative boldly stated, "It's quite obvious that if this had been done here in Iceland it would have resulted in a general strike" (interview with trade union representative, 8 March 2012, Iceland). Why, then, did trade unions accept such radical market-oriented reforms?

In short, they were willing to tolerate comprehensive market-oriented reform in exchange for compensatory social policies. This bargain is not immediately obvious. The formal tripartite pacts that curbed inflation in the early 1990s were allowed to lapse, prompting some observers to argue that Iceland is not a consensual society (Thorhallsson 2010; Thorhallsson and Kattel 2013). Indeed, Davíð Oddsson, governing in coalition with the center-right Progressive Party, threatened to launch a Margaret Thatcher–style attack on organized labor unless they acquiesced to neoliberal reforms. An official at the Ministry of Finance summarized their plan as follows:

> The strategy was such that we put forward that an agenda where we will change all laws that are in favor of the trade unions in the public sector. That was about the rights and responsibilities of the employees, of the pension funds, and the right to negotiate. And we'll launch a program where we say that we'd like to address all of these issues in a new way. And then all the unions went, "No, you don't do that! We'll call a massive strike." And then we said, "Okay, which one will you pick?" (interview with director, Ministry of Finance, 15 March 2012, Iceland)

Iceland's trade unions opted to strike a deal with the government. In the words of a trade union representative:

> [The government] tried to change the constitution in 1995 and 1996 to limit freedom of association more than before. They tried to tackle the priority clauses [which underpinned trade union strength]. They tried to diminish the power of the trade unions. So there was a very strong conflict. It didn't result in a general strike but we had a discussion with the prime minister . . . and we told him you are now backing the neoliberal forces in your party and this will surely end up with a very strong conflict in the labor market. We will not accept this. . . . We actually managed to, with polite threats, change that policy, and keep their hands off the labor market. (interview with trade union representative, 8 March 2012, Iceland)

The price for preempting labor market reform and defending the welfare state was financial deregulation and comprehensive market-oriented reform. From the perspective of organized labor, this was a small price to pay to avoid open conflict with the government. The representative continued: "It is one thing is to sell a bank, and banks should be privately owned anyway. We weren't very bothered by that. . . . [But the Independence Party] never tried to liberalize the health care system. They never tried to liberalize the welfare system" (interview with trade union representative, 8 March 2012, Iceland). In fact, while the government liquidated state-owned enterprises and the corporate tax plummeted, social expenditure actually increased during Davíð Oddsson's tenure, from 13.9 percent of GDP in 1991 to 17.4 percent by 2004 (OECD 2016).

Evocative of neocorporatist pacts in small countries such as Denmark, Finland, and Ireland (Ornston 2012b), Iceland's ability to exchange market-oriented reform for social concessions differs from the more contentious process of liberalization in more populous, polarized polities such as Germany, France, the United Kingdom, and the United States (Levy, Kagan, and Zysman 1997; Vail 2009).[14] Indeed, this bargain was as much about personal friendships as power and threats. According to one veteran:

> [Two individuals] sat down and said [the old system] leads us nowhere. And this was very informal, because they got along well and they had the same vision that the Icelandic people deserve better than living with these conditions. So as I gather, they just sat down over a cup of coffee and said, "Okay, now we have these discussions, how should we tackle this?" (interview with director, Ministry of Finance, 15 March 2012, Iceland)

An advisor close to the prime minister confirmed the importance of interpersonal relations in subsequent negotiations between the government and organized labor, commenting:

> There was good cooperation between them and Davíð Oddsson's government. I think it was also because he was pleasant and respectful to them. I remember that Davíð Oddsson said, "You should not attack the labor unions when they are as weak as they are." (interview with former advisor, 14 March 2012, Iceland)

The informal, highly personalized process of deal-making that secured trade union acquiescence extended to other reforms and other actors. For example, the Independence Party neutralized opposition to the privatization and deregulation of the Icelandic banking industry with generous side payments to traditional industrialists and rival political parties. In a process that was carefully managed after the upstart entrepreneur Jón Ásgeir Jóhannesson seized control of one bank, Landsbanki was auctioned off to Björgólfur Guðmundsson, who duly appointed Independence Party loyalists such as Kjartan Gunnarsson (Mixa 2015, 43), while Búnadarbanki (renamed Kaupthing) was sold to Progressive Party stalwarts. The latter used their bank to modernize the Icelandic cooperative industry, transforming it into a leading supplier of frozen food to the United

Kingdom (Bergmann 2014, 71–72). Although denounced as "crony capitalism" (Gylfason 2015; Wade 2009), it is important to recognize that the meticulously orchestrated sale of Iceland's largest financial institutions to privileged insiders was also an effective strategy to reduce opposition to privatization and neoliberal reform more generally.

Indeed, an emphasis on crony capitalism, although it captures important features of the Icelandic case, ignores the broader social dynamics that reinforced the bubble. The benefits of privatizing and deregulating Iceland's financial system were hardly limited to privileged insiders. The Social Democrats did not receive a bank, but privatization had the effect of democratizing finance by weakening the traditional "rule of halves" by the Independence and Progressive parties. In fact, Social Democratic politicians, along with most major parties, received campaign contributions and personal loans from the banks (Árnason 2015, 50).[15] At the height of the bubble in 2006, Icelandic financial firms contributed eight dollars for every citizen. To put this number in perspective, consider the United States. Although sometimes depicted as agents of Wall Street, US politicians received only sixty cents (per capita) from financial firms in 2010 (Árnason 2015, 51).

Meanwhile, trade unions benefited from the financialization of the Icelandic economy in the early twenty-first century as they invested heavily in the banks through occupational pension schemes (Bergmann 2014, 71). As consumers, the working class also enjoyed access to cheap credit, which had been rationed until the 1980s, and appreciating home values. Even traditional resource-extractive industries, which were vulnerable to a stronger *króna*, could protect themselves with foreign currency–denominated loans, happily supplied by Iceland's expanding banks (Willson and Gunnlaugsdóttir 2015, 139).[16]

At this point it should be clear that even if the Icelandic government enthusiastically championed the financial services industry, the politics of compensation was not predicated on a large, Nordic-style state. Just as Iceland's three largest commercial banks could independently influence Icelandic public opinion by purchasing newspapers and television stations, they could use their growing wealth to placate opposition political parties, trade unions, traditional industries, and rural communities. For example, Landsbanki owner Björgólfur Gudmundsson invested so heavily in the Icelandic arts that observers argue he was more influential than the Minister of Culture (Bergmann 2014, 72). Not even academia was immune from their influence. The banks channeled capital to business departments across the country and played a particularly influential role in the growth of Reykjavik University, a private institution established in 1998. Not surprisingly, the rector of Reykjavik University emerged as an enthusiastic champion of the Icelandic financial services industry, while other academics published dubious reports on the unique qualities of "homo oeconomicus islandicus," financed by financial firms (Pálsson and Durrenberger 2015, xxii–xxiii).

Iceland was hardly the only country where financial enterprises bought friends. As a small, tight-knit society, it was the threat of exclusion that most distinguished Iceland from larger, more fragmented countries. This was most conspicuous in the "cultish" working environment of the banks (Árnason 2015, 49). In a very small, highly interconnected sector, questioning the banks could not only cause you to lose your job but also to be blacklisted from the financial services industry more generally. One editor was quoted as saying:

> There were here a few corporations that dominated everything and if people wanted to work with certain trades they didn't have many options. If they came into opposition with one or two men even, they would literally not have any job opportunities. I think that this is at least part of the explanation, that people were afraid of losing their very subsistence. (Árnason 2015, 53)

This claim emerged frequently in interviews. Commenting on the anxiety he felt penning an article for a minor journal, a young banker remarked: "Criticism was not well received and did not help the people criticizing. It was about legitimacy and resources and people did not gain access to the right kind of jobs if they were criticizing industry" (interview, bank director, 7 March 2012, Iceland). A professor confirmed, "Being a critic of the banking system, or even voicing some concern even going to criticism, was something that was not good for your career in Iceland" (interview, professor, 8 March 2012, Iceland).

The threat of exclusion extended to other sectors outside of finance. In addition to the fact that Icelandic media was largely owned by the banks, many financial journalists were eventually hired by the banks and were reluctant to do anything that might jeopardize that lucrative career path. A journalist remarked: "We were fighting, in 2005, 2006, and 2007, to keep the journalists who were then were picked up by the banks. They were hired by the banks. And, in many ways, you could see the guys who were supposed to be the experts, they got too cozy with the bankers" (interview with journalist, 9 March 2012, Iceland).

Even university professors, who were less likely to jump ship for an investment bank, felt the pressure to conform to the narrative described above. A professor who questioned the banks at the height of the bubble remarked: "I was told that I was totally wrong. I was told that I was jealous and mentally ill and so on. . . . One of the CEOs of the banks said that his bank would never support the faculty while I was here" (interview with professor, 12 March 2012, Iceland). Another academic described how a research institute was closed after criticizing the government's pro-cyclical fiscal policies (interview with professor, 7 March 2012, Iceland). The opposition was quickly neutralized with the politics of compensation:

> The labor union was against [the closure] and they were very vocal. But what the government said was, "We'll give you money to operate your own unit if you stop criticizing." That's how things worked at the time. You criticized and you got something. So I think that's part of the reason why the union movement didn't oppose [the government]. (interview with professor, 7 March 2012, Iceland)

The collective impact of these developments was a strong consensus supporting both market-oriented reform and the growth of the Icelandic financial services industry. There is no question that a very small group of elites were responsible for the key political and corporate decisions that fueled the bubble (Gylfason 2015; Wade 2009). But it is also important to recognize that their ability to do so was predicated on their ability to persuade and compensate wide swaths of Icelandic society. Indeed, most Icelanders benefited from the growth of the financial services industry. Those that did not were easily silenced with the threat of exclusion or marginalization precisely because they were so few in number. This near absence of opposition, whether due to the politics of persuasion or compensation, enabled Iceland to coordinate public policy and corporate strategy to an unparalleled degree.

Societal Capture: The Politics of Coordination

In twenty-first-century Iceland, the politics of coordination extended to both public- and private-sector actors. Policy makers consistently weakened regulatory standards and used the power of the state to promote the domestic and international expansion of Iceland's three banks. Meanwhile, the banks were able to leverage tight-knit networks independently of the state, mobilizing capital and skilled labor to support their growth. This highly coordinated approach to public policy and corporate strategy not only accelerated the financialization of the Icelandic economy but also led to an exceptionally narrow pattern of specialization, as the banks made very similar bets and chased identical assets.

During the 1990s, the politics of coordination helped Iceland exit statism. Although Davíð Oddsson was unable to destroy the labor movement and actually increased social expenditures, these concessions enabled him to pursue more comprehensive neoliberal reforms. Iceland continued to rank fifty-second in the "size of government," but generous side payments enabled Oddsson and other center-right leaders to improve Iceland's position in the category of regulation from twenty-seventh in 1980 to fourth by 2005. Together with improvements to the legal system, property rights, and monetary policy, Iceland ranked eleventh in the world by 2005. It never eclipsed the United Kingdom, but did rank alongside historically liberal market economies such as Australia, Ireland, and Canada (Gwartney, Lawson, and Hall 2015).

The scope and magnitude of reform was most striking in the realm of financial regulation. In addition to privatizing the state-owned banks, the government consistently worked to eliminate regulations that might have impeded their growth. Some of these regulations were consistent with the broader trend toward liberalization within Europe and the world. In deregulating domestic interest rates in 1986 and abolishing capital controls in 1995, Iceland merely converged with international norms (Mixa 2015, 37). In other respects, however, Iceland not only caught up to other developed countries but surpassed them. The government made it easier for banks to pursue highly leveraged financial strategies by deregulating the operating structure of securities companies, permitting financial firms to invest directly in real estate, lowering reserve requirements, and legalizing the use of an enterprise's own shares as collateral for a loan. In fact, Iceland consistently elected to pursue the minimum regulations mandated by the European Union (Bergmann 2014, 78). More importantly, the chronically understaffed Financial Supervisory Authority elected not to enforce the country's anemic regulations (interview with two bank directors, 7 March 2012, Iceland). To cite one common example, when the British Financial Services Authority, hardly a stickler for detail, asked its Icelandic counterparts to address several irregularities in the governance of Kaupthing, its concerns were simply ignored (Boyes 2010, 121–22). Meanwhile, the Central Bank failed to enforce a 2001 law explicitly outlawing the indexation of loans to foreign currencies (Gylfason 2015, 325).

This was not simply a question of deregulation, as the government also actively intervened to promote the growth of Iceland's banks. The president, prime minister, foreign minister, and Central Bank governor all touted the strength of the Icelandic financial system (Bergmann 2014, 99). A professor remarked:

> The government not only opened the doors for the banks but very actively promoted what they were doing and supported them. They more or less only sent out these favorable signals and they were more than willing to speak out on behalf of the banks. High-ranking government officials, sometimes the [Central Bank] governor himself, would attend the opening of bank branches, especially overseas, and they helped the bankers gain access to high level politicians abroad. So they showed their support even if it wasn't really a question of devoting a lot of government resources. (interview with professor, 8 March 2012, Iceland)

This sets Iceland apart from other financialized societies such as the United Kingdom or the United States, where banks used their "structural power" to quietly veto undesired regulation or secure favorable reforms (Culpepper and Rienke 2014). In Iceland, by contrast, we observe a highly visible and deliberate campaign by policy makers to actively promote the growth of the financial services industry.

At the same time, the banks were capable of functioning as coordinating agents in their own right. For example, they controlled every major media outlet except for public radio and television (which towed the party line). When confronted with critical reports by foreign financial analysts, the Iceland Chamber of Commerce was able to write approvingly of a "joint effort of all stakeholders to convey correct information" as bank executives, government politicians, business associations, and the Icelandic media worked together to deliver a carefully coordinated rebuttal (Árnason 2015, 56). This coordinated media campaign not only reassured foreign investors but also reinforced the domestic image of the banks as an attractive place to invest and work. This positive picture enabled the banks to mobilize capital from across the country. For example, municipalities, local savings banks, and pension funds all invested heavily in the banks (Bergmann 2014; Willson and Gunnlaugsdóttir 2015).

Bank representatives, who relied principally on foreign capital to finance their expansion, dismissed this contribution as "pennies" (interview with bank director, 7 March 2012, Iceland), but they depended on Iceland in other ways. For example, the banks relied heavily on domestic human capital to support their expansion. More specifically, the banks used their positive image and formidable resources to recruit the "best and brightest" from across the country (interview with professor, 8 March 2012, Iceland). As students flocked en masse to the banks, universities responded to increasing demand. For example, math and engineering departments adapted their curricula to offer courses on financial engineering (Lewis 2009). Like Nokia in Finland, a responsive labor market supported their rapid, if short-lived, expansion.

Iceland was not the only country where banks influenced politics and society, but this went one step beyond the low-profile lobbying of Wall Street or the City of London. The Icelandic financial crisis was not simply a story about "regulatory capture" (Stigler 1971) or even the seizure of the state, which used regulatory policy, monetary policy, and even foreign policy to promote and protect the banks. The coordinated response to the 2006 "geyser crisis," which included officials from all relevant government agencies as well as all the major media outlets, was virtually unparalleled. Every significant media outlet in Iceland was owned by a bank or the (supportive) government, while many traditional enterprises had either invested in the banks or borrowed money from them.

In other words, Iceland is perhaps best characterized as a form of *societal capture*, in which all major stakeholders in the public *and* private sector were beholden to the financial services industry. Consider the 2006 Committee on the Future of Icelandic Society. Chaired by the rector of Reykjavik University (which was partly owned by the Chamber of Commerce and enjoyed close ties to the banks), the committee included representatives from two banks, the chairman of a major pension fund (which was heavily invested in the banks), the director of one of Iceland's largest accounting firms (which relied on the banks as clients), and representatives from the Association of Icelandic Artists, the rector of the Icelandic Academy of the Arts, and the director of the National Theater (all of which relied on the patronage of the banks). Not surprisingly, the committee concluded that the biggest challenge confronting Iceland was not financialization but rather excessive government intervention (Árnason 2015, 55). In a sense, the banks "purchased" coordination with their enormous wealth, and it was much easier to do so within a small, tight-knit society.

Naturally, the banks' capacity to capture Icelandic society was partly a function of its small size rather than its cohesive character. But the internal workings of the financial services industry capture a uniquely Icelandic form of cohesion that reflects much more than a small domestic market. In Iceland, banks artificially inflated the value of their assets by trading properties among their holding companies. As famously summarized by one hedge-fund manager: "You have a dog, and I have a cat. We agree that they are each worth a billion dollars. You sell me the dog for a billion, and I sell you the cat for a billion. Now we are no longer pet owners, but Icelandic banks, with a billion dollars in new assets" (Lewis 2009). Iceland's banks generated up to 25 percent of their assets or half of their core capital in this way with the tacit support of the Financial Supervisory Authority and the Central Bank, which extended credit without questioning the value of the commercial banks' collateral (Bergmann 2014, 95).

Although this pattern of trading pet assets often occurred within rather than between fiercely competitive banking blocs, rival owners worked together to inflate asset values in other ways. Because they grew up in the same tight-knit society and operated within similar social circles, they employed similar business models and copied one another closely. All three banks focused on investment banking and adopted a highly leveraged strategy. In the words of one economist: "They were clones of one another! Before the crash, I [called] the three banks to ask about their business model and they said, 'We have no business model, we grow to grow.' Inflating their assets was the only thing they could say and they all said the same thing" (interview with economist, 24 May 2016, Iceland). This marks a sharp contrast, not only with the United States or the United Kingdom, where some banks such as Goldman Sachs charted a relatively conservative course, but also with Sweden (see chapter 2). Even in Finland, where all banks participated in the credit bonanza of the 1980s, exposure varied. The highly aggressive SKOP Bank increased lending by 140 percent between 1986 and 1990, whereas the more conservative (and historically Swedish-speaking) Union Bank of Finland increased credit by only 55 percent (Vihriälä 1997, 57).

The similarities among Iceland's banks didn't end there. All three Iceland banks targeted very similar kinds of real estate, namely high-end retail operations, in the same locations, Copenhagen and London. When threatened by speculative attacks, each introduced overseas savings programs. In fact, the banks not only focused on similar asset classes but in many cases chased the *same* assets (Bergmann 2014, 82). In bidding for the same properties, rival banks were able to increase the value of their holdings. This unwitting and distinctive pattern of coordination, following directly from tight-knit social networks, helped transform Iceland into a global player in the banking industry. Unfortunately, it also contributed to the industry's abrupt collapse.

Good Governance Gone Bad: The Collapse of the Geyser Economy

Collectively, the politics of persuasion, compensation, and coordination completely transformed Iceland. Until the 1980s the economy revolved almost exclusively around the fishing industry. Fish and fish-related products represented 70 percent of Icelandic exports as recently as 1980, and postwar governments used everything from the banking system to foreign policy to maximize the exploitation of this natural resource. By 2006, however, the fishing industry accounted for only 50 percent of the country's exports (OECD 2016). Growth was based not on fishing, or even manufactured exports, but knowledge-intensive services.

Banking, in particular, had supplanted fishing as Iceland's flagship industry. Between 2003 and 2007 alone, employment in the financial services sector increased from 4.0 percent to 4.9 percent, leapfrogging fish-related industries, whose share of employment declined from 6.8 percent to 4.1 percent. By this point, financial services represented 8.8 percent of GDP, more than the historically dominant fishing industry and comparable to financial powerhouses such as the United Kingdom and the United States (Halldórsson and Zoega 2010, 16–17). By other metrics, Iceland's growth was even more remarkable. The banking sector's balance sheet exceeded 800 percent of GDP by 2007, far higher than the United States or the United Kingdom and eclipsed only by Switzerland and Luxembourg. Unlike these countries, which had taken decades, if not centuries, to accumulate capital and expertise, bank loans and other assets had represented just 100 percent of Icelandic GDP as recently as 2000 (Wade 2009, 15).

Unfortunately, the same characteristics that enabled Iceland to redefine itself as a high-end services center in less than a decade heightened its vulnerability to disruptive economic shocks. In expanding their balance sheets to almost nine times Iceland's GDP, its three largest commercial banks were not only too big to fail but too large to rescue. Moreover, their relentless expansion had left them highly leveraged. The loan to deposit ratio of Icelandic banks was more than twice as high as comparable institutions such as HSBC (Mixa 2015, 212). This risky profile was compounded by poor lending choices, often to the bank owners themselves or their holding companies, as well as their weak capital base (Bergmann 2014; Gylfason 2015).

In contrast to other financial powerhouses, there was also little variation among Iceland's largest financial institutions. All three commercial banks had expanded aggressively, with little effort to diversify either geographically or sectorally (Mixa and Sigurjónsson 2011, 210). These formidable risks were compounded by the fact that this highly leveraged growth strategy was not limited to the financial services industry. Traditional industries, encouraged by the commercial banks, had adopted more speculative strategies. Seventy percent of Icelandic businesses relied on foreign currency loans (a higher proportion than either 1980s Finland or Sweden), while fishing firms derived an increasing share of their profits from investment rather than fishing (Bergmann 2014, 125). Many had exited the fishing industry altogether. In the words of one former policy maker:

> There was a complete takeover by new types of entrepreneurs, new types of managers and investment companies. The privatized banks started offering loans. I know of several sectors, several individuals who sold their companies because they got such high offers that they knew they could not themselves make that kind of money profitably in their own company. As a result, they just sold, "We'll take the money and start investing in the financial sector." (interview with former official, Ministry of Economy, 24 May 2016, Iceland)

Consumers followed suit, using cheap credit and foreign currency loans to invest in equities or real estate. The Icelandic stock exchange increased ninefold between 2001 and 2007, beating out not only every country in Western Europe and North America but also developing countries such as Brazil, China, and India (Ólafsson 2011, 28–29). Although housing price appreciation started later in Iceland, it accelerated sharply after 2004, outstripping developments in Western Europe's most overheated economies and the United States (IMF 2015a, 42). By 2006 investment in real estate had reached 20 percent of GDP, higher than

Spain and twice as high as the United States (Montiel 2014, 259). By virtually any metric, the financialization of the Icelandic economy was unprecedented and unparalleled.

As a result, Iceland differed from other countries such as the United States, where complex derivatives obscured the amount of risk in the housing market and financial system. In Iceland, the warning signs were relatively clear. In macroeconomic terms, Iceland was spending far more than it earned, running large, persistent current account deficits. As early as 2004, the IMF drew attention to macroeconomic imbalances and the rapid expansion of credit in particular. In 2005 the Royal Bank of Scotland argued that Iceland's growth was unsustainable, pointing to its 15.7 percent current account deficit, the largest in the OECD (Bergmann 2014, 89). By 2006 it was 23.2 percent, four times greater than the US trade deficit (OECD 2016). In fact, the negative attention sparked a speculative attack on the Icelandic crown in 2006 that nearly exhausted the Central Bank's one billion Euro foreign currency reserve (Bergmann 2014, 92).

Meanwhile, private-sector analysts focused on risks in Iceland's financial sector. Unlike the United States, where complicated instruments confounded all but a handful of mavericks, Iceland's financial bubble was relatively easy to diagnose. Mainstream actors such as Fitch, Merrill Lynch, and Danske Bank published a series of critical reports in February and March 2006. The latter pulled its line of credit to Iceland's banks, commenting on "a stunning expansion of debt, leverage and risk-taking that is almost without precedent anywhere in the world" (Zoega 2011, 19).

The negative sentiment was not universal. Other credit agencies gave the major commercial banks solid ratings, and not only because of an effective Icelandic media campaign. These positive ratings also reflected solid growth based on abundant natural resources, market-friendly reforms, and a healthy fiscal picture. But the coverage was sufficiently mixed to spook many investors. The Norwegian Petrol Fund was the first major actor to short the Icelandic crown and was soon followed by a group of fifty other hedge funds (Bergmann 2014, 90). As a result, the price to insure against a default by an Icelandic bank remained 30–40 percent higher than comparable financial institutions after 2006 (Bergmann 2014, 96). One would imagine this worrisome development would inspire the Icelandic government or other major stakeholders to reduce the amount of risk in their financial system.

Icelandic policy makers, however, responded by doubling down on an increasingly overextended growth strategy. For example, when the National Economic Institute expressed concerns about an overheated economy in the early 2000s, the government continued to cut taxes and launched a massive public investment campaign to triple aluminum production.[17] To address worries about house price inflation, policy makers increased the value of a house covered by the state-owned Housing Financing Fund from 65 percent to 90 percent (Bergmann 2014, 76–77). The move was criticized by international institutions such as the OECD and the IMF for fueling a real estate bubble, but never reversed (IMF 2011; OECD 2011b).

Policy makers followed an equally reckless course when it came to bank supervision. When Danske Bank and Merrill Lynch questioned the health of Iceland's three largest commercial banks, Iceland responded with a coordinated media campaign. The minister of commerce and minister of education attributed the criticism to "jealousy," while the Icelandic Chamber of Commerce hired Frederic Mishkin to write a positive assessment with University of Iceland professor Tryggvi Thór Herbertsson (Bergmann 2014, 91–92). Prime minister Geir Haarde subsequently appeared with Mishkin in New York to reassure American investors, while the Icelandic media published reassuring interviews with banking representatives (Árnason 2015, 56). This was not an isolated case, as the government would employ similar strategies in 2007 and 2008 (Árnason 2015; Bergmann 2014).

These positive pronouncements would have been perfectly understandable if the government had been working behind the scenes to put Iceland's banks on firmer footing. The Central Bank of Iceland, however, which had lowered reserve requirements in 2002 to stimulate lending, made no effort to reverse course after 2006. While the government worked with the banks to secure access to foreign deposits through overseas programs such as Icesave in the UK, it took the puzzling step of eliminating reserve requirements on these accounts. In fact, the government, despite narrowly avoiding a currency crisis in 2006, allowed its own foreign reserves to dwindle from 20 percent of short-term foreign liabilities to just 7 percent by 2007, well below international standards (Gylfason et al. 2010, 145–49). Banks interpreted the positive media coverage and looser regulatory requirements as a sign of support, and lending actually accelerated after 2006 (interview with bank director, 7 March 2012, Iceland). Why did the banks increase their leverage in the face of clear risks, and why did the government allow them to?

This apparent puzzle makes more sense when one considers how easily the investment banks could purchase support within a small society. As noted above, the government was in no mood to rein in the banks because Icelandic politicians were far more dependent on campaign contributions from the financial services industry than their American counterparts, and these donations reached all but one of Iceland's largest parties (Árnason 2015, 50–51). Although institutions such as the Financial Supervisory Authority were nominally independent, staff members who adopted a conciliatory posture received lucrative contracts at the major commercial banks (Gylfason et al. 2010, 149). This was also true of the media, which was, in any case, largely owned by the banks (Boyes 2010, 65). In fact, the banks used their wealth to compensate virtually all major stakeholders in Icelandic society, from organized labor, which benefited from swelling pension funds (Macheda 2012), to traditional industry, which relied on foreign currency loans and increasingly used Icelandic financial markets to generate revenue (Bergmann 2014, 137).

By extension, the generous use of side payments facilitated the marginalization of dissenting actors. The three commercial banks, for example, suggested that they would move abroad if the government did not maintain favorable tax and regulatory policies (Bergmann 2014, 79), while the government threatened the Icelandic labor movement if it did not acquiesce to neoliberal reforms (interview with director, Ministry of Finance, 15 March 2012, Iceland). Those few individuals who did dissent faced enormous peer pressure and suffered real consequences, ranging from a curtailment of their professional responsibilities (Mixa 2015, 42) to the loss of their job (interview with former editor, 9 March 2012, Iceland) or the dissolution of their institute (interview with professor, 7 March 2012, Iceland). As noted above, the threat of marginalization was particularly acute in a tight-knit society, where ostracism could make it difficult to secure any form of gainful employment (Árnason 2015, 53).

Perhaps most importantly, however, many Icelanders genuinely believed in the sustainability of this highly leveraged developmental model. Favorable media coverage, shared values, and personal relationships blinded many to risk of a financial crisis. In the words of one editor:

> Our friendship developed many decades later and he became one of the owners of the newspaper I worked for. So when I as an editor of a newspaper, dealing with issues about his bank, I was dealing with a company owned by a man [with whom I] became close friends ten or fifteen years ago, before he bought the bank. This affected my view of the bank and my judgment of what was going on. I believed the [bank's investments] were not a big deal. I did not realize how dangerous they were. This, I believe, is the reason why nobody stopped the banks. (interview with former editor, 15 March 2012, Iceland)

Even the bankers themselves appear to have believed in the sustainability of their business model. Although bank directors used holding companies to limit their individual liability, many entered the financial crisis carrying substantial debt, as did the politicians and journalists who supported them. For example, Landsbanki owner Björgólfur Guðmundsson filed the largest personal bankruptcy in world history (Gylfason 2015, 321).

Collectively, the politics of persuasion, compensation, and coordination left Iceland in far worse shape in 2008 than it would have been if the government or private-sector actors had taken measures to curb lending in 2003, 2006, or even 2007. By the time the crisis hit in 2008, Iceland's three largest banks were managing assets eleven times the country's gross domestic product. Because they pursued such similar strategies, all three were bankrupted within a week. Their collective bankruptcy, which would rank as the third largest in US history, sent the Icelandic economy into a tailspin. The Icelandic crown lost 80 percent of its value by the end of the year. Because 70 percent of corporate loans were indexed to foreign currencies, even firms in traditional industries such as agriculture and fishing were insolvent (Bergmann 2014, 125). From peak to trough, the stock market lost 95 percent of its value. Fiscal costs were estimated at 44 percent of GDP. By these metrics, Iceland experienced the costliest banking crisis in the history of the developed world to date, eclipsed only by a handful of emerging economies, such as Argentina and Indonesia (Laeven and Valencia 2012, 19–20).

Epilogue: Economic Adjustment after the Financial Crisis

Although Iceland's banking crisis was unparalleled, the macroeconomic impact was more muted than one might expect. Output plummeted by 10 percent and unemployment approached 10 percent, but this only represented the third-worst decline in output within the OECD and the fourth-worst decrease in employment (Bergmann 2014, 125–26). Moreover, Iceland recovered more rapidly than other crisis-hit countries such as Greece, Ireland, and Spain, returning to its pre-crisis per capita income by 2015 (Eurostat 2016).[18] To a large degree, Iceland's recovery can be attributed to external institutions. The International Monetary Fund ratified heterodox strategies, including capital controls, to grapple with the crisis. Meanwhile, Iceland's arm's-length relationship with the EU enabled it to restore competitiveness by devaluing its currency and walking away from its international obligations to British and Dutch depositors (Armingeon and Baccaro 2012).

But Iceland's decision to devalue its currency is not simply a story about the European Union. It also reflects a broader willingness to abandon its neoliberal developmental strategy. In contrast to other countries such as the United Kingdom and the United States, where the banking industry successfully obstructed reform, Iceland passed more comprehensive legislation. The imposition of capital controls marks the clearest break with liberal orthodoxy, but Iceland also overhauled its regulatory framework, imprisoned bank executives, limited bonus pay, and imposed a "financial activity tax" (Helgason 2015; OECD 2015a, 65–68; OECD 2015b, 184). The financial activity tax marked a sharp shift away from the low-tax regime described above. In the wake of the crisis, the government increased the VAT, personal income, capital gains, and corporate tax rates, as well as introducing new taxes on inheritance and wealth (Bergmann 2014, 159). Combined with aggressive spending cuts and freezes, Iceland enacted some of the most drastic austerity measures in the world, exceeded only by Greece (IMF 2015b, 65–68).

In contrast to Greece, the adoption of new regulations and austerity measures in Iceland was relatively consensual. This reflects the fact that costs of retrenchment were widely distributed (Bergmann 2014, 159) and also shows a spirit of shared sacrifice. A government official remarked:

> The strange thing is that most people are okay with this. They accept it and say let's try to get out of this as fast as fucking possible. This is the difference between our society and the Greek society. That is one of the specificities of a small community such as ours. It's not difficult to get a consensus on how to tackle the problems that you face and find a way to break out of it. I guess that's the attitude of most of us. I personally suffered a very heavy loss like everyone else. I just accepted it. (interview with director, Ministry of Industries and Innovation, 13 March 2012, Iceland)

Although Iceland did experience mass protests, most notably the "pots and pans demonstrations" from October 2008 to January 2009, dissent was directed principally against the financial services industry, and the government that was perceived to have enabled it. Bankers described how swiftly and comprehensively public opinion shifted within a tight-knit society:

> I think [my colleague] is right on the "island effect." We are feeling that it is the same now as it was then. During the buildup of the financial market and liberalization, people were not allowed to criticize it. Now we have a complete shift.... [If I said] I would like to build financial services, like Luxembourg did, not balance sheet oriented, that's too risky, but service oriented, people would be furious, "Why, how dare you say these things? We tried this and it collapsed." [Before] everything the banking sector was doing was published in the newspapers. Now we send the press release and it is very hard to get things through. It seems that we are paying for the past in that respect. So you wonder, will we always be like this, like an island, with norms being very strong with regard to what thoughts can be expressed? I don't know, but we are still there. (interview with bank director, 7 March 2012, Iceland)[19]

This is not to overstate the amount of reform or consensus in contemporary Icelandic politics. Although bankers may complain about unfair persecution or excessive regulation, others remain frustrated by the slow pace of reform (Gylfason 2015, 328). A revolutionary "crowdsourced" constitution was effectively blocked by the Independence Party in 2012 (Bergmann 2014, 178–82). Public opinion remains deeply divided over fundamental cleavages, from the taxation of fishing quotas to EU membership. At the same time, the country has clearly abandoned its campaign to transform itself into a financial services center. The Independence–Progressive Party coalition that returned to power in 2013 did not defend the old regime. Although promising to cut taxes and (gradually) relax capital controls, the government instead promoted other interests, specifically mortgage owners, rural manufacturing, and fishing.

Perhaps the most striking development since the financial crisis is the remarkable growth of the tourism industry. Foreigners had traveled to Iceland since independence, but the financial crisis marked a clear break with earlier trends. The number of foreign visitors, which increased by 61 percent between 2000 and 2010, more than doubled between 2010 and 2014, outstripping the all-powerful fishing industry in employment and revenue (Icelandic Tourist Board 2015). Of course, Iceland's booming tourism industry is driven in part by a weaker *króna*, which makes the country relatively affordable to foreigners. But tourism was roughly constant in the immediate wake of the crisis, between 2007 and 2010, and deep devaluations did not spark a similar tourist boom in earlier decades.

In fact, until the financial crisis the Icelandic tourism industry suffered from its position in a small, tight-knit society. During the early postwar period, it was starved of resources as policy makers prioritized the fishing industry. Neoliberal reforms democratized the allocation of credit in the 1990s and 2000s, but workers instead flocked to the investment banks and traditional enterprises sought to mimic them. Tourism's historic position within the Ministry of Transportation reflects its low salience. Tourism existed, but it was not viewed as an industry or even a significant source of employment. Even when incorporated into the Ministry of Industry in early 2008, only one employee was responsible for promoting the sector. In the words of former industry chairman, Kjartan Lárusson, "The view was that this was not really business and if it was a business then it was dangerous, because then it might be something that threatened the usual order of things, i.e. agriculture, fisheries, and industry" (Jóhannesson and Huijbens 2010, 428).

By discrediting the banking industry, the financial crisis created space for alternative industries and tourism in particular. Like the growth of the financial services industry, this was not necessarily a top-down process. Committed to austerity, the government could not devote significant financial resources to tourism (interview with official, Ministry of Industries and Innovation, 20 May 2016, Iceland). But it could promote the industry through other channels.

The 2010 Eyjafjallajökull eruption represented a particularly important turning point as policy makers responded to negative media coverage with a three-month marketing campaign. The award-winning "Inspired by Iceland" campaign, which would last for three years, not only demonstrated the public sector's increasing commitment to tourism but its capacity to leverage cohesive social networks. Within a week one third of the country was involved in the innovative social media campaign, and after six weeks half the population had participated. In a striking example of how quickly news spreads within a tight-knit community, 96 percent of the country was aware of the initiative after four weeks (IPA 2014).

By raising awareness about tourism, the "Inspired by Iceland" campaign mobilized resources that the public sector lacked. Icelandair, for example, launched an aggressive advertising campaign, marketing Iceland as an attractive tourist destination to North American consumers. This campaign worked, because private-sector entrepreneurs invested in complementary services and infrastructure that did not exist a decade ago (interview with official, Ministry of Industries and Innovation, 20 May 2016, Iceland). Employment in the tourism industry increased by 37.5 percent between 2010 and 2014, supported mainly by the growth of hotels, restaurants, and tour operators (Icelandic Tourist Board 2015). This growth is most visible in Reykjavik, but even peripheral communities that relied on fishing in the early postwar period and debt-financed public investment in the early 2000s have turned to tourism. In a case study of Grundarfjördur, a small town with a population of less than a thousand, Margaret Willson and Birna Gunnlaugsdóttir (2015) describe how tourism, which was marginal before the crisis, had transformed the community. The local hotel, owned by a fishing family, has seen its profits double every year since 2008. Meanwhile, locally oriented businesses such as restaurants and supermarkets have adapted their strategy to appeal to foreign visitors (146).

The growth of the Icelandic tourism industry is encouraging for several reasons. First, it highlights the enduring capacity of small, cohesive communities to respond effectively to economic crises. In this particular case, Iceland did not even require a flagship firm or heavy public investment to reinvent itself. Second, the tourist industry almost certainly represents a safer and more sustainable development strategy than investment banking. In addition to lower levels of financial leverage, the industry is significantly less concentrated. In comments that apply just as well to banking as fishing, an economist concluded:

> The difference between fishing industry and the tourism industry is that fishing is dominated by a few firms within calling distance of the leading politicians, whereas the tourism industry is diversified. Their telephone numbers are unlikely to be on the phones of the powers that

> be. . . . I have a specific example in mind, Mauritius. Mauritius used to be run by plantation owners and then wisely the authorities decided to make Mauritius a tourist paradise. That meant that the plantation owners were no longer able to dictate to the government, and that's been a healthy influence on Mauritius. (interview with economist, 24 May 2016, Iceland)

Although these developments are certainly encouraging, the evidence in this book suggests that Icelandic policy makers and industry leaders should not be too complacent. Already there are worrisome signs that Iceland might be blowing another bubble, even without an Ericsson, Nokia, or Glitnir. In 2016 the number of tourists was projected to approach 1.7 million (up from 489,000 in 2010) and the trend shows no signs of slowing down. Asked to comment on the growth of the tourism industry, the economist quoted above remarked:

> It's happened in a sudden and almost violent way. . . . Some people say that Iceland now is like 2007 on steroids. Imported cars, there was no importation of cars for two or three years after the crash. But now they are flooding in again. You're seeing 4WD on the streets like never before. Many people think overcapacity will be a huge issue in Iceland a few years down the road. (interview with economist, 24 May 2016, Iceland)

A former policy maker was even more concerned: "The 30 percent or 40 percent growth we are experiencing is not healthy. It taxes our infrastructure, the hospitals, the hotels, the police, the roads. The growth is too rapid" (interview with former policy maker, Ministry of the Economy, 24 May 2016, Iceland).

Perhaps the biggest danger is not too little investment in infrastructure but too much. If Iceland invests in infrastructure, construction, and supporting services with the expectation that it will experience 30–40 percent annual growth, it will be vulnerable to any disruptive shock. There is, of course, the ever-present danger of another volcano. The country is also heavily dependent on Icelandair, which handles 70 percent of the air traffic at Keflavik (interview with official, Ministry of Industries and Innovation, 20 May 2016, Iceland). Any serious problem at the airline would represent a systemic threat to the Icelandic economy, disrupting the flow of tourists that have fueled recent growth. In this sense, little has changed. As one economist quipped, "Tourists can be fickle. Like fish in the sea, they can vanish overnight" (interview with economist, 24 May 2016, Iceland).

5
OVERSHOOTING IN COMPARATIVE PERSPECTIVE
Contrasting Cases

In this book I argue that the same cohesive, encompassing networks that facilitate radical reform and rapid restructuring in Nordic Europe simultaneously contribute to policy overshooting, overinvestment, and devastating economic crises. Cross-national variation within Nordic Europe supports this hypothesis. Reform and restructuring was the most muted in Sweden, the largest and least cohesive of the three societies surveyed here, regardless of whether we focus on the rise of the state in the mid-twentieth century, the dot-com boom, or the financialization of the economy at the turn of the millennium. Iceland, by contrast, is the most interconnected, particularly when we take informal relationships into account. Here we observe the most radical shifts, from an extreme form of statism to market fundamentalism and from fish to financial services. Finland represents an intermediate case, characterized by greater reform, restructuring, and overshooting than Sweden, but less than Iceland.

Of course, the fact that all three societies are relatively tightly knit limits the variation in chapters 2 through 4. To address this issue, I extend the scope of the analysis in these final chapters. Doing so enables me to address several questions. How unique are the Nordic countries? Surely other countries expanded the state in the middle of the twentieth century. Other societies were also affected by the growth slowdown of the 1970s and turned to financialization and high-technology markets, with mixed results. Are the Nordic countries truly outliers in the scope and pace of reform, restructuring, and overshooting? Does this reflect dense social ties or is another variable at play? Finally, do the benefits of cohesive and encompassing networks outweigh the costs? Should other countries attempt to emulate the Nordic model or should they respond to the challenges of globalization and rapid technological change by charting their own course?

I begin by analyzing four small European states: Austria, Greece, Portugal, and Switzerland. Small size may be a necessary condition for the broad and dense cross-sectoral networks that characterize Finland, Iceland, and Sweden, but these four cases demonstrate that this is not a sufficient one. Like their Nordic counterparts, Austria and Switzerland are small, open, coordinated market economies. But I argue that these countries are best understood as "segmented societies," with sharper religious, regional, linguistic, and industrial cleavages. Effective conflict-resolving institutions enabled these countries to invest in basic goods such as macroeconomic stability and industrial peace, but they militated against radical reform and delayed the pace of restructuring. As a result, these countries are characterized by gradual institutional change, incremental upmarket movement, and remarkable economic stability. These two Central European cases not only serve to isolate the impact of cohesive, encompassing networks but also demonstrate that countries can thrive in a globalized and digitalized economy without rapid, Nordic-style adaptation.

Because Austria and Switzerland industrialized earlier than their Nordic counterparts, I then turn to two late developers, Greece and Portugal. Although similar in size to Sweden and ethnically homogeneous, these fragmented and polarized polities present even starker contrasts with our Nordic cases. Conflict has hindered reform and restructuring, and the inability to invest in even basic collective goods has resulted in repeated economic crises. The Greek and Portuguese cases thus represent an important counterpoint, not only to the Nordic countries but also Austria and Switzerland. Whereas Austrian and Swiss cases highlight the opportunity cost of deep, Nordic-style solidarity, Greece and Portugal illustrate the price of excessive conflict and the benefits of fostering cohesion in deeply divided societies.

Incremental Upmarket Movement in Central Europe: Austria and Switzerland

The small states of Central Europe appear very similar to those of Scandinavia to the extent that Peter Katzenstein (1985) considered them collectively in his second book on small states. Austria (8.5 million) and Switzerland (8 million) approximate Sweden (10 million) or even Finland (5.5 million) in population.[1] Heavily dependent on international markets, they rival Sweden and Iceland in their reliance on foreign trade (OECD 2016).[2] Like the Nordics, elites know one another and have a tradition of cooperating within official, neocorporatist institutions as well as informal channels (Katzenstein 1984, 124). Measured in terms of strike activity, one could argue that these societies are even more consensual than Finland or Iceland (Merrien and Becker 2005, 117; Rehn 1996, 128).

Although highly organized, Austria and Switzerland are better understood as "segmented" societies, characterized by sharper religious, linguistic, regional, and sectoral cleavages. Like Germany, bicameral federal political systems reflect deep-seated regional differences. This is clearest in multilingual Switzerland, where local cantons have jealously safeguarded their authority since the highly decentralized political settlement of 1848 (Bonoli and Mach 2000, 134–35). The resulting "consensus," unlike Nordic Europe, is deeply conservative. In Katzenstein's (1984, 144) words, "The result, often discussed in Switzerland, is a decidedly status quo–oriented policy process, which prizes small steps. Large-scale policy changes are not easily accomplished."

This characterization also applies to Austria, which struggled with separatism in the early twentieth century and fought a civil war as recently as 1934.[3] Like Finland, Austria responded by engaging employers and trade unions within encompassing, neocorporatist institutions after World War II. With compulsory membership, employers are even more organized than their Finnish (or Swedish) counterparts, and Austria has been presented as the paradigmatic case of neocorporatism (Rehn 1996, 128). Like Germany and Switzerland, however, Austrian social partnership is less encompassing than its Nordic counterpart. First, trade union density is lower, resulting a less solidaristic approach to reform and restructuring. Second, and more importantly, industry-labor and even interfirm collaboration is generally organized along sectoral rather than national lines. For example, although wage bargaining is highly coordinated, wages are negotiated locally, and earnings dispersion is significantly higher than in the Nordic countries (Bonoli and Mach 2000; Hemerijck, Unger, and Visser 2000).

Moreover, compulsory associational membership masks significant heterogeneity. In sharp contrast to Sweden, Finland, and Iceland, postwar Austria was characterized not by one production regime but rather by three competing industrial orders. Like Finland, Austria relied heavily on large, state-owned enterprises after World War II, which employed almost a quarter of the industrial labor force in 1986 and specialized in capital-intensive, low-technology products such as basic metals and semi-finished products (Vartiainen 1999). But Austria was also exceptionally dependent on foreign multinationals, which accounted for almost 40 percent of the industrial labor force. Finally, the most politically influential force, domestic privately owned industry, is overwhelmingly composed of small and medium-sized enterprises, employing craft-based strategies to target narrow, specialized niches in medium-technology industries such as engineering (Rehn 1996, 136–37).[4]

The Swiss economy more closely resembles Finland or Sweden in its reliance on a relatively small number of large export-oriented firms. Overshooting, however, is not simply a function of firm size, as Switzerland simultaneously occupies an extraordinary number of markets for such a small state. Whereas Sweden, the most diverse economy examined in this book, achieved deep specialization in a narrow range of clusters, comparative studies suggest that Switzerland occupied a more modest position in a wider array of industries (Porter 1990). For example, the Swiss watch industry, comprising a relatively stable 12 percent of exports since 1970, was less dominant than other leading sectors such as Swedish automotives, Finnish papermaking, or Icelandic fishing (Feubli et al. 2013). In sum, reform-oriented actors in both Austria and Switzerland confronted not only a relatively fragmented political system but also a more pluralistic economy populated by very different enterprises, targeting distinct, largely unconnected markets.

In this less cohesive environment, consensus has the effect of delaying reform and restructuring. Of the two economies, Austria exhibits the greatest capacity for reform and restructuring, having nationalized large swaths of industry after World War II, most notably the country's two largest banks (Vartiainen 1999).[5] Unlike Finland and Iceland, however, Austrian policy makers were motivated by the more immediate threat of Soviet expropriation rather than any strategic long-term vision (Rehn 1996, 144). Any efforts to spearhead restructuring were undermined by political disagreements over how exactly to use nationalized enterprises, including the banking sector (Katzenstein 1984, 140–43). After Austrian business effectively vetoed efforts to diversify into higher value-added industries, state-owned enterprises became a vehicle for absorbing excess labor and compensating disadvantaged regions (Rehn 1996, 145–46).

Postwar stakeholders did manage to settle on a distinctive approach to Keynesianism, using expansionary fiscal policies, tight monetary policy, and coordinated wage bargaining to create a climate conducive to investment. There was no serious effort, however, to alter the sectoral or structural composition of industry after World War II. In addition to the constraints on state-owned industry, stakeholders blocked alternative strategies to accelerate the redistribution of capital or labor, such as Swedish-style active labor-market policies (Katzenstein 1984, 41). In Olli Rehn's (1996, 161) assessment, postwar economic policy was "impressive as far as macroeconomics are concerned, but relatively impotent as far as microeconomics are concerned."

Like Germany, the absence of a grand strategic plan was not necessarily a liability, as Austria's diversified industrial base insulated it from OPEC-induced oil shocks and shifting patterns of competition in the 1970s. State-owned enterprises were naturally hard-hit by the crisis, but the small and medium-sized enterprises described above played a stabilizing role and Austria actually increased its market share in the global market for industrial goods from 1.28 percent in 1970 to 1.35 percent by 1984 (Rehn 1996, 130). Partly as a result, Austria faced little pressure to diversify into new high-technology markets during the 1980s. Although Austria continued to excel at the acquisition and diffusion of new technologies into established industries, rival ministries and parties bickered over industrial policy, and the country adopted a "muddling-through" approach to the 1980s (Rehn 1996, 141). Expenditure on R&D, which closely resembled Finland at 1.16 percent of GDP in 1981, was only 1.89 percent of GDP in 2000, and the country trailed on a wide range of indicators from the share of high-technology manufactured exports (table A.3) to high-technology services, high-technology patenting, and venture capital (Eurostat 2016). The country has since responded to a perceived "technology gap," but reforms have been more effective in upgrading the research intensity of established industries rather than diversifying into fundamentally new ones. Moreover, and in sharp contrast to countries such as Finland, policy makers' efforts to boost R&D have not been matched by initiatives in other complementary areas such as university education and venture capital (Cooke et al. 2007, 220–21).

Similar dynamics prevail in other areas. Austria has liberalized considerably in recent years, privatizing state-owned industries, liberalizing trade, and deregulating financial markets (Hemerijck, Unger, and Visser 2000, 200–204). Austrian policy makers, however, moved more slowly than their Nordic counterparts (Rehn 1996, 134). In contrast to the ambitious, forward-looking discourse I document in chapters 2, 3, and 4, Austrian politicians were more likely to coin catchphrases such as, "The most important person in a bobsled is the one who handles the brake" and "Let up on the brakes, but don't step on the gas" (Hemerijck, Unger, and Visser 2000, 200). Austria was a late and gradual liberalizer insofar as trade was concerned (Katzenstein 1984, 52–53). Financial liberalization proceeded at an equally glacial pace as policy makers first tested the market's reaction to small reforms before lifting formal controls. The government did not even begin the process of privatizing state-owned banks until 1993, when financial liberalization was already well under way (Rehn 1996, 134).[6]

Newly privatized Austrian banks did prove vulnerable to the 2008 credit crunch, as they had expanded aggressively across Central and Eastern Europe, issuing loans totaling 60 percent of GDP. The fallout from the crisis, however, was limited for two reasons. First, risk was widely distributed across a dozen different countries.[7] Second, risk-taking never extended to the Austrian economy as a whole, in sharp contrast to the Nordic banking crises I describe in chapter 4. Equity prices soared between 2002 and 2007, but debt increased at an average pace and credit expansion was actually among the lowest in the OECD. Austrian bank assets, which already stood at 225 percent in 1995, increased to 379 percent of GDP by 2008 (OECD 2009a, 23). As a result, Austria was relatively immune to the 2008 financial crisis. Not only did the country escape a systemic banking crisis, the export-oriented economy outperformed Finland and Sweden (see table A.4).

Although sometimes depicted as an "institutional dinosaur" (Crepaz 1995) and criticized for its inability to compete in more dynamic high-technology industries (Cooke et al. 2007, 220), the country's unremarkable but stable growth has prompted some to comment on the "rewards of slowness" (Hemerijck, Unger, and Visser 2000, 193). I develop this point below. Before doing so, however, it is important to acknowledge that Austria has been exceptionally fortunate over the years. Its reliance on high-quality, craft-based production insulated it from the crisis of Fordism in the 1970s, and it was fortuitously positioned to benefit from German reunification and economic restructuring in Eastern and Central Europe during the 1990s. Would a more severe economic crisis have triggered radical Nordic-style reform and rapid restructuring?

The Swiss experience of the mid-1970s suggests that even an acute crisis may not be enough to provoke comprehensive reform or restructuring in a relatively fragmented polity. In the 1970s, the OPEC-induced oil shocks triggered the sharpest downturn in the OECD.[8] Even worse than the downturn of the early 1930s, Swiss output plunged over 7 percent between 1974 and 1976 (Bolt and van Zanden 2013), a reminder that even diversified countries can experience a crisis. In the Swiss case, diversification may have contributed to the country's ills. The crisis triggered safe-haven flows to the Swiss banking industry, causing the currency to appreciate. A stronger franc hurt domestically based Swiss manufacturers, but they were unable to overrule financial interests (Merrien and Becker 2005, 118) and large internationalized multinationals (Katzenstein 1984, 90–91).

This is not to imply that Switzerland took decisive measures to accelerate the redistribution of resources from traditional manufacturing into financial services. In contrast to the cases surveyed in this book, the economic crisis of the mid-1970s triggered little action. The sharp decrease in national output in the mid-1970s and in later decades was exacerbated by an unwillingness to employ countercyclical, Keynesian policies. Nor did Switzerland adopt ambitious, Finnish-style technology policies in response to the crisis (Blaas 1992, 374). This is not surprising given the country's historic reliance on market-based solutions to economic problems. For example, Switzerland was an early and consistent liberalizer in trade policy, a laggard in social policy, eschewed industrial policy, and adopted a laissez-faire attitude toward the financial services industry (Katzenstein 1984, 93–117).

Remarkably, Switzerland also refrained from liberalizing its economy in any significant way. Fiscal consolidation, although sufficient to prevent large budget deficits, was modest, particularly when measured over the entire 1970s (Katzenstein 1984, 107). Meanwhile, the country preserved the heavy agricultural subsidies, cartelized structures, and other barriers that were always an important part of its trade regime (Merrien and Becker 2005, 115). This was not an isolated example; the growth slowdown of the early 1990s elicited a similar (non) response (Bonoli and Mach 2000, 146). Economists, businesses, political parties, and other groups may have formulated an effective consensus on macroeconomic policy, but they disagreed with one another over the desirability of deeper market-oriented reforms (Merrien and Becker 2005, 117). As a result, the most important measures were imposed externally, following trade negotiations at the European and global level. Analysts have concluded that the impact of globalization was more muted in Switzerland than elsewhere (Bonoli and Mach 2000, 164–68) and argue that the policy making community has been "stuck" (Merrien and Becker 2005, 130).

One could argue that Switzerland's frozen but liberal economic regime creates ample space for private-sector actors to take more radical action. There is little evidence of this in practice. Swiss business responded to the downturn of the 1970s either by rationalizing or upgrading their manufacturing operations rather than diversifying into fundamentally new industries (Katzenstein 1984). The Swiss watch industry, for example, has evolved over time, moving into luxury watches in the 1970s and adding progressively more sophisticated components in recent decades (Thompson 2015), but it still represents the same share of manufactured exports (12 percent) that it did in the 1970s (Feubli et al. 2013).

As table A.3 shows, Switzerland does enjoy a strong position in high-technology markets, but this generally reflects existing strengths in industries such as electrical engineering and pharmaceuticals rather than rapid diversification into new industries or the proliferation of new growth-oriented enterprises. In the 1970s, the country was already the second largest exporter of technology after the United States (Katzenstein 1984, 100). After 1980 the growth of high-technology manufactured exports trailed Finland, Sweden, and the United States (table A.3).[9] R&D spending as a share of GDP actually decreased in subsequent decades from 2.4 percent to 2.33 percent (Archibugi and Pianta 1992, 23; Eurostat 2016), falling behind Finland and Sweden. Coupled with limited progress in other areas, from education to early-stage risk capital markets, the country's remarkably slow productivity growth is often attributed to its inability to develop new products or activities (Blaas 1992, 374; Merrien and Becker 2005).

The growth of financial services represents only a partial exception to this general trend. The Swiss have competed effectively in banking for almost a century and this can hardly be seen to represent a big leap into a new industry. The country attracted safe haven flows as early as the interwar period, lured by the conservative macroeconomic policies described above and laissez-faire regulatory policies, particularly when it comes to the disclosure of financial information (Katzenstein 1984, 96). Although vulnerable to periodic failures, such as the bankruptcy of Banque Leclerc in 1978, the comparatively gradual growth of the Swiss banking industry (OECD 2009b, 20) has insulated it from the banking crises that devastated Sweden, Finland, and Iceland.

The 2007–2009 financial crisis is instructive. UBS was heavily exposed to the crisis, principally because of its expansion to the United States, but policy makers preemptively raised capital requirements in 2007. Credit Suisse started unloading subprime debt even earlier, in 2006, while smaller banks were completely unaffected by the crisis (Campbell and Hall 2017, 125–28). Although financial losses were formidable, Switzerland more closely resembles large countries such as the United States or the United Kingdom, where exposure varied significantly, rather than Finland or Iceland where all the major banks pursued virtually identical strategies.

These highly organized but segmented societies thus mark a sharp contrast with the Nordic cases. Here linguistic, regional, and sectoral cleavages frustrated efforts to forge the kind of collective, strategic vision that characterized postwar Swedish economic policy, late twentieth-century Finnish technology policy or early twenty-first-century Icelandic society. Consensus was confined to macroeconomic issues such as fiscal policy, monetary policy, and collective wage bargaining. Even here, these countries charted a conservative course, eschewing comprehensive Nordic-style reforms.[10] Strategic industrial policies of the sort that might facilitate diversification into new industries were simply out of the question. Paul Hofmann (1981, 59) summarizes Swiss politics thusly:

> The people who really count in this country are a few hundred men who know one another, having gone to the same schools and served in the same army units. They may belong to different political parties or competing firms or interest groups, but there is a basic consensus among them to defend the status quo.

This is not to imply that there has been no change in Austria or Switzerland. As Peter Katzenstein (1984) has made clear, these societies experienced continuous reform and restructuring in the early postwar period. Today, both Austria and Switzerland are more liberal than they were in the 1980s. Adaptation, however, occurred through cumulative, small-scale reform rather than sharp policy reversals, and the most important changes were imposed externally, by organizations such as the European Union (Bonoli and Mach 2000, 164). Similar dynamics prevail in the private sector, which is characterized by incremental upmarket movement into higher value-added products or activities within existing industries and enterprises, rather than the creation of fundamentally new ones (Katzenstein 1984, 208–9, 228–29).

This conservative approach to contemporary economic challenges has earned Austria and Switzerland little praise, in contrast to the accolades heaped on Nordic Europe. But their capacity to gradually upgrade established industries has simultaneously generated steady growth and insulated them from the disruptive shocks that plagued Nordic Europe (table A.5) without sacrificing their prosperity. In fact, one could argue that these countries benefited from their conservative political and social institutions. Although some degree of cooperation is essential to resolve distributional conflicts and create a stable macroeconomic climate for investment (see below), the fragmentation described above may actually protect certain high value-added activities. This is clearest in the case of the Swiss banking industry, whose growth is predicated on the absence of significant policy reform. Some scholars suggest that this may also apply to specialized manufacturers, where veto-prone institutions protect specialized investments from the risk of expropriation by the state, radical regulatory shifts, or sudden reversals in investor sentiment (Hall and Soskice 2001).

It is tempting to praise Austria and Switzerland, more consensual than Greece or Portugal (below) but less tight-knit than Nordic Europe, for achieving a "Goldilocks" level of cooperation. But it is unclear whether this is a viable model for other regions, including Nordic Europe. Incremental upmarket movement into progressively higher value-added activities was predicated on a long standing presence in high-quality markets. Switzerland, and even Austria, could leverage strong, craft-based traditions and guild structures to set standards, upgrade skills, and diffuse technology throughout the economy (Culpepper 2007; Mjøset 1992). This conservative approach might prove less effective in countries with a weaker skill base operating in lower-technology industries. Indeed, one could argue that the Nordic countries belong in this second category, penalized by their status as late industrializers. To what extent is economic volatility in Nordic Europe simply a function of timing, with the latest industrializer (Iceland) experiencing wilder swings in policy and output than the earliest one (Sweden)? To answer this question, we travel farther south, to Portugal and Greece.

The Late Industrializers of Southern Europe: Greece and Portugal

One could attribute overshooting in Nordic Europe to late industrialization. Although collective responses to capital scarcity facilitated reform and restructuring, they also contributed to policy overshooting and overinvestment in low- and high-technology industries alike. But capital scarcity does not have to provoke a collective response. If the challenges associated with late industrialization united the Nordic countries, they divided Southern Europe. Much more fragmented and polarized than the small states of Central Europe, Southern European countries such as Greece and Portugal struggled to agree on basic macroeconomic policy, much less craft a single strategic vision for their economy.[11] This did not prevent economic development, especially in the early postwar period. But the failure to resolve basic collective action problems, most notably fiscal policy, delayed diversification into higher value-added activities and exposed these countries to recurring economic crises. In this case, the key driver of volatility was not too much change, but too little.[12]

Like Austria and Switzerland, the small states of Southern Europe resemble the Nordic countries in several ways. With approximately ten million inhabitants, Portugal and Greece rival Sweden in population. Politically, a powerful centralized state and a unicameral legislature create an ideal environment for reform (Nicholls 2015; Sotiropoulos 2012). Ethnically homogeneous, a Portuguese scholar characterized his country as an "almost perfect nation-state" with no major linguistic or regional cleavages (interview with historian, 5 July 2016, Portugal). Historically, this characterization may have been even more apt for Greece, where a weak aristocracy muted class divisions and generated a measure of "social cohesion" in the early twentieth century (Close 2002, 6). After World War II, both countries experimented with corporatist producer associations (Lavdas 2005; Royo 2002). These formal institutions were complemented by informal relationships. For example, the Greek Ship Owners' Union routinely leveraged close ties with Greek government officials, exchanging low taxes and anti-union policies in exchange for lucrative shipping jobs (Close 2002, 46). The so-called "one hundred families" of Portugal, connected through interlocking directorates, leveraged ties with the public sector, constructing state-sanctioned monopolies in a wide variety of industries during the Second Republic (Morrison 1981, 4).[13]

In other respects, however, Greece and Portugal were far more polarized than their Nordic or even Central European counterparts. In Portugal disputes over the pace and scope of modernization led to violent nineteenth- and twentieth-century conflicts between reform-oriented liberals and conservative landed elites and clergy (Pedaliu 2013, 10). Greek nation-building was even more problematic. In addition to inheriting a less capacious administrative apparatus from the Ottoman Empire (Koliopoulos and Veremis 2010), national independence was a product of great-power politics and did not generate a particularly strong sense of national identity. The new Greek state needed to use generous side payments to secure the allegiance of local notables (Nicholls 2015, 134). In both countries, patronage delivered a measure of stability but was not connected to a coherent economic strategy and would prove costly in the long run. During the nineteenth century, Greece and Portugal defaulted on ten separate occasions (Rogoff and Reinhart 2009). By the beginning of the twentieth century, chronic, fiscal mismanagement had taken a toll and Greece and Portugal were no longer more prosperous than their Nordic counterparts (Bolt and van Zanden 2013). Moreover, patronage failed to temper working-class radicalism and, in the case of Greece, persistent disputes over foreign policy. The twentieth century was characterized by repeated coups and, in Greece, a protracted civil war between 1946 and 1949. In contrast to Finland and Austria, which also suffered civil wars, Greece and Portugal were governed by authoritarian regimes as recently as the 1970s.

Authoritarianism, and a history of conflict more generally, had a polarizing effect on society, most notably a radicalized working class, which was divided along both sectoral and ideological lines (Lavdas 2005, 302; Royo 2002, 94–95). Greek and Portuguese employers were also more fragmented than their Nordic counterparts. In Greece membership rates were low and organizational capacity varied wildly by sector (Lavdas 2005, 303–4). While the shipping association carved out independent deals with the state, industry-state relations were characterized by considerable tension, even in the early postwar period (Lavdas 2005, 308). Associational membership was higher in Portugal, where Salazar attempted to construct a corporatist state. But even under the dictatorship, industry was divided between firms that were subject to formal corporatist regulation and enterprises that could secure separate concessions through informal channels (Morrison 1981, 4). Today Portuguese industry is organized into two competing confederations with different policy preferences (Watson 2015, 23), and its organizational capacity remains low (interview with economist, 12 July 2016, Portugal).

In this respect, Greece and Portugal differ from Nordic and Central Europe. Organizational fragmentation as well as pervasive distrust militate against even basic forms of cooperation (Lyberaki and Tsakalotos 2002). For example, an employee at the Confederation of Finnish Industries marveled at the fact that his Southern European colleagues could not agree on statistics that were widely accepted in Finland (interview with representative, Confederation of Finnish Industries, 14 June 2012, Finland). This is not surprising, particularly in the case of Greece. In contrast to the friendly relationships between labor- and employer-backed research institutes in Finland (see chapter 3), the Greek research community is highly politicized (Nicholls 2015, 138).[14] In this context, it is difficult to understand how Greek elites (or ordinary citizens) could agree on basic issues such as macroeconomic policy or wage setting, much less identify a coherent long-term vision for the economy. Table A.2 supports these claims. In contrast to Nordic Europe, only one individual argued that "everyone knows everyone and cooperation is relatively easy to establish." Most explicitly disagreed with this statement.

In Portugal order was imposed from above by an authoritarian state. The Salazar regime used the strength of the state to impose the fiscal discipline that had been absent in the nineteenth and early twentieth centuries. That said, the deeply conservative government had an ambivalent relationship with big business and was never particularly interested in moving labor from rural farms into large factories (interview with economist, 4 July 2016, Portugal). His successor launched an ambitious modernization campaign in the 1960s, channeling capital toward heavy industries such as steel and petrochemicals. But the Second Republic was just as likely to use corporatist regulations to protect small and medium-sized producers in low-technology and nontradable industries (Royo 2010, 211). Although Portugal grew rapidly, particularly during the modernization drive of the 1960s, agriculture was largely untouched by the modernization drive and continued to employ a third of the labor force as recently as 1970 (Morrison 1981, 7).

This schizophrenic approach to economic adjustment outlived the dictatorship. The immediate postrevolutionary period of the late 1970s was characterized by far-reaching reforms. For example, the government redistributed land and nationalized large swaths of industry, including most of Portugal's banks. In contrast to Sweden, Finland, and Iceland, however, this U-turn was deeply polarizing. In addition to undermining the (already limited) organizational capacity of industry,[15] the nationalization of Portugal's largest business blocs alienated Portuguese employers (Morrison 1981, 47–48). In the words of one economist, "Entrepreneurialism has been a very dirty word since the revolution" (interview with economist, 4 July 2016, Portugal).

Postrevolutionary reforms also divided the left. The revolution may have strengthened Portuguese civil society (Fernandes 2015), but it did so in ways that weakened the prospects for Nordic-style cooperation. More specifically, the transition radicalized the working class, enabling the Communists to assume a leading role in the Portuguese labor movement. Non-Communist parties on the right *and* left responded by systematically weakening the organizational capacity of labor. These reforms had the effect of fragmenting Portuguese labor markets and creating a "siege mentality" among Communist trade unions and party members (Watson 2015, 88). Although levels of industrial unrest would remain low, Portugal does not possess a Nordic-style ideology of social partnership (Watson 2015, 19). Interviewees instead characterized labor relations as a "constant war of attrition" (interview with economist, 8 July 2016, Portugal).

This polarized environment had predictable implications for economic adjustment. Instead of boosting investment, nationalization spooked industry and Portuguese capital formation plummeted after 1974 (Amaral 2007, 205–7). Although policy makers used state-owned enterprises, most notably banks, to stabilize employment and protect small and medium-sized enterprises (Fishman 2010, 293–97), they did not pursue the kind of systematic investment campaign that characterized the 1960s. Nor did policy makers introduce ambitious Finnish- or Swedish-style innovation polices. Research intensity increased during the 1980s and 1990s but only gradually, at the same pace as other Southern European countries such as Greece and Spain (Pessoa 2014, 123). As recently as 2005, Portugal was only investing 0.76 percent of GDP in R&D, trailing not only Finland (3.33 percent), Sweden (3.39), and Iceland (2.7) but also many countries in Southern and Eastern Europe (Eurostat 2016).

Of course, Portugal did not need to rely on public investment to accelerate restructuring. Other countries, such as Iceland and Ireland (which I cover in detail in the next chapter), relied on market competition to fuel growth. Portugal also pursued market-oriented reform, most notably the privatization of state-owned enterprises in the 1990s, but not on a scale that distinguished itself from other EU member-states. For example, foreign investment (including EU structural funds approaching 4 percent of GDP) emerged as an important driver of productivity growth after Portugal joined the European Union in 1986, and during the 1990s in particular (Amaral 2007, 205–7). But Portugal never pursued the kinds of systemic reforms that transformed countries such as Ireland into a hub for foreign direct investment. Efforts to attract individual enterprises such as Volkswagen, Siemens, or Embraer were offset by near-constant changes to the corporate tax regime (interview with economist, 8 July 2016, Portugal). This kind of instability was not limited to corporate taxation. Kate Nicholls (2015, 186) describes how the "pendulum principle" undermined the development of a knowledge economy, reversing reforms to higher education, labor-market policy, and immigration. Interviewees echoed this point, ruing the absence of a long-term strategic vision in the Portuguese public sector (interviews with an economist and an industry association representative, 12 July 2016, Portugal).

This inconsistent approach to policy making was perhaps most conspicuous and most problematic in fiscal policy. Portuguese governments periodically consolidated public finances in response to pressing external constraints such as

IMF intervention in the early 1980s or the run-up to the Euro in the 1990s. But budgetary consolidation was based on ad hoc measures and never reflected a new economic paradigm of the sort that emerged 1990s Sweden or even neighboring Spain (Royo 2012, 19). Within two years of adopting the Euro, Portugal had already overshot the 3 percent deficit ceiling. A permanent fix was undermined by partisan disagreement and frequent turnover in government (Royo 2012, 45). Chronic deficits were compounded by low levels of coordination in the labor market and the failure to adapt an admittedly fragmented system of collective bargaining to a low-inflation environment (Watson 2015, 86).

By 2008 Portugal was mired in a deep economic crisis that rivaled Finland and Iceland in severity (see table A.4). In the Portuguese case, however, the problem was fundamentally different. Whereas Finland and Iceland had relied too heavily on volatile new industries, such as banking or mobile communications, Portugal had failed to diversify into higher value-added activities (see table A.3). Portugal was not characterized by excessive dependence on a single sector (interview with economist, 6 July 2016, Portugal). Rather, policy makers and industry leaders had failed to develop an effective response to declining cost competitiveness in a wide variety of traditional low-technology industries. Expansionary fiscal policies stabilized employment during the 2000s (Fishman 2010) but they also rendered Portugal susceptible to tightening credit conditions after 2007. This was not a new problem. On the contrary, it mirrored the structural crises of the 1970s and 1980s, with the Troika now assuming the role that the IMF had played in earlier decades.

This is not to imply that Portugal is incapable of reform or restructuring. As in earlier decades, Portugal has consolidated public finances with relatively little social unrest (*Economist* 2015). This broad, if belated, commitment to austerity reflects the fact that Portugal, although much less cohesive than Nordic Europe, is not nearly as polarized as Greece. Indeed, interviewees were quick to note that although Portugal lacks an ideology of "social partnership" and coordinating capacity remains weak, it is possible to identify consensus on a wide variety of issues from foreign policy to education (interviews with political scientist, 4 July 2016, and economist, 12 July 2016, Portugal). This may explain why particularly talented or "enlightened" policy makers are sometimes able to introduce sweeping reforms, even in the absence of strong mediating institutions (Nicholls 2015, 225).

The 2005–2011 Sócrates administration's ambitious investments in research and education might fall into this category. Capitalizing on a widespread, if largely untapped, consensus that Portugal needed to boost investment in innovation, he proposed a Finnish-style "technological shock." Ambitious public- and private-sector investments effectively doubled Portuguese research expenditure in less than five years, from 0.76 percent of GDP in 2005 to 1.58 percent between

2009.[16] As Nicholls (2015, 225) notes, these types of reforms are intrinsically fragile. Subsequent administrations continue to prioritize innovation, but efforts to boost research intensity have been threatened by budgetary cutbacks as well as persistently low levels of industry-university and interfirm cooperation (interviews with economist and employee, Ministry of the Economy, 13 July 2016, Portugal). In the long run, however, these investments may enable Portugal to solve recurring problems with cost competitiveness (Royo 2010, 235–36).[17] For an even starker contrast with our Nordic cases, we must turn to Greece.

Greece represents an even clearer example of how the inability to resolve basic collective action problems can lead to recurring crises. Nineteenth-century cleavages may have been less pronounced than in Portugal, but twentieth-century Greece was sharply divided by foreign policy disagreements and class conflict (Close 2002, 8). These divisions did not prevent growth. In the Greek case, modernization was not imposed by an authoritarian regime but was spurred instead by a combination of US aid and market-oriented reform. Collectively, these developments fueled annual GDP growth of 6.5 percent between 1950 and 1973, one of the highest rates in the developed world. Mirroring Portugal's modernization campaign, the Greek government invested heavily in shipping and complementary industries such as steel, shipbuilding, and oil refining. By the beginning of the Third Republic in 1974, Greece boasted the largest merchant fleet in the world, and manufacturing had doubled in size as a share of GDP (Close 2002, 48–55).

Even at its most dynamic, however, Greece exhibited less capacity for reform and restructuring than Portugal. First, government policies were internally inconsistent. Like Portugal, the conservative government's commitment to modernization was undercut by its determination to protect agriculture and small and medium-sized industry from competitive pressures (Pagoulatos 2003, 68). The military junta that followed in 1967 sought to increase the scope of state intervention but simultaneously possessed an ideological aversion to any form of planning (Pagoulatos 2003, 28). In contrast to Portugal, which at least charted a relatively consistent course from its colonial empire to Western Europe, Greece vacillated between openness and autarky (Pagoulatos 2003, 22–26).

Second, it is unclear whether the government possessed the capacity to implement a more consistent and coherent growth strategy. Pagoulatos (2003, 61–62) characterizes Greek public administration during the 1960s as

> A mosaic of bodies inadequately coordinated and isolated from each other . . . a feeble, unassertive, under-resourced, and politically dependent bureaucratic apparatus leading to serious fragmentation and discontinuity of state policies. Greece offered a case of developmental policies without a, strictly speaking, developmental state.

This had important consequences, as the government's own heavy investments in infrastructure, designed to integrate rural regions, were often diverted to serve clientelistic purposes (Close 2002, 52). Even if the state had exhibited a greater capacity for coordination, it is unclear whether public efforts to promote industrialization would have succeeded without significant societal support. Whereas the government proved adept at some tasks, mainly the repression of organized labor (Pagoulatos 2003, 88), efforts to direct investment were less successful. For example, government grants to modernize agriculture were routinely used to speculate on urban real estate (Pagoulatos 2003, 37), and companies diverted funds specifically earmarked for industrial investment to other uses (Pagoulatos 2003, 64). As a result, rapid growth between 1950 and 1973 was driven largely by nontradable industries, most notably construction (Close 2002, 52).

The early postwar Greek experience suggests that a massive infusion of capital can transform even a fragmented, polarized society with limited reform capacity. The expansion of the Greek construction industry could even be seen as a nontradable analogue to overinvestment in Nordic Europe, particularly since it was propelled by a nationwide fixation with acquiring real estate (Close 2002, 52). Like Portugal, however, the key difference with Nordic Europe lies not in the (weakly coordinated) industrialization of the Greek economy in the early postwar period, but the response, or lack thereof, to the exhaustion of this capital-intensive model in the mid-1970s.

This is not to imply that there was no reform at all. Post-authoritarian leaders directly confronted the ship owners most closely associated with the military junta in the 1970s, while the Panhellenic Socialist Movement (PASOK) used its legislative majority to nationalize large swaths of industry, including the country's largest banks, during the early 1980s. Nationalization, however, differed from Nordic Europe in two respects. First, policy makers lacked a clear strategic vision for the future. The state did not use its expanded powers to systematically mobilize capital and modernize Greek industry (chapter 2), nor did it embark on a Finnish-style campaign of technological upgrading (chapter 3). Instead, PASOK used the public sector to reward party loyalists, most notably working-class constituents (Pagoulatos 2003, 92). This was an understandable reaction to the labor-repressive practices used by the military junta between 1968 and 1974, but it was not particularly conducive to restructuring.

Second, these expansionary public policies tended to divide rather than unite society. As in Portugal, nationalization was profoundly controversial. In the Greek case, cooperation between the government and the Federation of Greek Industries deteriorated considerably after 1974 (Lavdas 2005, 308) and capital investment plummeted (Close 2002, 170). Meanwhile, any effort to fundamentally transform the Greek society was undermined by the center-right New

Democracy Party, which thwarted the expansion of state-owned enterprises by pursuing a campaign of privatization when it entered office in the 1990s (Pagoulatos 2003, 127). At the same time, several forces blocked any systematic movement toward greater market competition. First, PASOK fiercely criticized any proposals by New Democracy. Dimitri Sotiropoulos (2012, 24), explaining the "paradox" of nonreform in Greece, writes:

> Even in policy sectors where both parties claim that there should be national consensus, such as in education, culture, and tourism, their political rhetoric remains inflammatory. Almost all legislation introduced by the incumbent government is rejected by the opposition and vice versa.

Second, socialist opposition to liberalization, or reform more generally, was compounded by the very real specter of industrial unrest, which surged in the early 1990s. Although smaller than their Nordic counterparts, Greek trade unions were far more disruptive, partly in reaction to labor-repressive strategies of the early postwar period. Between 1980 and 2006, Greece experienced thirty-three general strikes, three times as many as Italy, the second most strike-prone country in Western Europe (Hamann, Johnston, and Kelly 2013, 1037).

Finally, any effort to liberalize the Greek economy was further undermined by the tendency of New Democracy to use the public sector and anti-competitive regulations to deliver side payments to its own supporters beginning in the mid-1990s (Pappas 2013, 36). One could argue that this willingness to extract resources from the public sector (and by extension, society) represented a perverse form of coordination (interview with political scientist, 30 June 2016, Greece). Because policy makers targeted very different groups, however, Greek society was effectively paralyzed, experiencing neither state-led modernization nor market-driven restructuring. Dimitri Sotiropoulos (2012) describes the "paradox of non-reform in a reform-ripe environment," in which deteriorating economic conditions, a near-universal sense of crisis, and a clear legislative majority somehow failed to produce any significant change.

Greece, like Portugal, experienced some success in conforming to EU-imposed constraints, reducing barriers to trade, deregulating financial markets, and curbing public expenditures through a series of ad hoc measures in the run-up to the Euro. Progress was limited, however, and Greece was easily the worst-performing country in the OECD on measures of structural reform (Close 2002, 180–81). New Democracy stabilized gross government debt at 100 percent of GDP, highest in the European Union in the 1990s, but no progress was made toward the official target of 60 percent (Eurostat 2016). Political paralysis, combined with high levels of industrial unrest, discouraged private investment. Convergence, which proceeded at a rapid pace in the early postwar period, stalled between 1975 and 2000 (Pagoulatos 2003, 91). The share of high-technology exports rose between 1980 and 2000 (table A.3), but this occurred in a context of rapid deindustrialization (Close 2002, 171). The adoption of the Euro and access to cheap capital temporarily boosted growth in the 2000s, but the cost of failing to reform the public sector and restructure the economy was clear by 2008.

Circumstances have since changed, as Greece has implemented one of the most drastic fiscal consolidations in the history of the OECD. But consolidation, and the structural reforms associated with it, only occurred when subjected to heavy external pressure, including the direct supervision of the European Commission, the European Central Bank, and the International Monetary Fund. Moreover, in contrast to fiscal consolidation in Finland, Sweden, Iceland, or even Portugal, austerity has proven deeply controversial, triggering not only widespread and sustained social unrest but the apparent breakdown of the Greek party system (Verney 2014). This is a natural response to exceptionally painful austerity measures, but it is also difficult to see how one can forge a common approach to public-sector reform and economic restructuring in such a highly polarized environment (Fioretos 2013). The danger is that political paralysis and societal polarization will lead to continued volatility, albeit for very different reasons from those in Nordic Europe.

This rather pessimistic-sounding analysis should not obscure the fact that both Greece and Portugal have made significant progress since World War II (Amaral 2007; Close 2002). Both countries experienced rapid growth, most notably in the early postwar period, narrowing the gap with the developed world at a faster pace than most late industrializers. Comprehensive reform, however, remains elusive and these countries were only partially successful in their efforts to transition away from capital-intensive growth toward more knowledge-intensive activities after 1974. Portugal and Greece not only lacked the political consensus to pursue systematic structural reforms but also struggled to create a stable macroeconomic framework. Partly because of this, the private sector has not emerged as a particularly dynamic force either. There is some evidence of upmarket movement, particularly in Portugal (Amaral 2007, 224), but restructuring remains modest, and there is little evidence of Nordic-style leaps into fundamentally new industries.

As a result, there has been considerable volatility since 1974. Unlike Nordic Europe, this is less a function of rapid restructuring than a failure to address long-standing issues from industrial competitiveness to fiscal policy. These fundamental weaknesses were temporarily obscured by massive, temporary capital infusions from the European Union.[18] The failure to pursue more comprehensive patterns of reform and restructuring, however, was quickly exposed when credit dried up. Consequently, and in sharp contrast to Nordic Europe, the twenty-first-century downturns bear a strong resemblance to the turmoil of the 1970s.

In this respect, the Greek and Portuguese cases highlight the strength of the Nordic region. Although this book argues against lionizing the Nordic model, these societies are successful. The capacity of public- and private-sector actors to fundamentally restructure their economies has enabled them to escape the "middle-income trap," successfully transitioning from capital-based growth into more knowledge-intensive industries.[19] This process of continuous reinvention has been achieved at a cost: economic volatility. Countries that already occupy stable high-quality niches (such as Austria and Switzerland) might want to think twice before emulating the Nordic model. For countries that are still relatively dependent on low-technology industries and vulnerable to cost competition, on the other hand, the Greek and Portuguese cases suggest that the benefits of cooperation outweigh the risks (Doner and Schneider 2016).

Of course, it is unclear whether Greece and Portugal could develop more cohesive, encompassing, Nordic-style social networks even if they wanted to. The Finnish case suggests that it may be possible to develop cooperation over time by incentivizing membership in encompassing producer associations, subsidizing interfirm cooperation, connecting elites in courses on economic policy, and other network-building efforts. But this was a lengthy process, and Finland benefited from favorable historical conditions. Although early twentieth-century industry-labor relations were notoriously acrimonious, the country was fortunate enough to inherit a coherent administrative apparatus, equally distributed natural resources, and little in the way of religious conflict. This characterization applies to an even greater degree for Iceland and Sweden. Does this mean that only Nordic countries possess very cohesive, encompassing networks? If so, why should a non-Nordic reader care about the politics of interconnectedness and overshooting? In the following chapter, I generalize the argument to several other cases, beginning with Ireland. Like Greece and Portugal, this peripheral country trailed its continental counterparts and relied on EU structural funds, but it responded very differently to the challenges of late development.

6

OVERSHOOTING BEYOND NORDIC EUROPE

Ireland and Estonia

The rise and fall of heavy industry in Sweden, Finland's emergence as a high-technology leader, and Iceland's short-lived reign as a financial services center are all so dramatic that one could question whether the dynamics described in this book could possibly apply to other countries. In this chapter I argue that the politics of interconnectedness can be generalized. The Nordic countries represent one possible starting point. Although comparative studies suggest that sharper regional cleavages militate against Finnish-style coordination (Kristensen 2011, 233; Moen 2011b, 143), Denmark and Norway are still characterized by relatively dense, cross-cutting ties (Campbell and Hall 2009; Rokkan 1967). These connections facilitated radical reform, from the adoption of statist industrial policies in early postwar Norway (Grønning, Moen, and Olsen 2008, 285) to the recent reconfiguration of Danish labor-market institutions in the 1990s (Madsen 2006). These countries have also proven vulnerable to overshooting, from deep fiscal and banking crises several decades ago (Hyytinen and Pajarinen 2003, 24–25; Schwartz 1994, 533–34), to Denmark's more recent housing bubble (Campbell and Hall 2017, 42) and Norwegian dependence on oil (Benner 2003, 140).

The analytic payoff from a more detailed analysis of these Nordic countries, however, is limited. These cases do little to address alternative explanations for overshooting such as natural resources, the size of the public sector, labor-power resources, or employer coordination (see chapter 1). To maximize analytic leverage we should look further abroad, selecting societies that differ from our Nordic cases along as many dimensions as possible. To this end, I open with an account of Irish economic development. Although it is similar in population to Finland, the country could hardly be more different. More heavily influenced by Britain than Germany, the Republic of Ireland did not use large banks or the state to build up massive national champions. Instead, this liberal market economy relied on a low-tax, lightly regulated, employer-friendly environment to attract foreign direct investment. These differences notwithstanding, elites were nonetheless connected by a similar network of cohesive and encompassing relationships. These ties enabled Ireland to reform its economy with exceptional speed, adopting a highly coordinated campaign to recruit foreign direct investment. They also increased the country's vulnerability to disruptive shocks, from rising labor costs in the 1970s to the global credit crunch of 2007–2009.

Having demonstrated that the argument can be extended to liberal market economies such as Ireland, I then turn to the transitional economies of East Central Europe. Estonia represents a clear outlier in the early and enthusiastic adoption of market reforms. I suggest that Estonia's remarkable reform capacity is not necessarily a consequence of political polarization or societal weakness, but may instead reflect the cohesive and encompassing ties that bind decision makers across society. These tight-knit, cross-sectoral relationships accelerated the diffusion of new ideas and enabled Estonia to rapidly restructure its economy. Of course, they also increased the risk of overshooting. This alternative interpretation not only explains the pace and scope of market-oriented reform but also addresses Estonian leadership in unrelated areas, such as information and communication technology. Collectively, the Estonian and Irish cases suggest that the Nordic region is not unique. The theoretical framework advanced in this book could be applied to other small, cohesive communities within Europe and beyond.

Ireland: The Politics of Interconnectedness in a Liberal Market Economy

To demonstrate that overshooting is not limited to Nordic Europe, we begin in Ireland, which experienced a similar series of exaggerated boom-bust cycles.[1] In chapters 2 through 4 I address a variety of alternative explanations for overshooting, including labor power resources, employer coordination, state intervention, protectionism, and natural resources. None of these apply to Ireland. The Irish working class is less well organized than its Nordic counterparts. At 32.7 percent in 2010, Irish trade union density is less than half that of Finland, Iceland, or Sweden (OECD 2016). The Irish Labour Party, the only left wing party consistently represented in the legislature, never received more than 20 percent of the vote after World War II. To the extent that overshooting exists in Ireland, it is certainly not a product of Nordic-style labor power resources.

This characterization also extends to employers. Although interlocking directorates are more common than one might expect in a liberal market economy (see table A.1), Ireland did not construct Finnish- or Swedish-style industrial families. Irish financial institutions instead maintained an arm's-length relationship with their clients and were just as likely to send deposits abroad to London (Ó'Grada 1997, 176). This pattern was reinforced by Irish reliance on foreign (mostly US) direct investment after 1958. Industry associations, to the extent that they existed, were more committed to lobbying than investing in collective goods such as vocational training or technical standards (Ornston and Schulze-Cleven 2015, 571). Nor did the government attempt to take matters into its own hands. Staffed by generalists with few formal ties to civil society, Ireland is characterized by a relatively weak and closed administrative apparatus (Campbell and Hall 2017, 77). As a result, Ireland did not possess the legacy of "financial repression" that might have contributed to banking crises in Finland, Iceland, and Sweden. Nor can overshooting be attributed to natural resources, as Irish economic development was initially based on low labor costs rather than natural resources.

In this sense, Ireland more closely resembles the late industrializers of chapter 5 (Greece and Portugal) rather than Finland, Iceland, or Sweden. Indeed, one could question the decision to classify Ireland as a cohesive, encompassing society. Some scholars attribute Ireland's volatile economic performance to state weakness or societal fragmentation, suggesting that the country would benefit from a dose of Nordic-style cohesion (Campbell and Hall 2017; O'Riain 2014). I argue otherwise for two reasons. First, in chapters 2 through 4 I demonstrate that the Nordic countries are hardly immune from policy overshooting and overinvestment. Although greater solidarity might reduce inequality, it is by no means clear that more cohesive and encompassing ties would inoculate Ireland against policy errors or economic crises. On the contrary, they could make matters even worse.

Second and more importantly, Ireland is more similar to the Nordic countries than one might expect, particularly when we shift our focus away from formal measures of neocorporatism and coordination toward informal networks. With fewer than five million inhabitants, Irish elites routinely interact in corporate boards, public committees, and civic associations. In contrast to the small states of southern Europe, these interactions are also relatively harmonious. Like its Nordic counterparts, external vulnerability and weak internal divisions have forged a relatively strong sense of national identity. Initially, post-independence politics was contentious, but the postwar republic simply lacks deep-seated linguistic, regional, religious, or ideological cleavages (Kissane 2002). Like Iceland, a center-right party (Fianna Fáil) used nationalistic appeals to assume a near-hegemonic position in Irish politics, incorporating a wide range of actors, from agriculture to industry and the working class, with generous side payments (Nicholls 2015, 79). Unlike Greece or Portugal, observers routinely comment on the remarkable degree of continuity across governments and the near absence of "basic political conflict" when it comes to economic policy (Morrissey 1986, 80). Interdepartmental cooperation, although not necessarily formalized, is common and easy to establish (interviews with former minister, 17 May 2006, and former director, government agency, 6 June 2006, Ireland).

These ties extend to the private sector as well. Although the Industrial Development Authority (IDA) is not a neocorporatist body, the agency maintains close relationships with all of its clients (MacSharry and White 2000). In the private sector, Ireland's largest firms are connected, if not through interlocking directorates (Clancy, O'Conner, and Dillon 2010), then through informal ties (interview with former official, Department of Trade, Industry and Employment, 4 July 2012, Ireland). Even organized labor, if less central than its Nordic counterpart, was incorporated into a series of encompassing three-year collective wage agreements (Social Partnership) between 1987 and 2009 (Ornston and Schulze-Cleven 2015, 571–72). Policy makers also had little difficulty using interpersonal networks to reach pragmatic agreements with trade union representatives (interview with employee, National Center for Partnership and Performance, 14 June 2006, Ireland). In one particularly remarkable case, a policy maker successfully persuaded a trade union leader to refrain from organizing a factory out of concern for the chilling effect it would have on foreign investment (interview with former director, government agency, 6 June 2006, Ireland). As a result of these tight-knit, cross-sectoral ties, Irish interviewees use strikingly similar language to describe their society, differing only in the use of the term "village" rather than "club":

> [Ireland is] very small. It's a big village. I always use the expression it's a big village. People know each other from different strands of society, and they're known from different strands of society. . . . My understanding is that there are often informal parallel structures. Most important people of influence are in them and very few people are not in them. (interview with former official, Department of Trade, Industry and Employment, 4 July 2012, Ireland)

Table A.2 demonstrates that this sentiment was not unusual. Ireland rivaled Finland and Iceland in the substantial majority (72 percent) of interviewees who agreed with the claim that "everyone knows everyone and cooperation is relatively easy to establish," as well as the relatively small number (11 percent) who disagreed with this statement.

As the following section relates, Irish policy makers and other reform-oriented actors could use these tight-knit social networks to accelerate restructuring, employing the politics of persuasion to mobilize support, relying on the politics of compensation to neutralize opposition, and using the politics of coordination to pursue systemic reform. Of course, the specificities of adjustment differ. The fact that Ireland is a liberal market economy makes it difficult to engage in certain forms of collective action, from vocational training (Ornston and Schulze-Cleven 2015) to private sector–led rescue packages (Campbell and Hall 2017), and the benefits of growth are less equitably distributed. That being said, the parallels with Nordic Europe are no less striking. After pursuing an exaggerated form of import-substituting industrialization in the early postwar period, Ireland performed a complete about-face to redefine itself as one of the leading destinations for foreign direct investment in the world. When this export-led boom faltered at the end of the twentieth century, Ireland constructed the largest housing bubble in Western Europe.

Ireland has proven vulnerable to policy overshooting and overinvestment since it gained independence in 1922. Like its contemporaries, Ireland witnessed a shift from market competition to state intervention in the wake of the Great Depression. In the Irish case, concerns about economic dependence on Britain led policy makers to adopt an ambitious program of import-substituting industrialization, erecting barriers to trade and restricting foreign ownership of Irish firms (Mjøset 1992, 262). The shift to protectionism was surprisingly consensual, in part because Fianna Fáil compensated the agricultural interests that benefited the most from free trade (O'Riain 2014, 180). Most notably, Fianna Fáil suspended land annuity payments to Britain, sparking a six-year trade war. By the early 1950s, virtually all major actors defended protectionism, including not only agriculture but also the major industrial and labor associations, the Central Bank, and the Department of Finance (Ó'Grada 1997, 50–53; Ó'Grada and O'Rourke 1996, 399–400).

In the short run, high tariff walls protected domestic producers from foreign competition. Manufacturing employment more than doubled between 1931 and 1951 (O'Malley 1992, 32–33). Unlike Portugal, which created a mercantilist trade network with its colonies (see chapter 5), and Iceland, where high tariffs were offset by massive fish exports (see chapter 4), Ireland pursued a particularly extreme form of autarky, aiming to secure self-sufficiency in a market with just three million consumers. Unable to achieve economies of scale and suffering from chronic foreign exchange shortages, the result was an economic catastrophe. Dubbed the "worst decade since the famine," approximately 15 percent of the population left Ireland in search of employment during the 1950s (Girvin 1997, 61). Only when confronted with a demographic collapse and the threat of expulsion from the Organization for European Economic Cooperation did Irish decision makers reconsider their commitment to protectionism (Mjøset 1992, 269–71).

Once the limitations of import-substituting industrialization were clear, Irish elites responded with Nordic-style speed and effectiveness. Policy makers eliminated the taxation of export profits in 1958, eliminated quotas in 1959, (unsuccessfully) applied to join the European Union in 1961, unilaterally lowered tariffs in 1963 and 1964, and signed a free-trade agreement with the United Kingdom in 1965 (Mjøset 1992, 272). Of course, many late industrializers, including Portugal (chapter 5), reacted to the failure of import-substituting industrialization by liberalizing trade. But Ireland went a step further, not only liberalizing trade but conducting a complete volte-face, privileging foreign capital and export-led industry on a systematic level. Ireland is not just "more liberal" than it was in the 1950s, it now ranks among the most globalized and market-friendly societies in the world (A.T. Kearney Inc. 2003).

How should we explain this stunning policy reversal, which was far more dramatic than anything we observe in similarly positioned societies such as Greece and Portugal (Nicholls 2015)? I argue that cohesive and encompassing networks enabled reform-oriented actors to engage in the politics of persuasion, compensation, and coordination. In the Irish case, a single white paper, drafted under the supervision of the minister of finance, T. K. Whitaker, in 1958, completely transformed elite opinion (Breznitz 2012). Although personal relationships played an important role, Whitaker and his allies could also use a wide variety of tripartite institutions to educate skeptical policy makers, industrialists, and workers about the benefits of free trade and foreign direct investment (Morrissey 1986, 83).

That consensus-building tradition continued within bodies such as the National and Economic Social Council (NESC) (Culpepper 2002). As a result, few question Ireland's open, export-oriented growth regime.[2] In the words of one taskforce chairman:

> There is a huge [consensus] around FDI, to the point that one cannot question whether the pursuit of FDI is compatible with setting up a sustainable model for an open economy.... There is almost a conspiracy of silence that one should not talk about the [low corporate] tax rate. (interview with policy maker, 5 July 2012, Ireland)[3]

This near-universal commitment to free trade and foreign direct investment cannot be attributed solely to the persuasive powers of organizations such as the Committee on Industrial Organisation (CIO) and the National Economic and Social Council (NESC). The tripartite committees that educated actors on the benefits of trade liberalization also compensated enterprises that would be hardest hit by economic openness. For example, the CIO distributed adaptation grants to modernize vulnerable industries between 1962 and 1967 (Ó'Grada and O'Rourke 1996, 402). Meanwhile, labor was compensated with progressively more generous collective wage agreements beginning in the 1970s (Prondzynski 1998).

This broad consensus enabled Ireland to launch an exceptionally comprehensive campaign to attract foreign direct investment. The main coordinating actor was the Industrial Development Authority. Tasked with attracting multinational corporations to Ireland, the agency received sweeping powers in the wake of the 1958 White Paper. By the 1980s, it wielded a comprehensive arsenal of subsidies representing 12 percent of public investment (Ó'Grada 1997, 55). Viewed in this light, it is easy to interpret the IDA as a kind of developmental state, insulated from society and using its autonomy to spearhead restructuring (Breznitz 2007, 151–53). In practice, the IDA's effectiveness was always predicated on its ability to cooperate with domestic actors. A stable macroeconomic climate, peaceful labor market, and low-tax regime, achieved through Irish Social Partnership, proved critical in upgrading investment during the 1980s and 1990s (Ornston 2012b, 150–52). But cooperation was far more extensive than this. The IDA also secured skilled labor by codesigning educational curricula with regional technical colleges, lobbying the national government to create additional radio spectrum for a telecommunications firm, working with local governments to construct a bypass for commuters, and connecting corporate clients and academics in research consortia (interviews with former director, regional college, 23 May 2006; former executive officer, electronics firm, 1 June 2006; former executive, IDA, 6 June 2006; and director, electronics firm, 15 June 2006, Ireland). In fact, multinational representatives cited ease of access to government and other stakeholders as one of the biggest advantages to operating in Ireland (interviews with former manager, electronics firm, 3 May 2006; manager, electronics firm, 8 June 2006; and director, electronics firm, 8 June 2006, Ireland).

The shift from protectionism to foreign direct investment fueled rapid industrialization, enabling the country to converge with, and eventually surpass, the EU in per capita GDP (Eurostat 2016). Unlike Greece and Portugal, growth was predicated on a capacity to engineer "big leaps" (Ornston 2012b) into new industries, moving from food processing, footwear, and textiles into high-technology manufacturing and, more recently, knowledge-intensive services (see table A.3). This was not a smooth or straightforward process (see table A.5). Increasing labor costs triggered capital flight and a deep economic crisis in the 1980s (Mjøset 1992). The resulting turn to basic high-technology export and assembly operations supported rapid growth in the 1990s, but increased Ireland's vulnerability to the dot-com crash and EU enlargement at the turn of the millennium (Barry and Egeraat 2008; Ornston 2012b). Instead of unpacking these shifts, which are extensively documented in Breznitz (2007), Ó'Grada (1997), O'Riain (2014), and Ornston (2012b), I focus on the housing bubble of the early twenty-first century.

Ironically, the rise of this nontradable industry can be traced back to Ireland's export-led growth model and the IDA in particular. Recognizing that employment growth in manufacturing was limited and Ireland could no longer compete in low-skilled activities, the IDA targeted financial services as a high-skill, labor-intensive alternative in the 1990s. This shift began with the International Financial Services Centre in 1987, which employed a combination of conventional instruments including marketing, grants, tax concessions, and low-cost real estate (MacSharry and White 2000).[4]

As part of its campaign to lure foreign banks to Ireland, the IDA lobbied the government to reduce the regulatory burden on financial firms. This represents more than the "structural power" that enabled financial firms to veto unfavorable regulation in the United States or the United Kingdom (Culpepper and Rienke 2014). Irish interviewees speak of active collaboration, as the IDA united leading financial firms and policy makers within clearinghouses and similar working groups to coordinate with government and amongst themselves (interviews with representative, Irish Business and Employers Confederation, and employee, Ministry of Finance, 10 July 2012, Ireland). As the International Financial Services Centre grew in importance and manufacturing declined, the IDA secured a regulatory environment that was so permissive, pre-crisis outsiders dubbed Dublin the "Wild West" of European finance (Lavery and O'Brien 2005).[5] Of course, the Central Bank of Ireland and the financial supervisory authority, responsible for governing financial markets, were also threatened with the specter of capital flight. As a result, they not only refrained from imposing new regulations but also declined to use the few tools that it *did* possess. In the words of one employee, "My view was that the Central Bank was not willing to enforce its rules. I introduced [new instruments] that the Bank could apply without going to court, but there was definitely an unwillingness to use the powers they had" (interview with employee, Central Bank of Ireland, 5 July 2012, Ireland).

To be clear, the IDA was tasked with promoting foreign firms. Neither the agency nor Irish policy makers sought to promote the growth of Ireland's own domestic banks at the turn of the century. Much like Iceland, however, entrepreneurial private-sector actors, specifically Anglo-Irish Bank, used this lax regulatory environment, combined with cheap capital from the European Union, to experiment with risky new corporate strategies. As in Finland and Iceland, their aggressive debt-fueled strategy diffused rapidly within close-knit financial circles.[6] Allied Irish Banks and, to a lesser extent, the more conservative Bank of Ireland soon followed Anglo's lead into property markets (interview with employee, Central Bank of Ireland, 6 July 2012, Ireland). Even regional banks were affected. In the words of one policy maker: "Virtually all of the banks went 'bananas,' even the cooperative banks. Even our most conservative institution, the Educational Builders Society, succumbed and [had to be] acquired by the state" (interview with employee, Ministry of Finance, 10 July 2012, Ireland).

In this respect, Ireland more closely resembles Finland (or Iceland) than larger Anglo-Saxon societies such as the United Kingdom or United States. First, Ireland was characterized by an exceptional degree of isomorphism in which all banks, new and old, large and small, were exposed to the crisis (Honohan 2010).[7] Second, the Irish crisis did not involve complex, poorly understood financial instruments that were offloaded onto unsuspecting investors, but rather simple loans to a handful of housing developers. Inexplicably, the banks kept many of these loans on their books, trusting their clients to invest the money responsibly. A financial regulator explained:

> The nature of those relationships are quite interesting because what you would have particularly in Anglo and some other banks was a small number of individuals right up against the limit of the bank's ability to lend to an individual.... And those people were not being subjected to proper credit approval processes on a project-by-project basis. (interview with employee, Central Bank of Ireland, 5 July 2012, Ireland)

If the risks associated with this highly leveraged business model were so clear, why did Irish policy makers fail to address the bubble? As noted above, the IDA used the near-universal support for FDI to argue against any intervention that might spook foreign investors. By the early twenty-first century, domestic financial firms were in a position to advance similar arguments, employing nationalist rhetoric to do so. One regulator remarked:

> Top-level management bought into the issue. You see, if there was any mention internally within the [Central Bank] about trying to reign in lending practices, you had foreign competition coming into the Irish market.... One of the issues was that the Irish banks said, "If you try to regulate us, we'll lose massive share to foreign banks," and this took hold not just in the commercial banks but in the regulatory authority and in the Central Bank itself and in the Department of Finance. (interview with employee, Central Bank of Ireland, 6 July 2012, Ireland)

Nonfinancial interest groups expressed little interest in pressing the issue. In addition to accepting committee reports that Irish growth depended on new knowledge-intensive industries such as financial services, the benefits of cheap credit were widely distributed. Ireland may have lagged its Nordic counterparts in social spending, but Social Partnership delivered rising wages in a wide variety of industries. Meanwhile, rising home prices benefited consumers across the Irish economy. In fact, the property market represents a good example of how policy makers not only tolerated the credit bubble but actively supported it. For example, the government lowered real estate taxes at the height of the bubble and introduced a series of incentives to promote property investment (interviews with employee, Central Bank of Ireland, 6 July 2012, and professor, 9 July 2012, Ireland). This surprising decision reflected the political clout of the construction industry. Like Iceland, the industry not only captured individual regulatory agencies but "affected every level of Irish political life" (Mahon, Faherty, and Keys 2012, 5).

Although the Mahon Tribunal documented extensive corruption, there was also a genuine and widely held belief that the real estate boom was sustainable, driven by rapid economic growth and favorable demographics. For example, NESC, whose information-gathering and consensus-building capabilities enabled Ireland to reform macroeconomic policy in 1987 (Culpepper 2002), commissioned the Bacon Report to investigate the housing market during the late 1990s. The report acknowledged rapid property price inflation but concluded that Ireland suffered from insufficient supply rather than excessive demand (Peter Bacon & Associates 2000).[8]

Like Iceland (or Finland), interviewees describe how the same cohesive networks that facilitated the growth of financial services created a conformist environment that was inhospitable to dissenting views. One policy maker commented: "If you suggested there was a bubble [in your research], you met quite a lot of opposition to that work. They were reluctant for that work to be published and become the official viewpoint of the bank" (interview with employee, Central Bank of Ireland, 6 July 2012, Ireland). Although the Irish media was more open to alternative views than its Icelandic counterpart, coverage of the real estate bubble was overwhelmingly positive (Nyberg 2011, 95), and critics such as Richard Curran faced "collective annihilation by a torrent of criticism from most of the media, the estate agents, the IAVI, and the Construction Industry Federation" (Donovan and Murphy 2013, 162).[9] Investigative reports note that this type of criticism was particularly costly in a tight-knit society (Honohan 2010). In the words of a former board member:

> It wasn't good for your health to be too questioning. An important aspect of all of this is that the individual becomes visible in the networks of a small country and can feel lonely and exposed. So there is a lot of informal pressure to share [those ideas] and to not question it

robustly. (interview with former board member, financial services firm, 4 July 2012, Ireland)

In the short run, financialization sparked rapid restructuring and growth. Bank loans, directed in the late 1990s at high-technology enterprises in the form of commercial real estate and venture capital, were reoriented toward residential investment. The share of credit devoted to real estate increased from less than 10 percent in 2000 to over 25 percent by 2007 (O'Riain 2014, 83). Credit expansion was not quite as rapid as in Iceland (chapter 4) or Estonia (see below), but bank assets more than doubled in size to 791 percent of GDP between 2000 and 2008 (Christensen 2011, 109). Buoyed by cheap loans, housing prices increased by 240 percent between 1997 and 2007, eclipsing even paradigmatic property bubbles such as Spain (180 percent) and the United States (175 percent) (Dellepiane and Hardiman 2011, 11). At the height of the bubble, Irish real estate investment represented over a quarter of GDP (Christensen 2011, 109).

Unfortunately, this boom was not sustainable. The abrupt collapse of the Irish housing market in 2008 created a banking crisis and then a fiscal one when the government rashly agreed to guarantee the debts of Ireland's largest financial institutions.[10] Bailouts, which touched three quarters of the country's domestic banking industry, caused government debt as a share of GDP to balloon from 23.9 percent in 2007 to 120.2 percent by 2012. Ireland was hardly the only country caught up in the global financial crisis, but the bust was exceptionally severe. At 41 percent of GDP, the fiscal cost was second only to Iceland within the developed world. Unable to devalue its currency, the output loss was the highest in the OECD, eclipsed by only a handful of developing countries (Laeven and Valencia 2012, 19–20).

One can debate whether a blanket guarantee and fiscal austerity was the optimal choice (Campbell and Hall 2015; O'Riain 2014), but Ireland's capacity for collective action appears undiminished. Between 2008 and 2015, the population absorbed budget cuts totaling 20 percent of GDP, second only to Greece, with minimal social unrest (Hardiman and Regan 2013, 10).[11] Why was Ireland able to reduce public spending so effectively? In contrast to many other crisis-hit countries, all major actors in Ireland have prioritized macroeconomic stabilization and believe this should not be accomplished by raising the country's low corporate tax rate (Hardiman and Regan 2013, 11). As a result, although Social Partnership may not have survived the crisis, the government was nonetheless able to strike an agreement with public-sector workers to limit pay increases and recruitment between 2010 and 2014 (Hardiman and Regan 2013, 12). Those deals reflect the "silent conspiracy" described above, in which Ireland's future prosperity hinges on foreign investment. This consensus may be stronger than ever following the failure of indigenous growth engines such as software (Breznitz 2007) and banking (O'Riain 2014).

Indeed, foreign investment spearheaded an export-led recovery after 2008, transforming a 5 percent current account deficit into a 5 percent surplus by 2012 (Eurostat 2016). Like earlier decades, FDI-led growth reflects significant restructuring (Regan and Brazys forthcoming). Recognizing that Ireland needs to target more knowledge-intensive industries, policy makers have adapted regulations to eliminate the taxation of intellectual property (Barr and Francis 2014) and invested in new research infrastructure, such as Science Foundation Ireland and the Programme for Research in Third Level Institutions (O'Riain 2014, 74–75). Rapid restructuring has garnered significant praise, and the country is once again presented as a "model" reformer (Mayer 2012). But it is also risky. A single industry, pharmaceuticals, represented approximately one-fifth of the country's GDP in the wake of the crisis. As a result, the country is uniquely vulnerable to the looming cluster of patent expirations in the pharmaceutical industry (Regan 2014, 27–28). Any serious effort by the United States to crack down on the transfer pricing that attracts foreign direct investment would be even more devastating (interview with former employee, Science Foundation Ireland, 12 May 2006, Ireland). In short, Ireland's "rocky road" is not a relic of the twentieth century (Ó'Grada 1997), but an enduring aspect of its development and a common characteristic of tight-knit, cohesive communities.

Estonia: The Politics of Overshooting in East Central Europe

To what extent does this argument travel outside of Western Europe? In this section I argue that the theory advanced in this book can shed light on the transitional economies of East Central Europe. Reacting to the excesses and inefficiencies of the command economy, countries across the region privatized state-owned enterprises, reduced public spending, and liberalized trade in the 1990s. At the same time, some countries went much further than others in liberalizing their economies. The Visegrád states (the Czech Republic, Hungary, Poland, and Slovakia) pursued a more incremental approach, using tariffs, state aid, and social policies to protect and upgrade traditional Communist-era industries such as armaments and automotives (Bohle and Greskovits 2012, 138–39). By contrast, other societies, most notably the Baltic republics, pursued rapid and radical market-oriented reform (Bohle and Greskovits 2012, 96). Estonia, one of the first countries to adopt a hard currency regime, privatized virtually all state-owned enterprises, sharply reduced state aid, retrenched social spending, and adopted a low, flat income tax. The share of noncrisis state aid in 2009–11 (0.11 percent of GDP) represented a fraction of what policy makers spent in the Czech Republic (0.64 percent), Poland (0.73), or Hungary (1.33) (Kuokstis 2015, 117). These neoliberal reforms devastated traditional manufacturing firms, but enabled Estonia to engineer big leaps into new industries such as ICT and financial services.

The origins of this sharp divergence are not immediately obvious. Structurally, the production profile of the Baltic republics resembled the Visegrád group in the early 1990s, so it is difficult to attribute their neoliberal trajectory to comparative advantage (Bohle and Greskovits 2007, 459). Scholars have instead linked the scope and pace of market-oriented reform to executive autonomy or the weakness of societal actors, most notably organized labor (O'Dwyer and Kovalčík 2007; Raudla 2013; Thorhallsson and Kattel 2013). This makes sense. The case studies of prewar Sweden, prewar Finland, and postwar Ireland suggest that regimes where labor is poorly represented (or actively repressed) are more likely to favor market competition. But accounts that emphasize state autonomy or societal weakness fail to explain several distinctive aspects of Baltic adjustment. First, if the government relied on the power of the state to overpower societal actors, why did it enjoy such strong public support? Second, and perhaps even more puzzling, why did Estonia, an ostensible paragon of liberalism, undertake massive public investments in collective goods such as education, research, and ICT infrastructure? In the following case study, I argue that cohesive, encompassing networks shed new light on why Estonia embraced both comprehensive market-oriented reform and ambitious innovation policies. These reforms transformed the country into a "model pupil" within East Central Europe (Smith 2003) but also increased its vulnerability to disruptive shocks.

Like the example of Iceland, this claim may surprise some readers. Comparative studies suggest that Estonian society is fragmented and polarized. Certainly, neocorporatist institutions are much weaker than in Nordic Europe, not least because trade unions were tainted by their association with the Soviet occupation from 1940 to 1991 (Feldman 2006). Second, and directly related to this development, ethnic Estonians responded to decades of Russification by marginalizing the country's large Russian-speaking minority. After independence, the government effectively disenfranchised 40 percent of its residents. Although these restrictions were eventually relaxed, 19 percent of the population lacked Estonian citizenship as recently as 2003, and language requirements make it even harder for Russian speakers to work in the civil service, education, and other public-sector positions (Bohle and Greskovits 2012, 100). Since Russian speakers were disproportionately employed in Soviet-era manufacturing industries, this move had the effect of marginalizing working-class interests as well.

When we shift our focus to the informal ties that bind the Estonian-speaking community, however, the picture looks different. Like the Nordic cases and Ireland, Estonian speakers routinely cross paths within a small community of approximately one million inhabitants (interview with former employee, Estonian technology park, 9 June 2016, Finland). These ties may not extend to specific subgroups, namely Russian speakers, but it is important to recognize that Nordic social networks are not necessarily universal either. Early twentieth-century Sweden excluded organized labor (see chapter 2); contemporary Finland is not a particularly hospitable environment for libertarians (see chapter 3); and the cozy ties that characterize Denmark do not extend to recent immigrants (Campbell and Hall 2009, 565).[12] Estonian speakers, however, are united by informal ties that transcend individual regions, political parties, industries, and niches to connect a wide variety of different sectors, including the political class, civil servants, academics, and the business community (OECD 2011a, 137; Randma 2001, 48).[13] For example, Estonian-speaking *nomenklatura* were not systematically excluded from power, but participated actively in political and economic decision making after independence (Steen and Ruus 2002, 240).

Estonian interpersonal networks are not only encompassing in the way they cut across sectors, regions, and political parties but are also cohesive. Like Finland, proximity to Russia has forged an exceptionally strong sense of national identity. This sense of social solidarity is arguably even stronger in Estonia as a result of Soviet-era repression, its vulnerable geopolitical position, and its sizeable Russian-speaking minority. Comparative studies describe a civil service united by unusually strong esprit de corps (Kattel and Raudla 2013, 443), while industry distrust of the state is lower than other small, Northern European states (Steen 2015, 193). This consensus extends across the political system (Adam, Tomšič, and Kristan 2008, 51), encompassing left-leaning parties that would qualify as right-wing in other countries (Vogt 2003, 50). In contrast to other post-Communist societies, only 10 percent of Estonia's former Communist Party members expressed left-leaning political preferences by 1997 (Steen and Ruus 2002, 240). Nor is this broad bipartisan consensus confined to elites. According to public opinion surveys, satisfaction with the government and the economy was among the highest in East Central Europe (Bohle and Greskovits 2012, 136–37).[14]

These cohesive and encompassing networks facilitated rapid reform and restructuring. Of course, Estonia's more radical approach to economic restructuring was partly a reaction to Soviet-era legacies. More intrusive planning and geopolitical vulnerability influenced policy decisions, from the early adoption of a hard currency regime to the deregulation of traditional industry. But the politics of persuasion also helped unite elites across the political spectrum. Echoing Urho Kekkonen's call to restrain consumption (and working-class wages) in the name of national independence, Prime Minister Mart Laar presented monetary independence (and market-oriented reform more generally) as a question of national survival in the early 1990s. This national project not only received widespread support but had the effect of unifying the country. The Popular Front, precursor to the left-leaning Center Party, embraced the initial decision to adopt a currency board following the recommendation of a committee chaired by its (future) leader (Bohle and Greskovits 2012, 104–5).

Laar went one step beyond Kekkonen by promoting Estonia as a success story in the international media (Bohle and Greskovits 2012, 112). In doing so he crafted an attractive, coherent, and widely accepted narrative that paralleled Sweden's self-proclaimed status as a knowledge society and Iceland's twenty-first-century financial conquests. This compelling story gripped the public imagination, as evidenced by Siim Kallas's ability to build an entire political party around his seemingly uninspiring post as the first governor of the Bank of Estonia (Bohle and Greskovits 2012, 107).

As a result, one of the most striking features of economic policy making in Estonia is the consistent commitment to market-oriented reform despite fierce personal rivalries and high levels of turnover in government (Bohle and Greskovits 2012, 102). Although Greek and Portuguese interviewees identified the lack of continuity in government as a major impediment to structural reform, it made little difference in Estonia. Naturally, Mart Laar's right-leaning coalitions were always the most aggressive in promoting market competition. His first government passed a 26 percent flat tax, balancing the budget by cutting social spending, most notably pensions (Bohle and Greskovits 2012, 112). But centrist, social democratic, and agrarian parties exhibited little willingness to reverse these reforms in the mid-1990s. For example, a centrist-led coalition extended market-oriented pension reform in 1997 (Bohle and Greskovits 2012, 118) and liberalization continued apace in the 2000s, even after Estonia had concluded accession negotiations with the European Union (Bohle and Greskovits 2012, 132–33).

If many appear to have embraced Laar's radical market-oriented vision from a sense of ideological conviction or shared sacrifice, it also reflected carefully calculated concessions designed to compensate adversely affected (Estonian-speaking) citizens. The same Laar administration that introduced a flat tax and cut social spending simultaneously expanded public-sector employment, most notably in the field of education (Bohle and Greskovits 2012, 121). Although Estonia trails the Visegrád states in expenditure on state aid and social protection (Kuokstis 2015, 117), it invests significantly more in education and employs more workers within the public sector (Bohle and Greskovits 2012, 35). During the 1990s, the second Laar administration (1999–2002) also promoted home ownership with tax-deductible interest payments, loan guarantees, and subsidies (Bohle and Greskovits 2012, 134). Collectively, persuasion and compensation broadened support for market-oriented reform. As noted above, more Estonians expressed satisfaction with their government and economic system than in any other country in East Central Europe. Public protest, in sharp contrast to the Visegrád states, was virtually nonexistent (Bohle and Greskovits 2012, 136–37).

This relatively consensual and coordinated approach to economic reform radically transformed the Estonian economy. Although economic output declined alongside traditional industry in the early 1990s, the country soon boasted the highest growth rates in East Central Europe. By the mid-2000s, GDP growth approached double digits (Eurostat 2016). Expansion reflected the speed with which Estonia restructured its economy away from traditional Soviet-era manufacturing industries. Its proximity to Finland enabled it to enter high-technology manufacturing, attracting foreign direct investment from Nokia's chief subcontractor, Elcoteq. The share of high-technology products as a proportion of total manufactured exports skyrocketed from 10.9 percent in 1995 to 31.2 percent by 2000, eclipsing even Finland (OECD 2016).

Just like Finland, Iceland, Ireland, and Sweden, however, the same attributes that transformed Estonia into a "model pupil" increased its vulnerability to policy overshooting and the gross misallocation of resources. For example, high-technology production was concentrated in relatively low-end assembly and export activities that were sensitive to rapidly increasing labor costs and vulnerable to outsourcing (Bohle and Greskovits 2012, 127). R&D as a share of GDP was only 0.60 percent in 2000, trailing not only Finland (3.25 percent) but also post-Communist societies such as Poland (0.64 percent) and Hungary (0.79 percent). As a result, high-technology manufacturing was far less stable than in other East Central European countries. The share of high-technology manufactured exports plummeted from 31.2 percent in 2000 to 9.7 percent by 2007, *before* Nokia's collapse (OECD 2016).

As in Ireland, early twenty-first-century growth was based less on high-technology manufacturing than on nontradable services, most notably residential construction. But the housing boom rested on shaky ground, as the decline of new and traditional industry deprived the economy of foreign exchange. Inspired by favorable international evaluations, policy makers did little to rein in the boom, even following the proliferation of loans with zero or five percent down payments. On the contrary, the government contributed to the problem with a procyclical fiscal stance, refusing to raise property tax rates and carving out exemptions for second homes and corporate investment in real estate (Baudouin 2009, 3–4).

Although dissenting voices criticized high levels of inequality in Estonian society, few questioned its ability to handle shifting economic conditions. Collective confidence in Estonia's status as a "model pupil" enabled policy makers to discount warnings when external observers began to express concern (Bohle and Greskovits 2012, 232). The result, again in contrast to more incrementally oriented countries such as the Czech Republic, Hungary, and Poland, was a devastating recession that rivaled those in Iceland and Ireland. Estonian GDP shrank by nearly 15 percent in 2009 alone, far eclipsing declines in the Visegrád states (Eurostat 2016).

Consistent with the argument outlined above, Estonia did not stand still but responded to the crisis with radical reform. It established itself as a hardliner within Eastern and Central Europe and the European Union more generally with fiscal consolidation measures that exceeded 9 percent of GDP in 2009. Despite experiencing the third-steepest decline in GDP in the EU, Estonia ran the third-smallest budget deficit (Raudla 2013, 32). This policy stance is all the more remarkable because it was not imposed by an external actor such as the IMF or the EU. Estonia's ability to shoulder the massive costs associated with fiscal retrenchment reflects its collective commitment to the national project launched in 1991. The Euro functioned as an important focal point for policy makers (Raudla 2013, 42), while others cautioned against becoming a "serf" of the International Monetary Fund (Raudla and Kattel 2011, 175). Unified by this national project, initial fiscal consolidation was uncontentious, while subsequent disagreements were focused more on the substance of austerity rather than austerity itself (Raudla 2013, 40–41). Although some experts expressed concern, dissenting Estonian voices were few and far between (Raudla and Kattel 2011, 175). As a result, and in sharp contrast to other crisis-hit countries in Western or Southern Europe, trust in government remained high, while protest was virtually nonexistent (Bohle and Greskovits 2012, 232–36).

Moreover, and contrary to the emphasis on labor weakness (Bohle and Greskovits 2012; Bohle and Jacoby 2011), Estonian reforms were not simply a story about austerity. Estonia's commitment to fiscal retrenchment is virtually unparalleled, but it has also emerged as a regional leader in innovation. To be clear, Estonian innovation policy is not as broad as its Finnish counterpart, encompassing fewer policy instruments and fewer industries (Lember and Kalvet 2014). Within this space, however, policy makers have pursued specific objectives with exceptional focus. Education, discussed above, represents one such area. At 6.1 percent of GDP, Estonia ranked fifth in the EU in public educational expenditure in 2015, exceeding the Czech Republic (4.9 percent), Hungary (5.2 percent), and Poland (5.2 percent) (Eurostat 2016).

ICT represents another priority. Here, policy makers have coordinated activity across a wide variety of policy instruments, combining supply-side investment with sophisticated procurement policies. Virtually all schools were connected to the Internet by 1998, the government started accepting digital signatures in 2000, introduced a free national wi-fi network in 2001, adopted a digital ID system in 2002, recently expanded broadband access in rural communities, and has extended the digital ID system to foreigners by introducing the concept of "e-residency." Much like membership in the Euro, information and communication technologies represent a way for Estonia to define itself as a modern and "Western" society and have the effect of unifying the country with a single, ambitious national project.

Although Estonian innovation policy may leave room for improvement (Lember and Kalvet 2014), the contrast with the Visegrád region is stark. Poland provides an illustrative, if extreme, example of how difficult it is to coordinate innovation policy within a larger, more fragmented polity. A 2007 survey identified no fewer than 406 separate initiatives with no common goal and often working at cross-purposes (Rybinski and Kowalewski 2011), while a 2016 study failed to identify a single strategic vision for Polish innovation policy (NBP 2016). Although Polish innovation policy has evolved over time, reforms are imposed from the top level of government, with little societal input. These unpredictable changes have alienated Polish industry, which not only expressed confusion and skepticism but was also reluctant to participate in public initiatives. In this context, it is not surprising that Polish policy makers have struggled to foster innovation (Breznitz and Ornston 2017).

By contrast, the Estonian government had little difficulty enlisting private support for strategic initiatives such as information technology. Reassured by a clear and consistent vision, government procurement nurtured a nascent ICT cluster, contracting from Estonian start-ups and developing the pool of skilled labor. For example, the private sector took the lead in developing the technology for the digital ID card, which is accepted by a growing number of businesses (*Economist* 2013a; Kingsley 2012). Meanwhile, early successes, most notably Skype, emerged as a prominent role model for young Estonians and policy makers alike during the 2000s (interview with former employee, technology park, 9 June 2016, Finland). Inspired by the firm's success, policy makers ploughed resources into research and education during the 2000s. Between 2000 and 2014, R&D expenditure nearly tripled to 1.44 percent of GDP, surpassing Hungary (1.37 percent) and Poland (0.94 percent) (Eurostat 2016). Improvement in other areas was no less pronounced. The tertiary enrollment rate increased from 56 percent in 2000 to 77 percent by 2012, the fastest rate increase in the EU. The number of scientific publications more than doubled between 1998 (300) and 2008 (668), closing in on the EU average (Gorkey-Aydingolgu and Ozdemir 2015, 148). Although comparisons to Silicon Valley may be premature, the level of innovative and entrepreneurial activity is impressive (*Economist* 2013c). As of 2012, Estonia was leading the European Union in per capita–adjusted measures of start-up activity (Rooney 2012). These developments would have been hard to predict two decades ago (Bohle and Greskovits 2007, 459).

There is nothing intrinsically neoliberal about this coordinated campaign to rebrand the country "E-stonia" (Jansen 2011). Latvia, structurally and ideologically similar to Estonia, developed a very different collective vision of how to restructure its economy. The country also embraced market reform and eschewed traditional manufacturing. Unlike Estonia, however, Latvia recast itself as an entrepôt economy and financial services center, appealing to wealthy Russians with slogans such as "We're closer than Switzerland" (Bohle and Greskovits 2012, 130). Estonian decision makers explicitly rejected this entrepôt model, instead choosing to present their country as a highly educated high-technology leader (Bohle and Greskovits 2012, 128).

These ambitious investments in ICT are not unproblematic. Like Finland, a concentrated bet on rapidly evolving high-technology markets could increase the country's vulnerability to disruptive technological innovations, even if Estonia specializes in high value-added activities (Ornston 2014). Poland's fragmented and poorly coordinated innovation system, for all its weaknesses, has insulated the country from these shocks by fostering a highly diversified economy (Breznitz and Ornston 2017). Estonian reliance on ICT also exposes it to some novel risks. For example, Estonia's campaign to distance itself from its Soviet past by digitalizing its society had the ironic consequence of increasing its vulnerability to Russian cyberattacks (Davis 2007). As a result, there are reasons to suspect that the country's volatile post-independence performance will continue, even if it successfully transforms itself into an innovation leader.

Although I argue in chapter 5 that not all small states are characterized by cohesive and encompassing networks, the Estonian and Irish cases suggest that it is possible to generalize this argument beyond Nordic Europe. Both Estonia and Ireland are tightly knit societies, particularly when we shift our focus from labor organization and employer coordination to the informal ties that connect elites (and masses) across a wide variety of different sectors. These countries exhibit a common capacity for collective action, although the specificities of adjustment differ, and a similar vulnerability to overshooting. In the future, it would be valuable to extend the analysis by examining other small states, particularly outside of Europe. Are these societies also characterized by tight-knit networks or, like Greece and Portugal, does the politics of constrained geopolitical space play out differently? Because most readers do not live in small states, however, I instead conclude by discussing the implications for large countries. Although national-level dynamics are very different in large societies such as France, Germany, and the United States, these countries can still learn from and replicate small-state strategies at a regional level.

Conclusion

LESSONS FOR LARGE STATES

At first glance the Nordic countries would appear to hold few lessons for large states. Small size may not be a sufficient condition for the development of cohesive and encompassing networks (see chapter 5), but it appears to be a necessary one. Analyzing the rise of the state in the mid-twentieth century, the shift to high-technology markets in the late twentieth century, and the recent financialization of the economy, I demonstrate that large countries such as France, Germany, and the United States are fundamentally different from their Nordic counterparts. Reform-oriented actors have a harder time persuading their counterparts in the absence of dense, informal ties. It is more difficult to identify adversely affected actors and harder to make credible commitments, complicating the politics of compensation. This less consensual environment undermines the coordination of both public policy and private-sector activity. To be clear, these economies have evolved over time, but they have been less ambitious in reforming public policy, slower to restructure their economies, and less vulnerable to Nordic-style overshooting.

Although national-level dynamics are very different from Nordic Europe, I argue that the picture changes when we disaggregate these large societies. Smaller communities, such as San Diego, California, and Waterloo, Ontario, may be characterized by relatively cohesive and encompassing networks that span multiple sectors. Rather than stifling innovation, these tight-knit ties can accelerate reform and restructuring, enabling these regions to engineer Nordic-like leaps into new industries. Of course, the very act of doing so increases their vulnerability to disruptive shocks, from federal budget cuts to the collapse of Research in Motion. These risks may be less problematic for municipalities, however, since they are protected by state- and federal-level transfer programs. Since these protections do not apply to Finland, Iceland, or Sweden, I conclude by discussing how the Nordic countries and other small, tight-knit states should manage the risks of overshooting.

France, Germany, and the United States as Contrasting Cases

Throughout this book, I have implicitly argued that the Nordic countries differ from their larger counterparts in the scope of reform, the pace of restructuring, and the degree of overshooting. Here, I test that argument by examining the same three boom-bust cycles in chapters 2, 3, and 4 as they unfolded in three large countries. I use France, Germany, and the United States to test three alternative explanations for overshooting. Germany closely resembles Nordic Europe in its reliance on strategic cooperation. If strategic coordination is driving these developments, we should observe radical reform, rapid restructuring, and overshooting in Germany. France represents an extreme form of hierarchy, relying on a powerful centralized state to manage economic adjustment. If overshooting is a statist phenomenon, it should be particularly pronounced in France. Finally, the United States exemplifies the transformative power of the free market. If overshooting is caused by market competition, we would expect to observe greater restructuring and volatility in this liberal market economy. As this section illustrates, however, neither Germany, France, nor the United States rivaled Finland, Iceland, or Sweden in their capacity to redesign the "rules of the game" or redefine their production profile. This analysis thus underscores the relationship between cohesive, encompassing networks, radical reform, rapid restructuring, and overshooting.

Historically, the Nordic countries were more heavily influenced by Germany than by any other large society.[1] A late industrializer, Germany inspired everything from their engineer-oriented corporate culture (Rehn 1996, 286) to socialist ideology (Berman 1998). This is particularly evident when we focus on formal economic institutions. The Varieties of Capitalism literature, for example, identifies a number of parallels between Germany and Nordic Europe. As "coordinated market economies," the Nordic countries copied the German model of long-term, bank-based finance, integrating firms into encompassing industrial families and relying on these associations to deliver collective goods from technological standards to vocational training. After World War II, both Germany and the Nordic countries cooperated with organized labor in everything from national wage setting to firm management and introduced generous systems of social protection (Iversen and Pontusson 2000).

These similarities notwithstanding, Germany is clearly less tight-knit than any of the Nordic countries examined in this book. This is most evident in politics, where a "semi-sovereign" state shares power with subnational actors, the *Länder*, and is constitutionally prohibited from intervening in the labor market (Katzenstein 1987).[2] Commonly attributed to postwar constitutional engineering, this decentralized structure also reflects a delicate nineteenth-century compromise between regions with very different political institutions, religious traditions, and production profiles (Ziblatt 2006). As a result, even private-sector institutions are less cohesive than their Nordic counterparts. For example, although membership rates in employer associations are exceptionally high, interfirm and industry-labor cooperation generally occurs along sectoral rather than national lines (Kitschelt et al. 1999; Martin and Swank 2012).[3] Indeed, this more pluralistic financial and regulatory system protects an entire alternative industrial order, the *Mittelstand*, based on small and medium-sized enterprises (Herrigel 1996).

This decentralized political and economic structure influenced postwar adjustment. Adolf Hitler may have used totalitarian instruments to significantly expand the reach of the state during the interwar period (Berman 2006), but democratic postwar politicians proved considerably more conservative than their Nordic counterparts. For example, (West) German policy makers not only employed tight fiscal and monetary policies (Allen 1989) but eschewed the kinds of instruments that accelerated restructuring in postwar Finland, Sweden, and Iceland. For example, Germany did not rely on state-owned enterprises to spearhead growth, refrained from credit rationing, and never used labor-market institutions to pursue Swedish-style restructuring (Esser, Fach, and Dyson 1983).

This more conservative policy framework had important consequences for economic adjustment. Although postwar (West) Germany was even more dependent on manufacturing than Finland, Sweden, or Iceland, its industrial structure was more diverse. As table A.3 relates, Germany exported a larger proportion of high-technology goods in 1980. Its edge in medium-high technology goods such as automobiles and machine tools was even more pronounced (OECD 2016). Even within less research-intensive industries, Germany never favored capital-intensive firms as systematically as did their Finnish or Sweden counterparts. Manufacturing excellence was instead based, in part, on small and medium-sized enterprises producing high-quality, craft-style products in a wide array of narrow niches (Herrigel 1996; Piore and Sabel 1984). Partly as a result, by the 1980s the share of employment in large firms (35.8 percent) was significantly lower than in Sweden (60.6 percent). Although comparable figures are not available for Finland, the country more closely resembles Sweden (13) than Germany (9) in measures of average enterprise size (12) (Davis and Henrekson 1997, 362).[4]

This diversified industrial structure served (West) Germany well, insulating it from the kinds of disruptive shocks that led to stagnation in Sweden, increasing dependence on the Soviet Union in Finland, and economic volatility in Iceland (Streeck 1992). Partly as a result, reform and restructuring was more muted after the OPEC oil shocks. To be clear, the German government responded to the challenge of reunification with a series of measures, investing heavily in infrastructure, updating its vocational training system, and reforming its welfare state (Jacoby 2001; Vail 2009). Reform, however, generally unfolded at the margins of German society, through an incremental process of "layering" or "dualization" rather than the active conversion of core institutions as I document in chapters 2, 3, and 4 (Deeg 2010; Thelen 2014).

This is particularly evident in high-technology markets. Although some point to a surge in public investment in venture capital in the late 1990s as evidence of a new German "developmental" state (Adelberger 1999), it would be misleading to speak of Finnish- or Swedish-style innovation policies. There was no truly systemic effort to promote high-technology enterprise or even R&D more generally. In fact, industry studies suggest that high-technology enterprises succeeded by circumventing national economic institutions rather than leveraging them (Herrmann 2009; Lange 2009). Partly as a result of this, German high-technology start-ups were more likely to draw on established strengths such as enterprise resource planning rather than entering radically disruptive fields like their Swedish counterparts (Casper 2007a). It would be an exaggeration to label Germany a high-technology failure. Indeed, one advantage of Germany's more incremental and cumulative foray into high-technology markets is that it was less vulnerable to the dot-com crash (see table A.3).

But the differences with Nordic Europe are striking. As table A.3 relates, the share of high-technology manufactured exports increased, but not nearly as rapidly as in Finland or Sweden. German expenditure on R&D, already higher than in Finland, Sweden, or Iceland at 2.43 percent of GDP in 1981, peaked at 2.81 percent in 1991 (Archibugi and Pianta 1992, 21); this was hardly a systemic shift, and it stagnated at approximately 2.5 percent of GDP in subsequent years. Investment in early-stage risk capital markets, which reached 0.08 percent of GDP by 2000, was more impressive, buoyed by the government initiatives described above. But Finland, Sweden, and Iceland all eclipsed Germany here as well (Eurostat 2016).

Similar dynamics exist in financial markets, which exemplify the incremental, "dualistic" pattern of adjustment articulated above. A growing number of large German banks have reoriented themselves toward short-term securities markets, but others have maintained their traditional long-term relationships with small and medium-sized businesses (Deeg 2010). This diversified financial structure reduced German vulnerability to disruptive economic shocks. Although some German institutions were vulnerable to the 2008 credit crunch, there was no Finnish-, Icelandic-, or Irish-style isomorphism and exposure was uneven. The regional *Landesbanken* were exposed to US subprime debt and Deutsche Bank's financial health remains precarious, but other financial intermediaries, oriented toward the *Mittelstand*, were insulated from the crisis and actually expanded credit during the crisis (Detzer 2014). It is possible to identify exceptions at the sectoral or regional level (see below), but the German economy as a whole is characterized by considerable incrementalism. This is not necessarily a liability. Like Austria and Switzerland, this gradualist approach has delayed restructuring, but also has shielded Germany from the disruptive shocks that impacted Finland, Iceland, and Sweden.

Of course, one could argue that it is inappropriate to compare the unitary, centralized states of Nordic Europe to Germany's notoriously slow-moving political system. Perhaps France, with its powerful centralized state apparatus, is a better analogue. In fact, France's radical U-turn from classical liberalism to *dirigisme* in the middle of the twentieth century rivals Sweden's. Whereas laissez-faire economic policies in Sweden (and Finland) were a coordinated plan to accelerate restructuring, however, late nineteenth-century French liberalism reflected the Third Republic's notorious "stalemate society." Political and social paralysis would cause France to steadily cede ground to other late industrializers, principally Germany, but also Sweden and Finland, into the first half of the twentieth century (Hoffmann 1963).

Postwar policy makers responded to this economic and geopolitical crisis by delegating extraordinary powers to an elite cadre of civil servants, educated at elite schools and united by a strong esprit de corps. Whereas reform was negotiated in Sweden (and Finland), however, institutional change in France required the complete collapse of the government and built on the foundations of the authoritarian Vichy regime. It took yet another constitutional crisis, in 1958, to shield these bureaucrats behind a powerful, semi-presidential regime. At the height of their influence, civil servants were free to spearhead growth through the establishment of state-owned enterprises and also regulated the allocation of critical resources from foreign exchange to credit. Policy makers used these levers to favor large, capital-intensive enterprises, forcing small and medium-sized firms to merge into "national champions" and fueling some of the fastest growth rates in Western Europe (Zysman 1983).

French policy makers, however, never secured the full support of civil society like their Swedish (or Finnish or Icelandic) counterparts. To be clear, French civil servants were closely connected to one another and France's largest firms through a system of *pantouflage*, or circulation between the public and private sector. But ÉNA-educated elites did not control every large enterprise in France and were conspicuously absent from smaller enterprises, agriculture, and the labor movement (Levy 1999). Regions with strong Catholic or socialist-anarchist traditions stubbornly preserved traditional craft-based practices (Hancké 1997), while farmers, small shopkeepers, and workers represented a recurring threat to the regime (Berger and Piore 1980). Even large firms maintained an ambivalent relationship with the government, hiding information from central policy makers in order to maintain their independence (Zysman 1983). Although French civil servants could use their formidable authority, what Michael Mann (1986) refers to as "despotic" power, to impose reform on a fractured civil society, societal divisions limited the rate of change.

In this respect, France looks very different from Sweden (or Finland), where officials used virtually every policy lever available to favor large firms. French economic policy often worked at cross purposes, channeling cheap credit to large enterprises, but using agricultural subsidies and product market regulations to placate agriculture and small enterprises (Berger and Piore 1980). This had important implications for restructuring. Although the government was publicly committed to the creation of national champions, the average enterprise size in France (7) was almost half as high as Finland (12) or Sweden (13) by 1986, and the share of self-employment (10.5 percent) was almost twice as large (Davis and Henrekson 1997, 361–62). France was also slower to reallocate labor away from agriculture than either Sweden or Finland (Johansson 1997).

These inconsistent policies and the slower pace of restructuring were not necessarily a bad thing. Although French dependence on large firms increased its vulnerability to the OPEC oil shocks of the 1970s (Boyer 1997), the growth slowdown was not as severe as in Sweden (Sicsic and Wyplosz 1996). In contrast to Sweden's "narrow" and "deep" comparative advantage, France benefited from a more diverse manufacturing base. This included pockets of craft-based production, most notably in nonindustrial sectors such as agriculture (Berger and Piore 1980), as well as an array of new high-technology industries such as aerospace, armaments, and nuclear power (Zysman 1983).[5]

The differences between France and our three Nordic cases were even sharper after 1980. To be clear, France has changed considerably (Levy 1999; Vail 2009). In particular, deteriorating economic performance triggered one of the most dramatic and well-documented U-turns in modern economic history. In 1983 President Francois Mitterrand used the power of the state to renounce traditional industrial policies and rapidly liberalize the French economy (Levy 1999). Like his Nordic counterparts, Mitterrand employed a two part strategy. On the one hand, he relied on new innovation policies to target emerging high-technology industries. At the same time, he and his successors introduced greater competition into the French economy, privatizing state-owned enterprises, tightening fiscal policy, eliminating barriers to trade, and deregulating financial markets (Ornston and Vail 2016, 6).[6]

Reform, however, was less impressive than it first appeared, as French policy makers trailed their Nordic counterparts in both strategic vision and execution. As described earlier, the Swedish government's slogan "IT for everyone, before anyone else," the Finnish Science and Technology Policy Council's resolution to transform Finland into an "Innovative Society," and the Icelandic government's ambition to create a financial services center reflected a near-universal consensus, and each proposal was supported by significant public- and private-sector input. Twenty-first-century French economic policy, by contrast, has been characterized as "directionless" (Levy 2013). Resources rarely matched rhetoric and even the latter was strikingly inconsistent (Ornston and Vail 2016, 10–12).

For example, although the French government publicly prioritized innovation, and high-technology industry in particular, its ambitious targets were rarely met. Whereas Finland consistently increased public R&D spending, French government expenditure on R&D fell between 1981 and 2010, from 0.45 percent to 0.31 percent of GDP (Eurostat 2016).[7] Declining government expenditure on R&D was offset by tax credits, but total public R&D support remained lower than Finland (European Commission 2011, 83), and this tax-based strategy prevented France from constructing the kinds of broad-based research consortia that diffused new ideas and new technologies throughout Finnish society.[8] For example, the French government's latest network-based initiative, the *pôles de compétitivité*, reached only 2 percent of the country's firms (Fontagné et al. 2013, 913). As a result, the share of innovative small and medium-sized enterprises receiving funding was almost half the number of those in Finland (European Commission 2011, 87).

This narrower and more modest approach to technological innovation had important consequences for economic restructuring. France rivaled Sweden (but not Finland) in the growth of high-technology manufactured exports after 1980 (see table A.3), but growth was based principally on established strengths in aerospace, armaments, and nuclear power rather than fundamentally new enterprises or industries. In contrast to Finland (4.4 percent) and Sweden (4.2), which replaced manufacturing with knowledge-intensive services, the share of employment in high-technology services in France hovers at the EU average (2.8). There is also little evidence of increasing technological intensity in R&D statistics, which stagnated at approximately 2 percent of GDP after 1980 (Eurostat 2016). Of course, one accidental benefit of this was that France, like Germany, was less affected by the dot-com crisis (table A.3).

One could counter that French policy makers, like their Icelandic counterparts, were focused on expanding market competition rather than boosting innovation after 1980. Even here, however, policy making was less consistent and effective. In contrast to Finland, Sweden, and Iceland, side payments, such as the thirty-five-hour workweek, proved deeply controversial and were weakly linked to strategic objectives (Ornston and Vail 2016, 11).[9] In fact, that strategic vision was itself unclear. The same government that liberalized French financial markets in the early 1980s simultaneously sought to stabilize the industry by nationalizing vulnerable enterprises. Privatization, when it occurred, unfolded slowly and inconsistently between 1987 and 2002. Deregulation also proceeded at a more incremental pace, and France continues to exceed EU regulatory standards in several areas (Creel, Labondance, and Levasseur 2014, 64–67). This more conservative approach limited France's potential as a financial services center, particularly as it applies to investment banking. At the same time, the country's relatively diversified financial services industry has reduced its vulnerability to disruptive economic shocks (Hardie and Howarth 2009). Although not immune to problems such as the 1993 Credit Lyonnais debacle or the 2008 rogue trading incident at Société Générale, France, like Germany, has avoided a systemic banking crisis since liberalizing its financial services industry. While widely maligned for its inflexibility, France was among the least vulnerable to offshoring of high-technology industry after 2001 as well as to the 2008 credit crunch (see appendix 2).

The French case underscores the limited capacity of the state to restructure the economy without the kind of societal buy-in that existed in Sweden, Finland, and Iceland. Because of this, perhaps the United States, with its dynamic, market-based society, more closely approximates the small, open economies of Nordic Europe. This is obviously not true of policy making, where the United States is almost as incremental as Germany. The New Deal and the Great Society may have been transformative by US standards, but they were far less radical than mid-twentieth-century reforms in Finland, Sweden, and Iceland. In a comparative study of the United States and Sweden, Mark Blyth (2002, 61) describes how the expansion of the US public sector was limited in part by internal cleavages within the Democratic Party, which was sharply divided along regional, ideological, and ethnic lines. Business intransigence also blunted efforts to restructure industry through the National Industrial Recovery Act (Blyth 2002, 90).

Of course, market competition could drive restructuring in its own right, and US policies encouraged firms to adopt large-scale, capital-intensive business strategies during the interwar and postwar periods. The United States exemplified Fordism, in which large firms used economies of scale to corner the market for standardized goods (Piore and Sabel 1984). Because US policy makers never favored large firms as systematically as their Swedish (or Finnish) counterparts, however, nonagricultural self-employment remained higher in the United States (Davis and Henrekson 1997). Meanwhile, limited state intervention, a relatively light regulatory touch, and liquid equity markets created a more pluralistic environment, marked by greater turnover within the universe of large firms. In contrast to Sweden, Finland, and Iceland, where few large enterprises were established between 1945 and 1975 (and most of those were state-owned enterprises), the ranks of the Fortune 500 continually evolved. Partly as a result of this turnover, the United States was less dependent on capital-intensive heavy industries. US firms assumed a stronger position in consumer markets and high-technology industries. This diversified structure insulated it from the turmoil of the 1970s.

By the 1990s, the United States was a clear leader in the digital economy. Restructuring is less impressive, however, when one considers its advantageous starting point. The country's massive military-industrial complex had been developing cutting-edge technologies since World War II, contributing to the rise of large, established firms in a wide array of high-technology industries from aerospace to computing (Weiss 2014). Meanwhile, proximity to the largest consumer market in the world gave American firms a significant head start in technological standard-setting (Kristensen and Levinsen 1983). Finally, a massive liquid equity market created abundant exit opportunities for venture capital investors (Casper 2007a). As a result, the United States already enjoyed a large advantage in 1980. For example, the high-technology share of manufactured exports (24.0 percent) was roughly twice as high as Sweden, six times higher than Finland, and sixty times higher than Iceland (table A.3).

Despite the presence of a large, established high-technology sector, the United States was less committed to new innovation policies than Finland, Sweden, or even Iceland. Innovation policy was deeply divisive, and American policy makers instead had to rely on "hidden" institutions to funnel resources to technology-oriented firms (Block 2008). The most successful agencies were often low-profile, modestly funded organizations such as DARPA (Fuchs 2010), and the most transformative public policies were "small" initiatives such as the Small Business Innovation Research program (Keller and Block 2013). A larger commitment to innovation, much less Finnish-style coordination across multiple policy domains, was out of the question, and public R&D spending actually declined from approximately 0.7 percent of GDP in 1985 to 0.6 percent by 2000.

Of course, the United States could rely on alternative market-based mechanisms to redistribute resources to new high-technology firms. Even here, however, restructuring was more muted than one might expect, particularly when one takes the United States' starting position into account. As table A.3 relates, the high-technology share of manufactured exports increased by 160 percent between 1980 and 2000, less than Sweden (269 percent), Iceland (675 percent), or Finland (758 percent). Finland and Sweden surpassed the United States on other measures as well, particularly those related to technological innovation, including R&D expenditures as a share of GDP, population-adjusted measures of (triadic) patenting, and the share of researchers in the labor force. They even eclipsed the United States, a venture capital pioneer, in early-stage risk capital investment (Bitard, Hommen, and Novikova 2008, 515–16; Eurostat 2016; OECD 2016).

As I relate in chapter 3, rapid high-tech growth obscured important weaknesses within the Nordic region. For example, Finland and Sweden were both more specialized in a single industry, wireless communications, than the United States. They also trailed on broader measures of innovation from total venture capital investment (Cetindamar and Jacobsson 2003) to the share of the population employed in knowledge-intensive business and financial services (OECD 2016). The more gradual development of American high-technology industry created a breadth and maturity that protected the country from the dot-com crash at the turn of the millennium. Although venture capital investment plummeted, the United States could draw on a wider range of business models and had little difficulty retaining its status as a high-technology leader, even within the realm of manufacturing.

If high-technology growth is less volatile than we might assume, perhaps we might uncover evidence of Nordic-style overshooting within the financial services industry. Reform and restructuring, however, is less dramatic than one might expect. The United States not only benefited from its historical status as a liberal market economy but pursued deregulation less aggressively than its Nordic counterparts. Without denying the impact of regulatory changes such as the repeal of the Glass-Steagall Act, the United States did not actively reduce reserve requirements, nor did it ignore BIS guidelines like their Finnish and Icelandic counterparts (see chapters 3 and 4). On the contrary, some US analysts blame political gridlock, which prevented regulators from keeping pace with the rapidly evolving financial services industry, as opposed to active deregulation (Rosenthal, Poole, and McCarty 2013). This form of inaction proved deeply problematic, a reminder that polarization can be just as dangerous as excessive cohesion (see chapter 5). It does not, however, reflect Nordic-style overshooting.

If the "structural power" (Culpepper and Rienke 2014) of capital prevented US regulators from enforcing laws that were on the books, few countries ignored regulations as systematically as Iceland (Boyes 2010; Jännäri 2009, 121) or Ireland (Lavery and O'Brien 2005). This is partly because financialization occurred on an entirely different scale in the tight-knit Nordic countries (and Ireland). Finnish commentators spoke of a "Savings Bank Party," while Icelandic banks contributed over ten times as much to political campaigns (on a per capita basis) as their American counterparts (Árnason 2015, 51). Indeed, the Nordic banking bubbles and busts are less a story of "regulatory capture" than "societal capture," as financial actors penetrated the entire public sector and most societal institutions, including organized labor, the media, universities, and even (in Iceland) the arts.

These dynamics grossly inflated the size of the banking bubble. Only Finland, with its extremely underdeveloped financial system, never surpassed the United States as a banking center.[10] Sweden (temporarily) leapfrogged the United States in the share of value-added from financial intermediation in 1990 (6.9 percent), while Iceland (8.8 percent) and Ireland (10.7 percent) briefly overtook the United States in 2007. The discrepancy in bank assets was even more striking, particularly in Ireland and Iceland. Exceeding 600 percent of GDP in 2007, these countries operated in an entirely different league from the United States and eclipsed even the United Kingdom (Carey 2009).

The risks of rapid financialization were compounded by isomorphism, most notably in Iceland, but also in Finland and Ireland. In the United States, exposure varied widely. Some institutions, such as Merrill Lynch and Wachovia, were devastated by the crisis, but others, such as Bank of America and Wells Fargo, were strong enough to absorb troubled competitors. Some, most notably Goldman Sachs, had the foresight to profit from the crisis (Grunwald 2015). Similarly, real housing prices plummeted in heavily affected states such as Arizona and Florida, but decreased only modestly in regions such as Texas that were less dependent on financial services and residential construction. As a result, the direct fiscal costs of the 2007–2009 credit crunch were significantly lower in the United States (4.5 percent) than in Iceland (44.2 percent), Ireland (40.7 percent), or even 1990s Finland (12.8 percent) (Laeven and Valencia 2012, 24–26).[11]

This comparative exercise suggests that the Nordic countries adjust differently from their larger counterparts and that these differences cannot be attributed to strategic coordination, state capacity, or market competition. The Nordic countries adopted sweeping, coordinated reforms at each of the key junctures examined here. By contrast, reform-oriented actors in their larger counterparts struggled to persuade or compensate dissenters, resulting in a less sweeping institutional change in France, Germany, and the United States. The rapid diffusion of new business models enabled the Nordic countries to engineer big leaps into fundamentally new industries, whereas the large countries exhibit greater continuity. By the same token, radical reform and rapid restructuring exposed the Nordic countries to overshooting. As table A.5 demonstrates, France, Germany, and the United States were less volatile than Finland, Iceland, and Sweden.

The Politics of Interconnectedness in Large States: San Diego and Waterloo

If large countries are so different, what could policy makers, corporate executives, or individuals possibly learn from the Nordic region? Although US politicians periodically identify Denmark, Sweden, and Finland as a source of inspiration in social policy, financial regulation, and innovation policy, the preceding section demonstrates that the barriers to reform are equally conspicuous. As Peter Katzenstein (1985, 209) originally recognized, however, a different picture may prevail locally. At the municipal or regional level, elites (and masses) are more likely to interact on a regular basis, developing bonds that transcend linguistic, religious, ethnic, and sectoral cleavages.

Just as not all small states are characterized by cohesive, encompassing networks, this is not true of all regions. Large metropolitan areas such as Atlanta, Los Angeles, and Toronto may resemble Finland in population, but their social fabric is very different. Metropolitan Atlanta, where I started this book, is still characterized by sharp racial and socioeconomic divisions (Pomerantz 1996). In the Toronto metropolitan region, where I completed it, a highly pluralistic community complicates efforts to develop a consistent long-term plan for even the most basic collective goods such as transportation infrastructure (Bramwell and Wolfe 2014). Similar dynamics prevail in Los Angeles, which has been criticized for failing to foster a clearer collective identity or developmental strategy (Storper et al. 2015). Even small and medium-sized cities vary in the breadth and quality of their social connections. In Sean Safford's landmark study (2009, 93–95), Youngstown, Ohio, had a population of just 500,000 but lacked the civic institutions to connect different industries and socioeconomic classes.

Other regions, however, are characterized by high-quality social ties that transcend sectoral and social cleavages. This is particularly evident in the rich literature on European industrial districts. Regions such as northern Italy (Locke 1995), southwestern Germany (Schmitz 1991), and mainland Denmark (Kristensen 1999) are characterized by dense interfirm linkages that extend to organized labor, knowledge-bearing institutions, and local government. Much like their national counterparts, these cohesive, encompassing relationships permit investment in a wide variety of sophisticated goods. They are also conceptualized as an incremental force. European industrial districts are generally perceived to rely on incremental upmarket movement within established niches such as textiles (Locke 1995) or automobiles (Schmitz 1991) rather than engineering big leaps into new industries. When confronted by disruptive shocks, such as the OPEC oil crisis and shifting patterns of international competition in the 1970s, these "strong ties" led to functional, cognitive, and political lock-in (Grabher 1993, 260–64).

The Nordic experience suggests that one could conceptualize these cohesive networks differently, as a resource that can accelerate restructuring rather than inhibiting it. In Aalborg, Denmark, for example, entrepreneurial firms used dense interpersonal connections to transition from shipbuilding into mobile communications, transforming the North Jutland region from one of the least research-intensive metropolitan regions in Denmark into a "digital lighthouse" (Dahl, Pedersen, and Dalum 2003; Ornston 2012b, 112–18; Østergaard and Park 2015; Stoerring and Dalum 2007). Even Gernot Grabher's (1993, 266–68) influential study of regional "lock-in" comments on the speed with which firms adapted once confronted with clear and undeniable evidence of structural decline. Although adjustment was delayed, by the late 1980s firms across the board had abandoned steel manufacturing, instead positioning themselves as specialists in clean technology. Of course, the Ruhr region, like Aalborg, is a coordinated market economy, characterized by long-term strategic cooperation among producers, knowledge-bearing institutions, organized labor, and local policy makers. For a more demanding test of whether this argument about dense interpersonal networks can be extended to large countries, we should examine an environment where Nordic-style cooperation is least likely. Do the politics of interconnectedness extend to a highly pluralistic liberal market economy such as the United States?

As noted above, American cities such as Atlanta, Los Angeles, and Youngstown bear little resemblance to Nordic Europe. Other American communities, however, are characterized by a dense network of civic associations that connect elites (and ordinary citizens) from a wide variety of economic sectors (Safford 2009). Like European industrial districts, these high-trust relationships support investment in a variety of collective goods (Putnam 2000), albeit perhaps not the kinds of specialized inputs that characterize Aalborg and the Ruhr region (Ornston and Schulze-Cleven 2015). Until recently, these ties were perceived to stifle restructuring (Florida 2002). For example, Silicon Valley's success has been attributed to its fiercely competitive, atomistic culture rather than high levels of social capital (Cohen and Fields 2000). More recent scholarship has questioned these claims, however, noting that dense social networks can represent a source of dynamism when these ties bridge sectoral and socioeconomic cleavages (Safford 2009; Storper et al. 2015). The Nordic cases support this second interpretation, with the caveat that these relationships can also contribute to overshooting (see below).

San Diego, California, exemplifies these dense, widely distributed networks. Scholars describe high levels of social capital, a strong capacity for cross-sectoral collaboration, and a clear, collective vision for the future (Walshok and Shragge 2014). Instead of inhibiting restructuring, these ties have enabled the city to "reinvent" itself over time, evolving from a peripheral backwater to a military installation, a defense contractor, and, eventually, a leading innovator in consumer markets (Walshok and Shragge 2014).[12] This pattern of collaboration was visible as early as 1900, when the mayor, the city council, and the entire Chamber of Commerce focused on the United States Navy as "clean" way to develop their rural community, without jeopardizing either its natural beauty or its white Protestant values. The successful campaign, which spanned two decades, was a study in coordination, from the receptions hosted in the houses of wealthy elites to the 1915 Panama-California Exposition and the donation drives to purchase land for the naval base. Subjected to popular vote in 1919, the proposed transactions passed by a 100:1 margin (Walshok and Shragge 2014, 38–46). The naval base transformed a town hitherto dependent on tourism and fishing, sustaining it during the Great Depression and radically transforming it during World War II. Following an exceptionally severe recession from 1946 to 1950, the city upgraded its position as a defense contractor with a coordinated campaign to invest in research infrastructure, most notably the University of California at San Diego (UCSD) (Walshok and Shragge 2014, 68–81).

These investments enabled San Diego to flourish in the early postwar period. This defense-led growth strategy, however, was clearly exhausted by the early 1980s. Compounded by the virtual disappearance of traditional stalwarts such as fishing and aerospace, growth stagnated and unemployment approached 10 percent in 1984. The city's poor economic performance reflected its unbalanced industrial structure. Unlike Boston or Silicon Valley, the city possessed virtually no high-technology enterprises as recently as the late 1970s (Casper 2007b, 443). Although San Diego hosted numerous defense contractors, it suffered from a dearth of new firms and was poorly positioned to service consumer markets. The small and medium-sized enterprises that did exist lacked the absorptive capacity and supporting infrastructure to commercialize new technologies developed at UCSD (Walshok and Shragge 2014, 124–28). For example, the region possessed no major venture capital funds or intellectual property firms (Walshok and Shragge 2014, 137). It was not impossible to launch a new growth-oriented firm in this environment, but it was a risky, "hit-or-miss" proposition. The region's first biotechnology firm, Hybritech, established in 1978, had to import venture capital and managerial expertise from outside the region to succeed (Walshok and Shragge 2014, 134–35).

Together with a handful of other start-ups, however, Hybritech transformed San Diego. The firm's acquisition by Eli Lilly in 1986 was a game-changer. Although it never constructed a dense network of subcontractors such as Nokia and languished under Eli Lilly, the firm's success inspired others to follow in its footsteps. The number of biotechnology firms increased from seven in 1983 to thirty-eight by 1989 (Casper 2007b, 446). In addition to encouraging entrepreneurs to commercialize breakthrough innovations at UCSD, Hybritech and its early successors transformed workplace norms. Within the span of a decade, job-hopping became socially acceptable and employees no longer aspired to work at large, stable firms. By the 2000s, San Diego still depended on federal funding but was no longer defined by defense. Instead, it had established itself as one of the largest biotechnology clusters in the United States (Casper 2007b), flanked by strengths in wireless communications and other high-technology industries (Walshok and Shragge 2014, 146).

Although Hybritech played an instrumental role in transforming the corporate ecosystem in San Diego, high-technology industry was also embraced and supported by policy makers, university leaders, and local industrialists. For example, local policy makers, with broad industry support, partnered with the university to launch UCSD CONNECT in 1985. The networking initiative diffused knowledge about how to conduct business, connected start-ups to supporting resources such as risk capital, experienced management, and IP lawyers, publicized high-technology "success stories," and advertised the region's accomplishments to the rest of the world (Walshok and Shragge 2014, 135–44). In addition to these direct contributions, the program's perceived success placed San Diego on the map as a high-technology hub.

Over the course of the twentieth century, San Diego had transformed itself from a conservative military town into a high-technology hub with a "civic culture of innovation" (Walshok and Shragge 2014, 138). Naturally, the town benefited from its position in a liberal market economy, but scholars also highlight the importance of dense interpersonal networks, connecting not only high-technology firms but also academics, supporting services, policy makers, and civic associations such as the Chamber of Commerce. These actors claim that they were connected by strong ties, repeatedly emphasizing the region's culture of trust and mutual support (Walshok and Shragge 2014, 138). That sense of trust, in turn, reflected a clear collective vision of what the community should look like, shaped by common challenges and painful failures during the early 1980s (Casper 2007b; Walshok and Shragge 2014).

Not all US regions resemble San Diego in the breadth and quality of their social ties (see above), but the city is not an outlier. Comparative studies of Silicon Valley and Los Angeles suggest that cross-cutting social ties and a strong sense of collective identity enabled the former to penetrate new industries in ways that the latter could not (Storper et al. 2015). Similarly, Allentown, Pennsylvania, leveraged cross-cutting interpersonal networks to shift from steel into new, high-technology industries, while communities with more brittle structures such as Youngstown struggled to adapt (Safford 2009). Of course, one could argue it is easier for regions to enter new high-technology industries in the United States, with its large military (Weiss 2014). San Diego certainly benefited from massive public investment, from the US Navy in the early 1900s to generous federal research funding in the 2000s (Walshok and Shragge 2013).

Similar dynamics prevail in Canada, however, a country with a relatively small military, modestly funded innovation policies, and a historically weak position in high-technology markets. Like the United States the country is fragmented into regional business systems, with little evidence of Nordic-style cohesion in either politics or business. This characterization does not extend to the Waterloo region, however. Approximately one hundred kilometers west of Toronto with a population of roughly 500,000, the region is connected by a dense, century-old network of economic, educational, and civic associations (Nelles, Bramwell, and Wolfe 2005, 233). These interpersonal ties have fostered a strong sense of collective identity. Dubbed the "Waterloo way," this identity celebrates collaboration, as exemplified by ubiquitous references to its German heritage and collective "barn-building" campaigns (Nelles 2014, 94).

Until recently one might have claimed that these dense social ties delayed the pace of adjustment. The Waterloo region had a reputation as a conservative, albeit high-end manufacturing center (Leibovitz 2003, 2622). As recently as the 1970s the community was best known for its strengths in textiles, rubber, plastics, metalworking, machinery, and automotive components, as well as insurance, rather than high-technology industry (Munro and Bathelt 2014, 221). In the case of Waterloo, restructuring was driven less by an economic crisis than the introduction of an entrepreneurial actor, the University of Waterloo. Established as part of a coordinated regional scheme to upgrade production, the university sought to distinguish itself from more established Canadian competitors by focusing on new high-technology markets (Ornston 2016, 16).

WATCOM, a 1974 spinoff, represented a watershed moment in the development of the local high-technology industry. Like Hybritech in San Diego, the firm did not construct a Nokia-like network of subcontractors in the region, but it did present local industrialists, as well as university students, with an alternative to traditional manufacturing, inspiring successful high-technology start-ups such as OpenText and Research in Motion (RIM) in the 1980s (Munro and Bathelt 2014, 238). As these firms flourished, the University of Waterloo was quick to publicize their achievements. University administrators branded the region an innovation hub in the 1990s and adapted the curriculum to emphasize entrepreneurship. Individual professors traced the evolution of the local high-technology "cluster" and, in so doing, gave it a distinct identity (Bramwell and Wolfe 2008, 1184; Nelles, Bramwell, and Wolfe 2005, 241).

By the 1990s, these efforts had diffused beyond the university and a handful of entrepreneurs to encompass local government and industry. Regional policy makers established "Canada's Technology Triangle" in 1987 to publicize the region's status as a hotbed for technological innovation (Leibovitz 2003, 2622), while an industry association, Communitech, followed in 1998 (Nelles, Bramwell, and Wolfe 2005, 247). Communitech, in particular, emerged as a powerful focal point for discussion and coordination. Policy makers scrambled to tie themselves to the organization, while local firms felt pressure to join in order to signal their status as serious businesses (Leibovitz 2003, 2632–35). Much like UCSD CONNECT, Communitech inspired local entrepreneurs and successfully marketed the region to federal policy makers and external investors. As a result, the region was able to attract federal and provincial funds, as well as significant foreign direct investment (Bramwell, Nelles, and Wolfe 2008, 113; Bramwell and Wolfe 2008, 1178).

Like San Diego, economic adjustment was characterized by big leaps into new industries rather than the modernization of established ones. By the beginning of the twenty-first century, Waterloo was known as one of the most knowledge-intensive regions in Canada. Although heavily dependent on Research in Motion, the region hosted roughly five hundred high-technology firms, employing over twenty-five thousand workers (Bramwell, Nelles, and Wolfe 2008, 102). High-technology entrepreneurs did not perceive dense social networks as liabilities but rather as assets, accelerating the diffusion of new business models, facilitating the construction of infrastructure, and more effectively marketing the region to external investors (Nelles 2014).

This brief analysis of San Diego and Waterloo suggests that small and medium-sized cities can learn several lessons from the Nordic countries, even when situated within large and relatively fragmented nation-states. By shifting our focus from neocorporatist institutions and interfirm coordination to the less formal ties that bind actors in small states, we can identify parallels in small, highly interconnected communities. This does not apply to all regions (see above), and municipalities clearly lack the fiscal and regulatory tools of a nation-state (Ornston 2016), but tight-knit communities still can use cohesive, encompassing networks to adapt to disruptive economic shocks. Moreover, these case studies demonstrate that tight-knit relationships are more dynamic than we commonly recognize. Far from delaying the pace of restructuring, reform-oriented actors used widely distributed networks to more rapidly diffuse and scale new business models in San Diego and Waterloo. Clearly, policy makers and entrepreneurs in these communities are not confined to the incremental modernization of established industries.

At the same time, the Nordic experience suggests that a strong capacity for collective action can lead to too much change, contributing to policy overshooting and overinvestment. A single technological innovation, the iPhone, also threatened Waterloo, where RIM represented an even larger share of local ICT employment than did Nokia in Finland (Ornston 2017, 8). Although an impressive constellation of start-ups stabilized employment after the flagship firm declined, local observers have expressed concerns about the sustainability, if credit conditions tighten, of these young enterprises heavily dependent on venture funding (interview with journalist, 15 May 2016, Canada). Even San Diego, which appears to have reached the critical mass that enables it to automatically attract financial and human capital (Storper and Venables 2004), struggled in earlier decades. Defense-dependent San Diego was one of the hardest-hit American cities after World War II, as growth stagnated for five years (Walshok and Shragge 2014, 68). The region's sudden emergence as a high-technology cluster was inspired by Silicon Valley's success, but it also reflected an acute sense of crisis, as dependence on large defense contractors left the city with few alternative options during the recession of the 1980s (Walshok and Shragge 2014, 96).

This volatility underscores the danger of tight-knit networks and rapid restructuring more generally. Cohesive and encompassing networks may be hailed as a source of prosperity (Putnam 1993) and dynamism (Storper et al. 2015), but they do not inoculate communities from economic crises and can increase the risk of overshooting. Radical reform and rapid restructuring are often depicted as the best response to contemporary economic challenges such as globalization and technological change, but they can create as many problems as they solve. San Diego and Waterloo both used cohesive, encompassing networks to engineer Nordic-style leaps into new industries, but rapid restructuring also exposed them to new risks.

At the same time, there are several reasons to believe these risks are less pronounced at the municipal level. Perhaps most obviously, the limited number of policy levers in play diminishes the risk of policy overshooting and reduces the resources that can be mobilized around a single firm, industry, or business model. RIM may have dominated the Waterloo region, to the point where civic leaders felt pressured to carry Blackberry phones and defend the firm against negative press (interview with former policy maker, 7 March 2016, Canada), but the risks of state capture were significantly lower. RIM used its clout to influence land use and refashion the curriculum at the University of Waterloo. Unlike Nokia, however, its influence over federal and provincial policies such as innovation and immigration was more muted (Ornston 2017).

In fact, federal and provincial funding can act as an important buffer against overshooting. Unlike the Nordic countries, the largest public programs in cities such as San Diego and Waterloo were externally funded. For example, although RIM and its employees donated generously to the University of Waterloo, the institution was never seriously threatened by the firm's decline. Provincial funding and tuition revenue enabled the university to play a stabilizing role, not only as an employer but also by supporting student start-ups (Bramwell and Wolfe 2008). Even in San Diego, where defense cutbacks triggered severe recessions, income taxes and transfer payments represented an important counterweight, insulating citizens from the worst effects of overshooting (Walshok and Shragge 2014). Because these programs were administered by state- and federal-level actors, they were less vulnerable to local booms and busts.

Finally, cities benefit from labor mobility. Finns, Icelanders, and Swedes have left their countries to pursue better economic opportunities abroad, but inter-municipal labor mobility is naturally higher. When confronted with a disruptive economic shock, workers can move to a more prosperous region without securing a visa or learning a new language. This is not unproblematic. The decline of Detroit and other rust belt cities illustrates how brain drain and capital flight can send municipalities into a near-terminal spiral. This is a painful process for local policy makers tasked with managing decline and citizens who do not or cannot move, but the divergent fates of Europe and the United States after 2008 illustrate how labor mobility can reduce the human cost of a recession in hard-hit regions (Krugman 2013).[13] To the extent that this is true, it suggests that the benefits of replicating Nordic-style cooperation may outweigh the costs.

Lessons for Nordic Europe?

Unfortunately, the stabilizing forces that buffer municipalities during economic crises do not protect sovereign states. Where does that leave the Nordic countries? To the extent that policy makers are concerned about the region's volatile economic history, what can they do to reduce the risk of policy overshooting and overinvestment? There are several options but no easy solutions. Recent literature on institutional change suggests that policy makers can cultivate new ideas by creating small agencies to develop new policy instruments and business models. These "Schumpeterian developmental agencies" can use their low profile to experiment with fundamentally new business models, which may be embraced by mainstream policy makers or corporate executives (Breznitz and Ornston 2013). In Finland, for example, the public think tank Sitra piloted the new technology policies and venture capital investments that were later scaled by policy makers (Breznitz and Ornston forthcoming).

This process of under-the-radar experimentation may enable small countries to respond more effectively to disruptive shocks, but it does not necessarily ameliorate the pattern of overshooting articulated in this book. Although Sitra was able to present Finnish policy makers with tried and tested alternatives that accelerated the adoption of new innovation policies in the early 1980s and 1990s, these innovations were not embraced until after Finland had experienced a clear crisis. For example, the reports that Sitra issued during the late 1960s and 1970s, criticizing Finnish reliance on heavy industry and appealing for greater investment in R&D, were largely ignored until dependence on the Soviet Union was recognized as an existential threat in the early 1980s (Breznitz and Ornston forthcoming). In short, Schumpeterian developmental agencies may represent a valuable addition to a national innovation system (Karo and Kattel 2016), but they are not well equipped to combat policy overshooting and overinvestment.

A second, more radical solution to policy overshooting and overinvestment is political decentralization. Decentralizing authority to regional actors, introducing more veto points into government, or constraining the power of the state could reduce the coordinated policy shifts that increase dependence on a single business model, industry, or even firm. It would also ameliorate the kinds of "state capture" that contributed to overshooting in Finland and Iceland. In chapter 5 I describe how Switzerland, an extreme case of political decentralization, has resisted exaggerated policy shifts, from the turn to the state in the early postwar period (Immergut 1992) to the recent trend toward liberalization (Merrien and Becker 2005).

But political decentralization has its disadvantages. Chapter 5 also illustrates how too much decentralization can reduce a country's capacity to grapple with disruptive economic shocks. This was particularly clear in Greece and Portugal. Even Switzerland is not a paragon of flexible reform and its prosperity depends on its capacity to defend and upgrade relatively stable, centuries-old niches. Moreover, in chapter 4 I demonstrate that a key challenge for tight-knit communities is societal capture. In Iceland a handful of banks not only influenced policy making but transformed business models in traditional industries, controlled the media, and even penetrated seemingly unrelated spheres such as the arts. Political decentralization, by itself, is unlikely to eliminate these social dynamics and may make it even harder for policy makers to keep pace with rapid social change (Rosenthal, Poole, and McCarty 2013).

Any effort to combat Icelandic-style overshooting would likely have to go even further, decentralizing and diversifying decision making at all levels of society.[14] Luxembourg provides a blueprint of what this might look like. Situated in between Belgium, France, and Germany, the multilingual duchy of half a million people has long been penetrated by a variety of external influences. The duchy hosts numerous international organizations, while half the population is foreign-born (Powell 2013, 105). This was partly an accident of history, but it was also a strategic decision. Luxembourg's innovation policy, for example, has explicitly and relentlessly prioritized diversification, often at the expense of efficiency (Meyer 2008, 366). Until recently residents were sent abroad to pursue post-secondary education at a variety of institutions in several countries. The new national university has not fundamentally altered these dynamics by pursuing a highly internationalized strategy. Luxembourg's "hyper-diverse" society (Powell 2014) has also nurtured a surprisingly diverse economy. The country successfully, and relatively smoothly, transformed itself from a steel producer into a financial services hub and ICT producer over the course of the twentieth century (Powell 2013, 105).

The Nordic countries may already be moving in this direction, propelled less by deliberate policy choices than the gradual and cumulative impact of internationalization. Three interrelated changes are contributing to greater fragmentation in the Nordic region. First, technological innovation and internationalization have made it easier for firms to bypass national institutions altogether, securing not just clients but also financing, human capital, and managerial expertise from abroad (Herrmann 2009). Entrepreneurial software firms in Finland, for example, are significantly less wedded to national institutions than traditional manufacturing firms or even large high-technology enterprises such as Nokia (Ornston 2014). Although the sentiment was not universal, several executives claimed that they hardly ever interact with their Finnish colleagues, preferring to network at a global level (interviews with software executives 31 October 2005, and 23 November 2006, Finland). This is increasingly true of top-level firms as well. An innovation policy veteran glumly concluded:

> Ten years ago, you could have gotten all the major Finnish CEOs together to draft a joint letter about [this problem], but nowadays it doesn't work. . . . For example, the CEO of [leading Finnish firm] is too focused on China to think about Finnish innovation policy. (interview with former secretary, Science and Technology Policy Council, 7 June 2016, Finland)

Second, immigration is transforming hitherto homogeneous societies. Sweden's transformation to a multicultural society began decades ago, immigration is now reshaping Finland, and it may eventually transform Iceland as well. To the extent that immigrants are incorporated into decision-making circles, including policy formulation, corporate decision making, and media production, they may reduce the risk of overshooting and overinvestment by challenging dominant narratives and advancing alternative ideas. For example, Walshok and Shragge argue that San Diego's ability to develop a highly diversified high-technology base rested in large measure on its ability to attract and incorporate migrants from across the country and the world in a wide variety of sectors, most notably through the University of California at San Diego (Walshok and Shragge 2014).

Immigration may also reduce the risk of policy overshooting and overinvestment in other, less sanguine ways. The rise of populist right-wing parties in Finland and Sweden represents the third shift in the politics of these historically tightly knit societies (Nordensvard and Ketola 2015). Their brash, confrontational style has strained solidaristic social commitments, complicated consensual political processes, and it reflects the broader breakdown of the cohesive, encompassing, neocorporatist institutions that governed postwar adjustment (Lindvall and Sebring 2005). Considered collectively, it marks a clear, if gradual, shift away from the cohesive and encompassing networks that historically characterized the Nordic region.

The evolution of the Nordic region into a more diverse, contentious place is often portrayed as a negative development, not only weakening social solidarity (Nordensvard and Ketola 2015, 371; Pelkonen 2008, 412) but directly threatening the high-quality governance that underpins Nordic prosperity (Campbell and Hall 2009, 565; Putnam 2007, 157). This book presents a more nuanced picture, in which greater fragmentation and polarization could erode reform capacity, but also mute the exaggerated policy reforms and sharp shifts in corporate sentiment that caused so much volatility in the past. Although corporate elites may be less committed to national institutions than they were in the past, their willingness to experiment with heterodox business models could play an important stabilizing role. To the extent that immigrants view national narratives through a more skeptical lens, they might also be less likely to get caught up in the collective hysteria that marked Nokia's rise or Iceland's short-lived reign as a financial powerhouse. Political polarization is rarely perceived as a positive development, but it probably would have reduced Sweden's dependence on large capital-intensive enterprises in the early postwar period.

Of course, the gradual transformation of Finland, Sweden, and Iceland into more diverse, less cohesive societies is not without its risks. As noted above, the same dynamics that mute policy overshooting and overinvestment simultaneously weaken the reform capacity that enables these countries to respond so effectively to disruptive economic shocks. These societies are unlikely to descend into Greek-style polarization, but the margin for error is also lower in a more globalized, faster-paced international economy. Perhaps the clearest lesson from the Nordic region is that good governance remains an elusive goal. Without denying the negative impact of crony capitalism in other regions, the Nordic experience suggests that even the best-governed societies are vulnerable to economic crises. In other words, volatility is not a bug to be eliminated with judicious reform but rather an intrinsic feature of contemporary capitalism.

Appendix 1

MEASURING COHESIVE, ENCOMPASSING NETWORKS

Scholars have long claimed that the Nordic countries are characterized by unusually cohesive and encompassing networks (Campbell and Hall 2017, 34; Rothstein and Stolle 2003, 1). Networks are "cohesive" in the sense that actors trust one another and cooperation is relatively easy to establish. They are also "encompassing" in that relationships span different social groups. The measurement of these cohesive, encompassing relationships is not a straightforward task. This appendix reviews three quantitative approaches—neocorporatism, coordination, and network analysis—before introducing the methodology that underpins this book.

The first efforts to characterize cohesive, encompassing networks were associated with neocorporatism, a formal system of interest intermediation characterized by large, encompassing producer associations, specifically trade unions and employer associations (Goldthorpe 1984; Schmitter and Lehmbruch 1979). Neocorporatist indices proliferated after the concept was popularized in the 1970s. By 2003 Lane Kenworthy (2003) had identified no fewer than forty-two separate measures. In lieu of a comprehensive review, table A.1 presents data on trade union density or the share of the workforce affiliated with a trade union (Visser 2015). Column 1 demonstrates that the Nordic countries are clear outliers in their capacity to integrate workers and firms within encompassing producer associations.

These unions are also incorporated into economic and political decision making, which connects them to policy makers as well as employers. Column 2

APPENDIX 1

TABLE A.1 Conceptualizing Cohesive, Encompassing Networks

	TRADE UNION DENSITY (1991–2010)[i]	MACRO-CORPORATISM (1980–2000)[ii]	INTERLOCKING DIRECTORATES (2005)[iii]	AVERAGE SOCIAL TRUST (2004)[iv]
Primary Cases: Finland, Iceland, and Sweden				
Finland	74.8	0.57	0.21	6.4
Iceland	89.1	—	[0.33][v]	6.4
Sweden	79.0	0.79	0.22	6.1
Shadow Cases: Estonia and Ireland				
Estonia	20.1	—	—	5.2
Ireland	39.3	—	0.12	5.9
Contrasting Cases: Large States				
France	8.2	–0.41	0.24	4.5
Germany	25.2	0.21	0.43	4.8
United States	—	–1.56	—	—
Contrasting Cases: Central Europe				
Austria	36.4	0.23	0.15	5.1
Switzerland	20.4	–0.16	—	5.7
Contrasting Cases: Southern Europe				
Greece	27.1	—	0.07	3.9
Portugal	22.9	—	0.04	3.9

[i] Visser 2015.
[ii] Martin and Swank 2012.
[iii] Veen and Kratzer 2011.
[iv] European Social Survey 2004.
[v] Baldvinsdóttir 1998.

presents Martin and Swank's measure of "macro-corporatism," which includes employer as well as trade union organization and their functional incorporation into collective bargaining and policy formulation. Although the data are less comprehensive, the Nordic countries again rank high, not only into relation to pluralist societies such as the United States but also relative to highly centralized, statist countries such as France, where the strong esprit de corps that unites the senior civil service does not appear to extend to civil society as a whole. For this reason, several scholars have used the concept of neocorporatism to distinguish the highly interconnected small states of Nordic Europe from their larger, more fragmented counterparts (Katzenstein 1985; Pekkarinen, Pohjola, and Rowthorn 1992).

Although neocorporatism captures an important element of interconnectedness and I draw on this in the case studies, it is an incomplete measure of cohesive, encompassing networks. Most importantly, this emphasis on producer associations and industrial relations provides only limited insight into the inter-firm dynamics that govern the diffusion of new business models. This is not to deny that trade unions play an important role in economic restructuring by embracing technological change, lobbying for supportive policies, or blocking restructuring. For example, they facilitated the adoption of the postwar Swedish model and feature prominently in chapter 2. But they are rarely the driving force behind corporate strategy, particularly as it relates to recent developments such as the growth of high-technology industry or the financialization of the economy. This critique also extends to indicators such as "employer organization" (Martin and Swank 2012, 16–17), which are based principally on industrial relations and consequently yield limited insight into the relationships that facilitate (or inhibit) the diffusion of new ideas within the business community.

Precisely because of these shortcomings, the Varieties of Capitalism literature has emerged as a popular alternative to neocorporatism, distinguishing between arm's-length market competition and long-term strategic "coordination" (Hall and Soskice 2001, 8). This literature speaks more directly to corporate strategy by focusing on interfirm relations. Aggregated measures of coordination, however, are a poor proxy for small state networks for several reasons. In attempting to capture a particular pattern of capitalist relations, scholars have included measures such as stock market capitalization as a share of GDP, labor-market turnover, and the share of university graduates (Hall and Gingerich 2009, 456; Witt and Jackson 2016, 791–92). There is no question that these institutional features influence corporate strategy, but they are only loosely related to the concept of cohesive, encompassing networks.

To address this issue, we must disaggregate measures of coordination to focus on those components that specifically address interfirm relations. Recent advances in network analysis represent one promising way to do so by capturing the density of interlocking directorates or overlapping board memberships. Comprehensive cross-national data is scarce, but column 3 presents data on the density of interlocking directorates in the largest publicly listed firms in eight European countries (Veen and Kratzer 2011, 9). Although not directly comparable, the column also includes data from 1995 on the thirty largest publicly listed firms in Iceland (Baldvinsdóttir 1998, 233). This analysis suggests that the cohesive, encompassing relationships described above are not limited to industrial relations but also extend to interfirm relations.

At the same time, data on interlocking directorates (and coordination more generally) suffers from several shortcomings. First, measures of network density are not particularly sensitive to the geographical or sectoral scope of coordination. For example, some countries such as Italy rank high on measures of interlocking directorates (as well as coordination) but are characterized by competing regional orders rather than cohesive, encompassing national-level networks (Trigilia and Burroni 2009, 631). Coordination is similarly segmented in central European economies such as Austria, Germany, and Switzerland, albeit along sectoral rather than regional lines (Kitschelt et al. 1999, 434). The Nordic countries are distinct in the national scope of coordination. Unfortunately, efforts to distinguish between "sectoral" or "enterprise" level coordination and national coordination rely heavily on labor-market indicators and effectively reproduce the literature on neocorporatism above (Baccaro and Howell 2011, 130; Martin and Swank 2012, 16–17; Martin and Thelen 2007, 7).

Second, the density of interlocking directorates is heavily influenced by the legal system, which has evolved independently from cohesive and encompassing networks. Historically, Finland and Sweden were characterized by bank-based financial systems with weak shareholder protection. This enabled "stakeholders" to assemble firms into the "industrial families" in chapter 2 and the beginning of chapter 3. In 1976, for example, Finland (5%) exceeded West Germany (4%), Austria (3%), Switzerland (3%), France (3%), and the United States (3%) in measures of network density (Stokman and Wasseur 1985, 26).[1] The banking crises of the early 1990s, however, destroyed several leading "industrial families" in Finland and Sweden. It also led to regulatory reforms that advantaged minority shareholders over stakeholders (Hyytinen, Kuosa, and Takalo 2003, 74–80). By contrast, the higher density of interlocking directorates in France and Germany is partly a function of their economic and political stability.

Finally and perhaps most importantly, a narrow focus on interlocking directorates obscures the other ways in which individuals and firms are connected within Nordic Europe. In Finland, interviewees were more likely to credit idiosyncratic institutions such as Sitra's economic courses or Tekes's research consortia with the diffusion of new ideas rather than joint membership in corporate boards (see chapter 3). This is even more true of Iceland, where even less structured relationships connect different actors. For example, a study of interlocking directorates in the Icelandic financial services industry in the 1990s found that virtually *all* bank managers were connected when family ties were included (Baldvinsdóttir 1998, 68). This speaks to a broader problem with neocorporatism and coordination. Although all indicators suggest that the Nordic countries are highly interconnected, this emphasis on formal institutions fails to capture the informal ties that play such an important role in the small states of northwestern Europe (Campbell and Hall 2017, 34; Katzenstein 1985, 89; Rehn 1996, 234). Even recent advances in network analysis have not fully addressed this issue, as efforts to analyze civic associations focus on formal board membership (Safford 2009, 75) rather than the informal friendships or kinship ties that characterize small states such as Finland or Iceland.

The fourth column attempts to capture these informal ties with a measure of generalized social trust. Specifically, it presents responses, organized on a ten-point scale, to the claim that "people can generally be trusted" (European Social

Survey 2004). The data suggest that the connections that characterize Nordic Europe are not limited to peak- or elite-level institutions such as neocorporatist committees or corporate boards. They also speak to the quality of these relationships, suggesting that the encompassing ties in Nordic Europe are also relatively cohesive, characterized by a high level of trust.[2] Generalized social trust is still limited, however, in that it does not tell us much about the specific formal or informal ties that connect actors or the ways these ties shape economic adjustment.

To explore this, I complement these quantitative cross-national statistics with two additional sources of information. First, I use a comprehensive literature review to characterize relations in my twelve case studies (three main cases and nine shadow cases). This analysis addresses ties between different socioeconomic classes. Even more importantly, it focuses on interfirm relations and the extent to which these ties transcend regional, political, and sectoral cleavages. These findings are summarized in the first section of each case study, where I also acknowledge any discrepancies among my sources.

Second, I draw on original fieldwork. Between 2005 and 2016, I conducted 335 interviews as part of a series of projects on the politics of economic adjustment in Finland (117), Sweden (85), Ireland (90), Iceland (30), Portugal (9), and Greece (4). Because these interviews addressed sensitive issues, including corporate strategy and economic policy, many respondents requested anonymity. To accommodate this, I have stripped any identifying information from this book and provide only the general position, type of organization, date, and general location of each interview. Collectively, the interviews engaged a wide range of stakeholders, including academic experts, journalists, politicians, policy makers, trade union leaders, and representatives from several different industries (both high-tech and traditional), enabling me to characterize cross-class, private-public, and interfirm relations.

These interviews offered several advantages over the formal indicators above. First, they were particularly useful in characterizing informal relationships. Several Finns, for example, objected to an initial question about their "country" by noting that it was better analyzed as a "club" (interviews with journalist, 9 November 2005; official, Ministry of Finance, 11 June 2012; and former director, Pellervo, 12 June 2012, Finland). Several Irish interviewees advanced a similar argument, differing only in the decision to characterize their community as a "village" rather than a "club" (interview, former board member, financial services firm, 4 July 2012, Ireland). As the case studies relate, these interviewees continued by identifying the specific, often idiosyncratic institutions and relationships that connect different actors in their society. Second, interviews capture the quality of a relationship and the type of information being exchanged. For this reason, scholars often rely on this type of data to complement formal network analysis (Baldvinsdóttir 1998, 124–25). Finally, they permitted process tracing, testing the causal mechanisms that connect tight-knit interpersonal networks to reform, restructuring, and, ultimately, overshooting. The case studies draw on this interview data to test claims about the politics of persuasion, compensation, and coordination.

Skeptical readers might question whether individual quotes in this book accurately reflect my entire sample. To address this, it is possible to conduct a content analysis of the interviews that I conducted for this book. In my latest round of fieldwork, I opened each interview with the hypothesis that in small states "everyone knows everyone and cooperation is relatively easy to establish." Table A.2 presents this data, including 28 interviews in Finland (2012), 4 in Greece (2016), 30 in Iceland (2012 and 2016), 18 in Ireland (2012), 9 in Portugal (2012), and 22 in Sweden (2012). I do not include fieldwork from before 2012 or my 2016 interviews in Finland. Although small-state networks emerged as an important theme in these discussions, these interviews were conducted for other projects and often focused on other aspects of economic adjustment. These results would bias figures downward, most notably in Finland, where I conducted 89 additional interviews on related topics without explicitly asking about small state networks.[3]

The first column of table A.2 presents the share of interviewees who agreed that the claim above (everyone knows everyone and cooperation is relatively easy to establish) was an accurate characterization of their society. To be coded positively, an interviewee needed to specify that their society was different from large industrialized economies such as France, Germany, or the United States.[4] Second,

TABLE A.2 "Everyone Knows Everyone and Cooperation Is Relatively Easy to Establish"

	AGREE	DISAGREE
Iceland	23/30	2/30
	(77%)	(7%)
Ireland	13/18	2/18
	(72%)	(11%)
Finland	20/28	3/28
	(71%)	(11%)
Sweden	11/22	5/22
	(50%)	(18%)
Portugal	1/9	5/9
	(11%)	(56%)
Greece	0/4	3/4
	(0%)	(75%)

they needed to provide a specific and relevant example of these tight-knit networks.[5] Interviewees who specifically disagreed with this claim were coded negatively and appear in column 2 of table A.2. These individuals either argued that their country was relatively fragmented and polarized or insisted that it was no different from a large society such as Germany or the United States. Respondents who agreed with this statement but could not provide relevant examples or did not connect this to economic outcomes were coded neutrally. For clarity, these remaining responses are not presented in table A.2.

Although I did not conduct fieldwork in Austria, Estonia, France, Germany, Switzerland, or the United States, and the sample size for Southern Europe is extremely limited, the data in table A.2 support the characterization of the small states in this book. At least half of the interviewees in Finland, Iceland, Ireland, and Sweden agreed with the claim that "everyone knows everyone and cooperation is relatively easy to establish," whereas hardly anyone did in Greece and Portugal. Consistent with my categorization of the Nordic cases, Iceland appears to be the most tight-knit society. By contrast, fewer Swedish interviewees agreed with this claim and many who did were unable to furnish concrete examples. Finland, and Ireland despite its status as a liberal market economy, occupy an intermediate position between these countries.

This result also holds if we instead consider the number of interviewees who explicitly disagreed with the claim that "everyone knows everyone and cooperation is relatively easy to establish." A majority of respondents did so in Greece and Portugal, but only two individuals dissented in Iceland. Considered in combination with the quantitative data above, this simple content analysis suggests that Finland, Iceland, and Sweden, as well Ireland, are characterized by relatively cohesive, encompassing networks. These dense ties cut across cleavages to unite different actors within high-trust relationships. In chapters 2, 3, 4, and 6 I provide more details on the specific connections that bind actors and the ways they influence economic adjustment. In these chapters I also leverage the cross-national variation documented above to contrast Iceland at one extreme with Sweden (and four contrasting cases) at the other.

Appendix 2
CHARACTERIZING ECONOMIC ADJUSTMENT

In chapters 2, 3, and 4 I provide detailed evidence of radical reform, restructuring, and overshooting in Finland, Iceland, and Sweden, tracing rapid movement into capital-intensive manufacturing, the crisis of traditional industry, big leaps into new high-technology industries, the rapid financialization of the economy, and their susceptibility to devastating financial crises. Although in chapter 4 and the conclusion I juxtapose the Nordic countries to several contrasting cases, in this appendix I use cross-national, quantitative data to situate Finland, Iceland, and Sweden in comparative perspective.

High-quality cross-national data on the pace and character of industrialization in the early and mid-twentieth century are scarce, but it is possible to measure movement into new high-technology industries at the turn of the millennium. Table A.3 documents the exceptional pace of restructuring in Nordic Europe (and Ireland).[1] The rapid growth of high-technology manufactured exports, which eclipses every country except Greece, is particularly notable because the Nordic countries (and Ireland) did not occupy a very strong position in high-technology markets in 1980. Finland was especially dependent on low- and medium-technology goods.

As I relate in the empirical chapters, however, the rapid pace of high-technology growth was not sustainable. In part because high-technology competition was based on fundamentally new industries such as biotechnology and mobile communications rather than the organic upgrading of traditional medium-technology niches, the Nordic countries (as well as Estonia) were hard-hit by the dot-com

TABLE A.3 High-Technology Share of Manufactured Exports[i]

	1980	2000	2008
Primary Cases: Finland, Iceland, and Sweden			
Finland	3.6	27.3	17.2
Iceland	0.4	2.7	10.5
Sweden	10.7	28.8	19.0
Shadow Cases: Estonia and Ireland			
Estonia	—	31.2	9.1
Ireland	14.8	50.1	49.0
Contrasting Cases: Large States			
France	9.7	25.6	22.9
Germany	11.1	19.9	17.3
United States	24.0	38.3	30.7
Contrasting Cases: Central Europe			
Austria	6.4	15.7	12.7
Switzerland	23.7	33.8	44.0
Contrasting Cases: Southern Europe			
Greece	1.0	9.6	12.0
Portugal	8.3	10.3	—

[i] OECD 2016

crash. High-technology manufactured exports contracted more sharply between 2000 and 2008 than in any other region.[2]

The macroeconomic impact of the dot-com crash was muted in all countries (except Finland, which was affected by Nokia's decline after 2008). To better gauge the potential costs of overshooting, we must shift focus from high-technology competition to financial services. Comparable figures on the precrisis growth of financial services are scarce, but the fallout is easy to measure. Table A.4 presents the peak-to-trough decline in GDP during the Finnish and Swedish banking crises of the early 1990s. Ranking among the "big five" (along with Norway) at the turn of the millennium (Rogoff and Reinhart 2009, 159), these crises remain impressive, even by the standards of the 2007–2009 global financial crisis. As table A.4 relates, peak-to-trough declines were particularly dramatic in Finland, Iceland, and to a lesser extent Sweden, as well as Estonia and Ireland (see chapter 6). By contrast, large states (conclusion) and the small, open economies of Central Europe (see chapter 5) were less vulnerable to the crisis. Greece and Portugal also suffered sharp declines in GDP. Unlike the Finnish, Swedish, Icelandic, Irish, and Estonian banking crises, however, in chapter 5 I argue that these downturns reflected too little reform and restructuring rather than rapid liberalization and deregulation.

TABLE A.4 Economic Crises Compared: Peak-to-Trough Decline in Constant Per Capita GDP[i]

Swedish and Finnish Banking Crises (Early 1990s)	
Finland (1990–1993)	–11.1%
Sweden (1990–1993)	–6.1%
Primary Cases: Finland, Sweden, and Iceland	
Finland (2007–2009)	–8.7%
Iceland (2007–2010)	–8.9%
Sweden (2007–2009)	–7.2%
Shadow Cases: Estonia and Ireland	
Estonia (2007–2009)	–19.0%
Ireland (2007–2010)	–12.5%
Contrasting Cases: Large Countries	
France (2007–2009)	–3.8%
Germany (2008–2009)	–5.4%
United States (2007–2009)	–4.8%
Contrasting Cases: Central Europe	
Austria (2008–2009)	–4.1%
Switzerland (2008–2009)	–3.3%
Contrasting Cases: Southern Europe	
Greece (2007–2013)	–25.4%
Portugal (2008–2013)	–7.5%

[i] Federal Reserve Bank of St. Louis 2016.

Cross-national statistics on the rise (and fall) of high-technology industry and financial services suggest that countries with cohesive and encompassing networks such as Finland, Iceland, and Sweden (as well as Ireland and Estonia) are characterized by rapid restructuring, overshooting, and deep crises. These developments are more pronounced in relatively tight-knit societies such as Finland and are less conspicuous in larger, more fragmented countries such as Sweden. Do these individual boom-bust cycles accurately reflect broader trends in economic adjustment? To address this question, table A.5 presents data on "excess volatility" or variability in GDP output, controlling for differences in per capita income and the GDP growth rate (Rötheli 2012, 28). Averaged from 1970 to 2009, the data encompass the three main boom-bust cycles in this book.

Like the case studies, table A.5 demonstrates that the Nordic countries (plus Ireland) have enjoyed rapid growth but also suffered deep crises. As a result, they are characterized by greater volatility than large, advanced industrialized economies such as France, Germany, and the United States. Economic volatility is greatest in Iceland and the most muted in Sweden. This is not simply a story

TABLE A.5 Excess Volatility 1970–2009[i]

Primary Cases: Finland, Sweden, and Iceland	
Finland	1.393
Iceland	1.905
Sweden	0.587
Shadow Cases: Estonia and Ireland	
Estonia	—
Ireland	1.295
Contrasting Cases: Large Countries	
France	0.000
Germany	0.128
United States	0.130
Contrasting Cases: Central Europe	
Austria	0.222
Switzerland	0.000
Contrasting Cases: Southern Europe	
Greece	0.854
Portugal	0.534

[i] Rötheli 2012.

about population size or economic openness. As table A.5 illustrates, the small open economies of Central Europe, Austria and Switzerland, are significantly less volatile than their Nordic counterparts (whether controlling for income and GDP growth or not). Greece and Portugal do exhibit high levels of output volatility. As I relate in chapter 5, however, economic volatility does not reflect radical reform and rapid restructuring.

Notes

INTRODUCTION

1. In this book I focus solely on economic growth. I do not discuss other areas where the Nordic countries have flourished, such as employment, income equality, gender equality, or public health (Esping-Andersen 1990; Hall and Lamont 2009).

2. Even today, Finland ranks only twentieth in ratio of exports to GDP, trailing Chile, Poland, and most Western European economies (OECD 2016). Only Iceland ranks among the top ten in measures of economic openness, and this is a recent development; the country was highly protectionist in the early postwar period.

3. These two theories are not mutually incompatible. Andersen et al. (2007) point out that a larger public sector protects individuals from the risks of economic openness. On this point, see also Katzenstein (1985, 47).

4. Social democratic ideology and working-class power may yield greater insight into other outcomes such as equality (Esping-Andersen 1990).

5. For example, the Swedish financial system most closely approximated the ideal-typical case articulated by Hall and Soskice (2001), at least until the financial crisis of the early 1990s, as banks linked large firms within "industrial families" (Rehn 1996, 170). In Denmark, however, small and medium-sized enterprises were connected within informal local networks (Kristensen 1996). Finland, Norway, and Iceland all have relied heavily on the state (Moen 2011b; Rehn 1996; Wade 2009). These historically state-led economies fit awkwardly within the Varieties of Capitalism framework. Efforts to add a new "state-enhanced" or "mixed-market" category (Hancké, Rhodes, and Thatcher 2007; Schmidt 2002) yield little insight, as these countries bear little resemblance to the statist economies of Southern Europe (see chapter 5). For more details on the conceptual differences between cohesive, encompassing networks and strategic coordination, see appendix 1.

6. The Finnish case suggests that national cohesion cannot be attributed solely to ethnic or linguistic homogeneity. As I relate in chapter 3, the Soviet threat bridged historical divisions between Finnish and Swedish speakers, as well as outright hostility between employers and workers in the wake of a civil war.

7. As I demonstrate in chapter 6, cohesive and encompassing social networks are by no means limited to Nordic Europe.

8. The Nordic countries thus differ from Peter Hall's characterization of the large, advanced industrialized economies such as France, Germany, and the UK, which were characterized by considerable institutional continuity in the postwar period (Hall 1999).

9. In chapter 5 I argue that reform and restructuring has proceeded at a more gradual pace in Central Europe because these societies are less cohesive than Nordic Europe. Although consensual, they are characterized by strong regional cleavages and coordination generally occurs along sectoral lines. In the absence of a collective national-level vision of how to restructure the economy, policy making and production exhibit a strong status quo bias.

1. GOOD GOVERNANCE GONE BAD

1. As I relate in chapters 3 and 4, this was not always the case. Neocorporatism evolved later in Finland and, despite exceptional levels of trade union density, remains underdeveloped in Iceland.

2. For this reason, I argue that small, liberal market economies such as Estonia and Ireland may also possess relatively cohesive, encompassing networks (see chapter 6).

3. On the origin of these new ideas, see Breznitz and Ornston 2013, 2014, forthcoming.

4. This leads to a distinctive combination of continuity and change. Continuity in certain areas, such as social policy, permits radical and comprehensive restructuring in other domains, such as industrial policy (chapter 3) or financial regulation (chapter 4).

5. To the extent that the politics of persuasion generates a sense of "institutionalized sacrifice" (Campbell and Hall 2009), it may reduce the size of these side payments. A Greek academic argued that side payments had to be larger to bridge greater ideological distance and distrust in a polarized society (interview with professor, 30 June 2016, Greece).

6. For example, prime minister Davíð Oddsson agreed not to tinker with the Icelandic welfare state to avoid angering Icelandic trade unions, but their tacit support enabled him to pursue comprehensive, market-oriented reforms in a broad array of other domains from trade and taxation to privatization and financial regulation (see chapter 4).

7. In this book, I do not explore how these ideas are generated. For a more fully articulated theory of how societies, including Finland and Sweden, develop new ideas, see Breznitz and Ornston (2013, 2014, forthcoming).

8. Explanations that emphasize luck (Schwartz and Becker 2005b, 9) tend to overlook the degree to which comparative advantage is politically constructed. Although it seems "natural" for Finland to specialize in forest products, armchair industrialists forget that paper mills are expensive. Finland relied on collective institutions, such as the state and the universal bank, to capitalize on its forest resources (see chapter 3).

9. It also extends to areas that have nothing to do with international trade or economic policy, such as Iceland's unlikely emergence as a soccer powerhouse or the country's abrupt transformation from one of the most homophobic societies in Western Europe to one of the most tolerant (see chapter 4).

10. Even today, Finland, a paradigmatic example of overshooting, is less open to foreign trade than more incrementally oriented countries such as Austria, Belgium, Germany, and Switzerland (OECD 2016).

11. Large-scale quantitative studies suggest that this is not necessary true. Consistent with the argument advanced in this book, economic volatility is shaped by the degree of integration within a country rather than country size per se (Beenstock 2005, 35–37).

12. As I relate in chapter 5, Greece and Portugal are more fragmented and polarized than their Nordic counterparts. Austria and Switzerland are more consensual, but I characterize them as "segmented" societies because cooperation is generally organized along regional or sectoral lines. The national-level ties that distinguish Finland, Sweden, and Iceland are less salient in Central Europe.

2. MANUFACTURING A CRISIS

1. As recently as the 1990s, the group's investments represented 40 percent of the market value Stockholm stock exchange (Rehn 1996, 194).

2. As if to prove Ulf Hannerz's point, a representative from the Confederation of Swedish Industry (8 May 2012) and a newspaper editor (14 May 2012) used this precise language to characterize their country.

3. The working class was conspicuously absent from these networks. In the late 19th century, the franchise was sharply circumscribed and strike activity was brutally repressed.

As recently as the 1920s, industrial conflict was so intense that Sweden was known as the "strike capital of Western Europe" (Berman 1998, 42).

4. The Social Democratic minister of finance Fredrik Thorsson was such an enthusiastic champion of austerity after World War I that the resulting social dislocation was dubbed the "Thorsson effect" (Magnusson 2000, 196).

5. The SAF's intransigent position had softened when confronted with a decisive electoral defeat in 1936 and the prospect of a hostile SAP–Farmer's League coalition (Rehn 1996, 172).

6. The tax provisions for individuals were considerably less generous, ensuring that capital was allocated to (large) firms rather than individual consumers (Henrekson and Jakobsson 2001, 340).

7. Although the effective marginal tax rate on new share issues was at least 50 percent lower for institutional investors, it was still significantly higher than the effective marginal tax rate on debt, which was heavily negative.

8. Although by 1980, the share of nonagricultural employment in public-sector enterprises (8.3 percent) rivaled that of France (9.3 percent) (Clifton, Comín, and Fuentes 2003, 107).

9. From a socialist perspective, their workers were also much easier to organize

10. In this respect, Sweden differed from not only other countries but its own historical experience. Until the interwar period, Sweden was famous for the proliferation of "genius companies," start-ups built around novel technologies.

11. Erixon identifies TetraPak as an exception, but the company only reached the ranks of Sweden's largest firms by acquiring a century-old incumbent, Alfa-Laval, in 1991.

12. This proposal would have transferred profits from high-productivity firms into jointly managed funds. Swedish industry viewed this effort to socialize private property as a violation of its "right to manage."

13. Finland, which liberalized later, moved even more rapidly (see chapter 3).

14. In sharp contrast to Finland and Iceland, not all banks succumbed to the mania. Handelsbanken, committed to its traditional, conservative model, was virtually unaffected by the crisis.

15. Because the banking crisis was almost universally attributed to macroeconomic errors, financial supervision received relatively little attention (interview with economist, 11 May 2012, Sweden). As a result, the Swedish financial system confronted another, albeit rather different, crisis less than two decades later. One interviewee suggested that Sweden's highly concentrated exposure to Baltic debt could represent a similar example of groupthink within the financial services industry (interview with former government economist, 14 May 2012, Sweden). A full investigation of this hypothesis is beyond the scope of this book.

16. Because ICT was so universally popular, these venture capital funds and research foundations provided a convenient, uncontroversial way for the government to dispose of the wage earner funds of the 1980s (interview with policy maker, 16 October 2006, Sweden).

17. Data are not available for Iceland.

3. CONNECTING PEOPLE

1. This shift was less pronounced in Norway, which could rely on its oil deposits (Moen 2011b), and Iceland, which pursued a neoliberal strategy (see chapter 4).

2. This systemic focus is even more salient today as scholars seek to tackle so-called "grand challenges" (Cagnin, Amanatidou, and Keenan 2012).

3. In 1995 these banks merged into a single firm, Merita. Because the two banks were forced to dissolve their industrial holdings during the financial crisis of the early 1990s and Merita operated within a deregulated, shareholder-friendly environment, it was far less influential than the two firms that preceded it. By 2000 it had been absorbed into the pan-Nordic, Stockholm-based bank Nordea.

4. These sectoral associations were even more cohesive than their Swedish counterparts. In the words of one former forestry executive, "The formal cooperation between the different Finnish pulp and paper companies has always been much wider and closer than it ever was in Sweden." The executive spoke at length about differences in a wide range of areas, from research to sales (interview with former executive, 20 October 2006, Sweden).

5. To this we could add family-owned businesses such as the Ahlström group. But these entities, generally founded in the nineteenth century by wealthy, Swedish-speaking shipping magnates, were the exception rather than the rule (Stråth 2001, 62). Ahlström was the only family-owned firm to crack the top ten in 1975 and it was closely linked to the Union Bank of Finland (Ojala and Karonen 2006, 115).

6. Circumstances have since changed with the rise of the Finns Party. These developments are addressed in the conclusion.

7. Finland was a part of Sweden until 1809.

8. The most dramatic gains occurred after World War I. Finland was still 40 percent poorer than the Western European average in 1913 (Bolt and Zanden 2013).

9. The Bank of Finland did introduce two measures to curb lending growth in 1989, but the tightening of credit was mainly market-induced (Englund and Vihriälä 2003, 21)

10. The investment was exceptionally risky, as this enterprise alone was enough to bankrupt the firm in 1991 (interview with economist, 20 June 2012, Finland).

11. SKOP Bank's strategy of "cornering" firms and then selling them for a profit only worked if other financial actors also embraced this highly leveraged model (Englund and Vihriälä 2003, 17).

12. In other words, the number of politicians with ties to SKOP Bank outnumbered the members of the biggest political party in Parliament.

13. The crisis was exacerbated by other policies, including the stubborn defense of a fixed exchange rate. Like Sweden, participants suggest that these mistakes were aggravated by a form of groupthink that discouraged the expression of dissenting views (interviews with economists, 12 June 2012, 15 June 2012, 17 June 2012, and 20 June 2012, Finland).

14. A purely statist theory of Finnish success cannot explain the failure of traditional industrial policies, including Finland's inability to establish viable national champions in televisions and telecommunications equipment (Rehn 1996, 282–83).

15. While based in the United States, Motorola was involved in the NMT and GSM digital standards through its Danish subsidiary (Ornston 2012b, 121–22).

16. Established in 1968 to celebrate the Finnish parliament's fiftieth anniversary, Sitra functioned as a think tank and innovation policy lab, writing critical evaluations and launching small-scale pilot projects. Nominally supervised by the Bank of Finland, the organization enjoyed considerable freedom until the 1990s (Breznitz and Ornston 2013).

17. In his words, "It became evident to me that [we're] a big company and we have to contribute to the surrounding environment so that it's successful as well, so that [Finland has] good training systems and so that our technical universities are properly funded. Not only by Nokia but also by us." This is a good example of "institutionalized sacrificing" as described by John L. Campbell and John A. Hall (2009, 559).

18. Like innovation policy, retrenchment was achieved through a combination of persuasion and side payments (Kaitila et al. 2006; Saari 2001).

19. Although the center-right Aho administration attempted to reduce unemployment benefits and reduce labor-market regulation for young workers in the early 1990s,

it quickly backtracked when confronted with the threat of a general strike (Ornston and Rehn 2006, 89).

20. This was not universally true. Data security and gaming firms often described Tekes in more favorable terms (interviews with three software industry representatives, 3 November 2005 and 10 June 2016, Finland). But these niches were connected to mobile communications.

21. To place this in comparative perspective, Sweden would not introduce the Swedish Governmental Agency for Innovation Systems (VINNOVA) until 2001 (Gergils 2006, 343).

22. The fact that Finland ranked only fifth in total venture capital investment highlights the immaturity of the industry, a problem that is discussed in more detail below.

23. Ericsson was also a key coordinating agent in the Swedish innovation system, but it was never as central as Nokia. Government relations were more distant and punctuated by periods of tension (Linden 2012, 13).

24. The "Lex Nokia" was passed in 2009, when the firm's decline was already evident.

25. Again, this was less true of niches such as data security and gaming, both of which were linked to mobile communications.

26. A decade later, venture capitalists struggled to identify successful exits from the late 1990s (interview with venture capitalist 8 June 2016, Finland).

27. It would be unfair to direct all criticism at Finnish business. An employer organization representative argued that Finnish trade unions are no less conservative:

> The key difference [from Germany] is that when you mention digitalization the first thing that comes to mind is, "Is my work secure? Will I lose my job? Will automation delete my work or will it impact the sector in negative terms?" That's the stereotypical way of looking at things [in Finland]. In Germany, it's the other way around. . . . In Finland [trade unions] create resistance. But that's not only the fault of the trade unions, it's how digitalization has been presented. It's still being presented as an alternative to the traditional way of doing things in a way that cuts the work force. I don't know whose fault that is, not the trade unions alone, not the employers alone, not the media. (interview with employer association representative, 14 June 2016, Finland)

28. In the words of an industry veteran:

> The success of Rovio created a lot of things. . . . It gained the attention of investors outside of Finland and they were interested to see what is going on in this little country where new games are coming from. Might there be some new Rovios? The second thing is that it gave faith to the Finnish gaming industry. If they can do it, then we can do it. And of course Rovio employees have established like twenty companies. So Rovio is basically a school for the Finnish game developers. (interview with industry representative, 10 June 2016, Finland)

29. To put these numbers in comparison, the Finnish gaming industry employed fewer than two hundred people at the height of the dot-com bubble.

30. He also noted that the Swedish gaming industry as not as cohesive in this respect.

31. Nokia was a century-old conglomerate and its most prominent component producers (Elcoteq, Perlos) had long histories in manufacturing.

4. FROM BANKING ON FISH TO FISHY BANKS

1. It is important not to overstate these dynamics. Although industrial relations were contentious, industry and labor have been cooperating harmoniously on a wide range of other issues since the 1960s, most notably pension policy (Baldvinsdóttir 1998, 152).

2. Although cross-class cooperation has been attributed to a second cleavage between isolationists and integrationists (Karlsson 2000, 325), foreign policy was not an insurmountable barrier either. The Independence Party and the Progressive Party frequently overcame their differences to form successful governing coalitions. The two leftist parties might have done likewise, but they lacked the seats to form a majority government.

3. I am indebted to Bill Kissane for this insight. Originally used to distinguish between two different types of consensus in Finland and Ireland (see chapter 6), this formulation fits Iceland as well.

4. Organized labor's relationship with other neoliberal reformers like Margaret Thatcher and Ronald Reagan was notoriously contentious. As I relate in chapter 5, low levels of trust between policy makers, industry, and labor also hindered market-oriented reform in small European states like Greece and Portugal.

5. The fact that this pattern extends to noneconomic domains suggests that radical reform, rapid restructuring, and overshooting is not simply about comparative advantage, monetary policy, openness to foreign capital flows, or other economic institutions.

6. The first person to come out of the closet in Iceland did not do so until 1975 and then immediately moved to Copenhagen (Jóhannesson 2013, 123).

7. Although Iceland gradually liberalized trade throughout the postwar period, customs and import duty revenue remained among the highest in the OECD until the 1990s, eclipsed only by South Korea after 1980 (OECD 2016).

8. With the Cod Wars of 1958 to 1976, Britain supplanted Denmark as Iceland's principal bogeyman.

9. Occupational pensions emerged as a side payment to organized labor at this point (Ólafsson 2011, 13).

10. These figures do not include DeCode itself, which was domiciled in the United States, relied on American venture capital, and was a publicly listed company by 2000.

11. As noted above, Iceland's fishing quota was also reformed at this time.

12. For example, Iceland was significantly less dependent on public ownership than Sweden (2.91) or Finland (3.16).

13. The Swiss financial services industry was significantly larger than Iceland's in 1994, with bank assets totaling 350 percent of GDP (Wade 2009, 15).

14. Although more consensual, neoliberal reform in Iceland was also more radical, particularly when one considers how heavily regulated the country was in the early 1980s.

15. Only the Left-Green Party, which received approximately 9 percent of the popular vote in 1999 and 2005, did not receive campaign contributions from Iceland's banks.

16. The environment for small and medium-sized fisheries was less salubrious as the growing cost of a fishing quota and the stronger exchange rate favored larger producers. Always marginalized within the Confederation of Icelandic Employers, small and medium-sized fisheries struggled to secure the support of the Progressive Party after 1995. The Progressive Party's indifference to their plight may reflect the fact that the small communities most adversely affected by the consolidation of the Icelandic fishing industry were able to combat depopulation by using cheap foreign-denominated loans to invest in infrastructure such as schools and libraries (Willson and Gunnlaugsdóttir 2015, 141).

17. The National Economic Institute was closed in 2002, as the government argued that it could rely on Iceland's three major commercial banks for macroeconomic guidance. As noted above, when Iceland's largest trade union confederation expressed concerns about this development, they were compensated with their own research institute (interview with professor, 7 March 2012, Iceland).

18. Using PPP-adjusted measures of national output. The nominal decline in GDP was much sharper owing to the depreciation of the *króna*.

19. This claim is supported by polling data, which indicate that less than 10 percent of the population trusted the banking system in 2013 (Gylfason 2015, 330).

5. OVERSHOOTING IN COMPARATIVE PERSPECTIVE

1. By contrast, Belgium and the Netherlands are considerably larger than the Nordic states. Notoriously incremental, Belgium resembles the Central European countries examined here (Hemerijck, Unger, and Visser 2000). The larger but more cohesive Netherlands more closely approximates the Nordic countries in the way it radically reconfigured its welfare state during the 1980s (Visser and Hemerijck 1997), as well as its susceptibility to a housing bubble in the 2000s (Kurzer 2014).

2. The ratio of exports (and imports) to GDP is slightly lower in Finland.

3. In a 1918 referendum, Vorarlberg voted by a 60 percent margin to join Switzerland. This initiative was blocked by foreign powers, not least the Swiss themselves.

4. To this we could add Vienna, which, by virtue of its status as a former imperial capital, specializes in culture, tourism, and related services (I am indebted to Gernot Grabher for this point). The tourism industry alone generated a third of Austria's export revenues in the early 1970s, higher than any of the Nordic countries and second only to Spain within the OECD (Katzenstein 1984, 59).

5. This policy reversal was somewhat less dramatic than in Nordic Europe, because Austria was significantly less liberal than Sweden, Finland, or Iceland before World War II. The Hapsburg Empire was heavily protectionist and blocked the development of a modern financial system after the stock market crash of 1873 (Rehn 1996, 126).

6. Partly as a result, the expansion of credit in the 1980s was confined to the Austrian savings banks and the fallout from the crisis was limited.

7. In Sweden, the EU member with the second-largest exposure to Eastern Europe, banks had focused almost exclusively on the three diminutive Baltic economies.

8. The Swedish economy performed even more poorly after 1972, but the slowdown was spread out over a longer time period, extended in part by (unsuccessful) efforts to stabilize the economy with expansionary fiscal and monetary policies (see chapter 2 for an extended discussion).

9. By extension, reliance on established niches insulated Switzerland from the dotcom crash.

10. Although not the focal point of this book, Finland, Sweden, and Iceland have pursued very different macroeconomic policies since World War II (Mjøset 1987). For example, Sweden moved from an aggressive "bridging" policy in the 1970s to relatively tight fiscal policies by the 1990s. Finland, which relied on competitive devaluations for most of the postwar period, adopted a hard currency regime in the 1980s and now belongs to the Euro. Finally, Iceland engineered perhaps the most radical U-turn from an exceptionally inflationary regime to a tight monetary policy by the early 2000s. Participants suggest that these radical shifts were influenced by cohesive and encompassing networks (interview with director, Ministry of Economic Affairs, 6 March 2012, Iceland; former economist, Swedish Ministry of Finance, 11 May 2012, Sweden; former advisor to the Swedish prime minister, 14 May 2012, Sweden; executive, financial services firm, 12 June 2012, Finland; and three economists, Bank of Finland, 20 June 2012, Finland), but a full exploration of these dynamics is beyond the scope of this book.

11. In the language of Doner and Schneider (2016), these economies are "disarticulated."

12. This is not necessarily true of very small Southern European states. Greek scholars familiar with the Republic of Cyprus argue that the violent conflicts of the twentieth century created a much stronger spirit of solidarity among the Greek-speaking population (interviews with historian, 27 June 2016, and economist, 1 July 2016, Greece). Indeed, Cyprus more closely resembles Nordic Europe in its commitment to

tripartism, state-industry cooperation, and consensus on key policy issues (Natali and Pochet 2010; Panayiotopoulos 1995). This had predictable implications for economic adjustment. Overwhelmingly dependent on agriculture as recently as the 1970s, the state spearheaded rapid movement into light industry and tourism during the 1980s (Panayiotopoulos 1995). When increasing cost competition rendered Cyprus too dependent on volatile tourist revenues in the 1990s, the country transformed itself into a financial services center with remarkable speed, supported by a more stable macroeconomic framework, a low corporate tax rate, and complementary market-oriented reforms (Stephanou 2011). Partly as a result, Cyprus, less than half as prosperous as Greece in 1975, had leapfrogged the country in per capita income by 1987 and remains considerably wealthier today (Federal Reserve Bank of St. Louis 2016). Unfortunately, Cyprus has also proven exceptionally vulnerable to disruptive economic shocks, including not only sharp declines in tourism during the mid-1990s but also the recent, Iceland-style collapse of its banking industry after 2012 (Zenios 2013). Since the book has already presented three different examples of overshooting (Sweden, Finland, and Iceland), however, this section focuses instead on two contrasting cases, Portugal and Greece.

13. Several interviewees argued that early postwar Portugal was dominated by seven families, not one hundred (interviews with economists, 4, 8, and 12 July 2016, Portugal). Unlike the Nordic countries, however, these industrial families did not appear to copy each other and adopted different economic strategies (interview with economist, 12 July 2016, Portugal).

14. This does not appear to be an issue in Portugal.

15. In contrast to Finland, where industrial blocs copied one another closely (see chapters 3 and 4), economists saw little evidence of isomorphism in Portugal (interviews with economists, 4 and 6 July 2016, Portugal).

16. EU structural cohesion funds, which prioritized R&D under the 2007–2013 perspective, contributed significantly to this shift. In 2009 they represented roughly a quarter of Portuguese R&D expenditure (Godinho, Simões, and Zifciakova 2016). That said, EU funds alone cannot explain this transformation.

17. Of course, long-term investments in R&D require a more stable macroeconomic regime. Until this is achieved, Portugal is vulnerable to recurring crises.

18. EU structural funds and massive foreign direct investment did not inhibit restructuring in Ireland. In chapter 6 I elaborate on these differences.

19. The fact that they did so in such an egalitarian fashion makes the achievement even more impressive.

6. OVERSHOOTING BEYOND NORDIC EUROPE

1. In this chapter and throughout the book, "Ireland" refers to the Republic of Ireland.

2. For example, all major parties, left and right, supported Ireland's low corporate tax rate. Sinn Féin, one of the only dissenters, polled in the low single digits throughout the postwar period. When its electoral performance improved, the party immediately dropped its opposition to the low corporate tax rate.

3. A rare critic of the corporate tax rate confirmed: "They treat you like a traitor, like you should be hung. I always find it amusing. These guys like to think they're great internationalists, but when it comes to Ireland's corporate tax they wrap the green flag around them and they don the green jumper. We will die in the trenches defending our low corporate tax rate. They like you to conform and put immense pressure on you to conform" (interview with trade union representative, 4 July 2012, Ireland).

4. Unlike Iceland, the IDA thus sought to attract foreign firms to Ireland, rather than transforming Irish firms into global players.

5. By 2007 financial intermediation represented 13 percent of corporate profits, significantly higher than the United Kingdom or the United States (O'Riain 2014, 69).

6. Like Ireland's largest firms (Clancy, O'Conner, and Dillon 2010), Irish banks were connected through overlapping corporate boards (O'Riain 2014, 97). Although unable to invest in collective goods like their highly coordinated Danish counterparts (Campbell and Hall 2017), they followed one another closely and adopted similar corporate strategies.

7. In this respect Ireland also differs from Spain, where the housing bubble was regionally concentrated and bank exposure was uneven (interview with professor, 9 July 2012, Ireland).

8. In this respect groupthink was not confined to a handful of elite banks, property developers, or policy makers. It also extended to country's leading tripartite think tank.

9. Shortly after Curran's report, Prime Minister Bertie Ahern famously mused, "Sitting on the sidelines, cribbing and moaning is a lost opportunity. I don't know how people who engage in that don't commit suicide."

10. The political calculations behind the bank guarantee remain poorly understood. The available evidence suggests that neither the government nor the banks understood the full cost of the crisis in September 2008 (Donovan and Murphy 2013, 212).

11. In 2011, for example, Ireland lost only four thousand worker days to industrial action (Hardiman and Regan 2013, 11).

12. Much like early twentieth-century Swedish workers, Finnish neoliberals, and Danish immigrants, Russian speakers have been marginalized to the point of irrelevance. In 1994, before reforms weakened traditional industry, Russian speakers represented only 15 percent of the elites in state-owned enterprises and 6 percent of the elite in the private sector. The figures were even lower in the civil service (Steen 1997). Even if Russian speakers did participate in decision making, it is unclear whether it would make much of a difference. Much like the Swedish and Finnish Social Democratic parties in the early twentieth century, the (predominantly Russian-speaking) Center Party internalized many aspects of Estonia's economic model. The biggest difference between the Estonian and Russian-speaking parties appears to rest with foreign policy rather than economics.

13. This theme was echoed in interviews with those who had spent time in Estonia (interviews with venture capital investor, 9 March 2016, Canada, and policy consultant, 9 June 2016, Finland). In the words of a Swedish economist:

> I was doing some work on Estonia ... The thing that intrigued me was that at one level it seems that this small state was totally chaotic ... they would change governments all the time. But when I talked to people in Estonia, including the current president, they said, "Yeah, we have this, but at some level, the informal level, there is some set of institutions or glue." They had very clear ambitions and if they needed to change something they could do it. They had to change their policy regarding trade, abolish all duties, and it takes maybe two days. Maybe I exaggerate, but they could make very fast changes. (interview with academic, 9 May 2012, Sweden)

14. Since Russian speakers are generally less satisfied with the Estonian government and economy, the figures for Estonian speakers are even higher.

CONCLUSION

1. As I relate in chapter 4, this was less true of Iceland, which was constrained by its status as a Danish colony until 1944 and influenced by the United States after independence.

2. Although the German state has demonstrated greater willingness to intervene after reunification (Jacoby 2001; Vail 2009), it does not yet approximate the Nordic countries in its capacity for reform and restructuring (see below).

3. Compared to Sweden, German socialists not only had a more difficult time striking cross-class alliances before World War II but also struggled to bridge divisions within their own organization (Berman 1998).

4. There are no data for Iceland. As I relate in chapter 4, Icelandic policy makers systematically favored capital investment in the fishing industry but do not appear to have been particularly interested in building very large firms.

5. As noted above, Swedish industrial policies and even high-technology initiatives were decidedly defensive until the 1980s, promoting investment and technological diffusion within traditional manufacturing industries.

6. As I demonstrate in chapter 3, these strategies were not mutually exclusive, as market-oriented reform can create stronger framework conditions for the high-technology industries targeted by new innovation policies. Nokia, for example, benefited from a hard currency regime, liquid equity markets, and a more liberal trade regime as well as public support for R&D and human capital formation.

7. This decline in government R&D spending was somewhat offset by an increase in R&D spending by higher education, from 0.31 percent to 0.39 percent of GDP. But R&D expenditure by higher education increased at even more rapid clip in Finland, from 0.25 percent of GDP to 0.58 percent of GDP.

8. The emphasis on tax credits was partly a consequence of the fact that French businesses, still distrustful of the state, did not want to participate in government-sponsored initiatives (Ornston and Vail 2016).

9. By contrast, Sweden used active labor-market programs to redistribute labor to large capital-intensive enterprises, and later used pension funds to invest in new technology-based enterprises (see chapter 2).

10. In 1975 the share of value-added from financial services was the third lowest in the OECD, exceeding only Turkey and South Korea at 2.2 percent. By 1990 this had doubled, but only to 4.1 percent.

11. The Swedish banking crisis of the early 1990s was less expensive at 3.6 percent of GDP, although (like Finland, Ireland, and Iceland) output loss was higher.

12. I am indebted to John Zysman for pointing out the similarities between Finland and San Diego years ago.

13. Heightened labor mobility may also reduce vulnerability to the forms of groupthink that occurred in Finland, Iceland, and Sweden. In San Diego, for example, outsiders played an important role in diversifying the economy, from the wealthy philanthropists who funded research in the early twentieth century to professors who launched high-technology start-ups at the end of the century (Walshok and Shragge 2013).

14. As the case studies in this book relate, this is not captured by common measures of economic internationalization. Iceland might rank high on measures of economic openness in the early postwar period because of its dependence on fish exports, but the economy was heavily regulated and Icelandic society was exceptionally homogeneous. In Ireland foreign multinationals might play a key role in corporate decision making, but the country's highly consensual, carefully coordinated campaign to attract American FDI has led the country to specialize in a relatively narrow range of activities.

APPENDIX 1

1. Stokman and Wasseur's (1985) indicators of network density are significantly lower because they analyzed hundreds of firms. This is arguably a better measure of interconnectedness than a sample of several dozen large publicly listed firms.

2. This addresses another limitation of network analysis and the study of interlocking directorates in particular. Overlapping board memberships may represent a potential channel of communication, but it does not tell us about the quality of this relationship or the type of information that is being communicated (Scott 1985, 5).

3. These projects ranged from the evolution of neocorporatist institutions to Sitra's role as a radically innovative public agency and the recent rise of the "platform economy."

4. Many Swedish respondents insisted that their country was less tightly knit than other Nordic countries, but then used this same concept to distinguish themselves from larger communities such as Germany and the United States. These responses were coded positively.

5. Several respondents agreed with this claim but could not provide concrete examples. Alternatively, they agreed but then described features that did not reflect cohesive, encompassing social networks (such as the difficulty of achieving economies of scale in a small market). These responses were coded neutrally.

APPENDIX 2

1. As I relate in chapter 4, Iceland was slower to move into high-technology markets during the 1980s and 1990s. Here, structural reform was delayed until the 1990s, and then prioritized liberalization and financialization rather than innovation and high-technology competition.

2. This was less true of Ireland. Here, indigenous industry struggled (Breznitz 2007), but the country's status as a tax haven continued to attract large amounts of investment from high-technology US multinationals such as Apple and Google.

References

Adam, Frane, Matevž Tomšič, and Primož Kristan. 2008. "Political Elite, Civil Society, and Type of Capitalism: Estonia and Slovenia." *East European Quartlerly* 42 (1): 43–67.

Adelberger, Karen E. 1999. "A Developmental German State? Explaining Growth in German Biotechnology and Venture Capital." Berkeley: Berkeley Roundtable on the International Economy Working Paper, No. 134.

Agnarsson, Sveinn, and Ragnar Arnason. 2007. "The Role of the Fishing Industry in the Icelandic Economy." In *Advances in Fisheries Economics*, edited by Trond Bjørndal, Daniel V. Gordon, Ragnar Arnason, and U. Rashid Sumaila, 239–56. Oxford, UK: Blackwell.

Alesina, Alberto, and Francesco Giavazzi. 2006. *The Future of Europe*. Cambridge, MA: MIT Press.

Ali-Yrkkö, Jyrki. 2003. "Elcoteq—When Globalization Is Imperative: The Growth of a Telecom-Oriented EMS Company." In *Our Path Abroad: Exploring the Postwar Internationalization of Finnish Corporations*, edited by Pekka Mannio, Eero Vaara, and Pekka Ylä-Anttila, 365–76. Helsinki: Taloustieto Ltd.

———. 2010. "The Role of Nokia in the Finnish Economy." In *Nokia and Finland in a Sea of Change*, edited by Jyrki Ali-Yrkkö, 9–36. Helsinki: Taloustieto Ltd.

Ali-Yrkkö, Jyrki, and Raine Hermans. 2004. "Nokia: A Giant in the Finnish Innovation System." In *Embracing the Knowledge Economy: The Dynamic Transformation of the Finnish Innovation System*, edited by Gerd Schienstock, 106–27. Cheltenham, UK: Edward Elgar.

Allen, Christopher S. 1989. "The Underdevelopment of Keynesianism in the Federal Republic of Germany." In *The Political Power of Economic Ideas: Keynesianism across Nations*, edited by Peter A. Hall, 263–89. Princeton, NJ: Princeton University Press.

Amaral, João Ferreira do. 2007. "The Economy." In *A Portrait of Portugal*, edited by António Reis, 203–28. Rio de Mouro, PT: Temas and Debates.

Andersen, Torben M., Bengt Holmström, Seppo Honkapohja, Sixten Korkman, Hans Tson Söderström, and Juhana Vartiainen. 2007. *The Nordic Model: Embracing Globalization and Sharing Risks*. Helsinki: Taloustieto Ltd.

Ansell, Christopher K. 2000. "The Networked Polity: Regional Development in Western Europe." *Governance* 13 (2): 279–91.

Anthonsen, Mette, and Johannes Lindvall. 2009. "Party Competition and the Resilience of Corporatism." *Government and Opposition* 44 (2): 167–87.

Archibugi, Daniele, and Mario Pianta. 1992. *The Technological Specialization of Advanced Countries*. Dordrecht, NL: Kluwer Academic Publishers.

Armingeon, Klaus, and Lucio Baccaro. 2012. "Political Economy of the Sovereign Debt Crisis: The Limits of Internal Devaluation." *Industrial Law Journal* 41 (3): 254–75.

Árnason, Vilhjálmur. 2015. "Something Rotten in the State of Iceland: 'The Production of Truth' about the Icelandic Banks." In *Gambling Debt: Iceland's Rise and Fall in the Global Economy*, edited by E. Paul Durrenberger and Gísli Pálsson, 47–59. Boulder: University Press of Colorado.

A.T. Kearney Inc. 2003. "Measuring Globalization: Who's Up, Who's Down?" *Foreign Policy* 82 (1): 60–72.
Augustsson, Fredrik. 2005. *They Did IT: The Formation and Organisation of Interactive Media Production in Sweden*. Stockholm: National Institute for Working Life.
Baccaro, Lucio, and Chris Howell. 2011. "A Common Neoliberal Trajectory: The Transformation of Industrial Relations in Advanced Capitalism." *Politics & Society* 39 (4): 521–63.
Bain, Joe S. 1950. "Workable Competition in Oligopoly: Theoretical Considerations and Some Empirical Evidence." *American Economic Review* 40 (2): 35–47.
Baldvinsdóttir, Herdís Dröfn. 1998. "Networks of Financial Power in Iceland: The Labor Movement Paradox." PhD diss., Lancaster University.
Bärlund, Rafael, and Kielo Brewis. 2013. *Attracting Highly Qualified Third Country Nationals: National Contribution from Finland*. Helsinki: European Migration Institute.
Barr, Caelainn, and Theo Francis. 2014. "Ireland Moves to Close One Tax Break and Opens Another." *Wall Street Journal*, 4 November. http://www.wsj.com/articles/ireland-closes-one-tax-break-and-opens-another-1415149644.
Barry, Frank, and Chris van Egeraat. 2008. "The Decline of the Computer Hardware Industry: How Ireland Adjusted." *ESRI Quarterly Economic Commentary* (Spring): 38–57.
Baudouin, Lamine. 2009. "Estonia: Analysis of a Housing Boom." *ECFIN Country Focus* 6 (7): 1–7.
Beenstock, Michael. 2005. "Country Size in Regional Economics." In *Regional Disparities in Small Countries*, edited by Daniel Felsenstein and Boris A Portnov, 25–46. Berlin: Springer.
Beise, Marian. 2004. "Lead Markets: Country-Specific Drivers of the Global Diffusion of Innovations." *Research Policy* 33: 997–1018.
Ben-Aaron, Diana. 2010. "After Nokia, Can Angry Birds Propel Finland?" *Bloomberg Business Week*, December 2. https://www.bloomberg.com/news/articles/2010-12-02/after-nokia-can-angry-birds-propel-finland.
Benner, Mats. 2003. "The Scandinavian Challenge: The Future of Advanced Welfare States in the Knowledge Economy." *Acta Sociologica* 46 (2): 132–49.
Berger, Suzanne, and Michael Piore. 1980. *Dualism and Discontinuity in Industrial Societies*. Cambridge, UK: Cambridge University Press.
Berggren, Christian, and Staffan Laestadius. 2003. "Co-Development and Composite Clusters: The Secular Strength of Nordic Telecommunications." *Industrial and Corporate Change* 12 (1): 91–114.
Bergholm, Tapio. 2003. *A Short History of SAK*. Helsinki: SAK.
Bergmann, Eiríkur. 2014. *Iceland and the International Financial Crisis: Boom, Bust and Recovery*. New York: Palgrave Macmillan.
Berman, Sheri. 1997. "Civil Society and the Collapse of the Weimar Republic." *World Politics* 49 (3): 401–29.
——. 1998. *The Social Democratic Moment: Ideas and Politics in the Making of Interwar Europe*. Cambridge, MA: Harvard University Press.
——. 2006. *The Primacy of Politics: Social Democracy and the Making of Euorpe's Twentieth Century*. Cambridge, UK: Cambridge University Press.
Bilton, Nick. 2011. "The Engineer-Driven Culture of Nokia." *New York Times*, February 11. http://bits.blogs.nytimes.com/2011/02/11/for-nokia-design-will-be-key-to-future/.
Bitard, Pierre, Leif Hommen, and Jekaterina Novikova. 2008. "Appendix: Statistical Bases of Comparison for Ten 'Small Country' NSI." In *Small Country Innovation*

Systems, edited by Charles Edquist and Leif Hommen, 485–530. Cheltenham, UK: Edward Elgar.
Blaas, Wolfgang. 1992. "The Swiss Model: Corporatism or Liberal Capitalism?" In *Social Corporatism: A Superior Economic System?*, edited by Jukka Pekkarinen, Matti Pohjola, and Bob Rowthorn, 363–76. Oxford, UK: Clarendon Press.
Blickenstaff, Brian. 2014. "Life as Struggle: How Iceland Became the World's Best Pound-for-Pound Soccer Team." *Vice Sports*, December 17. https://sports.vice.com/en_us/article/life-as-struggle-how-iceland-became-the-worlds-best-pound-for-pound-soccer-team.
Block, Fred. 2008. "Swimming against the Current: The Rise of a Hidden Developmental State in the United States." *Politics and Society* 36 (2): 169–206.
Blyth, Mark. 2002. *Great Transformations: Economic Ideas and Institutional Change in the Twentieth Century*. Cambridge, UK: Cambridge University Press.
Bodley, John H. 2013. *The Small Nation Solution: How the World's Smallest Nations Can Solve the World's Biggest Problems*. Lanham, MD: AltaMira Press.
Bohle, Dorothee, and Béla Greskovits. 2007. "Neoliberalism, Embedded Neoliberalism, and Neocorporatism: Towards Transnational Capitalism in Central-Eastern Europe." *West European Politics* 30 (3): 443–66.
———. 2012. *Capitalist Diversity on Europe's Periphery*. Ithaca, NY: Cornell University Press.
Bohle, Dorothee, and Wade Jacoby (2011). "Flexibility Revisited: International Markets and the Small States of East-Central Europe." Annual Meeting of the American Political Science Association, Seattle, WA, August 1.
Bolt, Jutta, and Jan Luiten van Zanden. 2013. "The First Update of the Maddison Project: Re-Estimating Growth Before 1820." http://www.ggdc.net/maddison/maddison-project/data.htm.
Boltho, Andrea. 1982. "Growth." In *The European Economy: Growth and Crisis*, edited by Andrea Boltho, 9–39. Oxford, UK: Clarendon Press.
Bonoli, Giuliano, and André Mach. 2000. "Switzerland: Adjustment Politics within Institutional Constraints." In *Welfare and Work in the Open Economy*, edited by Fritz W. Scharpf and Vivien Schmidt, 131–74. Oxford, UK: Oxford University Press.
Bosworth, Mark. 2012. "Nokia Decline Sparks Finnish Start-Up Boom." *BBC News*, December 13. http://www.bbc.com/news/technology-20553656.
Boutin, Paul. 2010. "Analysts: How Nokia Lost the USA." *VentureBeat*, February 16. http://venturebeat.com/2010/02/16/nokia-us-cmda/.
Boyer, Robert. 1997. "French Statism at a Crossroads." In *Political Economy of Modern Capitalism: Mapping Convergence and Diversity*, edited by Colin Crouch and Wolfgang Streeck, 71–101. London: Sage.
Boyes, Roger. 2010. *Meltdown Iceland: How the Global Financial Crisis Bankupted an Entire Country*. London: Bloomsbury Publishing.
Bramwell, Allison, Jen Nelles, and David A. Wolfe. 2008. "Knowledge, Innovation, and Institutions: Global and Local Dimensions of the ICT Cluster in Waterloo, Canada." *Regional Studies* 42 (1): 100–116.
Bramwell, Allison, and David A. Wolfe. 2008. "Universities and Regional Economic Development: The Entrepreneurial University of Waterloo." *Research Policy* 37: 1175–87.
———. 2014. "Dimensions of Governance in a Mega-City: Scale, Scope and Coalitions in Toronto." In *Governing Urban Economies: Innovation and Inclusion in Canadian City-Regions*, edited by Neil Bradford and Allison Bramwell, 58–87. Toronto: University of Toronto Press.

Breznitz, Dan. 2007. *Innovation and the State: Political Choice and Strategies for Growth in Israel, Taiwan, and Ireland*. New Haven, CT: Yale University Press.
——. 2012. "Ideas, Structure, State Action, and Economic Growth: Rethinking the Irish Miracle." *Review of International Political Economy* 19 (1): 87–113.
Breznitz, Dan, and Darius Ornston. 2013. "The Revolutionary Power of Peripheral Agencies: Explaining Radical Policy Innovation in Finland and Israel." *Comparative Political Studies* 46 (10): 1219–45.
——. 2014. "Scaling Up and Sustaining Experimental Innovation Policies with Limited Resources: Peripheral Schumpeterian Developmental Agencies." In *Making Innovation Policy Work: Learning from Experimentation*, edited by Mark Dutz, Yevgeny Kuznetsov, Esperanza Lasagabaster, and Dirk Pilat, 247–77. Washington, DC: OECD/World Bank.
——. 2017. "EU Financing and Innovation in Poland." In *EBRD Working Paper*, No. 198. London: European Bank for Reconstruction and Development.
——. Forthcoming. "The Politics of Partial Success: Fostering Innovation in Innovation Policy in an Era of Heightened Public Scrutiny." *Socio-Economic Review*. http://dx.doi.org/10.1093/ser/mww018.
Breznitz, Shiri M., and Antti-Jussi Tahvanainen. 2010. "Cluster Sustainability in Peripheral Regions: A Case Study on Israel's and Finland's Biotechnology Industries." In *ETLA Discussion Paper*, No. 1212. Helsinki: Research Institute of the Finnish Economy.
Brown, J. Christopher, and Mark Purcell. 2005. "There's Nothing Inherent About Scale: Political Ecology, the Local Trap, and the Politics of Development in the Brazilian Amazon." *Geoforum* 36 (5): 607–24.
Burt, Ronald. 2005. *Brokerage and Closure: An Introduction to Social Capital*. Oxford, UK: Oxford University Press.
Cagnin, Cristiano, Effie Amanatidou, and Michael Keenan. 2012. "Orienting European Innovation Systems towards Grand Challenges and the Roles that FTA Can Play." *Science and Public Policy* 39 (2): 140–52.
Campbell, John L., and John A. Hall. 2009. "National Identity and the Political Economy of Small States." *Review of International Political Economy* 16 (4): 547–72.
——. 2015. "Small States, Nationalism and Institutional Capacities: An Explanation of the Difference in Response of Ireland and Denmark to the Financial Crisis." *European Journal of Sociology* 56 (1): 143–74.
——. 2017. *The Paradox of Vulnerability: States, Nationalism and the Financial Crisis*. Princeton, NJ: Princeton University Press.
Campbell, John L., and Øve K. Pedersen. 2007. "The Varieties of Capitalism and Hybrid Success: Denmark in the Global Economy." *Comparative Political Studies* 40 (3): 307–32.
Carey, David. 2009. "Iceland: The Financial and Economic Crisis." *OECD Economics Department Working Paper*, No. 725. Paris: OECD.
Carlsson, Bo, Lennart Elg, and Staffan Jacobsson. 2010. "Reflections on the Co-Evolution of Innovation Theory, Policy, and Practice: The Emergence of the Swedish Agency for Innovation Systems." In *The Theory and Practice of Innovation Policy*, edited by Ruud Smits, Stefan Kuhlmann, and Philip Shapira, 145–66. London: Edwin Elgar.
Casper, Steven. 2007a. *Creating Silicon Valley in Europe: Public Policy towards New Technology Industries*. Oxford, UK: Oxford University Press.
——. 2007b. "How Do Technology Clusters Emerge and Become Sustainable? Social Network Formation and Inter-firm Mobility within the San Diego Biotechnology Cluster." *Research Policy* 36: 438–55.

Castells, Manuel, and Pekka Himanen. 2002. *The Information Society and the Welfare State: The Finnish Model*. Oxford, UK: Oxford University Press.
Cetindamar, Dilek, and Staffan Jacobsson. 2003. "The Swedish Venture Capital Industry: An Infant, Adolescent or Grown-Up?" In *The Growth of Venture Capital: A Cross-Cultural Comparison*, edited by Dilek Cetindamar, 119–47. Westport, CT: Praeger.
Childs, Michael. 1936. *Sweden: The Middle Way*. New Haven, CT: Yale University Press.
Christensen, Jakob Ekholdt. 2011. "The Economic Crisis in Ireland, Iceland, and Latvia." *National Bank of Denmark Monetary Review* (1): 107–20.
Clancy, Paula, Nat O'Conner, and Kevin Dillon. 2010. "Mapping the Golden Circle." Dublin: TASC.
Clifton, Judith, Francisco Comín, and Daniel Díaz Fuentes. 2003. *Privatisation in the European Union: Public Enterprises and Integration*. New York: Springer.
Close, David H. 2002. *Greece Since 1945: Politics, Economy and Society*. London: Longman.
Cohen, Stephen S., and Gary Fields. 2000. "Social Capital and Capital Gains: An Examination of Social Capital in Silicon Valley." In *Understanding Silicon Valley: The Anatomy of an Entrepreneurial Region*, edited by Martin Kenney, 190–217. Stanford, CA: Stanford University Press.
Cooke, Philip, Carla De Laurentis, Franz Tödtling, and Michaela Trippl. 2007. *Regional Knowledge Economies: Markets, Clusters, and Innovation*. Cheltenham, UK: Edward Elgar.
Creel, Jérôme, Fabien Labondance, and Sandrine Levasseur. 2014. "The French Banking and Financial System and the Crisis." *Intereconomics* 2: 64–69.
Crepaz, Markus. 1995. "An Institutional Dinosaur: Austrian Corporatism in the Post-industrial Age." *West European Politics* 18: 64–88.
Culpepper, Pepper D. 2002. "Powering, Puzzling, and 'Pacting': The Informational Logic of Negotiated Reforms." *Journal of European Public Policy* 9 (5): 774–90.
———. 2007. "Small States and Skill Specificity: Austria, Switzerland, and Interemployer Cleavages in Coordinated Capitalism." *Comparative Political Studies* 40 (6): 611–37.
Culpepper, Pepper D., and Raphael Rienke. 2014. "Structural Power and Bank Bailouts in the United Kingdom and the United States." *Politics and Society* 42 (4): 427–54.
Cusack, Thomas R., Torben Iversen, and David Soskice. 2007. "Economic Interests and the Origins of Electoral Systems." *American Political Science Review* 101 (3): 373–91.
Dahl, Michael S., Christian Ø. R. Pedersen, and Bent Dalum. 2003. "Entry by Spinoff in a High-Tech Cluster." Aalborg: Danish Research Unit on Industrial Dynamics.
Dahlman, Carl J. 2006. "Conclusions and Lessons from Finland's Knowledge Economy for Other Economies." In *Finland as a Knowledge Economy: Elements of Success and Lessons Learned*, edited by Carl J. Dahlman, Jorma Routti, and Pekka Ylä-Anttila, 99–110. Washington, DC: World Bank Institute.
Dahlman, Carl J., Jorma Routti, and Pekka Ylä-Anttila, eds. 2006a. *Finland as a Knowledge Economy: Elements of Success and Lessons Learned*. Washington, DC: World Bank Institute.
———. 2006b. "Introduction." In *Finland as a Knowledge Economy: Elements of Success and Lessons Learned*, edited by Carl J. Dahlman, Jorma Routti, and Pekka Ylä-Anttila, 1–7. Washington, DC: World Bank Institute.
Dahmén, Erik. 1950. *Svensk Industriell Företagarverksamhet*. Lund: Band I. Industriens Utredningsinstitut.

Dalum, Bent. 1988. "Small Open Economies in the World Market for Electronics: The Case of the Nordic Countries." In *Small Countries Facing the Technological Revolution*, edited by Christopher Freeman and Bengt-Åke Lundvall, 113–38. London: Pinter.

———. 1992. "Export Specialisation, Structural Competitiveness, and National Systems of Innovation." In *National Systems of Innovation: Towards a Theory of Innovation and Interactive Learning*, edited by Bengt-Åke Lundvall. London: Pinter.

Davis, Joshua. 2007. "Hackers Take Down the Most Wired Country in the World." *Wired*, 21 August. http://www.wired.com/2007/08/ff-estonia/.

Davis, Steven J., and Magnus Henrekson. 1997. "Industrial Policy, Employer Size, and Economic Performance in Sweden." In *The Welfare State in Transition: Reforming the Swedish Model*, edited by Richard B. Freeman, Robert Topel, and Birgitta Swedenborg, 353–97. Chicago: University of Chicago Press.

Deak, Csaba, and Zoltan Peredy. 2015. "Policy Framework Conditions to Foster 'System Innovation' with Some Illustration from an International Perspective." *Journal of Innovation Management* 3 (1): 14–24.

Deeg, Richard. 2010. "Industry and Finance in Germany since Unification." *German Politics and Society* 28 (2): 116–29.

Dellepiane, Sebastian, and Niamh Hardiman. 2011. "Governing the Irish Economy: A Triple Crisis." *UCD Geary Institute Discussion Paper*, No. WP2011/03. Dublin: University College Dublin Geary Institute.

de Serres, Alain, Shuji Kobayakawa, Torsten Sløk, and Laura Vartia. 2006. "Regulation of Financial Systems and Economic Growth in OECD Countries: An Empirical Analysis." *OECD Economic Studies* 43: 78–113.

Detzer, Daniel. 2014. "Financial Systems in Financial Crisis: An Analysis of Banking Systems in the EU." *Intereconomics* 2: 56–64.

Doner, Richard F., and Benjamin Ross Schneider. 2016. "The Middle-Income Trap: More Politics than Economics." *World Politics* 68 (4): 608–44.

Donovan, Donal, and Antoine E. Murphy. 2013. *The Fall of the Celtic Tiger: Ireland and the Euro Debt Crisis*. Oxford, UK: Oxford University Press.

Economist, The. 2013a. "How Did Estonia Become a Leader in Technology?" *The Economist*, 31 July. https://www.economist.com/blogs/economist-explains/2013/07/economist-explains-21.

———. 2013b. "The Nordic Countries: The Next Supermodel." *The Economist*, February 2. https://www.economist.com/news/leaders/21571136-politicians-both-right-and-left-could-learn-nordic-countries-next-supermodel.

———. 2013c. "Not Only Skype." *The Economist*, 11 July. http://www.economist.com/blogs/schumpeter/2013/07/estonias-technology-cluster.

———. 2015. "Austerity without the Anger." *The Economist*, June 6. http://www.economist.com/news/europe/21653653-perhaps-surprisingly-anti-austerity-and-populist-parties-are-not-doing-well-austerity-without.

Edquist, Charles, ed. 1997. *Systems of Innovation: Technologies, Institutions, and Organizations*. London: Pinter.

Edquist, Charles, and Leif Hommen, eds. 2008. *Small Country Innovation Systems: Globalization, Change, and Policy in Asia and Europe*. Cheltenham, UK: Edward Elgar.

Eichengreen, Barry. 2006. *The European Economy since 1945: Coordinated Capitalism and Beyond*. Princeton, NJ: Princeton University Press.

Eklund, Magnus. 2007. "The Adoption of the Innovation System Concept in Sweden." PhD diss., University of Uppsala.

Englund, Peter, and Vesa Vihriälä. 2003. "Financial Crises in Developed Economies: The Cases of Sweden and Finland." *Pellervo Economic Research Institute Working Paper*, No. 63. Helsinki: Pellervo Economic Research Institute.

———. 2009. "Financial Crisis in Finland and Sweden: Similar but Not Quite the Same." In *The Great Financial Crisis in Finland and Sweden: The Nordic Experience of Financial Liberalization*, edited by Lars Jonung, Jaakko Kiander, and Pentti Vartia, 71–130. Cheltenham, UK: Edward Elgar.

Erixon, Lennart. 1982. "Why Did Swedish Industry Perform So Poorly in the Crisis?" *Skandinaviska-Enskilda Banken Quarterly Review* 4.

———. 1997. "The Golden Age of the Swedish Model: The Coherence between Capital Accumulation and Economic Policy in Sweden in the Postwar Period." Oslo: Institutt for Samfunnsforskning.

Esping-Andersen, Gösta. 1990. *The Three Worlds of Welfare Capitalism*. Princeton, NJ: Princeton University Press.

Esser, Josef, Wolfgang Fach, and Kenneth Dyson. 1983. "Social Market and Modernization Policy: West Germany." In *Industrial Crisis: A Comparative Study of the State and Industry*, edited by Kenneth Dyson and Stephen Wilks, 102–27. New York: St. Martin's.

European Commission. 2007. *Biopolis: Inventory and Analysis of National Public Policies that Stimulate Biotechnology Research, Its Exploitation and Commercialization by Industry in Europe in the Period 2002–2005: Final Report*. Luxembourg: Office for Official Publications of the European Union.

———. 2011. *European Competitiveness Report*. Luxembourg: Office for Official Publications of the European Union.

European Social Survey. 2004. "European Social Survey, Round 2." European Social Survey, accessed 15 November 2017. http://www.europeansocialsurvey.org/download.html?file=ESS2e03_5&y=2004.

Eurostat. 2016. "Data Explorer." Eurostat, accessed 1 December. http://epp.eurostat.cec.eu.int/.

Eythórsson, Einar. 2000. "A Decade of ITQ-Management in Icelandic Fisheries: Consolidation without Consensus." *Marine Policy* 24: 483–92.

Federal Reserve Bank of St. Louis. 2016. "FRED Economic Data." https://fred.stlouisfed.org.

Feldman, Magnus. 2006. "Emerging Varieties of Capitalism in Transition Countries: Industrial Relations and Wage Bargaining in Estonia and Slovenia." *Comparative Political Studies* 39 (7): 829–54.

Fellman, Susanna. 2008. "Growth and Investment: Finnish Capitalism, 1850s–2005." In *Creating Nordic Capitalism: The Business History of a Competitive Periphery*, edited by Susanna Fellman, Martin Jes Iversen, Hans Sjögren, and Lars Thue, 139–217. New York: Palgrave Macmillan.

Fellman, Susanna, Martin Jes Iversen, Hans Sjögren, and Lars Thue, eds. 2008. *Creating Nordic Capitalism: The Business History of a Competitive Periphery*. New York: Palgrave Macmillan.

Fernandes, Tiago. 2015. "Rethinking Pathways to Democracy: Civil Society in Portugal and Spain, 1960s-2000s." *Democratization* 22 (6): 1074–1104.

Feubli, Patricia, Emilie Gachet, Philipp Hänggi, and Damian Künzi. 2013. *Swiss Watch Industry: Prospects and Challenges*. Zurich: Credit Suisse Group AG.

Fioretos, Orfeo. 2013. "Origins of Embedded Orthodoxy: International Cooperation and Political Unity in Greece." *European Political Studies* 12: 305–19.

Fishman, Robert. 2010. "Rethinking the Iberian Transformations: How Democratization Scenarios Shaped Labor Market Outcomes." *Studies in Comparative International Development* 45 (3): 281–310.

Florida, Richard L. 2002. *The Rise of the Creative Class and How It's Transforming Work, Leisure, Community and Everyday Life*. New York: Basic Books.

Fontagné, Lionel, Pamina Koenig, Florian Mayneris, and Sandra Poncet. 2013. "Cluster Policies and Firm Selection: Evidence from France." *Journal of Regional Science* 53 (5): 897–922.
Fuchs, Erica. 2010. "Rethinking the Role of the State in Technology Development: DARPA and the Case for Embedded Network Governance." *Research Policy* 39: 1133–47.
Gargiulo, Martin, and Mario Benassi. 1999. "The Dark Side of Social Capital." In *Corporate Social Capital and Liability*, edited by Roger Leenders and Shaul Gabbay, 298–332. Boston: Kluwer.
Gehring, Keith. 2015. "The Role of Institutions and Policy in Knowledge Sector Development: An Assessment of the Danish and Norwegian Information Communication Technology Sectors." PhD diss., University of Denver.
Gergils, Hakan. 2006. *Dynamic Innovation Systems in the Nordic Countries*. Vol. 2. Stockholm: SNS Förlag.
Gingrich, Andre, and Ulf Hannerz. 2017. "Introduction: Exploring Small Countries." In *Small Countries: Structures and Sensibilities*, edited by Andre Gingrich and Ulf Hannerz, 1–44. Philadelphia: University of Pennsylvania Press.
Girvin, Brian. 1997. "Political Culture, Political Independence and Economic Success in Ireland." *Irish Political Studies* 12 (1): 48–77.
Glimstedt, Henrik, and Udo Zander. 2003. "Sweden's Wireless Wonders: The Diverse Roots and Selective Adaptations of the Swedish Internet Economy." In *The Global Internet Economy*, edited by Bruce Kogut, 109–51. Cambridge, MA: MIT Press.
Godinho, Manuel Mira, Vítor Corado Simões, and Jana Zifciakova. 2016. *RIO Country Report 2015: Portugal*. Luxembourg: European Commission.
Goldthorpe, John H., ed. 1984. *Order and Conflict in Contemporary Capitalism*. Oxford, UK: Clarendon.
Gorkey-Aydingolgu, Selda, and Zekai Ozdemir. 2015. "Governance of Technology and Innovation Policy Mix: The Estonian Experience Since 2000." *Review of European Studies* 7 (7): 144–51.
Gorodnichenko, Yuriy, Enrique G. Mendoza, and Linda L. Tesar. 2012. "The Finnish Great Depression: From Russia with Love." *American Economic Review* 102 (4): 1619–44.
Gourevitch, Peter. 1986. *Politics in Hard Times*. Ithaca, NY: Cornell University Press.
Grabher, Gernot. 1993. "The Weakness of Strong Ties: The Lock-in of Regional Development in the Ruhr Area." In *The Embedded Firm*, edited by Gernot Grabher, 255–77. London: Routledge.
Grímsson, Ólafur Ragnur. 1976. "The Icelandic Power Structure, 1800–2000." *Scandinavian Political Studies* 11 (1): 9–33.
Grønning, Terje, Svein Erik Moen, and Dorothy Sutherland Olsen. 2008. "Low Innovation Intensity, High Growth and Specialized Trajectories: Norway." In *Small Country Innovation Systems: Globalization, Change, and Policy in Asia and Europe*, edited by Charles Edquist and Leif Hommen, 281–318. Cheltenham, UK: Edward Elgar.
Grunwald, Michael. 2015. "Don't Break Up the Megabanks." *Politico*, May 27. http://www.politico.com/agenda/story/2015/05/sanders-dont-break-up-the-big-banks-000054.
Gustavson, Carl G. 1986. *The Small Giant: Sweden Enters the Industrial Era*. Athens: Ohio University Press.
Gwartney, James, Robert Lawson, and Joshua Hall. 2015. *Economic Freedom of the World: 2015 Annual Report*. Vancouver: Fraser Institute.

Gylfason, Thorvaldur. 2015. "Iceland: How Could This Happen?" In *Reform Capacity and Macroeconomic Performance in the Nordic Countries*, edited by Torben M. Andersen, U. Michael Bergman, and Svend E. Hougaard Jensen, 310–48. Oxford, UK: Oxford University Press.

Gylfason, Thorvaldur, Bengt Holmström, Sixten Korkman, Hans Tson Söderström, and Vesa Vihriälä. 2010. *Nordics in Global Crisis: Vulnerability and Resilience*. Helsinki: Taloustieto Ltd.

Häikiö, Martti. 2002. *Nokia: The Inside Story*. London: Prentice Hall.

Hall, Peter A. 1986. *Governing the Economy: The Politics of State Intervention in Britain and France*. Oxford, UK: Oxford University Press.

———. 1999. "The Evolution of Economic Policymaking in the European Union." In *From the Nation State to Europe?*, edited by Anand Menon and Vincent Wright, 214–45. Oxford, UK: Oxford University Press.

Hall, Peter A., and Daniel Gingerich. 2009. "Varieties of Capitalism and Institutional Complementarities in the Political Economy." *British Journal of Political Science* 39 (3): 449–82.

Hall, Peter A., and Michele Lamont, eds. 2009. *Successful Societies: How Institutions and Culture Affect Health*. Cambridge, UK: Cambridge University Press.

Hall, Peter A., and David Soskice. 2001. "An Introduction to Varieties of Capitalism." In *Varieties of Capitalism: The Institutional Foundations of Comparative Advantage*, edited by Peter A. Hall and David Soskice, 1–70. Oxford, UK: Oxford University Press.

Halldórsson, Ólafur G., and Gylfi Zoega. 2010. "Iceland's Financial Crisis in an International Perspective." Reykjavik: University of Iceland Department of Economics.

Hamann, Kerstein, Alison Johnston, and John Kelly. 2013. "Unions against Governments: Explaining General Strikes in Western Europe, 1980–2006." *Comparative Political Studies* 46 (9): 1030–57.

Hancké, Bob. 1997. "Modernisation without Flexible Specialisation: How Restructuring and Government Regional Policies Became the Step-Parents of Autarchical Regional Production Systems in France." *WZB Discussion Paper* 97 (304). Berlin: Wissenschaftszentrum.

Hancké, Bob, Martin Rhodes, and Mark Thatcher. 2007. "Introduction: Beyond Varieties of Capitalism." In *Beyond Varieties of Capitalism: Conflict, Contradictions and Complementarities in the European Economy*, edited by Bob Hancké, Martin Rhodes, and Mark Thatcher, 3–38. Oxford, UK: Oxford University Press.

Hannerz, Ulf. 2017. "Swedish Encounters: End Notes of a Native Son." In *Small Countries: Structures and Sensibilities*, edited by Andre Gingrich and Ulf Hannerz, 317–32. Philadelphia: University of Pennsylvania Press.

Hardie, Iain, and David Howarth. 2009. "Die Krise but not La Crise? The Financial Crisis and the Transformation of German and French Banking Systems." *Journal of Common Market Studies* 47 (5): 1017–39.

Hardiman, Niamh, and Aidan Regan. 2013. "The Politics of Austerity in Ireland." *Intereconomics* 48 (1): 9–14.

Helgason, Magnús Sveinn. 2015. "Bankers behind Bars: Is Iceland Living Up to That Meme?" *Reykjavik Grapevine*, March 24. http://grapevine.is/mag/articles/2015/03/24/bankers-behind-bars-is-iceland-living-up-to-that-meme/.

Hemerijck, Anton, Brigitte Unger, and Jelle Visser. 2000. "How Small Countries Negotiate Change: Twenty-Five Years of Policy Adjustment in Austria, the Netherlands, and Belgium." In *Welfare and Work in the Open Economy*, edited by

Fritz W. Scharpf and Vivien A. Schmidt, 175–263. Oxford, UK: Oxford University Press.

Henrekson, Magnus, and Ulf Jakobsson. 2001. "Where Schumpeter Was Nearly Right: The Swedish Model and Capitalism, Socialism, and Democracy." *Journal of Evolutionary Economics* 11: 331–58.

———. 2003. "The Transformation of Ownership Policy and Structure in Sweden: Convergence towards the Anglo-Saxon Model?" *New Political Economy* 8 (1): 73–102.

Henrekson, Magnus, Lars Jonung, and Joakim Stymne. 1996. "Economic Growth and the Swedish Model." In *Economic Growth in Europe since 1945*, edited by Nicholas Crafts and Gianni Toniolo, 240–89. Cambridge, UK: Cambridge University Press.

Herrigel, Gary. 1996. *Industrial Constructions: The Sources of German Industrial Power*. Cambridge, UK: Cambridge University Press.

Herrmann, Andrea M. 2009. *One Political Economy, One Competitive Strategy? Comparing Pharmaceutical Firms in Germany, Italy, and the UK*. Oxford, UK: Oxford University Press.

Hoffmann, Stanley. 1963. "Paradoxes of the French Political Community." In *In Search of France*, edited by Stanley Hoffman, 1–60. New York: Harper.

Hofmann, Paul. 1981. "The Swiss Malaise." *New York Times*, February 8.

Hölttä, Kirsi. 2011. "Rovion Johtaja Haluaa Rajat Auki Venäläisille ja Kiinalaisille [Rovio Boss Wants Open Borders to Russia and China]." *Aamulehti*, August 27. http://www.aamulehti.fi/Kotimaa/1194694300351/artikkeli/puheenaihe+rovion+johtaja+haluaa+rajat+auki+venalaisille+ja+kiinalaisille.html.

Hommen, Leif, and Charles Edquist. 2008. "Globalization and Innovation Policy." In *Small Country Innovation Systems: Globalization, Change, and Policy in Asia and Europe*, edited by Charles Edquist and Leif Hommen, 442–83. Cheltenham, UK: Edward Elgar.

Honkapohja, Seppo, Erkki Koskela, Stefan Gerlach, and Lucrezia Reichlin. 1999. "The Economic Crisis of the 1990s in Finland." *Economic Policy* 14 (29): 399–436.

Honohan, Patrick. 2010. *The Irish Banking Crisis: Regulatory and Financial Stability Policy, 2003–2008*. Dublin: Central Bank of Ireland.

Hyytinen, Ari, Iikka Kuosa, and Tuomas Takalo. 2003. "Investor Protection and Financial Development in Finland." In *Financial Systems and Firm Performance: Theoretical and Empirical Perspectives*, edited by Ari Hyytinen and Mika Pajarinen, 65–95. Helsinki: Taloustieto Ltd.

Hyytinen, Ari, and Mika Pajarinen. 2003. "Financial Systems and Venture Capital in the Nordic Countries: A Comparative Study." In *Financial Systems and Firm Performance: Theoretical and Empirical Perspectives*, edited by Ari Hyytinen and Mika Pajarinen, 19–63. Helsinki: Taloustieto Ltd.

Hyytinen, Ari, Petri Rouvinen, Otto Toivanen, and Pekka Ylä-Anttila. 2003. "Does Financial Development Matter for Innovation and Economic Growth? Implications for Public Policy." In *Financial Systems and Firm Performance: Theoretical and Empirical Perspectives*, edited by Ari Hyytinen and Mika Pajarinen, 379–456. Helsinki: Taloustieto Ltd.

Hyytinen, Ari, and Lotta Väänänen. 2003. "Government Funding of Small and Medium-Sized Enterprises in Finland." In *Financial Systems and Firm Performance: Theoretical and Empirical Perspectives*, edited by Ari Hyytinen and Mika Pajarinen, 325–78. Helsinki: Taloustieto Ltd.

Icelandic Tourist Board. 2015. "Tourism in Iceland in Figures." Reykjavik: Icelandic Tourist Board.

IMF [International Monetary Fund]. 2011. "International Monetary Fund, Article IV Consultations 2006 and 2008." In *Preludes to the Icelandic Financial Crisis*, edited by Robert Z. Aliber and Gylfi Zoega, 43–49. New York: Palgrave Macmillan.

———. 2015a. "Iceland: Selected Issues." Washington, DC: International Monetary Fund.

———. 2015b. "Now Is the Time: Fiscal Policies for Sustainable Growth." In *IMF Fiscal Monitor*. Washington, DC: International Monetary Fund.

Immergut, Ellen M. 1992. *Health Politics: Interests and Institutions in Western Europe*. Cambridge, UK: Cambridge University Press.

IPA [Institute of Practitioners in Advertising]. 2014. "Iceland Tourism: How Social Media Rescued Icelandic Tourism." London: Institute of Practitioners in Advertising.

Iversen, Torben, and Jonas Pontusson. 2000. "Comparative Political Economy: A Northern European Perspective." In *Unions, Employers, and Central Banks: Macroeconomic Coordination and Institutional Change in Social Market Economies*, edited by Torben Iversen, David Soskice, and Jonas Pontusson, 1–37. New York: Cambridge University Press.

Iversen, Torben, and David Soskice. 2009. "Distribution and Redistribution: The Shadow of the 19th Century." *World Politics* 61 (3): 438–86.

Jacoby, Wade. 2001. *Imitation and Politics: Redesigning Modern Germany*. Ithaca, NY: Cornell University Press.

Jalan, Bimal. 1982. "Classification of Economies by Size." In *Problems and Policies in Small Countries*, edited by Bimal Jalan, 39–48. London: Croom Helm.

Jännäri, Kaarlo. 2009. "Report on Banking Regulation and Supervision in Iceland: Past, Present and Future." Reykjavik: Prime Minister's Office.

Jansen, Sue Curry. 2011. "Redesigning a Nation: Welcome to E-stonia, 2001–2018." In *Branding Post-Communist Nations: Marketizing National Identities in the "New" Europe*, edited by Nadia Kaneva, 120–44. London: Routledge.

Jóhannesson, Guðni Thorlacius. 2013. *The History of Iceland*. Santa Barbara, CA: Greenwood.

Jóhannesson, Gunnar Thór, and Edward H. Huijbens. 2010. "Tourism in Times of Crisis: Exploring the Discourse of Tourism Development in Iceland." *Current Issues in Tourism* 13 (5): 419–34.

Johansson, Dan. 1997. "The Number and the Size Distribution of Firms in Sweden and Other European Countries." *IUI Working Paper*, No. 483. Stockholm: Research Institute on Industrial Economics.

Jónsson, Gudmundur. 2004. "Iceland, OEEC and the Trade Liberalisation of the 1950s." *Scandinavian Economic History Review* 52 (2–3): 62–84.

Jonung, Lars, Jaakko Kiander, and Pentti Vartia. 2009. "The Great Financial Crisis in Finland and Sweden: The Dynamics of Boom, Bust, and Recovery." In *The Great Financial Crisis in Finland and Sweden: The Nordic Experience of Liberalization*, edited by Lars Jonung, Jaakko Kiander, and Pentti Vartia, 19–70. London: Edward Elgar.

Kaitila, Ville, Heli Koski, Jorma Routti, Paula Tiihonen, and Pekka Ylä-Anttila. 2006. "Changes in the Economic and Institutional Regimes." In *Finland as a Knowledge Economy: Elements of Success and Lessons Learned*, edited by Carl J. Dahlman, Jorma Routti, and Pekka Ylä-Anttila, 25–38. Washington, DC: World Bank Institute.

Karlsson, Gunnar. 2000. *Iceland's 1100 Years: History of a Marginal Society*. London: C. Hurst & Co.

Karo, Erkki, and Rainer Kattel. 2016. "How to Organize for Innovation: Entrepreneurial State and Organizational Variety." *Working Papers in Technology Governance and Economic Dymanics*, No. 66. Tallinn: Tallinn University of Technology.

Kattel, Rainer, and Ringa Raudla. 2013. "The Baltic Republics and the Crisis of 2008–2011." *Europe-Asia Studies* 65 (3): 426–49.

Katzenstein, Peter J. 1984. *Corporatism and Change: Austria, Switzerland and the Politics of Industry*. Ithaca, NY: Cornell University Press.

———. 1985. *Small States in World Markets: Industrial Policy in Europe*. Ithaca, NY: Cornell University Press.

———. 1987. *Policy and Politics in West Germany: The Growth of a Semi-Sovereign State*. Philadelphia: Temple University Press.

Keller, Matthew R., and Fred Block. 2013. "Explaining the Transformation in the US Innovation System: The Impact of a Small Government Program." *Socio-Economic Review* 11: 629–56.

Kenworthy, Lane. 2003. "Quantitative Indicators of Corporatism." *International Journal of Sociology* 33 (3): 10–44.

Kern, Horst. 1998. "Lack of Trust, Surfeit of Trust: Some Causes of the Innovation Crisis in German Industry." In *Trust Within and In Between Organizations: Conceptual Issues and Empirical Applications*, edited by Christel Lane and Reinhard Bachman, 203–13. New York: Oxford.

Kiander, Jaakko. 2005. "The Evolution of the Finnish Model in the 1990s: From Depression to High Tech Boom." In *Employment Miracles: A Critical Comparison of the Dutch, Scandinavian, Swiss, Australian, and Irish Cases versus Germany and the US*, edited by Herman Schwartz and Uwe Becker, 87–112. Amsterdam: Amsterdam University Press.

Kiander, Jaakko, and Jaakko Pehkonen. 1999. "Finnish Unemployment: Observations and Conjectures." *Finnish Economic Papers* 12 (2): 94–108.

Kingsley, Patrick. 2012. "How Tiny Estonia Stepped Out of the USSR's Shadow to Become an Internet Titan." *Guardian*, 15 April. https://www.theguardian.com/technology/2012/apr/15/estonia-ussr-shadow-internet-titan.

Kissane, Bill. 2002. *Explaining Irish Democracy*. Dublin: University College Dublin Press.

Kitschelt, Herbert, Peter Lange, Gary Marks, and John D. Stephens. 1999. "Convergence and Divergence in Advanced Capitalist Societies." In *Continuity and Change in Contemporary Capitalism*, edited by Herbert Kitschelt, Peter Lange, Gary Marks, and John D. Stephens, 427–59. Cambridge, UK: Cambridge University Press.

Koliopoulos, John S., and Thanos Veremis. 2010. *Modern Greece: A History since 1821*. West Sussex, UK: Wiley & Blackwell.

Korpi, Walter. 1983. *The Democratic Class Struggle*. London: Routledge.

Korpi, Walter. 2006. "Power Resources and Employer-Centered Approaches in Explanations of Welfare States and Varieties of Capitalism: Protagonists, Consenters, and Antagonists." *World Politics* 58 (2): 167–206.

Koski, Heli, Liisa Leijola, Christopher Palmberg, and Pekka Ylä-Anttila. 2006. "Innovation and Education Strategies and Policies in Finland." In *Finland as a Knowledge Economy: Elements of Success and Lessons Learned*, edited by Carl J. Dahlman, Jorma Routti, and Pekka Ylä-Anttila, 39–62. Washington, DC: World Bank Institute.

Koski, Heli, and Pekka Ylä-Anttila. 2006. "Structural Changes in the Finnish Economy: From Agriculture to High-Tech." In *Finland as a Knowledge Economy: Elements* of Success and Lessons Learned, edited by Carl J. Dahlman, Jorma Routti, and Pekka Ylä-Anttila, 17–24. Washington, DC: World Bank Institute.

Kristensen, Peer Hull. 1996. "On the Constitution of Economic Actors in Denmark: Interacting Skill Containers and Project Coordinators." In *The Changing European Firm*, edited by Richard Whitley and Peer Hull Kristensen, 118–58. London: Routledge.

———. 1999. "When Labor Defines Business Recipes." In *Mobilizing Resources and Generating Competencies: The Remarkable Success of Small and Medium-Sized Enterprises in the Danish Business System*, edited by Peter Karnoe, Peer Hull Kristensen, and Poul Houman Andersen, 74–112. Copenhagen: Copenhagen Business School Press.

———. 2011. "Developing Comprehensive, Enabling Welfare States for Offensive Experimentalist Business Practices." In *Nordic Capitalisms and Globalization: New Forms of Economic Organization and Welfare Institutions*, edited by Peer Hull Kristensen and Kari Lilja, 220–58. Oxford, UK: Oxford University Press.

Kristensen, Peer Hull, and Jørn Levinsen. 1983. *The Small Country Squeeze*. Roskilde: Forlaget for samfundsøkonomi og Planlægning.

Kristensen, Peer Hull, and Kari Lilja, eds. 2011. *Nordic Capitalisms and Globalization: New Forms of Economic Organization and Welfare Institutions*. Oxford, UK: Oxford University Press.

Krugman, Paul. 2013. "Revenge of the Optimum Currency Area." In *NBER Macroeconomics Annual*, edited by Daron Acemoglu, Jonathan Parker, and Michael Woodford, 439–48. Chicago: University of Chicago Press.

Kuisma, Markku. 1999. "We Have No Rockefellers But We Have Cooperatives." In *The Pellervo Story*, edited by Markku Kuisma, Annastiina Henttinen, Sami Karhu, and Maritta Pohls, 9–24. Helsinki: Pellervo.

Kuokstis, Vytautas. 2015. "The Baltic States in World Markets: Does Peter Katzenstein's Framework Still Hold?" *Journal of Baltic Studies* 46 (2): 109–26.

Kurzer, Paulette. 2014. "How Different Are Northern and Southern Europe? A Look at Housing Bubbles and Crashes." Annual Meeting of the American Political Science Association, Washington, DC, 28–31 August.

Kuusi, Tero. 2015. "The Finnish Great Depression of the 1990s: Soviet Trade or Home-Made?" *ETLA Working Paper*, No. 32. Helsinki: Research Institute of the Finnish Economy.

Laeven, Luc, and Fabian Valencia. 2012. "Systemic Banking Crises Database: An Update." Washington, DC: International Monetary Fund.

Lange, Knut. 2009. "Institutional Embeddedness and the Strategic Leeway of Actors: The Case of the German Therapeutical Biotech Industry." *Socio-Economic Review* 7: 181–207.

Larsen, Hans Kryger. 2001. "Introduction." In *Convergence? Industrialization of Denmark, Finland and Sweden 1870–1940*, edited by Hans Kryger Larsen, 9–20. Helsinki: Finnish Society of Sciences and Letters.

Larsson, Mats, Håkan Lindgren, and Daniel Nyberg. 2008. "Entrepreneurship and Ownership: The Long-Term Viability of the Swedish Bonnier and Wallenberg Family Business Groups." In *Creating Nordic Capitalism: The Business History of a Competitive Periphery*, edited by Susanna Fellman, Martin Jes Iversen, Hans Sjögren, and Lars Thue, 75–103. London: Palgrave Macmillan.

Lavdas, Kostas A. 2005. "Interest Groups in Disjointed Corporatism: Social Dialogue in Greece and European Competitive Corporatism." *West European Politics* 28 (2): 297–316.

Lavery, Brian, and Timothy O'Brien. 2005. "Insurers' Trails Lead to Dublin." *New York Times*, April 1. http://query.nytimes.com/gst/fullpage.html?res=9805EED9103FF932A35757C0A9639C8B63.

Lee, Jane. 2009. "'Lex Nokia' Company Snoop Law Passes in Finland: Employee-Monitoring Law Waved Through." *The Register*, March 6. http://www.theregister.co.uk/2009/03/06/finland_nokia_snooping/.

Lehtonen, Heikki, Simo Aho, Jarmo Peltola, and Mika Renvall. 2001. "Did the Crisis Change the Welfare State in Finland?" In *Down from the Heavens, Up from the Ashes: The Finnish Economic Crisis of the 1990s in Light of Economic and Social Research*, edited by Jorma Kalela, Jaakko Kiander, Ullamaija Kivikuru, Heikki A. Loikkanen, and Jussi Simpura, 102–29. Helsinki: Government Institute for Economic Research.

Leibovitz, Joseph. 2003. "Institutional Barriers to Associative City-region Governance: The Politics of Institution-building and Economic Governance in 'Canada's Technology Triangle.'" *Urban Studies* 40 (13): 2613–42.

Lember, Veiko, and Tarmo Kalvet. 2014. "Estonia: Public Procurement, Innovation, and 'No Policy' Policy." In *Public Procurement, Innovation, and Policy*, edited by Veiko Lember, Rainer Kattel, and Tarmo Kalvet, 127–19. Berlin: Springer.

Lemola, Tarmo. 2004. "Finnish Science and Technology Policy." In *Embracing the Knowledge Economy: The Dynamic Transformation of the Finnish Innovation System*, edited by Gerd Schienstock, 268–84. Cheltenham, UK: Edward Elgar.

Levy, Jonah. 1999. *Tocqueville's Revenge: State, Society, and Economy in Contemporary France*. Cambridge, MA: Harvard University Press.

———. 2013. "Directionless: French Economic Policy in the Twenty-First Century." In *The Third Globalization: Can Wealthy Nations Stay Rich in the Twenty-First Century?*, edited by Dan Breznitz and John Zysman, 323–49. Oxford, UK: Oxford University Press.

Levy, Jonah, Robert Kagan, and John Zysman. 1997. "The Twin Restorations: The Political Economy of the Reagan and Thatcher 'Revolutions.'" In *Korea's Political Economy: An Institutional Perspective*, edited by Lee-Jay Cho and Yoon-Hyung Kim, 3–57. Boulder, CO: Westview Press.

Lewellen, Wilbur G. 1971. "A Pure Financial Rationale for the Conglomerate Merger." *Journal of Finance* 26: 521–37.

Lewis, Michael. 2009. "Wall Street on the Tundra." *Vanity Fair*, March 3. https://www.vanityfair.com/culture/2009/04/iceland200904-2.

———. 2011. *Boomerang: Travels in the New Third World*. New York: W.W. Norton.

Liimatainen, Karoliina, and Aleksi Teivainen. 2015. "Tekes CEO: Cuts in Science Funding Will Chip Away at Our Strengths." *Helsinki Times*, August 12. http://www.helsinkitimes.fi/finland/finland-news/domestic/13490-tekes-ceo-cuts-in-science-funding-will-chip-away-at-our-strengths.html.

Linden, Carl-Gustav. 2012. "National Champions in Combat: Nokia, Ericsson and the Sensemaking of Business News." PhD diss., University of Helsinki.

Lindvall, Johannes, and Joakim Sebring. 2005. "Policy Reform and the Decline of Corporatism in Sweden." *West European Politics* 28 (5): 1057–74.

Locke, Richard M. 1995. *Remaking the Italian Economy*. Ithaca, NY: Cornell University Press.

Loftsdóttir, Kristín. 2015. "Vikings Invade Present-Day Iceland." In *Gambling Debt: Iceland's Rise and Fall in the Global Economy*, edited by E. Paul Durrenberger and Gísli Pálsson, 3–14. Boulder: University of Colorado Press.

Lundvall, Bengt-Åke, ed. 1992. *National Systems of Innovation: Towards a Theory of Innovation and Interactive Learning*. London: Pinter.
———. 2002. *Innovation, Growth, and Social Cohesion: The Danish Model*. Cheltenham, UK: Edward Elgar.
Luukkonen, Terttu. 2006. "The Venture Capital Industry in Finland." *ETLA Discussion Paper*, No. 1003. Helsinki: Research Institute of the Finnish Economy.
Lyberaki, Antigoni, and Euclid Tsakalotos. 2002. "Reforming the Economy without Society: Social and Institutional Constraints to Reform in Post-1974 Greece." *New Political Economy* 7 (1): 93–114.
Macheda, Francesco. 2012. "The Role of Pension Funds in the Financialisation of the Icelandic Economy." *Capital and Class* 36 (3): 433–73.
MacSharry, Ray, and Padraic White. 2000. *The Making of the Celtic Tiger: The Inside Story of Ireland's Economic Boom*. Cork, IE: Mercier Press.
Madsen, Per Kongshøj. 2006. "How Can It Possibly Fly? The Paradox of a Dynamic Labor Market in a Scandinavian State." In *National Identity and the Varieties of Capitalism: The Danish Experience*, edited by John L. Campbell, John A. Hall, and Øve K. Pedersen, 323–55. Montreal: McGill University Press.
Magnusson, Lars. 2000. *An Economic History of Sweden*. London: Routledge.
Mahon, Alan, Mary Faherty, and Gerald Keys. 2012. "The Final Report of the Tribunal of Inquiry into Certain Planning Matters and Payments." Dublin: Government Publications Office.
Mann, Michael. 1986. *The Sources of Social Power*. Cambridge, UK: Cambridge University Press.
Martin, Cathie Jo, and Duane Swank. 2012. *The Political Construction of Business Interests*. Cambridge, UK: Cambridge University Press.
Martin, Cathie Jo, and Kathleen Thelen. 2007. "The State and Coordinated Capitalism: Contributions of the Public Sector to Social Solidarity in Postindustrial Societies." *World Politics* 60 (3): 1–36.
Mayer, Catherine. 2012. "The Celtic Comeback." *Time*, October 15.
Merrien, Francois Xavier, and Uwe Becker. 2005. "The Swiss Miracle: Low Growth and High Employment." In *Employment Miracles: A Critical Comparison of the Dutch, Scandinavian, Swiss, Australian, and Irish Cases versus Germany and the US*, edited by Uwe Becker and Herman Schwartz, 111–32. Amsterdam: Amsterdam University Press.
Meyer, Morgan B. 2008. "The Dynamics of Science in a Small Country: The Case of Luxembourg." *Science and Public Policy* 35 (5): 361–71.
Milne, Richard. 2015. "Finland's Economy: In Search of the Sunny Side." *Financial Times*, March 11. http://www.ft.com/intl/cms/s/0/35c8560c-c62f-11e4-add0-00144feab7de.html-axzz3kJDJisyD.
Mixa, Màr Wolfgang. 2015. "A Day in the Life of an Icelandic Banker." In *Gambling Debt: Iceland's Rise and Fall in the Global Economy*, edited by E. Paul Durrenberger and Gísli Pálsson, 33–46. Boulder: University Press of Colorado.
Mixa, Màr Wolfgang, and Thröstur Olaf Sigurjónsson. 2011. "Learning from the 'Worst Behaved': Iceland's Financial Crisis and the Nordic Comparison." *Thunderbird International Business Review* 53 (2): 209–24.
Mjøset, Lars. 1987. "Nordic Economic Policies in the 1970s and 1980s." *International Organization* 41 (3): 403–56.
———. 1992. *The Irish Economy in a Comparative Institutional Perspective*. Dublin: National Economic and Social Council.

Moen, Arild. 2011a. "Finland Lawmakers Still Split on Portugal Bailout." *Wall Street Journal*, May 10, 2011. http://online.wsj.com/news/articles/SB10001424052748703730804576315443832330746.

Moen, Eli. 2011b. "Norway: Raw Material Refinement and Innovative Companies in Global Dynamics." In *Nordic Capitalisms and Globalization: New Forms of Economic Organization and Welfare Institutions*, edited by Peer Hull Kristensen and Kari Lilja, 141–82. Oxford, UK: Oxford University Press.

Moen, Eli, and Kari Lilja. 2005. "Change in Coordinated Market Economies: The Case of Nokia and Finland." In *Changing Capitalisms: Internationalization, Institutional Change, and Systems of Economic Organization*, edited by Glenn Morgan, Richard Whitley, and Eli Moen, 352–79. Oxford, UK: Oxford University Press.

Montgomery, Arthur. 1962. "The Swedish Economy in the 1950s." *Scandinavian Economic History Review* 10 (2): 220–32.

Montiel, Peter. 2014. *Ten Crises*. New York: Routledge.

Morrison, Rodney J. 1981. *Portugal: Revolutionary Change in an Open Economy*. Boston: Auburn House.

Morrissey, Martin. 1986. "The Politics of Economic Management in Ireland, 1958–70." *Irish Political Studies* 1 (1): 79–95.

Munro, Andrew, and Harald Bathelt. 2014. "Innovation Linkages in New- and Old-Economy Sectors in Cambridge-Guelph-Kitchener-Waterloo (Ontario)." In *Innovating in Urban Economies: Economic Transformation in Canadian City-Regions*, edited by David A. Wolfe, 219–44. Toronto: University of Toronto Press.

Murto, Eero, Mika Niemelä, and Tapio Laamanen. 2006. *Finnish Technology Policy from the 1960s to the Present Day*. Helsinki: Finnish Ministry of Trade and Industry.

Natali, David, and Philippe Pochet. 2010. "The Recent Evolution of Social Dialogue in Cyprus and Malta: Any Scope for Social Pacts?" In *After the Euro and Enlargement: Social Pacts in the EU*, edited by Philippe Pochet, Maarten Keune, and David Natali, 281–316. Brussels: European Trade Union Institute.

NBP [Narodowy Bank Polski]. 2016. *Potencjał Innowacyjny Gospodarki: Uwarunkowania, Determinanty, Perspektywy* [The Innovative Potential of the Economy: Conditions, Determinants, and Perspectives]. Warsaw: Narodowy Bank Polski.

Nelles, Jen. 2014. "Myth Making and the 'Waterloo Way': Exploring Associative Governance in Kitchener-Waterloo." In *Governing Urban Economies: Innovation and Inclusion in Canadian City-Regions*, edited by Neil Bradford and Allison Bramwell, 88–109. Toronto: University of Toronto Press.

Nelles, Jen, Allison Bramwell, and David A. Wolfe. 2005. "History, Culture, and Path Dependency: Origins of the Waterloo ICT Cluster." In *Global Networks and Local Linkages: The Paradox of Cluster Development in an Open Economy*, edited by David A. Wolfe and Matthew Lucas, 227–52. Montreal: McGill-Queen's University Press.

Neogames. 2014. *The Game Industry of Finland: Report 2014*. Helsinki: Neogames Finland.

Nicholls, Kate. 2015. *Mediating Policy: Greece, Ireland and Portugal before the Eurozone Crisis*. New York: Routledge.

Nordensvard, Johan, and Markus Ketola. 2015. "Nationalist Reframing of the Finnish and Swedish Welfare States: The Nexus of Nationalism and Social Policy in Far-Right Populist Parties." *Social Policy and Administration* 49 (3): 356–75.

Nyberg, Peter. 2011. *Misjudging Risk: Causes of the Systemic Banking Crisis in Ireland*. Dublin: Ministry of Finance.

O'Dwyer, Conor, and Branislav Kovalčík. 2007. "And the Last Shall Be First: Party System Institutionalization and Second-Generation Economic Reform in Postcommunist Europe." *Studies in Comparative International Development* 41 (4): 3–26.

OECD [Organisation for Economic Co-operation and Development]. 2001. *OECD Economic Surveys: Iceland 2001*. Paris: OECD.

———. 2005. *Science, Technology and Industry Scoreboard*. Paris: OECD.

———. 2006. *OECD Economic Surveys: Iceland*. Paris: OECD.

———. 2009a. *OECD Economic Surveys: Austria*. Paris: OECD.

———. 2009b. *OECD Economic Surveys: Iceland*. Paris: OECD.

———. 2010. *Strong Performers and Successful Reformers in Education: Lessons from PISA for the United States*. Paris: OECD.

———. 2011a. *OECD Governance Reviews Estonia: Towards a Single Government Approach*. Paris: OECD.

———. 2011b. "OECD Survey of Iceland, 2006 and 2008." In *Preludes to the Icelandic Financial Crisis*, edited by Robert Z. Aliber and Gylfi Zoega, 50–53. New York: Palgrave Macmillan.

———. 2014. *OECD Economic Surveys: Poland 2014*. Paris: OECD.

———. 2015a. *OECD Economic Surveys: Iceland 2015*. Paris: OECD.

———. 2015b. *OECD Science, Technology and Industry Scoreboard 2015*. Paris: OECD.

———. 2016. "OECD.Stat." OECD, accessed 18 May 2016. http://stats.oecd.org/.

Ó'Grada, Cormac. 1997. *A Rocky Road: The Irish Economy since the 1920s*. Manchester, UK: Manchester University Press.

Ó'Grada, Cormac, and Kevin O'Rourke. 1996. "Irish Economic Growth, 1945–1988." In *Economic Growth in Europe since 1945*, edited by Nicholas Crafts and Gianni Toniolo, 388–426. Cambridge, UK: Cambridge University Press.

Ojala, Jari, and Petri Karonen. 2006. "Business: Rooted in Social Capital over the Centuries." In *The Road to Prosperity: An Economic History of Finland*, edited by Jari Ojala, Jari Eloranta, and Jukka Jalava, 93–126. Helsinki: Suomalaisen Kirjallisuuden Seura.

Ólafsson, Stefán. 2011. "Icelandic Capitalism: From Statism to Neoliberalism and Financial Collapse." *Comparative Social Research* 28: 1–51.

O'Malley, Eoin. 1992. "Problems of Industrialisation in Ireland." *Proceedings of the British Academy* 79: 31–52.

O'Riain, Sean. 2014. *The Rise and Fall of Ireland's Celtic Tiger*. Cambridge, UK: Cambridge University Press.

Orlowski, Andrew. 2011. "Nokia's 15-Year Tango to Avoid Microsoft." *The Register*, February 11. http://www.theregister.co.uk/2011/02/11/nokia_microsoft_history/.

Ornston, Darius. 2006. "Reorganising Adjustment: Finland's Emergence as a High Technology Leader." *West European Politics* 29 (4): 784–801.

———. 2012a. "Old Ideas and New Investments: Divergent Pathways to a Knowledge Economy in Denmark and Finland." *Governance* 25 (4): 687–710.

———. 2012b. *When Small States Make Big Leaps: Institutional Innovation and High-Tech Competition in Western Europe*. Ithaca, NY: Cornell University Press.

———. 2013. "Creative Corporatism: Explaining High-Technology Competition in Nordic Europe." *Comparative Political Studies* 46 (6): 702–29.

———. 2014. "When the High Road Becomes the Low Road: The Limits of High Tech Competition in Finland." *Review of Policy Research* 31 (5): 454–77.

——. 2016. "Small States and Small Cities: Using Interpersonal Networks to Accelerate Restructuring." *IPL White Paper* 2016–03. Toronto: Innovation Policy Lab.

——. 2017. "When Flagships Falter: Comparing Finland and Waterloo." Creating Digital Opportunity Conference, Montreal, Canada, May 2.

Ornston, Darius, and Olli Rehn. 2006. "An Old Consensus in the 'New' Economy? Institutional Adaptation, Technological Innovation and Economic Restructuring in Finland." In *How Revolutionary Was the Revolution? National Responses, Market Transitions, and Global Technology*, edited by John Zysman and Abraham Newman, 78–100. Stanford, CA: Stanford Business Books.

Ornston, Darius, and Tobias Schulze-Cleven. 2015. "Concertation and Coordination: Two Logics of Collective Action." *Comparative Political Studies* 48 (5): 555–85.

Ornston, Darius, and Mark Vail. 2016. "The Developmental State in Developed Societies: Power, Partnership, and Divergent Patterns of Intervention in France and Finland." *Comparative Politics* 49 (1): 1–21.

Østergaard, Christian Richter, and Eunkyung Park. 2015. "What Makes Clusters Decline? A Study on Disruption and Evolution of a High-Tech Cluster in Denmark." *Regional Studies* 49 (5): 834–49.

Ostrom, Elinor. 1990. *Governing the Commons: The Evolution of Institutions for Collective Action*. Cambridge, UK: Cambridge University Press.

Ottosson, Jan. 1997. "Interlocking Directorates in Swedish Big Business in the Early 20th Century." *Acta Sociologica* 40 (1): 51–77.

Pagoulatos, George. 2003. *Greece's New Political Economy: States, Finance, and Growth from Postwar to EMU*. Houndmills, UK: Palgrave Macmillan.

Paija, Laura. 2000. "ICT Cluster: The Engine of Knowledge-Driven Growth in Finland." *ETLA Discussion Paper*, No. 733. Helsinki: Research Institute of the Finnish Economy.

Paija, Laura, and Christopher Palmberg. 2006. "Sectoral Perspectives on the Finnish Knowledge Economy: From Forest-Related Industries to ICT." In *Finland as a Knowledge Economy: Elements of Success and Lessons Learned*, edited by Carl J. Dahlman, Jorma Routti, and Pekka Ylä-Anttila, 63–86. Washington, DC: World Bank.

Pajarinen, Mika, and Petri Rouvinen. 2013. "Nokia's Labor Inflows and Outflows in Finland: Observations from 1989 to 2010." *ETLA Report*, No. 10. Helsinki: Research Institute of the Finnish Economy.

Pálsson, Gísli, and E. Paul Durrenberger. 2015. "Introduction: The Banality of Financial Evil." In *Gambling Debt: Iceland's Rise and Fall in the Global Economy*, edited by E. Paul Durrenberger and Gísli Pálsson, xiii–xxxi. Boulder: University Press of Colorado.

Panayiotopoulos, Prodromos I. 1995. "Cyprus: The Developmental State in Crisis." *Capital and Class* 57: 13–53.

Pappas, Takis S. 2013. "Why Greece Failed." *Journal of Democracy* 24 (2): 31–45.

Pedaliu, Effie. 2013. "The Making of Southern Europe: An Historical Overview." In *A Strategy for Southern Europe*, edited by Eirini Karamouzi, Effie Pedaliu, Emma de Angelis, and Zoi Koustoumpardi, 8–14. London: London School of Economics.

Pekkarinen, Jukka, Matti Pohjola, and Bob Rowthorn, eds. 1992. *Social Corporatism: A Superior Economic System?* Oxford, UK: Clarendon.

Pelkonen, Antti. 2008. "Reconsidering the Finnish Model: Information Societ Policy and Modes of Governance." *TRAMES* 12 (4): 400–420.

Pessoa, Argentino. 2014. "Structural and Technological Change in the European Periphery: Painful Lessons from the European Periphery." In *Structural Change, Competitiveness and Industrial Policy: Painful Lessons*, edited by Aurora A. C. Teixeira, Ester Silva, and Ricardo Mamede, 105–32.
Peter Bacon & Associates. 2000. *The Housing Market in Ireland: An Economic Evaluation of Trends and Prospects*. Dublin: National Economic and Social Council.
Piore, Michael J., and Charles F. Sabel. 1984. *The Second Industrial Divide: Possibilities for Prosperity*. New York: Basic Books.
Pohjola, Matti. 1996. *Tehoton Pääoma* [Inefficient Capital]. Porvoo: WSOY.
Pomerantz, Gary. 1996. *Where Peachtree Meets Sweet Auburn: The Saga of Two Families and the Making of Atlanta*. New York: Scribner.
Pontusson, Jonas. 1992. *The Limits of Social Democracy: Investment Politics in Sweden*. Ithaca, NY: Cornell University Press.
———. 2011. "Once Again a Model: Nordic Social Democracy in a Globalized World." In *What's Left of the Left: Democrats and Social Democrats in Challenging Times*, edited by James Cronin, George Ross, and James Shoch, 89–115. Durham, NC: Duke University Press.
Pontusson, Jonas, and Peter Swenson. 1996. "Labor Markets, Production Strategies, and Wage Bargaining Institutions: The Swedish Employer Offensive in Comparative Perspective." *Comparative Political Studies* 29 (2): 223–50.
Porter, Michael E. 1990. *The Competitive Advantage of Nations*. New York: Free Press.
Portes, Alejandro. 1998. "Social Capital: Its Origins and Applications in Modern Sociology." *Annual Review of Sociology* 24: 1–24.
Powell, Justin J. W. 2013. "Small State, Large World, Global University? Comparing Ascendant National Universities in Luxembourg and Qatar." *Current Issues in Comparative Education* 15 (1): 100–113.
———. 2014. "International National Universities: Migration and Mobility in Luxembourg and Qatar." In *Internationalisation of Higher Education and Global Mobility*, edited by Bernhard Streitwieser, 119–33. Oxford, UK: Oxford University Press.
Prondzynski, Ferdinand von. 1998. "Ireland: Corporatism Revived." In *Changing Industrial Relations in Europe*, edited by Anthony Ferner and Richard Hyman, 55–73. Oxford, UK: Blackwell Publishers.
Putnam, Robert D. 1993. *Making Democracy Work*. Princeton, NJ: Princeton University Press.
———. 2000. *Bowling Alone: The Collapse and Revival of American Community*. New York: Simon & Schuster.
———. 2007. "E Pluribus Unum: Diversity and Community in the Twenty-first Century." *Scandinavian Political Studies* 30 (2): 137–74.
Randma, Tiina. 2001. "A Small Civil Service in Transition: The Case of Estonia." *Public Administration and Development* 21 (1): 41–51.
Raudla, Ringa. 2013. "Fiscal Retrenchment in Estonia during the Financial Crisis: The Role of Institutional Factors." *Public Administration* 91 (1): 32–50.
Raudla, Ringa, and Rainer Kattel. 2011. "Why Did Estonia Choose Fiscal Austerity after the 2008 Crisis?" *Journal of Public Policy* 31 (2): 163–86.
Regan, Aidan. 2014. "What Explains Ireland's Fragile Recovery from the Crisis? The Politics of Comparative Institutional Advantage." *CESifo Forum* 15 (2): 26–31.
Regan, Aidan, and Samuel Brazys. Forthcoming. "Celtic Phoenix or Leprechaun Economics? The Politics of an FDI-led Growth Model in Europe." *New Political Economy*.

Rehn, Olli. 1996. "Corporatism and Industrial Competitiveness in Small European States: Austria, Finland, and Sweden, 1945–1995." PhD diss., Oxford University.

Rodrik, Dani. 2007. *One Economics, Many Recipes: Globalization, Institutions, and Economic Growth*. Princeton, NJ: Princeton University Press.

Rogers, Joel, and Joshua Cohen. 1995. *Associations and Democracy*. New York: Verso.

Rogoff, Kenneth, and Carmen M. Reinhart. 2009. *This Time Is Different: Eight Centuries of Financial Folly*. Princeton, NJ: Princeton University Press.

Rokkan, Stein. 1967. "Geography, Religion, and Social Class: Cross Cutting Cleavages in Norwegian Politics." In *Party Systems and Voter Alignments*, edited by Seymour Martin Lipset and Stein Rokkan, 368–69. New York: Free Press.

Rooney, Ben. 2012. "The Many Reasons Estonia Is a Tech Start-Up Nation." *Wall Street Journal*, 14 June. http://blogs.wsj.com/tech-europe/2012/06/14/the-many-reasons-estonia-is-a-tech-start-up-nation/.

Rosenthal, Howard, Keith Poole, and Nolan McCarty. 2013. *Political Bubbles*. Princeton, NJ: Princeton University Press.

Rötheli, Tobias F. 2012. "Output Growth and Output Variability: Quantifying Connections and Tradeoffs." *Review of Economics* 63 (1): 1–17.

Rothstein, Bo, and Dietlind Stolle. 2003. "Introduction: Social Capital in Scandinavia." *Scandinavian Political Studies* 26 (1): 1–26.

Royo, Sebastian. 2002. "A New Century of Corporatism? Corporatism in Spain and Portugal." *West European Politics* 25 (3): 77–104.

——. 2010. "Portugal and Spain: Paths of Economic Divergence (2000–2007)." *Análise Social* 45: 209–54.

——. 2012. "From Boom to Bust: Portugal, Spain, and the Global Financial Crisis." Annual Meeting of the American Political Science Association, New Orleans.

Rüdiger, Ahrend, Jens Arnold, and Fabrice Murtin. 2009. "Prudential Regulation and Competition in Financial Markets." *OECD Economics Department Working Paper*, No. 735. Paris: OECD.

Rybinski, Krzysztof, and Oskar Kowalewski. 2011. "The Hidden Transformation: The Changing Role of the State after the Collapse of Communism in Central and Eastern Europe." *Oxford Review of Economic Policy* 27 (4): 634–57.

Rydström, Jens. 2011. *Odd Couples: A History of Gay Marriage in Scandinavia*. Amsterdam: Aksant Academic Publishers.

Saari, Juho. 2001. "Bridging the Gap: Financing Social Policy in Finland, 1990–1998." In *Down from the Heavens, Up from the Ashes: The Finnish Economic Crisis of the 1990s in Light of Economic and Social Research*, edited by Jorma Kalela, Jaakko Kiander, Ullamaija Kivikuru, Heikki A. Loikkanen, and Jussi Simpura, 189–214. Helsinki: Government Institute for Economic Research.

Saarinen, Jani. 2005. "Innovations and Industrial Performance in Finland 1945–1998." PhD diss., Lund University.

Sabel, Charles, and Annalee Saxenian. 2008. *A Fugitive Success: Finland's Economic Future*. Helsinki: Finnish National Fund for Research and Development.

Safford, Sean. 2009. *Why the Garden Club Couldn't Save Youngstown: The Transformation of the Rust Belt*. Cambridge, MA: Harvard University Press.

Sajari, Petri. 2009. "Nokia—Stronger than Law?" *Helsingin Sanomat*, February 1. http://www.hs.fi/english/article/Nokia+-+stronger+than+law/1135243256669.

Salovaara-Moring, Inka. 2009. "Mind the Gap? Press Freedom and Pluralism in Finland." In *Press Freedom and Pluralism in Europe: Concepts and Conditions*, edited by Andrea Czepek, Melanie Hellwig, and Eva Nowak, 213–28. Bristol, UK: Intellect Books.

Schmidt, Vivien. 2002. *The Futures of European Capitalism*. Oxford: Oxford University Press.
Schmitter, Philippe C., and Gerhard Lehmbruch, eds. 1979. *Trends toward Corporatist Intermediation*. Beverly Hills, CA: Sage.
Schmitz, Hubert. 1991. "Industrial Districts: Model and Reality in Baden-Württemberg, Germany." In *Industrial Districts and Local Economic Regeneration*, edited by Frank Pyke and Werner Sengenberger, 3–29. Geneva: International Institute for Labor Studies.
Schrank, Andrew, and Marcus J. Kurtz. 2005. "Credit Where Credit Is Due: Open Economy Industrial Policy and Export Diversification in Latin America and the Caribbean." *Politics and Society* 33 (4): 671–702.
Schwartz, Herman. 1994. "Small States in Big Trouble: The Politics of State Reorganization in Australia, Denmark, New Zealand, and Sweden in the 1980s." *World Politics* 46 (4): 527–55.
Schwartz, Herman, and Uwe Becker. 2005a. *Employment 'Miracles': A Critical Comparison of the Dutch, Scandinavian, Swiss, Australian, and Irish Cases versus Germany and the US*. Amsterdam: Amsterdam University Press.
———. 2005b. "Introduction: Miracles, Mirages, and Markets." In *Employment 'Miracles': A Critical Comparison of the Dutch, Scandinavian, Swiss, Australian, and Irish Cases versus Germany and the US*, edited by Uwe Becker and Herman Schwartz, 11–38. Amsterdam: Amsterdam University Press.
Schybergson, Per. 2001. "Large Enterprises in Small Countries." In *Convergence? Industrialization of Denmark, Finland, and Sweden, 1870–1940*, edited by Hans Kryger Larsen, 97–155. Helsinki: Finnish Society of Sciences and Letters.
Science and Technology Policy Council. 1990. *Review 1990: Guidelines for Science and Technology Policy in the 1990s*. Helsinki: Government Printing Center.
Science and Technology Policy Council. 1993. *Towards an Innovative Society*. Helsinki: Government Printing Center.
Scott, James C. 1999. *Seeing Like a State: How Certain Schemes to Improve the Human Condition Have Failed*. New Haven, CT: Yale University Press.
Scott, John. 1985. "Theoretical Framework and Research Design." In *Networks of Corporate Power: A Comparative Analysis of Ten Countries*, edited by Frans N. Stokman, Rolf Ziegler, and John Scott, 1–19. Cambridge: Polity Press.
Sejersted, Francis. 2011. *The Age of Social Democracy: Norway and Sweden in the Twentieth Century*. Princeton, NJ: Princeton University Press.
Seppälä, Timo. 2010. "Transformations of Nokia's Finnish Supplier Network from 2000 to 2008." In *Nokia and Finland in a Sea of Change*, edited by Jyrki Ali-Yrkkö, 37–68. Helsinki: Taloustieto Ltd.
Sicsic, Pierre, and Charles Wyplosz. 1996. "France, 1945–1992." In *Economic Growth in Europe Since 1945*, edited by Nicholas Crafts and Gianni Toniolo, 210–39. Cambridge, UK: Cambridge University Press.
Sigurjónsson, Thröstur Olaf. 2011. "Privatization and Deregulation: A Chronology of Events." In *Preludes to the Icelandic Financial Crisis*, edited by Robert Z. Aliber and Gylfi Zoega, 26–40. New York: Palgrave Macmillan.
Sjögren, Hans. 2008. "Welfare Capitalism: The Swedish Economy, 1850–2005." In *Creating Nordic Capitalism: The Business History of a Competitive Periphery*, edited by Susanna Fellman, Martin Jes Iversen, Hans Sjögren, and Lars Thue, 22–74. London: Palgrave MacMillan.
Skippari, Mika, and Jari Ojala. 2008. "Nokia and Tampella after the Second World War." In *Creating Nordic Capitalism: The Business History of a Competitive*

Periphery, edited by Susanna Fellman, Martin Jes Iversen, Hans Sjögren, and Lars Thue. London: Palgrave Macmillan.

Skog, Albin, Mats Lewan, Michael Karlström, Sergey Morgulis-Yakushev, Yixin Lu, and Robin Teigland. 2016. "Chasing the Tale of the Unicorn: A Study of Stockholm's Misty Meadows." Stockholm: Center for Strategy and Competitiveness, Stockholm School of Economics Institute for Research.

Smith, David. 2003. *Estonia: Independence and European Integration*. London: Routledge.

Sölvell, Orjan, Ivo Zander, and Michael Porter. 1991. *Advantage Sweden*. Stockholm: Norstedts.

Soskice, David. 1990. "Wage Determination: The Changing Role of Institutions in Advanced Industrialized Countries." *Oxford Review of Economic Policy* 6 (1): 36–61.

Sotiropoulos, Dimitri A. 2012. "The Paradox of Non-Reform in a Reform-Ripe Environment: Lessons from Post-Authoritarian Greece." In *From Stagnation to Forced Adjustment: Reforms in Greece, 1974–2010*, edited by Stathis Kalyvas, George Pagoulatos, and Haridimos Tsoukas, 9–29. London: Hurst & Company.

Steen, Anton. 1997. "The New Elites in the Baltic States: Recirculation and Change." *Scandinavian Political Studies* 20 (1): 91–112.

———. 2015. "Small States and National Elites in the Neoliberal Era." In *Small States in the Modern World: Vulnerabilities and Opportunities*, edited by Harald Baldersheim and Michael Keating, 183–201. Cheltenham, UK: Edward Elgar.

Steen, Anton, and Jüri Ruus. 2002. "Change of Regime—Continuity of Elites? The Case of Estonia." *East European Politics and Society* 16 (1): 223–48.

Steinbock, Dan. 2000. *The Nokia Revolution: The Story of an Extraordinary Company That Transformed an Industry*. New York: Amacom.

———. 2004. *What Next? Finnish ICT Cluster and Globalization*. Helsinki: Ministry of the Interior.

Steinmo, Sven. 2010. *The Evolution of Modern States*. Oxford, UK: Oxford University Press.

Stephanou, Constantinos. 2011. "The Banking System in Cyprus: Time to Rethink the Business Model?" *Cyprus Economic Policy Review* 5 (2): 123–30.

Stigler, George J. 1971. "The Theory of Economic Regulation." *Bell Journal of Economics and Management Science* (2): 3–21.

Stoerring, Dagmara, and Bent Dalum. 2007. "Cluster Emergence: A Comparative Study of Two Cases in North Jutland, Denmark." In *Creative Regions: Technology, Culture, and Knowledge Entrepreneurship*, edited by Philip Cooke and Dafna Schwartz, 127–47. London: Routledge.

Stokke, Torgeir Aarvaag, and Christer Thornqvist. 2001. "Strikes and Collective Bargaining in the Nordic Countries." *European Journal of Industrial Relations* 7 (3): 245–67.

Stokman, Frans N., and Frans W. Wasseur. 1985. "National Networks in 1976: A Structural Comparison." In *Networks of Corporate Power: A Comparative Analysis of Ten Countries*, edited by Frans N. Stokman, Rolf Zeigler, and John Scott, 20–44. Cambridge, UK: Polity Press.

Storper, Michael, Thomas Kemeny, Naji Makarem, and Taner Osman. 2015. *The Rise and Fall of Urban Economies: Lessons from San Francisco and Los Angeles*. Stanford, CA: Stanford University Press.

Storper, Michael, and Anthony J. Venables. 2004. "Buzz: Face-to-Face Contact and the Urban Economy." *Journal of Economic Geography* 4 (4): 351–70.

Stråth, Bo. 2001. "Nordic Capitalism and Democratization." In *The Democratic Challenge to Capitalism: Management and Democracy in the Nordic Countries*, edited by Haldor Byrkjeflot, Sissel Myklebust, Christine Myrvang, and Francis Sejersted, 51–86. Bergen: Fagbokforlaget.

Streeck, Wolfgang. 1991. "On the Institutional Conditions of Diversified Quality Production." In *Beyond Keynesianism: The Socio-economics of Production and Full Employment*, edited by Egon Matzner and Wolfgang Streeck, 21–61. Aldershot, UK: Elgar.

———. 1992. "Productive Constraints: On the Institutional Preconditions of Diversified Quality Production." In *Social Institutions and Economic Performance*, edited by Wolfgang Streeck, 1–40. London: Sage.

Streeck, Wolfgang, and Kathleen Thelen. 2005. "Introduction: Institutional Change in Advanced Political Economies." In *Beyond Continuity: Institutional Change in Advanced Political Economies*, edited by Wolfgang Streeck and Kathleen Thelen, 1–39. Oxford, UK: Oxford University Press.

Swenson, Peter. 1991. "Bringing Capital Back In, or Social Democracy Reconsidered." *World Politics* 43 (4): 513–44.

Tainio, Risto, Kari Lilja, and Timo Santalainen. 2002. "Organizational Learning in the Context of Corporate Growth and Decline: A Case Study of a Major Finnish Bank." In *Helsingin Kauppakorkeakoulun Julkaisuja*. Helsinki: Helsingin Kauppakorkeakoulu.

Tainio, Risto, Matti Pohjola, and Kari Lilja. 1997. "Economic Performance of Finland after the Second World War: From Success to Failure." In *National Capitalisms, Global Competition, and Economic Performance*, edited by Sigrid Quack, Glenn Morgan, and Richard Whitley, 277–90. Amsterdam: John Benjamins.

Taylor, Mark Zachary. 2004. "Empirical Evidence against Varieties of Capitalism's Theory of Technological Innovation." *International Organization* 58 (3): 601–31.

Tell, Fredrik. 2008. "From ASEA to ABB: Managing Big Business the Swedish Way." In *Creating Nordic Capitalism: The Business History of a Competitive Periphery*, edited by Susanna Fellman, Martin Jes Iversen, Hans Sjögren, and Lars Thue, 104–36. New York: Palgrave Macmillan.

Thelen, Kathleen. 2014. *Varieties of Liberalization and the New Politics of Social Solidarity*. Cambridge, UK: Cambridge University Press.

Thompson, Clive. 2015. "Can the Swiss Watchmaker Survive the Digital Age?" *New York Times*, June 3. http://www.nytimes.com/2015/06/07/magazine/can-the-swiss-watchmaker-survive-the-digital-age.html?_r=0.

Thorhallsson, Baldur. 2010. "The Corporatist Model and Its Value in Understanding Small European States in the Neo-Liberal World of the Twenty-First Century: The Case of Iceland." *European Political Science* 9: 375–86.

Thorhallsson, Baldur, and Rainer Kattel. 2013. "Neo-Liberal Small States and Economic Crisis: Lessons for Democratic Corporatism." *Journal of Baltic Studies* 44 (1): 83–103.

Toivonen, Tuukka. 2014. "Success of Angry Birds Reflects Growth of Young Entrepreneurship in Finland." *Guardian*, September 8. http://www.theguardian.com/sustainable-business/2014/sep/08/finland-entrepreneurship-young-social-problems-lifestyle-angry-birds.

Transparency International. 2010. *Corruption Perception Index*. Berlin: Transparency International.

Trigilia, Carlo, and Luigi Burroni. 2009. "Italy: Rise, Decline and Restructuring of a Regionalized Capitalism." *Economy and Society* 38 (4): 630–53.

Vail, Mark. 2009. *Recasting Welfare Capitalism: The Changing Dynamics of Economic Adjustment in Contemporary France and Germany*. Philadelphia: Temple University Press.
Vartiainen, Juhana. 1998a. *The Labour Market in Finland: Institutions and Outcomes*. Helsinki: Prime Minister's Office.
———. 1998b. "Understanding Swedish Social Democracy: Victims of Success?" *Oxford Review of Economic Policy* 14 (1): 19–39.
———. 1999. "The Economics of Successful State Intervention and Industrial Transformation." In *The Developmental State*, edited by Meredith Woo-Cumings, 200–234. Ithaca, NY: Cornell University Press.
Veen, Kees van, and Jan Kratzer. 2011. "National and International Interlocking Directorates within European Corporate Networks within and among Fifteen European Countries." *Economy and Society* 40 (1): 1–25.
Verney, Susannah. 2014. "'Broken and Can't be Fixed': The Impact of the Economic Crisis on the Greek Party System." *Italian Journal of International Affairs* 49 (1): 18–35.
Vihriälä, Vesa. 1997. *Banks and the Finnish Credit Cycle: 1986–1995*. Helsinki: Bank of Finland.
Visser, Jelle. 2015. "Data Base on Institutional Characteristics of Trade Union, Wage Setting, State Intervention and Social Pacts, 1960–2014 (ICTWSS)." http://www.uva-aias.net/en/ictwss.
Visser, Jelle, and Anton Hemerijck. 1997. *A Dutch Miracle: Job Growth, Welfare Reform and Corporatism in the Netherlands*. Amsterdam: Amsterdam University Press.
Vogel, Steven K. 1996. *Freer Markets, More Rules: Regulatory Reform in Advanced Industrial Countries*. Ithaca, NY: Cornell University Press.
Vogt, Henri. 2003. "Coalition-Building and Consensus: Comparative Observation of the Three Baltic States." In *Baltic Democracy at the Crossroads: An Elite Perspective*, edited by Sten Berglund and Kjetil Duvold, 81–104. Kristiansand: Hoyskoleforlaget AS.
Wade, Robert. 2009. "The Crisis: Iceland as Icarus." *Challenge* 52 (3): 5–33.
Walshok, Mary Lindenstein, and Abraham J. Shragge. 2014. *Invention and Reinvention: The Evolution of San Diego's Innovation Economy*. Palo Alto, CA: Stanford University Press.
Watson, Sara. 2015. *The Left Divided: The Development and Transformation of Advanced Welfare States*. Oxford, UK: Oxford University Press.
Weiss, Linda. 2014. *America Inc.? Innovation and Enterprise in the National Security State*. Ithaca, NY: Cornell University Press.
Wilensky, Harold. 2002. *Rich Democracies: Political Economy, Public Policy, and Performance*. Berkeley: University of California Press.
Willson, Margaret, and Birna Gunnlaugsdóttir. 2015. "The Resilience of Rural Iceland." In *Gambling Debt: Iceland's Rise and Fall in the Global Economy*, edited by E. Paul Durrenberger and Gísli Pálsson, 137–49. Boulder: University Press of Colorado.
Witt, Michael A., and Gregory Jackson. 2016. "Varieties of Capitalism and Institutional Advantage: A Test and Reinterpretation." *Journal of International Business Studies* 47 (7): 778–806.
Ylä-Anttila, Pekka, and Christopher Palmberg. 2005. "The Specifities of Finnish Industrial Policy: Challenges and Initiatives at the Turn of the Century." *ETLA Discussion Paper*, No. 973. Helsinki: Research Institute of the Finnish Economy.
Zahariadis, Nikolaos. 2002. "Asset Specificity and State Subsidies in Industrialized Countries." *International Studies Quarterly* 45 (4): 603–16.

Zenios, Stavros A. 2013. "The Cyprus Debt: Perfect Crisis and a Way Forward." *Cyprus Economic Policy Review* 7 (1): 3–45.

Zhou, Jianping. 2007. "Danish for All? Balancing Flexibility with Security: The Flexicurity Model." Washington, DC: International Monetary Fund.

Ziblatt, Daniel. 2006. *Structuring the State: The Formation of Italy and Germany and the Puzzle of Federalism*. Princeton, NJ: Princeton University Press.

Zoega, Gylfi. 2011. "The Chapters in This Volume." In *Preludes to the Icelandic Financial Crisis*, edited by Robert Z. Aliber and Gylfi Zoega, 13–25. New York: Palgrave Macmillan.

Zysman, John. 1983. *Governments, Markets, and Growth: Financial Systems and the Politics of Industrial Change*. Ithaca, NY: Cornell University Press.

Index

Page numbers followed by letter *t* refer to tables.

Aalborg, Denmark, 192
Aalto Entrepreneurship Society, 99, 100
Actavis, 114
Aho, Esko, 102, 218n19
Allentown, Pennsylvania, 194–95
Allied Irish Banks, 167
Anglo-Irish Bank, 167, 168
Angry Birds (video game), 81, 98
ASEA, 28, 31, 42, 49
Association of Swedish Engineering Industries, 28
Atlanta, Georgia, 191
Augustsson, Fredrik, 56
austerity measures: in Estonia, 176; in Greece, 137, 158; in Iceland, 137; in Ireland, 170; in Sweden, after World War I, 217n4
Austria: banks in, 145–46; conservative approach to economic challenges in, 145, 149; diversified economy of, 143, 144; divisions in, 9; global financial crisis of 2007-2009 and, 146, 213*t*; incrementalism in, 5, 17, 142, 149, 184; liberalization in, 145; neocorporatism in, 143, 204*t*; Nordic states compared to, 9, 142–43, 148, 149; OPEC-induced oil crises of 1970s and, 144–45; postwar economic policy of, 143, 144; reform and restructuring in, 9, 144, 148–49, 215n9; as segmented society, 141, 142; small and medium-sized enterprises (SMEs) in, 143–44; tourism industry in, 221n4

Bagge, Gösta, 35, 36
Baltic republics: neoliberal reform in, 171–72. *See also* Estonia; Latvia
bank(s): Austrian, 145–46; Finnish, 61–62, 65, 66, 67, 68, 69, 71, 72, 131, 218n3; French, 187; German, 183–84; Icelandic, 117–36; Icelandic, artificial inflation of assets of, 2, 130; Icelandic, as coordinating agents, 129–31; Icelandic, before 1990, 109, 117; Icelandic, narrow specialization of, 127, 131, 132, 190; Icelandic, privatization and deregulation of, 120–22, 124–25, 128; Icelandic, risks taken by, 132–35; Icelandic, societal capture by, 18, 130, 134–35, 189–90, 199; Icelandic, wide-ranging influence of, 18, 125–26; Irish, 167–68, 190, 223n6; Swedish, 27–28, 32, 41, 45, 49, 54, 190; Swiss, 146, 148, 149; U.S., 130, 189–90, 224n10. *See also* banking crises; *specific banks*
banking crises: in Cyprus, 222n12; in Finland, 19, 65, 72–73, 77, 190, 213*t*; in Iceland, 2, 9, 21, 102, 103, 117–18, 129, 135–36, 138, 190, 213*t*; in Ireland, 161, 167–70; in Sweden, 54, 72, 213*t*, 217n15, 224n11; in U.S., 117, 133, 189–90, 213*t*
Bank of America, 190
Bank of Finland, 71, 72
Belgium, 93, 216n10, 221n1
Big Five (Sweden), 28
Bildt, Carl, 55, 102
biotechnology industry: in Finland, 74, 80, 93–94; in San Diego, California, 193–94
Birgersson, Jonas, 56
Bjarnason, Brynjólfur, 118
Björgólfsson, Björgólfur Thor, 121
Blyth, Mark, 37, 187
Bonnier family, 42
boom-bust cycles: in Finland, 73; in Iceland, 135–36; in Ireland, 161, 170, 171; in Nordic region, 1–2, 11, 22–23, 213–14, 214*t*; in Sweden, 54. *See also* economic crises; overshooting and overinvestment
Branting, Hjalmar, 36
Buchanan, James, 115, 118–19
Búnadarbanki, 124

Canada: Toronto region in, 191; Waterloo region in, 180, 195–96
Cassel, Gustav, 35, 36
Central Bank of Ireland, 167, 168
Central Europe: incrementalism in, 5, 17, 142, 149, 184; reform and restructuring in, 215n9. *See also* Austria; East Central Europe; Switzerland

253

cities/regions: cohesive networks in, 10, 180, 191–93, 194, 195; Nordic countries' experience and lessons for, 196–97; stabilizing forces in, 197–98
cohesive and encompassing networks, 12, 203; and asset-specific investments, 16–17; and boom-bust cycles, 213; in cities/regions, 10, 180, 191–93, 194, 195; and collective goods, investment in, 4, 6, 13–14, 15; comparative perspective on, 141–42; and conformism, 16, 20, 49, 135, 169–70; coordination as measure of, 204*t*, 205–6; and cross-class collaboration, 34; in Denmark, 160, 173, 191, 192; in Estonia, 9, 161, 171, 173, 178; external threat and, 66, 67, 173, 215n6; in Finland, 8, 23, 60, 61–65, 159, 173, 208*t*, 209, 215n6; and good governance, 7; in Iceland, 8, 23, 102–9, 130, 131, 141, 208*t*, 209; and industry-university cooperation, 83; and innovation, 5, 98–99, 113–14; and interfirm relations, 204*t*, 205; international openness combined with, 4, 21; interviews used to measure, 207–9, 208*t*; in Ireland, 9, 161, 162–64, 178, 208*t*, 209; neocorporatism as measure of, 203–5, 204*t*; in Nordic states, 5, 6, 11–15; in Norway, 160; and policy overshooting and overinvestment, 2, 5–6, 7, 11, 19–24, 26, 108, 197; politics of persuasion in, 7, 17, 19–20, 165; and reform and restructuring, 4–5, 6, 7, 11, 15–19, 26, 60, 70, 75–76, 102, 108, 137, 141, 172, 192, 193, 196; and response to economic crises, 5, 11, 22, 30, 139; in San Diego, California, 180, 192–93, 194; shift away from, 200–201; in Silicon Valley, California, 192, 194; size of state and, 12, 178–79, 180; and spread of ideas, 26, 37–38, 98–99; in Sweden, 8, 23, 27, 29–30, 141, 173, 208*t*, 209; trust as measure of, 204*t*, 206–7; in Waterloo, Ontario, 180, 195
collective goods, investment in: cohesive networks and, 4, 6, 13–14, 15; conflict as barrier to, 142
Communitech, 196
compensation. *See* politics of compensation
Confederation of Icelandic Employers, 104, 107, 220n16
conformism, in tight-knit societies, 16, 20, 49, 135, 169–70; in Finland, 20, 63, 64–65, 87, 91; in Iceland, 20, 108, 122, 126–27, 129, 133, 134, 135; in Ireland, 169–70, 222n3; in Sweden, 42–43, 50. *See also* politics of persuasion

construction industry: in Greece, 156; in Ireland, 169
cooperative relationships: benefits vs. risks of, 4–5, 7, 16–17, 159; possibility of developing, 159. *See also* cohesive and encompassing networks
coordination. *See* politics of coordination; strategic coordination
corporatism: in Greece, 150; in Portugal, 150, 151, 152. *See also* neocorporatism
Credit Lyonnais debacle, 187
credit rationing: in Finland, 67, 69, 71; in Iceland, 109–10; in Sweden, 8, 32, 45, 50, 52, 53
Credit Suisse, 148
criticism, stifling of. *See* conformism
cross-class collaboration: cohesive networks and, 34; in Finland, 64; in Iceland, 104, 107, 220n2; in Sweden, 33–34, 36, 41
Curran, Richard, 169
Cyprus, 221n12
Czech Republic, incrementalism in, 171, 176

Danske Bank, 133, 134
DARPA, 188
decentralization: as buffer to policy overshooting, 199; in Germany, 182; in Switzerland, 199
DeCode Genetics, 114, 115
de Gaulle, Charles, 33
Denmark: cohesive networks in, 160, 173, 191, 192; criticism of Icelandic banks, 20, 133, 134; "flexicurity" in, 92; housing bubble in, 2, 160; Iceland's independence from, 109, 112; liberalization in, 21; reform and restructuring in, 160; welfare state in, 25
deregulation: in Estonia, 9; in Finland, 71, 102; in Iceland, 9; in Nordic Europe, 58–59; in Sweden, 52–54, 102; in U.S., 189
Detroit, Michigan, 198
diversification, economic: in Austria, 143, 144; barrier to, in Finland, 89–91; as buffer to policy overshooting, 199–200; in France, 185; in Germany, 182–83; immigration/labor mobility and, 201, 224n13; in Switzerland, 143, 144
divisions: in Austria, 9; in Estonia, 172–73; in Iceland, 103, 106; in Nordic region, trend toward, 200–201; in Southern Europe, 9, 142, 150, 151–52, 155, 156–57, 158, 208*t*, 209; in Sweden, 30–31; in Switzerland, 9; in U.S., 189

dot-com crash of 2000: and contraction of high-technology industries, 211–12, 212*t*; in Finland, 94, 212; in France, 186; in Germany, 183; in Iceland, 114–15; in Sweden, 2, 55–57; in Switzerland, 221n9; in U.S., 189

East Asia, low-cost rivals in, impact on Nordic states, 48
East Central Europe, transitional economies of, 171. *See also* Visegrád states
economic crises: cohesive networks and response to, 5, 11, 22, 30, 139; cross-country comparison of, 213*t*; in Nordic Europe, 1, 2, 9, 202; in Southern Europe, 9, 142, 154. *See also* banking crises; dot-com crash of 2000; global financial crisis of 2007-2009
education policies: in Estonia, 174, 176–78; in Finland, 82–84, 87; in Iceland, 129; in Ireland, 166; in Luxembourg, 200. *See also* universities
Elcoteq, 88, 175, 219n31
electronic banking, Finland's pioneering role in, 17
employer associations: in Austria, 143; in Germany, 182; in Greece, 151; in Iceland, 104, 107, 220n16; in Ireland, 162; in Portugal, 151; in Sweden, 28, 39, 40
entrepreneurship: cohesive networks and, 11, 98–99; Finnish policies discouraging, 89–91; Finnish policies promoting, after 2005, 99–100; Icelandic policies discouraging, 107, 109–10; Icelandic policies promoting, after 1980, 117; Swedish policies discouraging, 44, 45, 46, 48, 49, 51; Swedish policies promoting, after 1980, 52, 54–55
Ericsson, 28, 49, 54, 56, 86, 219n23
Estonia, 171–78; austerity measures in, 176; cohesive networks in, 9, 161, 171, 173, 178; global financial crisis of 2007-2009 and, 176, 212, 213*t*; high-technology industries in, 175, 177–78, 212*t*; housing bubble in, 175–76; Ireland compared to, 170, 175; liberalization and deregulation in, 9, 171–75; neocorporatism in, 172; Nordic states compared to, 24, 173, 174, 175, 176, 178; overshooting and overinvestment in, 175–76, 178; politics of compensation in, 174–75; politics of persuasion in, 174; public investment in collective goods in, 172, 174–78; reform and restructuring in, 161, 171–75; Russian-speaking minority in, marginalization of, 172–73, 223n12; taxation in, 174; Visegrád states compared to, 171, 174, 175, 176, 177; vulnerability to external shocks, 9, 178
European Union: and Central European states, 149; and Estonia, 174, 176, 178; and Greece, 157, 158; and Iceland, 128, 136; and Ireland, 165, 167; and Portugal, 153; structural funds from, impact of, 158, 159, 167, 222n16

FDI. *See* foreign direct investment
Fennoman, 65, 66
Fianna Fáil, 163, 164
fieldwork, 207
financial crises. *See* banking crises; economic crises; global financial crisis of 2007-2009
Finland: Austria compared to, 143, 145; banking crisis in, 19, 65, 72–73, 77, 190, 213*t*; banks in, 61–62, 65–69, 71, 72, 131, 218n3; biotechnology industry in, 74, 80, 93–94; civil war in, 62, 66; cohesive networks in, 8, 23, 60, 61–65, 159, 173, 208*t*, 209, 215n6; conformism in, 20, 63, 64–65, 87, 91; consensual approach to politics in, 63; and cost competitiveness, new focus on, 97–98; cross-class collaboration in, 64; deregulation of financial markets in, 71, 102; dot-com crash of 2000 and, 94, 212; economic development in 19th century, 65–66; economic growth in 20th century, 1, 69; electronic banking in, 17; entrepreneurship in, obstacles to, 89–91; Estonia compared to, 173, 175, 176, 178; external threat and national solidarity in, 66, 67, 173, 215n6; famine in, 65, 66; France compared to, 184, 185, 186, 187; Germany compared to, 182, 183; global financial crisis of 2007-2009 and, 95, 190; government-business cooperation in, 82–83, 87; high-technology industries in, 59–60, 74, 75–79, 84, 85–89, 93–94, 98–100, 212*t*; Iceland compared to, 103–4, 106–15, 118, 119, 129, 131; immigration reshaping, 200; industrial families in, 206; industrialization of, 65–66, 68–69; innovation policy in, 8, 70, 71, 74–85, 91–95, 96, 198–99; interfirm relations in, 82, 204*t*, 206; Ireland compared to, 161, 167, 168, 169; labor-industry cooperation in, 80–81; large firms in, policies favoring, 69–70; macroeconomic policies in, 221n10; neocorporatism in, 81–82, 76, 81, 97, 204*t*, 216n1; neoliberal revolution in, 101, 102; Nokia's role in, 8, 18, 85–91, 93, 95, 102; OPEC-induced oil crises of 1970s and, 70; overshooting and overinvestment in, 60,

Finland (*continued*)
61, 89–95; politics of compensation in, 18, 68, 72–73, 79–82; politics of coordination in, 82–85; politics of persuasion in, 19, 20, 72, 75–79; populist right-wing parties in, rise of, 201; Portugal compared to, 154; R&D investment in, 3, 18, 59, 74, 76, 77–79, 83–85, 89, 90, 93, 96; reform and restructuring in, 8, 15, 59–60, 70–72, 73–85, 96–97, 141; software product (gaming) industry in, 81–82, 98–99, 100, 200; Soviet-style command economy compared to, 67; statist turn in early 20th century, 25, 65, 66–69; Sweden compared to, 53–56, 59, 61–65, 67–70, 71, 72, 74, 75, 81, 83, 91; taxation in, 67; trade unions in, 2, 3, 18, 62, 80–81, 92–93, 219n27; trade with Soviet Union, 67, 68, 69, 70, 73, 199; vulnerability to external shocks, 2, 60, 85, 86, 89–95, 214*t*

Finnish Agency for Technology and Innovation. *See* Tekes

Finnish National Fund for Research and Development. *See* Sitra

fishing industry, in Iceland, 109, 110, 111–13, 131, 138, 139, 220n16

foreign direct investment (FDI): in Estonia, 175; in Finland, 65, 88; in Ireland, 9, 153, 161, 162, 164, 165–66, 167, 170–71, 224n14, 225n2; in Waterloo, Canada, 196

fragmentation: in Southern Europe, 9, 142, 150, 151–52, 155, 156–57, 158, 208*t*, 209. *See also* divisions

France, 184–87; diversified economy of, 185; financial services industry in, 187; global financial crisis of 2007-2009 and, 213*t*; Iceland compared to, 105; innovation policy in, 186; interfirm relations in, 204*t*, 206; large firms in, policies favoring, 184, 185; Nordic countries compared to, 9–10, 180, 184–87; OPEC-induced oil crises of 1970s and, 185; policy makers in, cohesive network of, 31; reform and restructuring in, 185–86; statist turn in, 25; Sweden compared to, 8, 27, 31, 32, 33, 43, 44, 51, 184, 185, 186, 187; taxation in, 32

Freeman, Christopher, 59

Freemasons, in Iceland, 104–5

Friedman, Milton, 115, 118–19, 121

gaming industry, in Finland, 81, 98–99, 100

genius companies, in Sweden, 32, 217n10

Germany, 181–84; decentralization in, 182; diversified economy of, 182–83; financial markets in, 183–84; global financial crisis of 2007-2009 and, 184, 213*t*; high-technology industries in, 183, 212*t*; incrementalism in, 183, 184; interfirm coordination in, 204*t*, 206; Nordic countries compared to, 9–10, 180, 181–84; southwestern, cohesive social networks in, 191, 192; statist turn in, 25

Gísladóttir, Ingibjörg, 121

Gissurarson, Hannes Hólmsteinn, 118, 120

Glitnir, 117, 121

global financial crisis of 2007-2009, impact of: in Austria, 146, 213*t*; cross-national statistics, 212, 213*t*; in Estonia, 176, 212, 213*t*; in Finland, 95, 190; in Germany, 184, 213*t*; in Greece, 158, 212, 213*t*; in Iceland, 135–36, 190, 212, 213*t*; in Ireland, 170, 190, 212, 213*t*; in Portugal, 154, 212, 213*t*; in Sweden, 217n15; in Switzerland, 148, 213*t*; in U.S., 190, 198, 213*t*

Goldman Sachs, 130, 190

Grabher, Gernot, 192, 221n4

Greece, 150, 155–58; austerity measures in, 137, 158; construction industry in, 156; economic volatility in, 9, 142, 214, 214*t*; global financial crisis of 2007-2009 and, 158, 212, 213*t*; inconsistent government policies in, 155–56, 174; labor relations in, 156, 157; Nordic states compared to, 9, 12, 142, 150, 158–59, 209; politics of compensation in, 151, 157; social fragmentation in, 9, 142, 150, 151–52, 155, 156–57, 158, 208*t*, 209

Grímsson, Ólafur Ragnar, 121

GSM digital standard, 75, 81, 86

Guðjohnsen, Eiður, 108

Gudmundsson, Björgólfur, 117, 124, 135

Gunnarsson, Kjartan, 118, 124

Gunnlaugsdóttir, Birna, 139

Haarde, Geir, 118, 134

Handelsbanken, 41, 72, 217n14

Hansson, Per Albin, 35

Hayek, Friedrich, 118–19

Heckscher, Eli, 35

Herbertsson, Tryggvi Thór, 134

high-technology industries: dot-com crash of 2000 and, 211–12, 212*t*; in Estonia, 175, 177–78, 212*t*; in Finland, 59–60, 74, 75–79, 84, 85–89, 93–94, 98–100, 212*t*; in Germany, 183, 212*t*; in Iceland, 102, 103, 113–15, 212*t*, 225n1; Nordic countries' turn to, 1, 9, 59, 211, 212*t*; in San Diego, California, 193–94, 201; in Sweden, 48–49, 54–57, 212*t*; in Switzerland, 147; in U.S., 188–89, 195; in Waterloo, Ontario, 195–96

Hitler, Adolf, 182
Hofmann, Paul, 148
Holstein, Staël von, 56
housing bubble: in Denmark, 2, 160; in Estonia, 175–76; in Iceland, 132–34; in Ireland, 164, 167–70; in Spain, 170, 223n7; in U.S., 133, 170
human capital: cohesive networks and investment in, 11; and entrepreneurship, 90, 100; Finland's investment in, 83–84, 87; Icelandic banking and, 117, 121, 129; Varieties of Capitalism literature on, 13
Hungary, incrementalism in, 171, 176
Hybritech, 193–94

Iceland: austerity measures in, 137; banking crisis in, 2, 9, 21, 102, 103, 117–18, 129, 135–36, 138, 190, 213*t*; banks in, 2, 18, 109, 117–36, 190; "cod wars" with UK, 106, 111, 220n8; cohesive networks in, 8, 23, 102–9, 130, 131, 141, 208*t*, 209; conformism in, 20, 108, 122, 126–27, 129, 133, 134, 135; contentious image of, 103, 106; "Corporate Vikings" in, 19; cross-class collaboration in, 104, 107, 220n2; economic adjustment after financial crisis, 136–40; Estonia compared to, 174, 175; Finland compared to, 103–4, 106–15, 118, 119, 129, 131; fishing industry in, 109, 110, 111–13, 131, 138, 139, 220n16; founding myth of, 110; France compared to, 105, 187; Germany compared to, 182; global financial crisis of 2007-2009 and, 135–36, 190, 212, 213*t*; government-business cooperation in, 2, 107, 124–25, 127, 128–29; high-technology industries in, 102, 103, 113–15, 212*t*, 225n1; housing bubble in, 132–34; independence from Denmark, 109, 112; Independence Party in, 3, 104, 105, 107, 118, 119, 121, 124, 125, 138; interfirm relations in, 204*t*, 206; Ireland compared to, 164, 167, 168, 169, 170; liberalization and deregulation in, 8, 108; macroeconomic policies in, 221n10; national solidarity in, 106; neocorporatism in, 102–3, 119; neoliberal reform in, 102, 115, 116–20, 127–28, 136, 220n14; overshooting and overinvestment in, 108, 131–36; politics of compensation in, 18, 110–11, 119, 122–27, 134–35, 216n6, 220n17; politics of coordination in, 111–12, 127–31; politics of persuasion in, 107, 118–22, 134; Portugal compared to, 154; privatization of banks (crony capitalism) in, 124–25; reform and restructuring in, 23, 102, 103, 108, 113–15, 117–32, 136–40, 141; societal capture by banks in, 18, 130, 134–35, 189–90, 199; statist turn in, 25, 103, 109–11; Sweden compared to, 53–54, 56, 103–4, 106–10, 113–15, 118, 119, 131; taxation in, 116, 119, 136–37; tourism industry in, 138–40; trade unions in, 103, 104, 107, 110, 119, 120, 122–24, 125, 127, 135; tripartite social pact in, 116, 123; vulnerability to external shocks, 23, 106, 117, 132, 140, 213, 214*t*; welfare state in, 109, 111, 123–24
Icelandair, 139, 140
IDA. *See* Industrial Development Authority (Ireland)
ideas, cohesive networks and spread of, 26, 37–38, 98–99
IMF. *See* International Monetary Fund
immigration, and transformation of Nordic societies, 200–201
incrementalism: in Austria and Switzerland, 5, 17, 142, 149, 184; in Belgium, 216n10, 221n1; as economic asset, 16–17; in Germany, 183, 184; in Visegrád states, 171, 176
Independence Party (Iceland), 3, 104, 105, 107, 118, 119, 121, 124, 125, 138
Industrial Development Authority (IDA, Ireland), 163, 166, 167, 168, 222n4
industrialization: of Finland, 65–66, 68–69; of Iceland, 110–13; of Ireland, 164, 166–67; of Nordic states, 4, 19; of Sweden, 31–32; timing of, hypothesis regarding, 23, 142, 149, 150
innovation policy: as alternative to capital-intensive manufacturing, 59; cohesive networks and, 5, 98–99, 113–14; in Estonia, 176, 177–78; in Finland, 8, 70, 71, 74–85, 91–95, 96, 198–99; in France, 186; in Germany, 183; in Iceland, 113–15; in Luxembourg, 200; in Poland, 177, 178; in Portugal, 153, 154–55; reliance on, and vulnerability to economic shocks, 2, 8; in San Diego, California, 194; Schumpeterian development agencies and, 198–99; in Sweden, 55, 59; in Switzerland, 147–48; "systemic" approach to, 82–83; in U.S., 188; in Waterloo, Ontario, 195. *See also* R&D, investment in
interfirm relations, 204*t*, 205–6; in Austria, 143; in Finland, 82, 206; in Germany, 182, 191; in Iceland, 104, 107, 220n16; in Ireland, 162; in Portugal, 151, 155; promoting, 159; in Sweden, 28, 29, 39, 40; Varieties of Capitalism literature on, 3, 13, 205. *See also* strategic coordination

interlocking directorates, as measure of cohesive networks, 204t, 205–6
International Financial Services Centre (Ireland), 167
International Monetary Fund (IMF): Greek financial crisis and, 158; Icelandic financial crisis and, 133, 134, 136; on Nordic achievements, 1; Portuguese financial crisis and, 154
interviews, 13, 207; and evaluation of cohesive networks, 207–9, 208t
iPhone, 2, 8, 197
Ireland, 161–71; austerity measures in, 170; banks in, 167–68, 190, 223n6; boom-bust cycles in, 161, 170, 171, 213; cohesive networks in, 9, 161, 162–64, 178, 208t, 209; conformism in, 169–70, 222n3; Estonia compared to, 170, 175; foreign direct investment in, 9, 153, 161, 162, 164, 165–66, 167, 170–71, 224n14, 225n2; global financial crisis of 2007-2009 and, 170, 190, 212, 213t; housing bubble in, 164, 167–70; industrialization of, 164, 166–67; Nordic states compared to, 9, 24, 161, 162, 164; overshooting and overinvestment in, 164, 178; pharmaceutical industry in, 171; politics of compensation in, 166; politics of coordination in, 167; politics of persuasion in, 165; protectionism in, 164–65; reform and restructuring in, 161, 165, 171; taxation in, 165, 166, 169, 170, 171, 222n2; trade unions in, 161–62, 163; vulnerability to external shocks, 161, 171
Italy, northern, cohesive networks in, 191

Jóhannesson, Jón Ásgeir, 106, 107, 121, 124

Kairamo, Kari, 76–77, 86
Kallas, Siim, 174
Katzenstein, Peter, 142, 143, 148, 191
Kaupthing, 117, 124, 128
Keflavik air base (Iceland), 110, 115, 140
Kekkonen, Urho, 62, 68
Kenworthy, Lane, 203
Keynesianism: Austrian approach to, 144; Finnish commitment to, 62; Swedish commitment to, 37, 50
knowledge-intensive industries. See high-technology industries
Kouri, Pentti, 20, 72
Kreuger, Ivar, 19, 32
Kymmene, 65

Laar, Mart, 174, 175
Landsbanki, 117, 124

large firms, policies favoring: Finnish, 69–70; French, 184, 185; German, 182; Swedish, 18, 20, 27, 28, 34, 41, 43–50, 217n6; U.S., 188
large states: global financial crisis of 2007-2009 and, 212, 213t; Nordic countries compared to, 9–10, 180, 190; reform and restructuring in, 10, 190. See also France; Germany; United States
Lárusson, Kjartan, 138
Latvia, economic restructuring in, 178
liberalization, financial: in Austria, 145; in Denmark, 21; in Estonia, 9, 171–75; in Finland, 71; in Iceland, 8, 108; in Sweden, 21
libertarianism, in Iceland, 118–19
Liinanmaa Agreement, 62
Lindahl, Erik, 35, 36
Lindhagen, Carl, 36
literacy, and cohesive social networks: in Iceland, 106; in Sweden, 27
literature review, 207. See also small states, literature on; Varieties of Capitalism literature
LO. See Swedish Trade Union Congress
local communities. See cities/regions
Los Angeles, California, 191
Lutheranism: in Iceland, 106; in Sweden, 27
Luxembourg, 199–200; Icelandic banking industry compared to, 117, 131

Mann, Michael, 185
Marel, 114
market competition: as imperfect disciplinary device, 22; inefficient strategies exposed by, 21, 22; in Nordic region, 2; and policy overshooting, hypothesis of, 181; social policies used to neutralize opposition to, 18, 123–24; and social solidarity, optimal combination of, 21; trade union weakness and, 172. See also neoliberalism
marketing: Finnish neglect of, 92–93; Icelandic use of, 134, 139
media: Finnish, 84–85, 87, 91; Icelandic, 104, 105, 107, 110, 119, 120–21, 122, 126, 129, 134, 135; Irish, 169; Swedish, 28
medical technology, in Iceland, 114, 115
Meidner, Rudolf, 41
Merita, 218n3
Merrill Lynch, 190; criticism of Icelandic banks, 133, 134
Metsä Serla, 62
Mishkin, Frederic, 120, 134
Mitterand, Francois, 185
Motorola, 218n15
Myrdal, Gunnar, 35, 36

INDEX   259

nationalization: in Austria, 144; in Finland, 66, 67; in Greece, 156; in Iceland, 109, 110; in Portugal, 152, 153; in Sweden, 51
National Share Bank (Finland), 61, 65, 69
Nelson, Richard, 59
neocorporatism, 12–13, 203; in Austria, 143, 204t; cohesive networks and, 14, 203–5, 204t; in Estonia, 172; in Finland, 61–62, 76, 81, 97, 204t, 216n1; in Iceland, 102–3, 119; positive economic outcomes of, 13; shortcomings of, 14; in Sweden, 28–29, 204t; in Switzerland, 143
neoliberalism, 101; in Estonia, 171–72; in Finland, 101, 102; in Iceland, 102, 115, 116–20, 127–28, 136, 220n14; in Nordic Europe, 58, 101, 102; in Sweden, 101, 102
Netherlands, 221n1
New Democratic Party (Greece), 156–57
Nicholls, Kate, 153, 155
Nicolin, Curt, 31, 42
Nokia: decline and collapse of, 93, 95, 98; diversification hindered by, 89–91; dot-com crash of 2000 and, 94; exports to Communist bloc, 69, 70; Finland's dependence on, 60, 75, 85–87, 89–91, 95, 102; market-oriented reform and, 86, 224n6; media coverage of, 84–85, 87, 91, 95–96; RIM compared to, 195, 197; success of, factors responsible for, 93; supplier network of, 87–89, 102; and technological innovation, 76–77, 78, 85–89; and transformation of Finland, 8, 18, 85–86; universities and, 83
Nordic states: adaptation and transformation of, 4, 5, 19; Austria and Switzerland compared to, 9, 142–43, 148, 149; cohesive networks in, 5, 6, 11–15; dot-com crash of 2000 and, 211–12, 212t; economic success of, common explanations for, 2–4, 12; economic volatility in, 1–2, 9, 11, 22–23, 202, 213–14, 214t; fragmentation in, trend toward, 200–201; high-technology industries in, 1, 9, 59, 211, 212t; large states compared to, 9–10, 180, 190; lessons from, 6, 180, 196–97; neocorporatism in, 13, 204t; neoliberalism (market-oriented reform) in, 58, 101, 102; politics of persuasion in, 19–20; populist right-wing parties in, rise of, 201; radical reform and restructuring in, 8, 15, 17, 22, 26, 141; social policies of, 3, 18, 53, 101–2, 123–24; social solidarity and market competition in, 21; societal capture in, 18, 130, 190, 199; Southern European states compared to, 9, 12, 142, 150–51, 158–59, 209, 221n12; stabilizing forces in, suggestions for, 198–99; statist turn in, 25–26; as supermodel, 1, 21; vulnerability to policy overshooting and overinvestment, 2, 5–6, 7, 11, 19–24, 26; welfare state in, 3, 19, 25, 101. *See also specific states*
Norway: cohesive networks in, 160; path to economic success in, 2; reform and restructuring in, 160; welfare state in, 25

Octopus, the (Iceland), 104, 107, 110
Oddsson, Davíd, 106, 107, 114, 116, 118, 119, 120, 122, 123, 124, 127, 216n6
Ohlin, Bertil, 35, 36
Ollila, Jorma, 91, 96
OPEC-induced oil crises of 1970s: impact on Austria, 144–45; impact on Finland, 70; impact on France, 185; impact on Switzerland, 146; Sweden's vulnerability to, 48; Swedish response to, 37, 50
OpenText, 195
organized labor. *See* trade unions
Ossur, 114
overshooting and overinvestment: alternative explanations for, 23–24, 60, 160, 161, 162, 181; cities/regions and risk of, 197–98; cohesive networks and vulnerability to, 2, 5–6, 7, 11, 19–24, 26, 108, 197; decentralization as buffer to, 199; in Denmark, 160; diversification as buffer to, 199–200; in Estonia, 175–76, 178; in Finland, 60, 61, 89–95; in Iceland, 108, 131–36; immigration as buffer to, 200–201; in Ireland, 164, 178; in Norway, 160; in Sweden, 46–51

Pagoulatos, George, 155
Palme, Olaf, 53, 55
Palmstierna, Erik, 36
Pálsson, Thorsteinn, 118, 119
PASOK (Panhellenic Socialist Movement, Greece), 156, 157
persuasion. *See* conformism; politics of persuasion
pharmaceutical industry: in Finland, 94; in Ireland, 171
Poland: incrementalism in, 171, 176; innovation policy in, 177, 178
policy overshooting. *See* overshooting and overinvestment
politics of compensation: in Estonia, 174–75; in Finland, 18, 68, 72–73, 79–82; in France, 187; in Greece, 151, 157; in Iceland, 18, 110–11, 119, 122–27, 134–35, 216n6, 220n17;

politics of compensation (*continued*)
and increased costs of social exclusion, 20; in Ireland, 166; in large states, 180; and reform and restructuring, 7, 17, 18, 22; in Sweden, 18, 34, 38–42

politics of coordination: in Finland, 82–85; in Greece, 157; in Iceland, 111–12, 127–31; in Ireland, 167; in large states, 180; in Nordic states, 3, 13; and policy overshooting and overinvestment, 20–21; and reform and restructuring, 7, 17, 18, 22; in Sweden, 28–29, 34, 43–46

politics of persuasion: in Estonia, 174; in Finland, 19, 20, 72, 75–79; in Iceland, 107, 118–22, 134; in Ireland, 165; in large states, 180; and reform and restructuring, 7, 17, 22; in Sweden, 34–38; in tight-knit societies, 7, 17, 19–20, 165

Portes, Richard, 120

Portugal, 150, 152–55; economic volatility in, 9, 142, 214, 214*t*; global financial crisis of 2007-2009 and, 154, 212, 213*t*; inconsistent government policies in, 153–54, 174; Ireland compared to, 164; labor relations in, 152–53, 154; nationalization in, 152, 153; Nordic states compared to, 9, 12, 142, 150, 158–59, 209; reform and restructuring in, 153, 154–55, 158; social fragmentation in, 9, 150–51, 208*t*, 209

Postipankki, 67

Progressive Party (Iceland), 104, 110, 121, 124, 125, 138, 220n16

protectionism: in Finland, 67; in Iceland, 109, 110; in Ireland, 164–65; in Nordic states, 12

R&D, investment in: in Austria, 145; in Estonia, 175, 177–78; in Finland, 3, 18, 59, 74, 76, 77–79, 83–85, 89, 90, 93, 96; in France, 186; in Germany, 183; in Iceland, 113, 114; in Portugal, 153, 154–55, 222n16; in Sweden, 83; in Switzerland, 147; in U.S., 188. *See also* innovation policy

Reagan, Ronald, 101, 220n4

real estate bubble. *See* housing bubble

reform and restructuring: in Austria, 9, 144, 148–49, 215n9; cohesive networks and, 5, 6, 7, 11, 15–19, 26, 60, 70, 75–76, 102, 108, 137, 141, 172, 192, 193, 196; consensual approach to, 9, 15, 174–75; in Cyprus, 222n12; in Denmark, 160; in Estonia, 161, 171–75; in Finland, 8, 15, 59–60, 70–72, 73–85, 96–97, 141; in France, 185–86; in Germany, 183; in Iceland, 23, 102, 103, 108, 113–15, 117–32, 136–40, 141; inconsistent government policies as impediment to, 153–56, 174; in Ireland, 161, 165, 171; in large states, 10, 190; in Nordic states, 8, 15, 17, 22, 26, 141; in Norway, 160; in Portugal, 153, 154–55, 158; in smaller communities, 180; social fragmentation as impediment to, 142; social policies during, 18, 53, 123–24; in Sweden, 8, 15, 32–34, 51–57, 141; in Switzerland, 9, 15, 148–49, 215n9; in U.S., 188–89

regulatory capture, 18, 87. *See also* societal capture

Rehn, Gösta, 41

Rehn, Olli, 144

relational capitalism, 16

research and development. *See* R&D

Research in Motion (RIM), 195, 196, 197

Reykjavik University, 125, 130

Rovio, 96, 98, 99, 219n28

Ruhr region, Germany, 192

SAF. *See* Swedish Employers' Association

Safford, Sean, 191

Salazar, Antonio de Oliveira, 151, 152

Saltsjöbaden Agreement, 39, 50

San Diego, California, 192–94; buffers against policy overshooting in, 198; cohesive social networks in, 180, 192–93, 194; impact of migrants in, 201, 224n13; vulnerability to economic shocks, 197

SAP. *See* Swedish Social Democratic Party

Schumpeter, Joseph, 59

Schumpeterian development agencies, 198–99

Science and Technology Policy Council (STPC, Finland), 76, 77, 79, 83, 84

SEB (Stockholm's Enskilda Banken), 27, 28, 41, 53

segmented societies, 141, 142

Serlachius, Gösta, 66, 67

side payments: size of, social cohesion and, 216n5. *See also* politics of compensation

Silicon Valley, California: cohesive networks in, 192, 194; Estonia compared to, 178; San Diego compared to, 193, 197

Silicon Vikings, 56

Sitra, 70, 75–76, 82, 84, 85, 198–99, 206, 218n16

SKOP Bank, 61, 62, 72, 131, 218n11

Skype, 177

Slovakia, incrementalism in, 171

Slush conference, 99, 100

small and medium-sized enterprises (SMEs): in Austria, 143–44; Finnish support for, 84; Swedish policies disadvantaging, 44 small states: and cohesive networks, 12, 178–79, 180; definition of, 6; social policies to neutralize opposition to free trade, 18, 123–24

small states, literature on, 142; applicability to Nordic states, 3–4, 11, 12–15; arguments counterbalancing, 7; shortcomings of, 4–5

Smárason, Hannes, 121

social cohesion. *See* cohesive and encompassing networks

Social Democrats: in Finland, 62, 68; in Iceland, 107, 120, 121, 125; in Sweden, 33, 34, 35–36, 37, 41, 50, 51

social divisions. *See* divisions; fragmentation

social policies, in Nordic Europe, 3; enduring commitment to, 53, 101–2; to neutralize opposition to free trade, 18, 123–24. *See also* welfare state(s)

societal capture: in Ireland, 169; in Nordic states, 18, 130, 134–35, 190, 199

Société Générale, 187

Sócrates, José, 154

software industry, in Finland, 81–82, 98–99, 100, 200

solidaristic wage bargaining, in Sweden, 40–41, 43, 44, 50

Sotiropoulos, Dimitri, 157

Southern Europe: economic volatility in, 9, 142, 154, 214, 214*t*; Nordic states compared to, 9, 12, 142, 150–51, 158–59, 209, 221n12; social fragmentation in, 9, 142, 150, 151–52, 155, 156–57, 158. *See also* Greece; Portugal

Soviet Union: collapse of, impact on Finland, 73; fear of invasion by, and Finnish national solidarity, 66, 67, 173, 215n6; Finland's economy compared to, 67; Finland's trade with, 67, 68, 69, 70, 73, 199; impact on Estonia, 172–73

Spain: fiscal policy in, 154; housing bubble in, 170, 223n7; tourism in, 221n4

Squid, the (Iceland), 104

state-owned enterprises: in Austria, 143, 144, 145; in Finland, 67, 68; in France, 184; in Sweden, 51

statism, in postwar era, 25–26, 101; in Austria, 143; in Finland, 25, 65, 66–69; in Iceland, 25, 103, 109–11; and policy overshooting, hypothesis of, 181; in Sweden, 8, 26–27, 32–34, 37

Stefánsson, Karí, 114

Stockholm School of Economics, 35

Stockholm's Enskilda Banken (SEB), 27, 28, 41, 53

STPC. *See* Science and Technology Policy Council

strategic coordination (among firms): vs. informal ties, 13, 190; as measure of cohesive networks, 205; and policy overshooting, hypothesis of, 181; Varieties of Capitalism literature on, 3, 13, 181, 205

Supercell, 98, 99

Svenskt Näringsliv, 28

Sweden: banking crisis in, 54, 72, 213*t*, 217n15, 224n11; banks in, 27–28, 32, 41, 45, 49, 54, 190; cohesive networks in, 8, 23, 27, 29–30, 141, 173, 208*t*, 209; conformism in, 42–43, 50; as contrasting case, 7–8, 30; cross-class alliances in, 33–34, 36, 41; deregulation of financial markets in, 52–54, 102; deteriorating economic performance in 1980s, 49–51; divisions in, 30–31, 50; dot-com crash of 2000 and, 2, 55–57; East Asian industrialization and, 48; economic growth in (1930s-1970s), 1, 47; entrepreneurship in, after 1980, 52; entrepreneurship in, policies discouraging, 44, 45, 46, 48, 49, 51; Estonia compared to, 174, 175; Finland compared to, 53–56, 59, 61–65, 67–70, 71, 72, 74, 75, 81, 83, 91; France compared to, 8, 27, 31, 32, 33, 43, 44, 51, 184, 185, 186, 187; genius companies in, 32, 217n10; Germany compared to, 182; government-business cooperation in, 28–29; high-technology industries in, 48–49, 54–57, 212*t*; Iceland compared to, 53–54, 56, 103–4, 106–10, 113–15, 118, 119, 131; immigration and transformation of, 200; industrial conflict in, history of, 216n3; industrial families in, 28, 206; industrialization of, 31–32; interfirm collaboration in, 28, 29, 39, 40; labor-industry cooperation in, 29, 31; large firms in, policies favoring, 18, 20, 27, 28, 34, 41, 43–50, 217n6; liberalization in, 21, 52–53; macroeconomic policies in, 221n10; neocorporatism in, 28–29, 204*t*; neoliberal revolution in, 101, 102; OPEC-induced oil crises of 1970s and, 37, 48, 50; overshooting and overinvestment in, 46–51; politics of compensation in, 18, 34, 38–42; politics of coordination in, 28–29, 34, 43–46; politics of persuasion in, 34–38; populist right-wing parties in, rise of, 201; reform and restructuring in, 8, 15, 32–34, 51–57, 141; size and diversity of, 27, 31; small enterprises in, policies disadvantaging, 42; Social Democrats in, 33, 34, 35–36, 37, 41, 50, 51;

Sweden (*continued*)
  solidaristic wage bargaining in, 40–41, 43, 44, 50; statist turn in, 8, 26–27, 32–34, 37; taxation in, 32, 40, 44–45, 51, 217n6; trade unions in, 2, 29, 31, 33; universal banking in, 27–28, 32, 49; vulnerability to external shocks, 48, 49–50, 214*t*; welfare state in, 2, 25, 26–27, 33, 39, 42, 43
Swedish Board for Technical Development (STU), 50
Swedish Employers' Association (SAF), 41, 217n5; agreement with LO, 39, 41; large capital-intensive firms favored by, 44, 46; and solidaristic wage bargaining, 40, 43, 50
Swedish Forest Industries Association, 28
Swedish model, 35, 41–42
Swedish Social Democratic Party (SAP), 35; alliance with industry and middle class, 39–41; and "cow trade" with Farmer's League, 38–39; and cross-class connections, 36; and LO, 35–36, 37; side payments by, 38; and welfare state, 43
Swedish Trade Union Congress (LO), 29; large capital-intensive firms favored by, 44, 46; and Social Democratic Party (SAP), 35–36, 37; and solidaristic wage bargaining, 40, 41, 43; and Swedish Employer's Association (SAF), 39, 41
Switzerland: asset-specific investments in, 17; banking industry in, 146, 148, 149; conservative approach to economic challenges in, 147, 149; decentralization in, 199; diversified economy of, 143, 144; divisions in, 9; dot-com crash of 2000 and, 221n9; global financial crisis of 2007-2009 and, 148, 213*t*; Icelandic banking industry compared to, 117, 131; incrementalism in, 5, 17, 142, 149, 184; innovation in, 147–48; market-based solutions to economic problems, 146–47; neocorporatism in, 143; Nordic states compared to, 9, 142–43, 148, 149; OPEC-induced oil crises of 1970s and, 146; reform and restructuring in, 9, 15, 148–49, 215n9; as segmented society, 141, 142; watch industry in, 144, 147

taxation: in Estonia, 174; in Finland, 67; in Iceland, 116, 119, 136–37; in Ireland, 165, 166, 169, 170, 171, 222n2; in Portugal, 153; in Sweden, 32, 40, 44–45, 51, 217n6
technological innovation: reliance on, and vulnerability to economic shocks, 2, 8; tight-knit relationships and, 5, 113–14. *See also* high-technology industries; innovation policy

Technology Industries of Finland, 92, 96
Tekes, 21, 76, 77, 79–80, 81, 82, 83, 84, 86, 92, 96, 99, 100, 206
TetraPak, 217n11
Thatcher, Margaret, 101, 220n4
tight-knit relationships. *See* cohesive and encompassing networks
Toronto metropolitan region, Canada, 191
tourism industry: in Austria, 221n4; in Cyprus, 222n12; in Iceland, 138–40; in Spain, 221n4
trade: Austria and, 145; Central European states and, 142, 145, 147; East Central European states and, 171; Estonia and, 175; Finland and, 59, 66, 67–70, 73, 74, 79, 86, 89, 95, 199; France and, 186; Germany and, 182, 183; Greece and, 158; Iceland and, 102, 103, 109–12, 116, 131, 133; Ireland and, 164–65, 166, 167, 171; Nordic states and, 2, 211, 212*t*; Sweden and, 8, 27, 47, 54, 56; Switzerland and, 144, 145, 147; U.S. and, 188–89. *See also* market competition; protectionism
trade unions: in Austria, 143; in Estonia, 172; in Finland, 2, 3, 18, 62, 80–81, 92–93, 219n27; in Greece, 156, 157; in Iceland, 103, 104, 107, 110, 119, 120, 122–24, 125, 127, 135; in Ireland, 161–62, 163; in Portugal, 152–53; role in economic restructuring, 204–5; in Sweden, 2, 29, 31, 33, 35–36, 37, 40–41; weakness of, and market competition, 172
trust, culture of: and cohesive social networks, 14, 204*t*, 206–7; in experts, 52–53, 71–72; and Finland's pioneering role in electronic banking, 17; in Iceland, 107; and policy overshooting, 19; in San Diego, California, 194; and Swedish reform and restructuring, 52–53

UBS, 148
UCSD (University of California at San Diego), 193, 194, 201
UCSD CONNECT, 194, 196
Union Bank of Finland, 61, 65, 69, 131
United Kingdom: "cod wars" with Iceland, 106, 111, 220n8; Icelandic banking industry compared to, 117, 129, 130, 131, 134, 136; statist turn in, 25; Sweden compared to, 51
United States: banks in, 130, 189–90, 224n10; fragmentation in, 189; global financial crisis of 2007-2009 and, 190, 198, 213*t*; high-technology industries in, 188–89; housing bubble in, 133, 170; Icelandic

banking industry compared to, 117, 125, 129, 130, 131, 133, 136, 189–90; influence on Iceland, 115, 118–19, 120; large firms in, policies favoring, 188; large metropolitan areas in, 191; Nordic states compared to, 9–10, 180, 187–90; reform and restructuring in, 188–89; regions with cohesive social networks in, 180, 192–95; statist turn in, 25; Sweden compared to, 31; Wall Street and Treasury in, close ties between, 31; Wall Street contributions to politicians in, 125. *See also specific cities/regions*

universities: Finnish, cooperation with industry, 82–83, 84; Icelandic, banking industry and, 125–26, 129, 130; Swedish, resistance to applied R&D, 83; and technological innovation, in San Diego, 193, 194; and technological innovation, in Waterloo, 195–96

University of California at San Diego (UCSD), 193, 194, 201

University of Waterloo, 195–96, 197, 198

Varieties of Capitalism literature, 3, 13, 181, 205

venture capital investment: in Finland, 84–85, 219n22; in Sweden, 55–56, 57; in U.S., 189

Vesterbacka, Peter, 96

Vigo accelerator program, 99, 100

Visegrád states, Estonia compared to, 171, 174, 175, 176, 177

volatility, economic: cohesive social networks and, 5–6; of Finland, 2, 60, 85, 86, 89–95, 214*t*; of Iceland, 23, 106, 117, 132, 140, 213, 214*t*; of Ireland, 161, 171; of Nordic Europe, 1–2, 9, 11, 22–23, 202, 213–14, 214*t*; of Southern Europe, 9, 142, 214, 214*t*; of Sweden, 48, 49–50, 214*t*. *See also* economic crises; overshooting and overinvestment

Wachovia, 190

Waldén, Rudolf, 67

Wallenberg, André Oscar, 27

Wallenberg family, 28, 41

watch industry, Swiss, 144, 147

WATCOM, 195

Waterloo, Ontario, 195–96; buffers against policy overshooting in, 198; cohesive social networks in, 180, 195; vulnerability to economic shocks, 197

welfare state(s): in Denmark, 25; in Iceland, 109, 111, 123–24; in Nordic Europe, 3, 19, 25, 101; in Norway, 25; in Sweden, 2, 25, 26–27, 33, 39, 42, 43

Wells Fargo, 190

Whitaker, T. K., 165

Wicksell, Knut, 34

Wigforss, Ernst, 35, 36, 38

Willson, Margaret, 139

Youngstown, Ohio, 191, 195

CPSIA information can be obtained
at www.ICGtesting.com
Printed in the USA
BVHW08s1818090918
526887BV00001B/50/P